Immigration
and the Law
A Dictionary

CONTEMPORARY LEGAL ⬛ ISSUES

Immigration and the Law

A Dictionary

Bill Ong Hing

ABC-CLIO

Santa Barbara, California
Denver, Colorado
Oxford, England

Library of Congress Cataloging-in-Publication Data
Hing, Bill Ong.
    Immigration and the law : a dictionary / Bill Ong Hing.
        p. cm. — (Contemporary legal issues)
    Includes bibliographical references and index.
    ISBN 1-57607-120-0 (alk. paper)
1. Emigration and immigration law—United States—
Dictionaries. I. Title. II. Series.

KF4817 .H56   1999
342.73'082'03—dc21   99-051982

05 04 03 02 01 00 99   10 9 8 7 6 5 4 3 2 1 (cloth)

ABC-CLIO, Inc.
130 Cremona Drive, P.O. Box 1911
Santa Barbara, California 93116-1911

This book is printed on acid-free paper ∞.
Manufactured in the United States of America

To the souls who were excluded by misguided immigration policies: Jews attempting to flee Nazi Germany aboard the SS *St. Louis;* Chinese turned back under the auspices of the Chinese exclusion laws after prison-like detention on Angel Island; citizens and other workers of Mexican descent rounded up in Operation Wetback; Haitians interdicted on the high seas; Guatemalans and El Salvadorans spurned by hostile agents unwilling to discuss asylum; and all the others.

Contents

Preface

United States immigration law and policy are mazelike, cobbled together over the past 150 years by presidents, members of Congress, and those who end up enforcing the laws. Perhaps next to tax law, no other area of law involves a more complex statutory and regulatory scheme. One federal judge described the field this way:

> We have had occasion to note the striking resemblance between some of the laws we are called upon to interpret and King Minos's labyrinth in ancient Crete. The Tax Laws and the Immigration and Nationality Acts are examples we have cited of Congress's ingenuity in passing statutes certain to accelerate the aging process of judges. In this instance, Congress, pursuant to its *virtually unfettered power* to exclude or deport natives of other countries, and apparently confident of the aphorism that human skill, properly applied, can resolve any enigma that human inventiveness can create, has enacted a baffling skein of provisions for the INS and courts to disentangle. [*Tim Lok v. INS*, 548 F.2d 37, 38 (2nd Cir. 1977) (emphasis added)]

Welcome to the world of immigration law, where this virtual "unfettered power" to exclude or deport aliens, sometimes referred to as "plenary power," has given rise to a hodgepodge of rules that reflect the biases and whims of policy makers and bureaucrats believing that they know what's best for the nation.

Immigration issues have taken center stage in recent years. How many immigrants we should allow into the country and from what areas of the world are hotly debated. The pressure placed on the United States to be generous toward refugees seeking to enter from many regions of the world is enormous. Whether we should extend public benefits, rights, and other services to those immigrants and refugees who are already here is a source of contention. In short, these questions are the common subject of headlines, political debates, pundit shows, classrooms, and dinner talk.

An understanding of basic immigration terms and issues is an important element of what we should all know. The need for this understanding is essential not just for policy makers, but for employers, educators, students, and anyone who desires to keep abreast of current affairs or to intelligently contribute to the debate.

This volume is intended to provide a solid resource for comprehending immigration issues. I have set forth more than the most common terms and phrases related to immigration issues; many entries needed for a more sophisticated understanding of current immigration policy are included. Several important historical entries have also been selected. And many of the most important cases have been digested. I have also included descriptions of organizations and individuals who have had lengthy track records of involvement in the immigration arena.

I could not have completed this project without the able assistance of faculty secretaries, Paula Buchignani, Sara Buck, Ann Graham, and Sue Williams, at U.C. Davis School of Law, and my research assistant Lena Sims. Furthermore, the support of Dean Rex Perschbacher and Associate Dean Kevin Johnson is deeply appreciated.

Introduction

A History of Immigration Policies

Although immigration laws did not become a permanent fixture in U.S. statutes until the mid-1800s, debate over newcomers was a part of the political and social discourse even before the Declaration of Independence. As early as 1751, no less an icon of the New World than Benjamin Franklin opposed the influx of German immigrants, warning that "Pennsylvania will in a few years become a German colony; instead of their learning our language, we must learn theirs, or live as in a foreign country." He later expanded his thoughts:

> [T]hose who came hither are generally the most stupid of their own nation, and as ignorance is often attended with great credulity, when knavery would mislead it, and with suspicion when honesty would set it right; and few of the English understand the German language, and so cannot address them either from the press or pulpit, it is almost impossible to remove any prejudices they may entertain. . . . Not being used to liberty, they know not how to make modest use of it.

These critical statements of one of the framers of the U.S. Constitution should be contrasted with the sentiments of George Washington, who in 1783 proclaimed, "The bosom of America is open to receive not only the opulent and respectable stranger, but the oppressed and persecuted of all nations and religions." His words are strikingly reminiscent of the famous lines of the Jewish American poet Emma Lazarus engraved at the base of the Statue of Liberty in 1886:

> *Give me your tired, your poor,*
> *Your huddled masses yearning to breathe free,*
> *The wretched refuse of your teeming shore,*
> *Send these, the homeless, tempest-tost to me.*
> *I lift my lamp beside the golden door!*

So which sentiment would guide America: Franklin's disgust of the "most stupid of their own nation," or the open arms of Washington and Lazarus to the poor and oppressed? The contrast is emblematic of the debate on immigration that has been a constant part of the American psyche since the nascent stages of the country. Refugees, immigrants, and their advocates have come to rely on rhetorical examples of Washington and Lazarus. But this sentimental language is not part of the constitution, and has no legal meaning.

From Open Doors to Early Restrictions: 1798–1908

In spite of Franklin's influence, the first hundred years of the nation was characterized by open borders. An early attempt to regulate aliens, in the Alien Act of 1798, authorized the president to expel dangerous aliens. The law proved very unpopular, however, and expired without fanfare two years later.

Scholars generally trace the beginning of restrictive U.S. immigration policies to racial nativist laws directed at various Asian immigrant groups, national origin quotas that disfavored southern and eastern Europeans, and policies that alternately attracted and deported Mexican migrants, depending on the nation's economic needs. However, voluntary African immigration also was not favored. African Americans were slaves for the first one hundred years of this nation's history. By the time they were freed, slavery had destroyed much of the African ancestral family and cultural structure. Familial and social ties with Africa had long been severed, so reunification with African relatives was impossible. Moreover, what African in his or her right mind would have wanted to come to the United States during or immediately after slavery? Thus, a formal African exclusion law was not necessary to discourage African immigration.

Prior to 1870, the subordination of people of African descent was further underscored by the fact that people from Africa could not become U.S. citizens through naturalization. The Nationality Act of 1790 limited naturalization to "free white persons" and specifically excluded African Americans and Native Americans. However, in 1870, Congress extended naturalization rights to outlanders of African descent. Still, African immigrants were not widely accepted in the United States.

In 1912, Congress began consideration of legislation that would eventually result in a literacy requirement for immigrants. In the midst of this debate, a Mississippi senator offered an amendment to exclude persons of African descent, which was narrowly rejected, twenty-eight to twenty-five, with forty-two not voting. But two years later, a Missouri senator succeeded in persuading the Senate to pass immigration legislation that included a provision requiring exclusion of "all members of the African or black race." However, the Senate was forced to back away from the African exclusion when the legislation went to conference committee.

When Congress did enact laws of sufficient popularity to have a lasting impact, Asian immigrants were targeted. Federal limitations on immigration began in 1862 and 1875, with prohibitions upon the importation of indentured labor from Asia, prostitutes, and alien convicts. In 1870, Congress extended the right to naturalize to aliens of African descent, but deliberately denied Chinese that right because of their "undesirable qualities." Clamor against Chinese, especially in California, reached fever pitch by 1882, when Congress enacted the first Chinese exclusion act, which was made permanent in 1904.

Similar nativist sentiment eventually led to limitations on Japanese immigration. But because Japan had emerged as a major world power at the turn of the century, defeating both China and Russia in war, the United States could not restrict Japanese immigration in the same heavy-handed fashion with which it had curtailed Chinese immigration. Instead an informal agreement with Japan was negotiated. Under the terms of the so-called Gentlemen's Agreement reached in 1907 and 1908, the Japanese government refrained from issuing travel documents to laborers destined for the United States.

The reduction in Japanese immigration contrasted sharply with general immigration policies at the time. The first decade of the century actually witnessed expanded tolerance toward other immigrants because of a national economic recovery. This resulted in the largest influx ever, particularly of European immigrants, mostly from southern and eastern Europe. The decade's record-setting influx fed exclusionist sentiment, however, providing sufficient impetus by 1907 to convene the Dillingham Commission to investigate the immigration system.

The Literacy Requirement and Expansion of Racial and Ethnic Exclusion: 1917–1934

Restrictive immigration policies with broader implications were enacted in 1917 and 1924. In 1917 legislation, Congress responded to continued anti-Asian clamor, much of it directed at immigrants from India, and a renewed xenophobia aroused by the influx of southern and eastern Europeans. A controversial section of this legislation was the literacy test. The constant flow of Italians, Russians, and Hungarians, which peaked in the first decade of the century, fueled racial nativism and anti-Catholicism, culminating in the requirement that excluded aliens "who cannot read and understand some language or dialect." But the act also created the "Asiatic barred zone" by extending the Chinese exclusion laws to all other Asians. The zone covered South Asia from Arabia to Indochina, as well as the adjacent islands. It included India, Burma, Thailand, the Malay States, the East Indian Islands, Asiatic Russia, the Polynesian Islands, and parts of Arabia and Afghanistan. China and Japan did not have to be included because of the Chinese exclusion laws and the Gentlemen's Agreement with Japan.

The reactionary, isolationist political climate that followed World War I, manifested in the Red Scare of 1919–1920, led to even greater exclusionist demands. The landmark Immigration Act of 1924, opposed by only six senators, once again took direct aim at southern and eastern Europeans, largely Catholics or Orthodox Christians whom the Protestant majority in the United States viewed with dogmatic disapproval. The act restructured criteria for admission and created a general selection policy that remained in place until 1952. It provided that immigrants of any particular country be limited to 2 percent of their nationality in 1890. The law struck most deeply at Jews, Italians, Slavs, and Greeks, who had immigrated in great numbers after 1890, and who would be most disfavored by such a national origins quota system. The harshness of the laws was illustrated by a pre–World War II incident involving the SS *St. Louis,* a ship carrying over 900 Jews sent from Nazi Germany first to Cuba and then the United States, only to be turned away from this country partly on the basis of quotas.

Though sponsors of the act were primarily concerned with limiting immigration from southern and eastern Europe, they simultaneously eliminated the few remaining categories for Asians. The act provided for the permanent exclusion of any "alien ineligible to citizenship." Since Asians were barred from naturalization under the 1870 statute, the possibility of their entry was cut off indefinitely. The prohibition even included previously privileged merchants, teachers, and students. The primary target was the Japanese, who, while subject to the Gentlemen's Agreement, had until then never been totally barred by federal immigration law.

Around this same era, from 1915 to 1921, a California-sponsored Americanization program took aim at Mexican immigrants. Within a hundred years, Mexicans had become the strangers in the land that was once theirs. In 1821, Mexico had taken control of California, Texas, New Mexico, and Arizona, and parts of Colorado, Utah, and Nevada, when it declared its independence from Spain. Within twenty-five years, however, Texas was annexed by the United States. At the end of the Mexican-American War in 1849, the Treaty of Guadalupe Hidalgo gave all Mexicans living in these areas the option of becoming U.S. citizens or relocating within the new Mexican borders. Although some Mexicans moved to Mexico, most remained in what became U.S. territory. In the years following the treaty,

Mexicans and Americans paid little attention to the newly created international border. Miners, shepherds, and seasonal workers traveled in both directions to fill fluctuating labor demands in what was essentially a single economic region.

While restrictionists and employers who claimed a need for cheap labor battled over future Mexican immigration, a third group of "Americanists" sought to assimilate Mexican immigrants. By 1913, California established a Commission on Immigration and Housing that directed efforts to teach English to immigrants and involve them in Americanization programs. The commission focused its attention on Mexican immigrant women, in the belief that they were primarily responsible for the transmission of values in the home. School districts employed special classes and "home teachers," hoping that Mexican women would pass on their newfound values to their children and husbands. English training, family planning, and developing a work ethic outside the home were considered important so that Mexican women could fill the labor need for domestic servants, seamstresses, laundresses, and service workers in the Southwest. The programs taught food and diet management; Mexicans were to give up their penchant for fried foods, tortillas would be replaced with bread, and lettuce served instead of beans. By the time of the Great Depression in the 1930s, the Americanization program stopped, restrictionist sentiment carried the day, and about half a million Mexicans were coerced by U.S. officials to return to Mexico.

Around this time, anti-Filipino sentiment surged as well. Filipinos were not affected by the national origins quotas of the 1924 law because the Philippines became a U.S. colony in 1898 following the Spanish-American War. Filipinos were noncitizen nationals who could come and go as they pleased. They became a convenient source of cheap labor after Japanese immigration was restricted in 1908. Initially they were attracted to Hawaii, but by the 1920s Filipinos came to California, predominantly to work on citrus and vegetable farms. In the off-season they provided service labor for hotels, restaurants, and private homes as busboys, cooks, hotel chauffeurs, dishwashers, domestic help, and gardeners. Exclusionists viewed Filipinos as an economic threat, taking jobs from whites and lowering standards for wages and working conditions. Eventually, an unlikely coalition of exclusionists, anticolonialists, and Filipino nationalists banded together to promote the passage of the Tydings-McDuffie Act in 1934. Under the law, the Philippines would become independent in twelve years (1946), and all Filipinos in the United States would lose their status as U.S. nationals. Those in the United States would be deported unless they became immigrants, but their annual immigrant quota was only fifty visas.

The Impact of World War II: 1940–1952

World War II had great influence over many immigration and refugee policies. Fear of foreign subversives led to the enactment of the Alien Registration Act of 1940. Fingerprinting and registration of aliens became the norm, as did the deportation of those who posed threats to national security.

The war reopened the door for others. For example, after the United States and China became allies against the Japanese, Congress agreed to repeal some aspects of the exclusion laws. The 1943 Chinese Repealer allowed Chinese to naturalize and become American citizens; it also struck from the books most of the Chinese exclusion laws. China was allotted a yearly quota of 105 immigrants. In 1946, Congress extended nonquota immigration status to Chinese wives of citizens. The same year, two days before the Philippines regained independence under Tydings-McDuffie, Congress extended naturalization rights to Filipinos and Indians. The Humanitarian Displaced Persons Acts in 1948 and 1950 permitted the entry of over 400,000 refugees into the United States within a four-year period, although their entry would affect the immigration quotas for their homelands for years to come. The spouses and children of U.S. servicemen benefited under the War Brides Act, which admitted 118,000 persons. Another 5,000 benefited from the Fiancées Act.

Substantial Change without Racial Remedies: The 1952 Act

The biases of the 1924 national origins quota system remained visible and came under heavy fire after the war, especially when the United States assumed leadership at the United Nations and other international organizations. The ideological Cold War between capitalism and communism made the United States acutely conscious of how its domestic policies, including immigration, were perceived abroad.

Following years of considerable study, Congress passed the McCarran-Walter Act of 1952. President Harry Truman vetoed the bill, disappointed that the national origins quota system was retained and critical of the severity of the grounds of exclusion, deportation, and denaturalization, and the lack of authority to alleviate hardships. However, postwar anxieties about enemy aliens and divided loyalties carried the day, and Congress overrode the veto.

The grounds of exclusion under the new law were extensive, with provisions relating to health, criminality, morality, poverty, and subversion. The grounds of deportation were similar, providing for the removal of those who entered without inspection, those who overstayed visas, and criminals, subversives, narcotics violators, prostitutes, and violators of registration and reporting requirements. Deportation procedures through a fair hearing process were also established, although no right to government-appointed counsel was provided.

The 1952 act ostensibly removed racial bars to immigration, previously applied to Chinese, as well as eliminating the "ineligible for citizenship" barrier to naturalization. But although it abolished the 1917 Asiatic barred zone, the law created a new restrictive zone—the Asia-Pacific triangle—that consisted of countries from India to Japan and all Pacific islands north of Australia and New Zealand. A maximum of two thousand Asians from this new triangle were allowed to immigrate annually. Once again Congress's actions proved schizophrenic: foreign policy dictated an end to absolute exclusion, but domestic exclusionist ideology would not permit immigration beyond a token quota of two thousand immigrants yearly from the entire Asia-Pacific region.

The McCarran-Walter Act has been repeatedly amended, but still remains the basic statute dealing with immigration.

The Successful Campaign against the National Origins Quotas: The 1965 Amendments

A national origins quota system continued to exasperate many observers. They felt the system perpetuated the philosophy that "some people are more equal than others," and they pointed to the creation of the Asia-Pacific triangle as evidence. After the congressional override of Truman's veto, critics were resigned to citing the law as an embarrassment that was inconsistent with America's stature as leader of the free world.

Truman and other critics did not relent. Soon after the enactment of the 1952 law, he appointed a special Commission on Immigration and Naturalization to study the system. Its report, issued in 1953, strongly urged the abolition of the national origins system and recommended quotas without regard to national origin, race, creed, or color. President Dwight Eisenhower embraced the findings, but his push for corrective legislation failed. Despite repeated attempts at new legislation, no major action was taken on any of the commission's recommendations until more than ten years later.

After years of unsuccessful efforts by Truman and Eisenhower to eliminate the quota system, President John F. Kennedy submitted a comprehensive program that provided the impetus for ultimate reform. He assailed the nativism that led to the national origins system of the 1924 law and called for the repeal of the racial constraints of the Asia-Pacific triangle. Kennedy envisioned a system governed by the skills of the immigrant and family reunification. For him, the proposed changes meant an increase both in fairness to applicants and in benefits to the United States. His approach recognized the interdependence among nations, making the old system appear anachronistic.

Although Kennedy's global vision was not without its detractors, it remained the driving theme for the proponents of reform who sought more open movement across international borders. In that manner, they believed the United States would stand both as a leader and as an example. Their high rhetoric was meant to evoke a romantic allegiance to the highest sort of aspirations. People were supposed to feel as if they could transcend the world in which they were living.

After his assassination in 1963, Kennedy's vision might have died but for the dedication of his brothers, Attorney General Robert Kennedy and Senator Edward Kennedy. The attorney general lobbied hard and the senator became the floor manager of the reforms. Kennedy's successor, Lyndon Johnson, became a strong proponent of reform, and the legislation was debated at the height of congressional sensitivity over civil rights.

President Kennedy's hopes for abolishing the quota system were realized when the 1965 amendments were enacted. But his vision of visas on a first-come, first-served basis gave way to a narrower and more historically parochial framework. The new law allowed twenty thousand immigrant visas for every country not in the Western Hemisphere. The allotment was made regardless of the size of the country, so that mainland China had the same quota as Tunisia. Of the 170,000 visas set aside for the Eastern Hemisphere, 75 percent were for specified "preference" relatives of citizens and lawful permanent residents, and an unlimited number were available to immediate relatives of U.S. citizens.

Two occupational preference categories and a nonpreference category were also established. The occupational categories helped professionals and other aliens who filled jobs for which qualified U.S. workers were not available. Under the nonpreference category, an alien who invested $40,000 in a business could qualify for immigration to the United States.

Reductions in Mexican Immigration: 1965–1976

Although the national origins quota system and statutory vestiges of Asian exclusion laws were abolished in 1965, the changes represented a blow to Mexican immigrants. Between 1965 and 1976, while the rest of the world enjoyed an expansion of numerical limitations and a definite preference system, Mexico and the Western Hemisphere were suddenly faced with numerical restrictions for the first time. Additionally, while the first-come, first-served basis for immigration sounded fair, applicants had to meet strict labor certification requirements. Of course, waivers of the labor certification requirement were obtainable for certain applicants, such as parents of U.S. citizen children. As one might expect given the new numerical limitations, by 1976 the procedure resulted in a severe backlog of approximately three years and a waiting list with nearly 300,000 names. By that time Mexicans were using about 40,000 of the Western Hemisphere's 120,000 annual allocation.

In 1976, legislation overhauled the Western Hemisphere immigration system, purportedly placing those countries in line with those of the Eastern Hemisphere. The first-come, first-served Western Hemisphere system was replaced with the statutory preference system along with the 20,000-visa-per-country numerical limitation. Thus, Mexico's annual visa usage was virtually cut in half overnight, and thousands were left stranded on the old system's waiting list. Some of those on the waiting list were rescued by litigation (*Silva v. Levi*) that recaptured some previously misallocated visas. Most, however, were left out.

"Diversity" Visas for Non-Asians and Non-Mexicans and Stricter Enforcement: 1986–1996

From the end of the 1970s and through the 1990s, immigrant visa demand from Mexico remained high and demand from certain Asian countries surged. By 1990, immigrants from Mexico, the Philippines, India, and Korea, and Chinese from China, Taiwan, and Hong Kong dominated the family reunification categories. Given the per-country numerical limitations, Mexico and Asian countries shared (and continue to share) the largest backlogs in family reunification categories. This was especially true for siblings of U.S. citizens and relatives of lawful permanent resident aliens.

The fact that Asian immigration would reach such high levels was not foreseen by policy makers who enacted the 1965 amendments. At the time the legislation passed, those who would benefit most from a family-based system would be those who were here in greater numbers in 1965, namely, those of European ancestry. However, European immigration actually declined after 1965 because family reunification for those nationalities largely had been completed.

Instead, the number of Asian immigrants began to increase in the early 1970s, then exploded in the late 1970s and 1980s, when Asian and Latin immigrants represented over 80 percent of the total. This did not go unnoticed by modern-day nativists. In 1982 as part of a major legislative package, Republican Senator Alan Simpson of Wyoming initiated a crusade to eliminate the immigration category allowing U.S. citizens to be reunited with siblings. He persisted in his efforts to abolish the category until he retired in 1996. These efforts were a direct assault on Asians and Mexicans who combined to make up the vast majority of sibling-of-citizen immigrants.

A different approach was used to respond to the rising domination of Asians and Latinos in immigration totals in the 1980s. Although the country's population was still overwhelmingly white, Congress in 1986 added a provision to the Immigration Reform and Control Act to help thirty-six countries that had been "adversely affected" by the 1965 changes. To be considered "adversely affected," a country must have been issued fewer visas after 1965 than before. Thus, the list included such countries as Great Britain, Germany, and France, but no countries of Africa who sent few immigrants prior to 1965. The 1986 law provided an extra 5,000 such visas a year for 1987 and 1988, but the number increased to 15,000 per year for 1989 and 1990 through additional legislation.

In 1988, Congress set aside an extra 20,000 visas to increase immigration diversity over a period of two years. This time, the lottery for the visas was available to nationals of countries that were "underrepresented," namely a foreign state that used less than 25 percent of its 20,000 preference visas in 1988. As a result, all but thirteen countries in the world (e.g., Mexico, the Philippines, China, Korea, India) were eligible. Over 3.2 million applications were received for the 20,000 visas.

Legislation in 1990 extended the diversity visa concept. Until October 1, 1994, a transition diversity program provided 40,000 visas per year for countries "adversely affected" by the 1965 amendments, except that 40 percent of the visas were effectively designated for Ireland. The justification for special treatment for Irish nationals was the recognition that under the primarily family-based immigration system, a special seed or pipeline category needed to be established in order to get a significant number of people in who could then take advantage of the family categories. This had not occurred in the case of Irish nationals. Beginning October 1, 1994, 55,000 diversity visas have been available annually in a lottery-type program to natives of countries from which immigration was lower than 50,000 over the preceding five years. The State Department determines the distribution of lottery visas using a complicated formula that weights countries and regions of the world and relative populations as well. To qualify for these post-1994 diversity visas, the applicant must have a high school education or its equivalent or within five years of application have at least two years of work experience in an occupation that requires at least two years of training or experience.

The 1990 legislation signaled important changes to immigration selection categories, with most impact on employment-related immigrant visas. The preference system that had previously mixed relative categories with employment categories was divided into a family preference system and an employment-related preference system. A slight increase was made to the number of visas available for relatives of U.S. citizens and lawful permanent residents (to about 465,000 visas), but the number of employment-related visas almost tripled to 140,000 visas per year. Family reunification remained the main principle for immigration categories.

Changes to enforcement concepts in the immigration laws are best epitomized by changes to the laws made in 1996. Congress continued the expansion of the "aggravated felony" category, which precludes many forms of relief, instituted mandatory detention policies for many criminal aliens, eliminated judicial review for many types of cases, imposed strict filing timelines for asylum applicants, and instituted expedited removal procedures for many aliens caught at the border.

Refugee and Asylum Policies

The United States takes considerable pride in its long history of providing refuge to foreign nationals displaced by the ravages of war or persecuted by totalitarian governments. Since George Washington's expression of open arms to the "oppressed and persecuted" to the admission of some Kosovar refugees in 1999, two centuries of similar statements from leaders and citizens alike have helped to project a certain national generosity of spirit—even if that spirit was not always evident.

Thousands of refugees, sometimes hundreds of thousands, have been escorted here by an array of congressional acts that, on an ad hoc basis, superseded the national quota systems. Prominent among these was the 1948 Displaced Persons Act, which enabled 400,000 refugees and displaced persons to enter, primarily from Europe. The 1953 Refugee Relief Act admitted another 200,000 refugees, including 38,000 Hungarians and about 2,800 refugees of the Chinese Revolution.

Refugee migration to the United States finds its origin in the noble pursuit of humanitarian foreign policy objectives. Refugee sympathizers invariably invoke the need to respond compassionately to those in other countries confronted with life-threatening crises. In passing the Displaced Persons Act, Congress explicitly adopted the definition of the terms *displaced person* and *refugee* set forth in the 1946 Constitution of the International Refugee Organization.

Rhetoric notwithstanding, refugee law and policy have reflected the tensions between humanitarian aims and practical domestic and international concerns. These tensions—evident over the years in even the least obvious situations—make plain the link between refugee and immigration policy. In the 1930s, for example, the United States turned away thousands of Jews fleeing Nazi persecution (such as those on the SS *St. Louis*) in large part because of the powerful restrictionist views then dominating immigration laws. Congress and U.S. consular officers consistently resisted Jewish efforts to emigrate, and impeded any significant emergency relaxation of limitations on quotas. A 1939 refugee bill would have rescued 20,000 German children had it not been defeated on the grounds that the children would exceed the quota for Germany. And in 1972 the U.S. Coast Guard and Naval Intelligence, confused over proper asylum procedures and indecisive in the face of conflicting objectives, returned an asylum-seeking Lithuanian seaman to his Soviet ship.

As if collectively to deny these tensions, policy makers showed every sign through the early 1970s of being pleased by their system of policies, laws, and ad hoc decisions. As they saw it, whenever large numbers of deserving refugees appeared, new legislation could be enacted or existing laws and regulations manipulated. That sort of flexibility in a legal regime was, to their minds, to be unashamedly admired. It also permitted policymaking consistent with their political preference for refugees from Communist countries.

A closer look at the basic structure of the system and the policies that informed it bears witness to this ideological bias. Consider the 1952 McCarran-Walter Act, which granted the attorney general discretionary authority to "parole" into the United States any alien for "emergent reasons or for reasons deemed strictly in the public interest." Although the original intent was to apply this parole authority on an individual basis, the 1956 Hungarian refugee crisis led to its expanded use to accommodate those fleeing Communist oppression. The parole authority was also used to admit more than 15,000 Chinese who fled mainland China after the 1949 Communist takeover and more than 145,000 Cubans who sought refuge after Fidel Castro's 1959 coup.

Using the parole authority, the attorney general also permitted over 400,000 refugees from Southeast Asia to enter between 1975 and 1980. By 1980, 99.7 percent of the more than one million refugees admitted under the parole system were from countries under Communist rule. These figures betray any claim that refugee policy was based solely on humanitarian considerations.

The preference afforded refugees from Communist countries is also reflected in the 1965 reforms, when Congress created the first permanent statutory basis for the admission of refugees. Incorporating prior refugee language into a seventh preference category, conditional entry was provided for refugees fleeing Communist-dominated areas or the Middle East. Immigration controls were manifest as well in this category, since it included a worldwide annual quota of 17,400 and a geographic restriction that limited its use through 1977 to countries outside the Western Hemisphere. Until its repeal in 1980, the seventh preference was used by tens of thousands of refugees fleeing China, the Soviet Union, and other Communist societies.

Shortly after the creation of the seventh preference, the United States agreed in 1968 to the United Nations Protocol Relating to the Status of Refugees. The protocol obligated compliance with the guidelines established by the United Nations Convention Relating to the Status of Refugees. The ideological and geographic restrictions of the seventh preference, however, were inconsistent with the ideologically neutral protocol, so the United States attempted to jury-rig compliance by using the attorney general's discretionary parole authority. But that authority did not conform to the protocol's principles of neutrality either.

Few complaints about refugee policies and laws were registered on the floors of Congress during most of the 1970s. Some liberal observers did challenge the bias favoring refugees from Communist countries, but mostly as it affected applications for political asylum filed by individuals who had already gained entry. As for the greater numbers seeking refugee status from abroad, policy makers seemed satisfied with the status quo.

After 1975, policy makers became less complacent as Asians began entering in increasing numbers under existing guidelines. Only about 2,800 Chinese benefited before then from the 1953 Refugee Relief Act. Through 1966, about 15,000 were admitted under the parole provision. These low numbers were not perceived as threatening, since the seventh preference category restricted Chinese refugees through an annual worldwide limitation of 17,400, which had to be shared with others. Indeed, until the provision was repealed in 1980, only 14,000 who fled mainland China were able to take advantage of the seventh preference.

Following the military withdrawal from Vietnam in April 1975, however, the flow of Asian refugees increased markedly almost overnight. Invoking numerical restrictions in the midst of a controversial and devastating war would have been unacceptable; too many understood such inflexibility as morally treacherous and politically high priced. Consequently, the attorney general on several occasions used the parole authority to permit Asians to enter—the first time it was so employed since the 1965 amendments.

The United States initially wanted to evacuate from Vietnam only American dependents and government employees—fewer than 18,000. Immediately before the fall of Saigon in April 1975, however, authorities moved to include former employees and others whose lives were threatened. These evacuees included approximately 4,000 orphans, 75,000 relatives of American citizens or lawful permanent residents, and 50,000 Vietnamese government officials and employees. Mass confusion permitted many who did not fit into these categories also to be evacuated. Between April and December 1975, the United Status thus admitted 130,400 Southeast Asian refugees, 125,000 of whom were Vietnamese.

The exodus did not stop there. By 1978 thousands more were admitted under a series of Indochinese Parole Programs, authorized by the attorney general. The number of Southeast Asian refugees swelled to 14,000 a month by the summer of 1979. Following the tightening of Vietnam's grip on Cambodia in the late 1970s, several hundred thousand "boat people" and many Cambodian and Laotian refugees entered. In fact, annual arrivals of Southeast Asian refugees increased almost exponentially: 20,400 in 1978, 80,700 in 1979, and 166,700 in 1980.

In general the flow of Southeast Asians was poorly coordinated. The executive branch repeatedly waited until the number of refugees in the countries of "first asylum" (those first reached by refugees) reached crisis proportions before declaring an emergency. Only then would a new parole program be instituted. Attacks on the inconsistent treatment of refugees and calls for a consistent policy became commonplace. Many were uncomfortable with the attorney general's considerable unstructured power to hastily admit tens of thousands of refugees under the parole mechanism. Others were genuinely concerned with the government's erratic response to the plight of Southeast Asian refugees. Dissatisfaction with ad hoc admissions provided the impetus for reform and, ultimately, the passage of the 1980 Refugee Act.

The new refugee law was an attempt by Congress to treat refugee and immigration policies as separate and distinct. A major catalyst for the new refugee law was a disturbing anxiety felt by some members of Congress that thousands of Southeast Asians would destabilize many communities. Concerns about controlling immigration have dominated Refugee Act applications ever since.

Those who passed the 1980 Refugee Act and those who enacted earlier legislation claimed that they desired a less biased system. The new law provided two tracks for refugee admission into the United States. The first provided the president with the power to admit refugees who are outside the United States only after consultation with Congress, while the second related to procedures by which aliens in the United States or at ports of entry may apply for asylum.

As for the first track for refugees from abroad, the numbers have been much more regulated than under the previous parole authority, although the United States has allowed in more than a million refugees since 1980. The ideologically and geographically restrictive seventh preference category was replaced with a general provision that allowed any person with a "well-founded fear of persecution" to enter as a refugee. The act required the president, after "appropriate consultation" with Congress, to determine who will be offered refuge and to establish corresponding limits on how many will be admitted. The reforms restricted the attorney general's authority to parole refugees, thereby foreclosing large, ex parte admissions.

In practice, however, the new law has been administered in a manner reminiscent of the heavy-handed use of the seventh preference and parole provisions. Without much congressional opposition, presidents have continued to favor refugees from Communist countries while consistently ignoring pleas of those from nonaligned or anticommunist countries such as Haiti and Guatemala. The number of Asian refugees has declined dramatically.

The executive branch and Congress established a limit of 234,000 refugees for fiscal 1980. Of that number, the Jimmy Carter administration designated 169,000 places for Southeast Asia, 33,000 for the Soviet Union, 19,500 for Cuba, and 1,000 for the remainder of Latin America. By 1985, the total number of refugees allotted by the Ronald Reagan administration dropped to 70,000, with 50,000 reserved for East Asia. For 1992 under the George Bush administration, the total was increased to 142,000, primarily to accommodate an increase to 61,000 for the former Soviet Union. The number for East Asians remained at 52,000, despite dire circumstances in Asian refugee camps. By 1998 under the Bill Clinton administration, the total number was down to 83,000, with 14,000 for East Asia and 51,000 for Europe.

In contrast, only between 5,000 and 10,000 asylum applications have been approved per year since 1980. To say the least, the United States has not reacted warmly to notable groups who have reached U.S. borders seeking asylum under the second track of refugee admissions. When Haitians, El Salvadorans, Guatemalans, and Chinese boat people began arriving in significant numbers, the administrations were quick to label them economic rather than political refugees.

This response has manifested itself in humiliating ways. In the early 1980s, the INS implemented an efficiency plan in Miami by which Haitian asylum hearings were often limited to fifteen minutes, immigration judges were ordered to increase productivity and hear at least eighteen cases per day, and some attorneys were scheduled for hearings at the same time for different clients in different parts of the city. The federal court of appeals ultimately chastised immigration officials for violating due process and ordered a new plan for the reprocessing of asylum claims (*Haitian Refugee Center v. Smith*). A similar suit concluded with the INS agreeing to reevaluate potentially up to half a million Salvadoran and Guatemalan asylum cases from the 1980s, in light of strong evidence of INS political bias and discrimination against these applicants (*American Baptist Churches v. Thornburgh*).

The great influence that anti-immigrant groups have had in recent years is no doubt rooted in the exposure of the INS's illegal actions against Haitian, Guatemalan, and El Salvadoran asylum applicants. The illegal actions of the INS in processing their applications were the agency's response to complaints that the asylum system was too generous or manipulable. But once the agency's illegal actions were exposed, exclusionist complaints about the asylum system increased dramatically, leading to many of the restrictive measures placed on asylum applicants in the 1990 legislation.

When boatloads of Chinese began arriving in 1992 and 1993, the exclusionists were given new fuel. At first, this created a dissonant situation for the INS. After all, Chinese were fleeing communism; but the situation seemed somehow different. Two incidents that occurred in late 1992 only days apart demonstrated the dilemma. In one, a Cuban commercial pilot commandeered a flight and landed in Miami. All aboard who wanted asylum, including the pilot, were welcomed with open arms, and none were taken into custody. Yet, a few days later, a boatload of Chinese seeking asylum landed in San Francisco Bay, and every single person on board who could be rounded up was incarcerated. Many applied for asylum, arguing that they feared persecution because of their opposition to China's one-child-per-family birth policy, or because they had supported the protesting students at Tiananmen Square in 1989. It was the nature of these claims that exclusionists labeled outrageous, citing the Chinese as perfect examples of how the asylum system was being exploited. After several Chinese boats arrived—particularly the highly publicized *Golden Venture* in New York Harbor in 1993—exclusionists were able to rally great public and political support for their cause, and asylum and undocumented immigration played on the front page for some time after that. Ironically, a coalition of Chinese asylum supporters and right-to-life proponents were able to convince Congress in 1996 to add an automatic asylum eligibility provision for those Chinese fleeing China's one-child policy.

Humanitarianism toward refugees has occasionally taken precedence over the need for control. Consider the 1982 and 1987 legislation concerning "Amerasian" children. These children, fathered by American servicemen in Korea, Vietnam, Laos, Cambodia, and Thailand over the past forty years, have suffered racial discrimination and ostracism in their native lands, leading to inadequate housing, substandard medical care, and nutritional deficiencies. Legislation designed to enable such children to enter more easily allows them the exceptional option of either filing on their own behalf or having an immigration visa petition filed for them. Other prospective family-based immigrants cannot petition on their own behalf. The consequences of this technical accommodation are significant.

Similarly, the Nicaraguan Adjustment and Central American Relief Act of 1997 (NACARA) established two programs to address the long-standing plight of many Central Americans who fled to the United States in the 1980s. The first allowed certain Nicaraguans and Cubans in the United States to adjust their status to lawful permanent residence. The second gave certain Salvadorans, Guatemalans, and nationals of several former Soviet bloc and Eastern European nations the opportunity to apply for suspension of deportation.

Those Cubans and Nicaraguans who were physically present in United States could adjust to lawful permanent residence if they were phy cally present in the United States for a continuous period beginning not later than December 1, 1995, and filed an application by April 1, 2000. In general, Guatemalans, Salvadorans, and Eastern bloc nations had to meet more rigorous standards. They had to have entered by 1990 and must have filed for asylum in 1990 or 1991. They also had to demonstrate (1) continuous physical presence in the United States for seven years, (2) good moral character, (3) extreme hardship to themselves or to a child or parent who is a U.S. citizen or lawful permanent resident, and (4) facts that showed they were deserving of favorable discretion. While the legislation represented an important step, the bias demonstrated in favor of Nicaraguans and Cubans over similarly situated individuals from Guatemala, El Salvador, and the Eastern bloc was difficult to justify from an ideologically neutral perspective. The discrepancy was finally resolved in late 1999 through additional legislation.

The decency of legislation such as NACARA or that on behalf of Amerasian children cannot conceal the ideological bias that has permeated refugee practices. A couple of examples of U.S. beneficence cannot negate the tensions between humanitarianism and political concerns that regularly condition and constrain refugee law and policymaking. More often than not, the impulse to conceal and deny actual motivations has been followed.

Immigration Reform and Control Act of 1986

The Immigration Reform and Control Act of 1986 (IRCA), a last-minute compromise reached in the closing days of Congress's term in 1986, came as a surprise to many observers of immigration policy. IRCA was enacted to reform certain aspects of existing immigration law and to reduce the numbers of undocumented aliens coming to the United States. The plan to reduce the number of undocumented workers was twofold: (1) grant amnesty or legalization to many of the undocumented workers, and (2) make it unlawful for employers to hire undocumented workers in order to remove the incentive for unauthorized workers to come to the United States (employer sanctions). The two methods of controlling undocumented workers represented a political compromise. Because Congress was concerned that some employers might use the threat of sanctions to justify discriminating against "foreign-looking" workers, IRCA also added prohibitions against certain unfair immigration-related employment practices. Specifically, the law regards as unlawful an employer who discriminates against someone because of that person's national origin or because of his or her citizenship or immigration status (citizenship discrimination).

Viewing the grant of amnesty or legalization to undocumented aliens as a means of controlling undocumented immigration was a puzzling concept to many. At the time the legislation was enacted, as well as today, there was no clear idea of how many undocumented aliens there were in the country. The range of estimates was wide. Legalization supporters predicted between 1.5 million and 9 million potential applicants, while the opponents claimed up to 20 million would apply. Two opponents opined that a third of the population of Mexico would use IRCA to legalize themselves in the United States. To make matters worse, argued the doomsayers, each legalization applicant would eventually petition for family members, thus creating a calamitous "chain migration" effect. Some estimated that within a decade, IRCA would add 70, 90, or 100 million new citizens to the United States! But what else could Congress do to deal with the undocumented population already in the country? There were only a handful of alternatives: first, legalize some or all of the aliens; second, find and deport some or all of them; or third, do nothing. The second alternative would have required a huge effort to "round up" aliens, would probably have violated the civil rights of many and therefore engendered a hoard of lawsuits, would have cost a fortune, and simply would never have worked. The third alternative was politically impossible, since Congress was under pressure to do something about the perceived undocumented problem. Legalization was the only viable option.

The legalization programs for undocumented aliens consisted of one for those who had resided in the United States since January 1, 1982, and the other was for special agricultural workers (SAWs) who had performed agricultural work for at least ninety days between May 1, 1985, and May 1, 1986.

Ultimately, 1.7 million applicants filed under the pre-1982 program, and 1.2 million applied as SAWs. About 70 percent who ultimately applied under the pre-1982 program were Mexican; the next largest groups were El Salvadoran (8.1 percent) and Guatemalan (3 percent). Those qualifying under the farmworker program were also mostly Mexican. Mexicans filed 81.6 percent of the SAW applications, Haitians 3.4 percent, El Salvadorans 2 percent, and Guatemalans and Asian Indians 1.4 percent each.

The passage of IRCA represented the culmination of years of social, political, and congressional debate about the perceived lack of control over the United States' southern border. The belief that something had to be done about the large numbers of undocumented workers who had entered the United States from Mexico in the 1970s was reinforced by the flood of Central Americans that began to arrive in the early 1980s. While the political turmoil of civil war in El Salvador, Guatemala, and Nicaragua drove many Central Americans from their homelands, they, along with the Mexicans who continued to arrive, were generally labeled economic migrants by the Reagan administration, the INS, and the courts. Beginning in 1971, legislative proposals featuring employer sanctions as a centerpiece were touted as resolutions to the undocumented alien problem. By the end of the Carter administration in 1980, a Select Commission on Immigration and Refugee Policy portrayed legalization as a necessary balance to sanctions.

While strong congressional sentiment to respond to the perceived problem of undocumented aliens drove Congress to pass IRCA, congressional endorsement of the idea of balancing employer sanctions and legalization does not mean that there was strong support for legalization per se. Congress essentially concluded that with a flood of aliens crossing illegally and unchecked, the southern border was out of control. It was widely believed that the nation shared this fear. Opposition to legalization was intense and the program narrowly survived the House of Representatives. In the eleventh hour, on October 10, 1986, Representative Bill McCollum introduced an amendment to completely delete legalization from IRCA. The House defeated the amendment—thereby saving the legalization program—though only by a vote of 199 to save it, 192 to kill it, with 41 absent. A swing vote of only four members would have reversed the result.

Casual observers of immigration policy in the 1980s might cite IRCA as an example of a congressional swing toward a pro-immigration position because of the legalization provisions. However, the amnesty provision just barely eked through the House of Representatives while the employer sanctions provisions received overwhelming legislative support.

Immigration Enforcement Agencies

The major enforcement responsibilities under the immigration laws are assigned to the attorney general. It is the attorney general's job to guard the frontiers, to determine the admissibility of those who seek to enter, and to expel those not entitled to remain in the United States. The attorney general discharges those responsibilities through the Immigration and Naturalization Service and the Executive Office for Immigration Review (EOIR), both agencies within the Department of Justice.

A second enforcement agency is the State Department, acting through the department's Bureau of Consular Affairs and the U.S. consuls stationed all over the world. It is the responsibility of these officials, chiefly the consuls, to determine in the first instance the admissibility of aliens who seek to enter the United States and to issue visas to those found eligible for admission.

The Department of Labor also has important responsibilities, acting through its Employment and Training Administration. Immigrants who seek to enter the United States to perform labor, except those who have immigrated on the basis of being relatives of U.S. citizens or lawful permanent resident aliens, cannot come unless they first obtain an alien employment certification (labor certification) that U.S. workers are unavailable to perform such labor and that their entry will not adversely affect wages and working conditions in the United States.

Today's Immigration System

Many people abroad and many visitors and foreign students in the United States are interested in becoming lawful permanent resident aliens and obtaining a "green card" (I-551 lawful permanent resident card). In other words, they are seeking lawful immigrant status. The basic immigrant categories are divided into those for relatives (family reunification) and those related to employment (employment-based).

Family Reunification Categories

The family reunification categories include a category for "immediate relatives" of U.S. citizens that is not limited by quotas or numerical limitations, and a list of preference categories that are subject to numerical limitations.

Immediate Relative Category

The immediate relative category of immigration is for the spouses, children (unmarried and under age twenty-one), and parents of U.S. citizens who can immigrate immediately if proper applications are submitted and the grounds of inadmissibility are satisfied. Unlimited numbers of immigrants may enter the United States each year in the immediate relative category.

In order to be a spouse, the marriage must be valid in the country where the marriage took place, and must not have been entered into solely for immigration purposes (i.e., a sham marriage). The spousal category includes widows or widowers of U.S. citizens if the marriage lasted at least two years before the citizen died, as long as they were not legally separated at the time of death. The spousal category does not, however, include same-sex marriages.

Children of citizens qualify as immediate relatives if the child is unmarried and under the age of twenty-one. An adopted child can qualify if the child was adopted while under the age of sixteen, has been in legal custody of the adopting parents for two years, and has resided with the parents for two years. A stepchild can qualify if the child was under the age of eighteen at the time of the marriage creating the step relationship.

U.S. citizens can petition for their parents if the citizen is at least twenty-one years old. Many aliens incorrectly believe that giving birth to a child in the United States will gain immediate immigration rights for the parents. Although the child becomes a citizen at birth, the offspring cannot petition for the parent until the age of twenty-one.

Family Preference System

The family preference system, which is subject to numerical limitations, has four categories for adult sons, daughters, and siblings of U.S. citizens, and certain relatives of lawful permanent residents.

First Preference: Unmarried Adult Sons and Daughters. First preference is reserved for the unmarried sons and daughters of U.S. citizens who are age 21 or over. Those under age 21 would go in the unlimited immediate relative category. The term *unmarried* includes persons who were previously married but who are presently unmarried.

Second Preference: Relatives of Lawful Permanent Residents. Second preference is the only category under which lawful permanent residents of the United States ("green card" holders) can petition for relatives. This preference has two subcategories: the 2-A category for the spouses and children (unmarried and under 21), and the 2-B category for unmarried sons and daughters (age 21 and over). As the only category available to lawful permanent-resident petitioners, the popularity of second preference has resulted in significant backlogs for immigrants from countries such as Mexico and the Philippines. Therefore it may be wise for a second-preference petitioner who is eligible for naturalization to do so in order to upgrade the petition to first preference or the immediate relative category in order to avoid such backlogs.

Since second preference is the only category available to permanent resident petitioners, lawful permanent residents cannot petition for parents, married sons or daughters, or siblings, as U.S. citizens can. In order to petition for such a relative, a lawful permanent resident would first have to become a citizen, usually through naturalization.

Third Preference: Married Sons and Daughters. Third preference is reserved for the married sons and daughters of U.S. citizens. Only U.S. citizens, not lawful permanent residents or noncitizen nationals, can petition for married sons and daughters. The spouse and children of the primary immigrant (beneficiary) will also be able to immigrate. Those family members are commonly referred to as "derivative beneficiaries."

Fourth Preference: Siblings. U.S. citizens can petition for brothers and sisters. Fourth preference requires that the petitioning citizen be at least 21 years of age. The beneficiary (primary immigrant) can be married or unmarried.

Thus, an adult U.S. citizen could petition under fourth preference for a 10-year-old sister or a 5-year-old brother. Half brothers or half sisters can qualify if both the petitioner and the beneficiary are the child of a common parent. Similarly, stepbrothers and stepsisters can also qualify. If the beneficiary is married, his or her spouse and minor, unmarried children will also be able to immigrate with the beneficiary as derivative beneficiaries.

Employment-Based Preferences

The employment-based preference system has five categories for individuals ranging from professionals to ministers and investors. These categories are also subject to numerical limitations.

First Preference for Professionals and Extraordinary Workers

The employment first preference is for immigrants of extraordinary ability, outstanding professors and researchers, and certain executives and managers. Unlike second and third preference immigrants, these outstanding individuals do not need to obtain a labor certification (or alien employment certification) from the Department of Labor indicating that there is a shortage of qualified workers in the particular field.

The term *extraordinary ability* means a "level of expertise indicating that the individual is one of the small percentage who have risen to the very top of the field of endeavor" in the sciences, arts, education, business, or athletics. The ability must be documented by sustained national or international acclaim. The rules set forth ten criteria to assess the qualifications for aliens of extraordinary ability. A petitioner who satisfies three of the ten criteria qualifies.

1. Receipt of lesser nationally or internationally recognized prizes or awards for excellence in the field of endeavor
2. Membership in associations in the field for which classification is sought, which required outstanding achievements of their members, as judged by recognized national or international experts in their disciplines or fields
3. Published material about the individual in professional or major trade publications or other major media, relating to his or her work in the field for which classification is sought
4. Participation, either individually or on a panel, as a judge of the work of others in the same or an allied field of specification for which classification is sought
5. Original scientific, scholarly, artistic, athletic, or business-related contributions of major significance in the field

6. Authorship of scholarly articles in the field, in professional or major trade publications or other major media
7. Display of work in the field at artistic exhibitions or showcases
8. Performance in a leading or critical role for organizations or establishments that have a distinguished reputation
9. Command of a high salary or other significantly high remuneration for services, in relation to others in the field
10. Commercial successes in the performing arts, shown by either box-office receipts or record, cassette, compact disc, or video sales

First preference applicants who are individuals of extraordinary ability do not require job offers by U.S. employers. Immigrant petitions may be filed by the individual or any person on their behalf.

Outstanding professors and researchers usually qualify if they are recognized internationally as outstanding in a specific academic field; have at least three years of experience in teaching or research in the academic area; and are entering for (1) a tenured position (or tenure-track position) within a university or institution of higher education to teach in the academic area, (2) a comparable position with a university or institution of higher education to conduct research in the area, or (3) a comparable position to conduct research in the area with a department, division, or institute of a private employer. A petition for an outstanding professor or researcher may be filed by any U.S. employer.

The multinational executive and manager option is for an immigrant who has been employed for at least one year (in the three years preceding the application) by a firm or corporation or other legal entity or an affiliate or subsidiary and must be entering to continue to render services to the same employer in a capacity that is managerial or executive.

Managerial capacity means an assignment in which the primary activity of the employee falls into one of these categories:

1. Manages the organization, or a department, subdivision, function, or component of the organization;
2. Supervises and controls the work of other supervisory professionals, or managerial employees, or manages an essential function within the organization, or a department or subdivision of the organization;
3. If another employee is directly supervised, has the authority to hire and fire or recommend those as well as other personnel actions (such as promotion and leave authorization) or, if no other employee is supervised, functions at a senior level within the organization hierarchy or with respect to the function managed; or
4. Exercises discretion over the day-to-day operations of the activity or function for which the employee has authority.

The term *executive capacity* means an assignment with an organization in which the employee primarily:

1. Directs the management of the organization or a major component or function of the organization;
2. Establishes the goals and policies of the organization, component, or function;
3. Exercises wide latitude in discretionary decision-making; and
4. Receives only general supervision or direction from higher-level executives, the board of directors, or stockholders of the organization.

The multinational executive and manager category also requires an employer petitioner.

Second Preference: Advanced Degree
Professionals and Exceptional Ability Workers

Second preference employment-based immigration visa classification provides for two separate means of qualification: those who are individuals of "exceptional ability" or those "members of the professions holding advanced degrees." Generally a job offer and an alien employment certification (labor certification) are required demonstrating that qualified U.S. workers are unavailable, but in some instances, these requirements can be waived by the INS if it would be in the national interest to do so.

Advanced Degree Professionals. The term *profession* means "any occupation for which a U.S. baccalaureate degree or its foreign equivalent is the minimum requirement for entry into the occupation," and includes but is not limited to architects, engineers, lawyers, physicians, surgeons, and teachers in elementary or secondary schools, colleges, academies, or seminaries. Second preference is limited to professionals with advanced degrees, which is any U.S. academic or professional degree or a foreign equivalent degree above that of baccalaureate.

Exceptional Ability Workers. For those seeking classification as individuals of exceptional ability, the ability must be in the sciences, arts, or business. It must also be shown that the person's immigration will substantially benefit the national economy, cultural or educational interests, or welfare of the United States. *Exceptional ability* means a degree of expertise significantly above that ordinarily encountered in the sciences, arts, or business. Generally, the petition must be accompanied by at least three of the following six types of documents:

1. An official academic record showing a degree, diploma, certificate, or similar award from a college, university, school, or other institution of learning relating to the area of exceptional ability
2. Letters from current or former employers showing at least ten years of full-time experience in the area of exceptional ability
3. A license to practice the profession or certification for a particular profession or occupation
4. Proof of having earned a salary, or other remuneration for services, that demonstrates exceptional ability
5. Evidence of membership in professional associations
6. Evidence of recognition for achievements and significant contributions to the industry or field by peers, governmental entities, or professional or business organizations.

National Interest Waiver. The national interest exemption provides an opportunity for individuals to immigrate in second preference without a job offer and an alien employment certification. Seven factors are considered in determining whether a national interest waiver should be granted:

1. Improving the U.S. economy
2. Improving wages and working conditions of U.S. workers
3. Improving education and training programs for U.S. children and underqualified workers
4. Improving health care
5. Providing more affordable housing for young and/or older, poorer U.S. residents
6. Improving the environment of the United States and making more productive use of its natural resources
7. A request from an interested U.S. government agency

Third Preference: Skilled Workers, Professionals, and Others

The third preference classification is available to skilled workers, professionals, and other types of workers. Any U.S. employer may file a petition for classification of an alien under this category. However, an alien employment certification (labor certification) demonstrating that a qualified U.S. worker is unavailable is necessary.

Skilled Worker. A skilled worker is an individual immigrating to the United States in order to perform a job that requires at least two years of training or experience. Relevant postsecondary education can be considered as training.

Professionals. As noted above, the term *profession* means "any occupation for which a U.S. baccalaureate degree or its foreign equivalent is the minimum requirement for entry into the occupation," and includes but is not limited to architects, engineers, lawyers, physicians, surgeons, and teachers in elementary or secondary schools, colleges, academies, or seminaries. The standing of an occupation as a profession can evolve with time as the minimum educational requirements needed for entry into that occupation increase. The common denominator is that professions require specialized training that is normally obtained though higher education or for which a bachelor's degree can be obtained. Equivalent specialized instruction and experience may also suffice.

Accountants, engineers, biochemists, biologists, chemists, dentists, dieticians, veterinarians, zoologists, economists, mathematicians, sociologists, hotel managers, journalists, librarians, pharmacists, and social workers have been classified as professionals. Professional standing has been denied to translators, laboratory assistants, school counselors, and mechanical technologists.

Other Workers. Other workers are those who are immigrating to the United States to perform jobs requiring less than two years of training or experience. Any applicant in this category must satisfy the training or experience required for the job offered. The job offered cannot be of a temporary or seasonal nature. Since an alien employment certification (labor certification) is required, qualified U.S. workers cannot be available for the job offered.

Fourth Preference: Religious Workers

The fourth preference for employment-based visas sets aside visa numbers for certain special immigrants, with particular attention to religious workers. In the religious worker area, the prospective immigrant must have been a member of a religious denomination for at least two years immediately preceding the filing of the immigrant visa petition. A *religious denomination* is "a religious group or community of believers having some form of ecclesiastical government, a creed or statement of faith, some form of worship, a formal or informal code of doctrine and discipline, religious services and ceremonies, established places of religious worship, religious congregations, or comparable indicia of a bona fide religious denomination."

The types of religious workers may qualify for the benefits of this fourth preference classification include ministers, professionals in a religious occupation, and individuals in religious occupations or vocations.

A *minister* is "an individual duly authorized by a recognized religious denomination to conduct religious worship and to perform other duties usually performed by authorized members of the clergy of that religion." There must be a reasonable connection between the duties of the position offered and the religious calling of the minister; lay preachers are expressly disqualified.

Professionals in a religious occupation qualify if the duties of the position offered are for a religious vocation or occupation and a U.S. baccalaureate degree or a foreign equivalent degree is required as a minimum in order to perform the vocation satisfactorily. Other religious occupations that fall into this preference include liturgical workers, religious instructors, religious counselors, cantors, catechists, workers in religious hospitals or religious health care facilities, missionaries, religious translators, and religious broadcasters. Religious vocations such as nuns, monks, and religious brothers and sisters qualify. Expressly excluded are janitors, maintenance workers, clerks, fund-raisers, and persons solely involved in the solicitation of donations. Unlike the minister of religion category that has no time constraints, the religious worker category is due to expire on September 30, 2000.

Fifth Preference: Investors

The immigrant investor category, sometimes referred to as the "employment creation" category, is for those immigrants seeking to enter for the purpose of engaging in a new commercial enterprise. The statute requires that the investment be at least $1 million, although the amount may be adjusted down to a low of $500,000 if the enterprise is located in a rural area or any area that has experienced high unemployment of at least 150 percent of the national average. The enterprise must create ten new jobs for citizens and lawful residents of the United States. Of the 10,000 visas set aside annually for the fifth preference investor category, not less than 3,000 are reserved for applicants whose enterprise will be located in a targeted employment area.

Labor Certification

Since immigration in the second and third preference employment categories are inextricably linked to a labor certification requirement, understanding that requirement is important. Prospective immigrants who would like to immigrate on the basis of a particular job skill usually must obtain an alien employment certification (AEC) or labor certification from the Department of Labor. Investors, certain executives and managers of multinational corporations (intracompany transferees), and immigrants of extraordinary abilities are exempted from the AEC requirement. The purpose of the AEC requirement is to protect American workers from having job opportunities taken away from them by foreign workers. The two main requirements for the labor certification are that the alien's services are required due to the unavailability of qualified workers in the United States, and that the alien will receive the prevailing rate of pay in the locality of intended employment. Additionally, the position must be permanent in nature.

Labor certification procedures require consultation with the state employment office, advertising the job for others to apply, making other employees at the place of employment aware of the opening, determining the prevailing wage for the job, interviewing all qualified applicants and explaining why any available U.S. workers are not qualified, and getting final approval from the Department of Labor. The process is a lengthy one, often taking up to three years. In some situations, reduction in recruitment can be sought in order to shorten the processing time.

Once a labor certification is issued, the employer can file a visa petition for the alien. When a visa becomes available to the alien, the person can become a lawful permanent resident of the United States under one of the employment preference system categories. A person who immigrates in this manner is not bound to work for the sponsoring employer forever. However, the person must intend to work for the sponsoring employer upon entering the United States with the immigrant visa.

The burden of establishing unavailability of U.S. workers is on the prospective employer. Recruitment efforts can take place either prior or subsequent to submission of the application for certification. The advertisement must describe the job with particularity, state the salary at a rate not below the prevailing wage for the job, specify the minimum requirements and the hours, and offer prevailing working conditions. The employer must contact potentially qualified U.S. applicants as soon as possible after receiving resumes or applications.

After completion of review by the local job service office, the labor certification application is forwarded to the office of the certifying officer of the regional Department of Labor. At this point the certifying officer either grants the labor certification or issues a notice of findings. If the labor certification is granted, the final determination form is sent to the employer or representative. If a notice of findings is issued, the employer has to submit additional evidence to cure the defects or rebut the basis of the determination.

The Department of Labor has prepared two lists that are relevant to labor certifications. Schedule A is a listing of occupations that DOL has precertified as demonstrating a shortage of available U.S. workers, and for which employment of immigrants will not adversely affect the wages and working conditions of others similarly employed. Schedule B is a list of occupations for which it has been determined there is a surplus of U.S. workers. In general, an application for certification of an occupation that appears on Schedule B will be denied.

Numerical Limitations

Immediate relatives of U.S. citizens are not subject to immigration quotas or numerical limitations. However, all prospective immigrants under the family or employment-based preference categories are subject to annual numerical limitations that are imposed on a per-country as well as worldwide basis.

When a person wants to immigrate to the United States, he or she must fit into an immigration category and not be subject to a ground of inadmissibility. Additionally, a visa must be available. Immediate relatives of U.S. citizens may immigrate to the United States without being subject to numerical limitations or quotas. Thus, visas are always available to immediate relatives of U.S. citizens as long as they are not inadmissible. However, other prospective immigrants who immigrate under the preference system are subject to two types of numerical limitations: a worldwide numerical cap and a country or territorial limit. The preference system provides separate systems for family immigration and for employment-related immigration.

Under the law, at least 226,000 family-preference category visas are available annually on a worldwide basis. Although in theory the worldwide quota can be increased to 480,000 annually, the level will likely not be much more than 226,000. This is because the family-preference category level is determined by subtracting the number of immediate relative entrants— generally well over 200,000 annually—from the maximum (480,000), with an absolute floor of 226,000. A separate worldwide numerical limitation of 140,000 is set aside for employment-based immigrants.

The law also provides an annual limitation of visas per country of 7 percent of the worldwide quotas. Thus, assuming a 226,000 worldwide family visa numerical limitation and 140,000 limit for employment visas, 7 percent of the total (366,000) is 25,620 for each country. But 75 percent of the visas issued for spouses and children of lawful permanent residents (family second preference 2-A) are not counted against each country's quota.

Prospective immigrants from countries with great visa demands such as the Philippines and Mexico face long backlogs. Until a visa becomes available, these individuals cannot immigrate to the United States.

Priority Dates and Visa Availability

Because of the numerical limitations on the preference immigration categories, backlogs exist in some categories for some countries. Immigration applicants must wait in accordance with a priority date that is assigned to each preference applicant, and his or her priority date must be monitored on a visa bulletin that provides information on visa availability.

Priority Dates. Because preference system visa demand for several countries often surpasses the per-country numerical limitations, as reflected in the monthly visa bulletin, a system of priority dates is used to determine the order of processing family and employment preference category immigrants. A priority date is generally established on the date a visa petition is filed on behalf of the prospective immigrant by a relative or employer. For alien employment certification (labor certification) cases, the priority date is established on the date the labor certification application is filed.

For example, if a first, second, third, or fourth preference family visa petition form is filed on December 10, 1999, that date becomes the beneficiary's priority date, even though the petition may not be approved until later. Similarly, when a person seeks to immigrate through the labor certification process under the third preference employment category, the date on which the application for labor certification is filed with labor officials establishes the priority date. If a labor certification is not needed, the date of the filing of the employer's visa petition establishes the priority date.

If the status of the beneficiary changes during a waiting period, the beneficiary can retain the same priority date so long as he or she still falls into an immigrant category. For example, if a third preference family beneficiary (married son or daughter of a U.S. citizen) becomes unmarried, the petition is automatically converted to first preference (or immediate relative if under the age of 21).

Visa Bulletin. Each month the Visa Office of the State Department issues a bulletin that charts the availability of visas around the world for purposes of the preference system. A sample visa bulletin is contained in the Appendix.

The chart contains a list of certain countries, as well as a general category for areas of the world that are not listed separately. The chart indicates visa availability using letters and dates. The letter C on the chart means that visas are currently available. The letter U indicates that visas are not available for that category. A date on the chart indicates that beneficiaries whose relative visa petition or labor certification applications were filed on or before that date may now apply for an immigrant visa. In other words, visas would be available to those beneficiaries whose priority dates have been reached.

Priority dates must be monitored month by month. As soon as a visa becomes available, the beneficiary should immediately apply for an immigrant visa abroad or for adjustment of status in the United States.

Inadmissibility Grounds

Although a visa may be available to aliens under one of the immigrant categories, the prospective entrant may still be denied the visa or denied admission into the United States if one of the grounds of inadmissibility is not satisfied. Dozens of categories and subcategories of inadmissible aliens are included in the law—ranging from physical or mental disability grounds to those relating to crimes and terrorism. The grounds of inadmissibility were formerly referred to as *exclusion grounds.*

Examples of grounds of inadmissibility include aliens with communicable diseases (e.g., tuberculosis, venereal diseases, HIV), those who are likely to become a public charge (usually those below 125 percent of the federal poverty guidelines), those who have not met vaccination requirements, those convicted of moral turpitude or narcotics crimes, those who have entered without inspection, those who by fraud or willful misrepresentation have sought a visa or other immigration benefit, those who have made a false claim to U.S. citizenship to obtain an immigration benefit, those who are guilty of unlawful presence in the United States for at least one year and who have departed, and those who have committed document fraud.

A waiver of inadmissibility is available for some grounds of inadmissibility if certain conditions are met. If a waiver is granted, then the person can immigrate.

Procedures for Immigrating

Under certain conditions, if the prospective immigrant is in the United States (e.g., as an H-1B nonimmigrant worker or F-1 foreign student), he or she can seek adjustment of status. If conditions for adjustment of status are not met, or if the person is out of the United States, then an immigrant visa application is processed abroad at a U.S. consulate. The procedures for immigrating are fairly straightforward.

Filing a Petition. A petition must be filed on behalf of the prospective immigrant (beneficiary) with supporting documents. In the family categories, the petition is a Form I-130 (filed by the citizen or lawful permanent resident petitioner); in the employment-based system, the petition is a Form I-140 (filed by the employer). In the employment-based second or third preference, the Form I-140 is not filed until a labor certification has been issued by the Department of Labor, or a national interest waiver of the labor certification has been granted.

If everything is in order, a notice of approval is sent to the petitioner.

Adjustment of Status in the United States. Nonimmigrant aliens who qualify under one of the immigrant categories usually prefer completing the immigration process in the United States rather than traveling abroad to process an immigrant visa application. The process of adjustment of status in the United States is not, however, available to everyone. Strict requirements must be met.

In order to qualify for adjustment of status, the person must have entered the United States with inspection (this disqualifies many undocumented aliens who entered surreptitiously along the border), must not have entered as a crew member of a ship or airplane, must not have worked without authorization (although those married to U.S. citizens are not penalized for working without permission), and a visa must be available.

Assuming these requirements are met, the person can submit an application for adjustment of status. This also involves being fingerprinted to check for any past criminal activity and a medical examination to check for any disqualifying problems. In marriage cases, the petitioner and the beneficiary may undergo strict questioning at this point as a test of whether the marriage is simply a sham for immigration purposes.

If approved, the adjustment-of-status applicant becomes a lawful permanent resident alien of the United States. In marriage cases, the approval is conditioned on the couple returning to the INS for another interview two years later to determine if the marriage has remained viable.

Consular Procedures Abroad. If the prospective immigrant is not eligible for adjustment of status in the United States or is already out of the United States, the final immigration process will be sought at a U.S. consulate abroad. This generally occurs at the consulate in the person's native country. Again, this process cannot occur unless a visa is available, which means that the visa bulletin in preference cases must be consulted.

Involvement by consular officials usually begins when the petitioner designates which U.S. consulate the approved I-130 or I-140 should be sent to. Once the approved petition is received by the U.S. consul and a visa is available, the consul will send a set of forms to the prospective immigrant. These forms, often referred to collectively as "Packet III," are to be completed and processed at the consulate. This also involves being fingerprinted to check for any past criminal activity.

Once all the forms are in order and a visa is available, the applicant will be given an appointment for an interview. A medical examination is also required to check for any disqualifying problems. The interview is conducted by a consular official.

If all goes well, the immigrant visa is issued to the applicant. The visa is valid for four months and must be used within that period of time. By using the visa, the person becomes an immigrant. The person's passport is stamped with a temporary I-551 (indicating employment authorization) and within a few weeks, the person is mailed a permanent resident alien registration card.

Important Policy Issues Today

Debating immigration policy has been a regular activity in the United States since the founding of the country. The state of the economy, racial views, social movements, the composition of the nation's leadership, media perspectives, and the effectiveness of particular spokespersons all affect the outcome of the debate from year to year. Broad or specific legal policies and enforcement priorities toward immigrants can mean humane treatment and openness at times, or restrictions and callousness at other times.

Much of the debate over the years has occurred at state and local levels. The historical anti-immigrant sentiment that was manifested in local and state laws directed against documented immigrants, such as alien land laws and restrictions on doing business (e.g., *Yick Wo v. Hopkins*), has a modern corollary in attempts to limit certain occupations and professions to citizens. As a general rule, such state restrictions have been deemed unconstitutional by the Supreme Court. For example, in *In re Griffiths,* the exclusion of lawful permanent residents from the practice of law in Connecticut was invalidated, and in *Sugarman v. Dougall,* a New York law providing that only U.S. citizens could hold permanent state civil service positions was struck down.

However, the protection that the Supreme Court had provided in this area began to erode around the time that more flexibility was being given to INS enforcement activities (e.g., *United States v. Martinez-Fuerte* and *Immigration and Naturalization Service v. Lopez-Mendoza*). Beginning with *Foley v. Connelie* in 1978, the Supreme Court has deferred to states requiring U.S. citizenship when the government job entails a public function, or involves the "formulation, execution, or review of broad public policy." Thus, in *Foley,* the Court held that New York could bar aliens from holding state law enforcement positions. A year later in *Ambach v. Norwick,* the Court ruled that public school teaching (even teaching French in high school!) fell within the public functions exception and could be limited to citizens as well.

In recent years, much anti-immigrant sentiment has originated in California. For example, when the state faced a severe budget problem in 1992, then-governor Pete Wilson fanned the flames of xenophobia by blaming many of the state's fiscal woes on immigrants. He charged that immigrants were costing state taxpayers billions in public assistance, medical care, and education. With gubernatorial support, the main lobbyist for the Federation for American Immigration Reform (FAIR) in California, former national INS commissioner Alan Nelson, and a former INS regional official, Harold Ezell, joined forces with other neonativists in California to place Proposition 187 on the 1994 ballot. The proposition's targeting of undocumented immigrants proved to be a smart political tactic that enabled its proponents to attract supporters who were otherwise not opposed to immigration.

Throughout the Proposition 187 debate, its major proponents claimed to be motivated only by a concern with undocumented immigrants, and that documented immigrants were beneficial to the country. They lied. As soon as Proposition 187 passed, the proponents of Proposition 187 and other neonativists immediately set their sights on reducing the flow of legal immigrants. Thus, responding to political pressure, the Commission on Legal Immigration Reform, chaired by the late former Congresswoman Barbara Jordan, recommended reducing legal immigration by a third. Congressman Lamar Smith and Senator Alan Simpson also introduced proposals that would make cuts. Even before Proposition 187, Republicans in Congress attacked legal immigrants by proposing to exclude lawful permanent residents and refugees from benefits that ranged from Supplemental Security Income to school lunch programs for their children. The welfare-cutting legislation was signed by a reluctant President Clinton in 1996. Within two years, benefits and food stamps were restored for some immigrants and refugees after the harshness and unfairness of the 1996 welfare reform were revealed.

Issues affecting immigration and immigrant policies continue to be debated today, from the broad to the specific. Restrictionists call for a moratorium on immigration for a number of years, in part to get "breathing" time and catch up on the process of Americanization. Most cultural pluralists say the United States is doing fine under the current system, and that Americans should instead be working on common respect and core values. Restrictionists attack the family reunification priority for the selection system, arguing that it should be replaced with a skills-based system. Proponents of family-based immigration say that the family system is fair and has always been good for our country, especially given the psychic value of family reunification for productive workers in the United States. Assimilationists want the naturalization residency period to be expanded from five years to as much as twenty years, to ensure that new citizens are really loyal to our country. Immigrant service providers argue that the current rules are adequate, that INS should place more resources into clearing naturalization backlogs, and that those applying for citizenship are among the most enthusiastic and productive citizens in the country. Nativists argue that new immigrants are undeserving of public benefits, while immigrants argue that they contribute much more to the economy than they take back in services or benefits. Restrictionists believe that the number of professionals entering in categories such as H-1B nonimmigrant categories are taking away jobs from U.S. workers. Businesses in the United States argue that they need these H-1B workers to be productive and that there are insufficient numbers of qualified U.S. professionals.

Such debates will continue, from Proposition 187–type proposals (whether benefits or schooling should be afforded to undocumented aliens), to asylum concerns (how much process should be afforded to asylum seekers), to basic selection criteria. Clearly, the historically recurring backlashes against immigration can sway political opinion and become manifested in exclusionist legislation. Demographic changes across the country over the last several decades and predictions of continued change in the future provide the impetus for much of the nativist sentiment today, especially for those uncomfortable with notions of diversity and change.

A

ABANDONMENT OF PERMANENT RESIDENCE Under certain conditions **lawful permanent resident alien**s who travel out of the United States on a regular basis or who spend more than a year abroad run the risk of being stripped of lawful permanent residence status (and their **alien registration receipt card**) on the grounds that they have abandoned their lawful permanent residence status.

Many lawful permanent resident aliens operate under the misconception that as long as they do not spend more than a year out of the United States, their lawful permanent residence status is maintained. Permanent residence can be deemed abandoned after a series of lengthy trips abroad over the period of a few years. Many immigrants who continue to work or operate a business abroad run a similar risk of losing permanent residence status. The law also provides that a lawful permanent resident may not be readmitted if he or she has been absent from the United States continuously for more than 180 days.

In making the determination of whether a person has abandoned permanent residence, an **immigration judge** will want to know whether the person maintains a residence in the United States; other evidence of residence such as bank accounts, belongings, family, employment, and other contacts, along with the intent to return, will be important. See *Matter of Kane.*

A permanent resident possessing a valid **reentry permit** has a better chance of establishing that permanent residence has not been abandoned. However, intent at the time of departure from the United States is the critical factor. While the reentry permit is a strong indicator of the alien's intent to return at the time of departure, the presumption of intent to retain status applies only to valid permits not procured by **document fraud** or **material misrepresentation.** Statements given during the application for readmission that contradict those given while obtaining the reentry permit may bring into question the validity of the permit. [8 C.F.R. §§211.1; 223.3]

ABASCAL, RALPH S. (1934–1997) Ralph S. Abascal was a pioneering legal services lawyer who won landmark decisions on behalf of farmworkers and undocumented immigrants. For more than twenty years, he was the general counsel and guiding spirit of California Rural Legal Assistance (CRLA), one of the nation's largest legal services programs. He also worked as the director of litigation at the San Francisco Neighborhood Legal Assistance Foundation from 1970 to 1975.

Abascal was the grandson of a stonemason from Spain. His father traveled to Cuba, helped build a railroad in Mexico, and then walked across the border to San Diego. Abascal's mother came from a family of immigrant fruit-pickers. Abascal saw the 1960 film *Inherit the Wind,* which depicted the debate over evolutionary theory waged by Clarence Darrow and William Jennings Bryan in the 1925 Scopes trial. That helped shift the focus of Abascal's studies; he had already received an M.B.A. from the University of California at Berkeley, and was nearing the completion of his Ph.D. in economics. But after viewing the movie, he studied the Progressive Era in American history, quit economics, and opted for law school. He later said, "I switched from seeking truth to seeking justice."

After earning a law degree, Abascal immediately went to work as a staff attorney for CRLA, one of the many legal services programs born of the War on Poverty. He started out in Salinas, quickly joining forces with the leaders of California's nascent farmworkers' union, Cesar Chavez and Dolores Huerta. Their collaboration resulted in several groundbreaking cases. One led to a ban on the use of the short-handled hoe, a symbol of harshness in the lettuce fields that allowed foremen to assume that their laborers were slacking off if they were not hunched over. In another more contentious case, nineteen farmworkers challenged the right of the University of California to conduct publicly financed research intended to develop labor-saving farm machinery.

His defense of farmworkers led Abascal into frequent battles with California's biggest farmers. A suit filed in 1969 on behalf of six nursing mothers who were working in the fields eventually led to a ban on the pesticide DDT. Two decades later, two other cases in the federal courts led to limits on dozens of pesticides thought to cause cancer. In 1971, he won a case before the California Supreme Court against Madera County, which attempted to force children over the age of ten whose families received welfare checks to help grape farmers in emergency harvests. In 1993, he argued before the U.S. Supreme Court in a class action challenging the 1986 Immigration Reform and Control Act, winning deportation stays for tens of thousands of undocumented aliens. He was also a leader in the ongoing court challenge to Proposition 187, the 1994 California initiative that attempted among other things to exclude undocumented children from public schools.

Abascal served on the boards of many legal and public interest organizations and received many awards for his work, including the American

Bar Association's Thurgood Marshall Award in 1995, the Kutak-Dodds Prize of the National Legal Aid Defender Association and the Robert Kutak Foundation, the California State Bar's 1983 award for legal services to the poor, and a similar award from the Mexican American Legal Defense and Education Fund. Abascal received his J.D. from Hastings College of Law in 1968.

ABC ASYLUM CLASS In *American Baptist Churches v. Thornburgh* [760 F. Supp. 796 (N.D. Cal. 1991)], known as the *ABC* case, a settlement was reached requiring the INS to readjudicate the asylum claims of certain Salvadorans and Guatemalans who were present in the United States as of 1990, and who registered for the *ABC* case benefits or, in the case of Salvadorans, for **temporary protected status.** The *ABC* litigation began in 1985 as a nationwide class action on behalf of Salvadorans and Guatemalans. The plaintiffs alleged that the INS and the Executive Office of Immigration Review were biased in their asylum adjudication process for those two nationalities. Under the settlement, Salvadorans are eligible for new asylum interviews. New asylum interviews for *ABC* class members began on April 7, 1997.

ACCULTURATION See **Assimilation.**

ACQUISITION OF CITIZENSHIP The Fourteenth Amendment to the U.S. Constitution provides, in pertinent part, that "all persons born or naturalized in the United States, and subject to the jurisdiction thereof, are citizens of the United States and of the State wherein they reside." Thus, in general, all persons born in the United States, even of alien parents, acquire U.S. citizenship at birth. Because foreign diplomats are not subject to the jurisdiction of the United States, their children born here do not acquire citizenship. Their children are treated as **lawful permanent resident alien**s. [8 U.S.C. §1401(a); *United States v. Wong Kim Ark,* 169 U.S. 649 (1898); 8 C.F.R. §101.3(a)(1)]

In addition to the fifty states and the District of Columbia, persons born in Puerto Rico, the Virgin Islands, and Guam are citizens of the United States at birth. Birth in the United States includes birth in its ports, harbors, bays, and a marginal belt of the sea extending three miles from the coastline. [8 U.S.C. §1403]

Under certain conditions, a person can acquire U.S. citizenship at birth even though the birth place is outside the United States. The basis for such a citizenship claim is generally one of transmission from a parent who is a U.S. citizen. The rules have changed many times. For a person born outside the United States after 1952, if both parents were U.S. citizens at the time, and one of the parents had a residence in the United States, the person is automatically a U.S. citizen at birth. If the child had one parent who was an alien and one who was a U.S. citizen, transmission of citizenship could occur if the citizen parent was physically present in the United States or outlying possession for a total of five years prior to the child's birth. At least two of the five years must have been accrued after attaining the age of fourteen. Different requirements apply if the child was born out of wedlock. [8 U.S.C. §§1401, 1409]

In essence, the United States follows both the **jus soli** and **jus sanguinis** rules of acquiring citizenship and nationality.

ⅠⅠⅠⅠ *ADAMS V. HOWERTON*   This case [673 F.2d 1036 (9th Cir. 1982)], involving a marriage of two gay men, exemplifies the standard view under U.S. immigration policy that same-sex marriages are not recognized for the purpose of conferring an immigration benefit.

Following the expiration of Sullivan's visitor's visa, Adams, a U.S. citizen, and Sullivan obtained a marriage license from the county clerk in Boulder, Colorado, and were married by a minister. Adams then petitioned the INS for classification of Sullivan as an **immediate relative** of a U.S. citizen, based upon Sullivan's status as Adams's spouse. The **visa petition** was denied, and through various appeals, the case ended up before the court of appeals.

Two questions were presented in the appeal: first, whether a citizen's spouse within the meaning of U.S. immigration law must be an individual of the opposite sex; and second, whether the statute, if so interpreted, is constitutional.

It was unclear to the court whether Colorado would actually recognize a same-sex marriage. But even if the Adams-Sullivan marriage were valid under Colorado law, it was clear to the court that Congress did not intend the mere validity of a marriage under state law to be controlling. Nothing in the law or the legislative history suggests that the term *spouse* in the law was intended to include a person of the same sex as the citizen petitioner. The term *marriage* ordinarily contemplates a relationship between a man and a woman. Congress has not indicated an intent to enlarge the ordinary meaning of those words. In view of the legislative history and statutory provisions, Congress intended that only partners in heterosexual marriages be considered spouses under the law.

As to the constitutionality of this law, the court noted that Congress has almost **plenary power** to admit or exclude aliens, and the decisions of Congress are subject only to limited judicial review. Congress's decision to confer spouse status under the law only upon the parties to heterosexual marriages has a rational basis and therefore comports with constitutional requirements.

Congress manifested its concern for family integrity when it passed laws facilitating immigration of the spouses of some valid heterosexual marriages. This distinction is one of many drawn by Congress pursuant to its determination to provide some—but not all—close relationships with relief from immigration restrictions that might otherwise hinder reunification in this country. In effect, Congress has determined that preferential status is not warranted for the spouses of homosexual marriages. Perhaps this is because homosexual marriages never produce offspring, because they violate traditional and often prevailing societal mores. In any event, having found that Congress rationally intended to deny preferential status to the spouses of such marriages, the court felt no need to further "probe and test the justifications for the legislative decision."

Although same-sex marriages may not confer immigration benefits, the **Board of Immigration Appeals** has recognized that persecution on account of sexual orientation may be grounds for claiming **asylum.** See *Matter of Toboso-Alfonso.*

ADJUSTMENT OF STATUS   Nonimmigrants who qualify under one of the **immigrant** categories and meet other requirements are able to adjust their status to that of a **lawful permanent resident alien** in the United States without having to travel abroad to process an immigrant visa application. Most immigrants become immigrants by processing their paperwork at an **American embassy** or consulate abroad. Many nonimmigrants, such as students, visitors, or temporary workers, prefer to process their paperwork in the United States through adjustment of status as a matter of convenience and to avoid travel expenses. Refugees and asylees who have resided in the United States for a year may also adjust their status to lawful permanent residence.

Generally, in order to adjust status in the United States without having to file paperwork abroad, nonimmigrants must have entered with inspection (i.e., not surreptitiously or through a false claim of U.S. citizenship), must not have engaged in unauthorized employment, and must not have overstayed their permitted time to remain in the United States. However, nonimmigrants who seek adjustment of status in the United States on the basis of a marriage to a U.S. citizen are generally not penalized for unauthorized work or overstaying their visa as long as the marriage is bona fide and the person did not enter with the intent of getting married. Only those nonimmigrants who enter with fiancé visas may enter with the intent of getting married. [8 U.S.C. §§1158, 1159, 1255]

ADMINISTRATIVE APPEALS UNIT   The Administrative Appeals Unit (AAU) is located in the central office of the INS in Washington, D.C. Many issues involving visa matters that are decided at the local **district offices** can be appealed to the AAU.

ADMINISTRATIVE LAW JUDGE   In general, administrative law judges (ALJs) are judges who hear cases involving civil (as opposed to criminal) laws and regulations that one of the agencies in the executive branch of government is in charge of enforcing. ALJs can impose monetary fines and other actions to enforce these laws. For example, ALJs hear and decide cases involving **employer sanctions** and charges of immigration-related employment discrimination, such as **citizenship discrimination** and **national origin discrimination.** ALJs also have jurisdiction to hear complaints involving **document fraud.** Immigration-related employment discrimination cases are heard by ALJs who are part of the **Office of the Chief Administrative Hearing Officer,** a branch of the **Executive Office of Immigration Review.**

ADMISSION   The term used in the **Illegal Immigration Reform and Immigrant Responsibility Act of 1996** (IIRAIRA) to mean lawful entry of the alien into the United States after **inspection** and authorization by an immigration officer. Whether an **alien** has been inspected and admitted is an important question, for example, if the person is later seeking **adjustment of status** to **lawful permanent resident alien** status in the United States; generally only those aliens who have been inspected and admitted or **paroled** into the United States are eligible for adjustment of status.

Aliens who have been paroled into the United States and those who have been permitted to land temporarily as alien **crew members** are not considered to have been admitted.

An alien who is already a lawful permanent resident and is returning from a trip abroad is not regarded as seeking admission upon return. This is most important because the person will not have to satisfy the **inadmissibility grounds** on each departure and return to the United States. This 1996 approach in large part implements the Supreme Court decision in *Rosenberg v. Fleuti.* There are, however, exceptions to this rule. A lawful permanent resident will be regarded as seeking an admission if the person (1) has abandoned or relinquished status [see a**bandonment of permanent residence**], (2) has been absent from the United States for a continuous period in excess of 180 days, (3) has engaged in illegal activity after having departed the United States [see *Matter of Contreras*], (4) has committed a crime, or (5) is seeking to enter without inspection. [U.S.C. §1101(a)(13)]

ADVANCED PAROLE   The INS district director can grant advanced parole or permission to an alien (usually someone without permanent status in the country) to return to the United States who must travel abroad because of an emergency. For example, an **adjustment of status** applicant may desire to leave the United States and return before the application has been decided. Such a departure and return are proper only if advanced parole has been authorized by the district director. When the person returns to the United States, he or she is said to be in the United States pursuant to advanced parole, for example for the purpose of completing adjustment of status processing. The district director may also terminate advanced parole status if the public interest does not warrant the person's continued presence in the United States. [8 C.F.R. §§212(d), 245.2(a)]

AFFIDAVIT OF SUPPORT   An affidavit of support (Form I-864) is a legal document that must be submitted on behalf of a prospective immigrant by a relative in the United States who is filing immigration papers on behalf of the prospective immigrant. The affidavit of support is legally binding on the person who signs it. The person signing the affidavit is often referred to as a sponsor. In the affidavit of support, the sponsor agrees to provide financial support to maintain the sponsored immigrant at an annual income that is not less than 125 percent of the federal poverty line. If the sponsor fails to abide by this promise, the sponsor can be sued by the immigrant, the federal government, or the state in which the immigrant resides. The affidavit is enforceable until the immigrant has become a citizen of the United States or has worked forty qualifying quarters for purposes of Social Security coverage. The major purpose of the affidavit of support is to ensure that immigrants will not need to resort to welfare and become **public charge**s. An example is included in the Appendix.

AFROYIM V. RUSK   In this case[387 U.S. 253 (1967)], the Supreme Court made clear that congressional attempts to strip citizens of their citizenship through **expatriation** cannot be enacted without close constitutional scrutiny. Afroyim immigrated to the United States from Poland in 1912 and became a citizen through **naturalization** in 1926. He went to Israel in 1950, and in 1951 he voluntarily voted in an election for the Israeli Knesset, the legislative body of Israel. In 1960, when he applied for renewal of his U.S. passport, the **State Department** refused to grant it on the grounds that he had lost his U.S. citizenship under a provision of the immigration laws that provided that a U.S. citizen shall "lose" his citizenship if he votes "in a political election in a foreign state." Afroyim brought this action arguing that the law violated his constitutional rights.

The Supreme Court agreed with Afroyim. Under the Fourteenth Amendment, "All persons born or naturalized in the United States … are citizens of the United States." Once obtained, this means that citizenship is kept unless the person voluntarily relinquishes it. Citizenship is no light trifle to be jeopardized at any moment Congress decides to do so under the name of one of its general or implied grants of power. The Fourteenth Amendment was designed to, and does, protect all citizens of this nation against a congressional forcible destruction of their citizenship by congressional action, regardless of creed, color, or race. See also *Vance v. Terrazas.*

AGGRAVATED FELON   An alien convicted of an aggravated felony can be removed from the United States. For the purpose of immigration law, an aggravated felony is murder, rape, sexual abuse of a minor, trafficking in any controlled substance (including drugs, firearms, or destructive devices), money laundering, or any crime of violence or theft (except for purely political offenses) for which the term of imprisonment imposed is at least one year. The term also includes treason; child pornography; operation of a prostitution business; fraud or deceit in which the loss to the victim or victims exceeds $10,000; tax evasion in which the loss to the United States government exceeds $10,000; crimes relating to the Racketeer Influenced and Corrupt Organizations (RICO) Act or selling false government documents, if the term of imprisonment imposed is at least one year; alien smuggling (except in the case of a first offense involving the assisting, abetting, or aiding of the alien's spouse, child, or parent); failure to appear to serve a sentence if the underlying offense is punishable by imprisonment for a term of five years; and bribery, counterfeiting, or forgery for which the time of imprisonment is at least one year. An attempt or conspiracy to commit any of these crimes is also included. An offense that is not a felony under federal law cannot be considered an aggravated felony even though it is a felony under state law.

A **lawful permanent resident alien** who has been convicted of an aggravated felony can be placed in **removal proceedings** even before release from incarceration. An alien convicted of an aggravated felony who is not a lawful permanent resident can be removed through an expedited procedure without a hearing before an immigration judge. [8 U.S.C. §§1101(a)(43), 1227(a)(2), 238; *Aguirre v. INS*, 79 F.3d 315 (2d Cir. 1996)]

AGUILERA-ENRIQUEZ V. INS   This decision [516 F.2d 565 (6th Cir. 1975)] affirms the proposition that aliens in **removal proceedings** do not have the right to government-appointed counsel.

Jesus Aguilera-Enriquez was a **lawful permanent resident alien** farmworker. Returning from a trip to Mexico, he was subjected to a search and was found with two grams of cocaine. He pleaded guilty in federal court of knowingly possessing cocaine and received a suspended one-year sentence, was placed on probation for five years, and was fined $3,000. He was not informed that a narcotics conviction would almost certainly lead to his removal from the United States.

Deportation (removal) proceedings were then brought against Aguilera-Enriquez. When he appeared before the **immigration judge,** he requested appointed counsel, but his request was denied. After a hearing, Aguilera-Enriquez was ordered deported and was not afforded the option of **voluntary departure.** This case represented a due process challenge to the judge's ruling that Aguilera-Enriquez had no right to counsel at government expense.

The court of appeals ruled that the test for whether due process requires the appointment of counsel for an indigent alien is whether, in a given case, the assistance of counsel would be necessary to provide fundamental fairness. Here, since Aguilera-Enriquez was effectively represented by counsel on appeal of the immigration judge's appeal, lack of counsel before the judge did not prevent full administrative consideration of any arguments that could be made. Counsel could have obtained no different administrative result. Fundamental fairness, therefore, was not abridged during the administrative proceedings.

ALIEN   An alien is any person in the United States who is not a **citizen** or **national** of the United States, including **lawful permanent resident alien**s, nonimmigrant students and visitors, **refugee**s, and **undocumented alien**s.

ALIEN EMPLOYMENT CERTIFICATION   Prospective immigrants who would like to immigrate on the basis of a particular job skill usually must obtain an **alien employment certification** (AEC) from the **Department of Labor** (DOL). **Intracompany transferees,** investors [see **investor visa**], and immigrants of extraordinary abilities are exempted from the AEC requirement. The purpose of the AEC requirement is to protect American workers from having job opportunities taken away from them by foreign workers. The two main requirements for the certification are that the alien's services are required due to unavailability of qualified workers in the United States and that the alien will receive the prevailing rate of pay in the locality of intended employment. The position must also be permanent in nature.

Certification procedures require consultation with the **state employment office,** advertising the job for others to apply, making other employees at the place of employment aware of the opening, determining the **prevailing wage** for the job, interviewing all qualified applicants and explaining why any available U.S. workers are not qualified, and getting final approval from the DOL. The process is a lengthy one, often taking up to three years. In some situations, **reduction in recruitment** can be sought in order to shorten the processing time. [8 U.S.C. §1182(a)(5); 20 C.F.R. §656]

Once an alien employment certification is issued, the employer can file a **visa petition** for the alien. When a visa becomes available to the alien, the person can become a **lawful permanent resident alien** of the United States under one of the employment **preference system** categories. A person who immigrates in this manner is not bound to work for the sponsoring employer forever. However, the person must intend to work for the sponsoring employer upon entering the United States with the immigrant visa. See *Jang Man Cho v. INS.*

The burden of establishing unavailability of U.S. workers is on the prospective employer. Recruitment efforts can take place either prior or subsequent to submission of the application for certification. The advertisement must describe the job with particularity, state the salary at a rate not below the prevailing wage for the job, specify the minimum requirements and the hours, and offer prevailing working conditions. The employer must contact potentially qualified U.S. applicants as soon as possible after receiving resumes or applications.

After completion of review by the local job service office, the alien employment certification application is forwarded to the certifying officer at the regional offices of the DOL. At this point the certifying officer either grants the certification or issues a notice of findings. If the certification is granted, the final determination form is sent to the employer or representative. If a notice of findings is issued, the employer has to submit additional evidence to cure the defects or rebut the basis of the determination.

The DOL has prepared two lists that are relevant to labor certifications. **Schedule A** is a listing of occupations that DOL has precertified as demonstrating a shortage of available U.S. workers, and for which employment of immigrants will not adversely affect the wages and working conditions of others similarly employed. **Schedule B** is a list of occupations for which it has been determined there is a surplus of U.S. workers. In general, an application for certification of an occupation that appears on Schedule B will be denied.

ALIEN LAND LAWS As part of the efforts to discourage Asian immigration in the early twentieth century, states such as California and Washington enacted laws restricting landownership. In addition to continued racial animosity, a sense of economic competition persisted. For example, by the 1910s, Japanese immigrants using intensive farming techniques produced more than 10 percent of California produce while owning only 1 percent of its farmland. So in 1913, the California legislature passed the Alien Land Law, which provided that only aliens eligible to citizenship could hold an interest in real property. Since the immigration laws denied Asians the right to become citizens, the land law precluded Japanese from owning property. The laws were upheld by the Supreme Court in 1923, and it was not until 1953 that the laws were reexamined and struck down as racially discriminatory. See *Masaoka v. California* [39 Cal. 2d 883 (1952)]; *Fujii v. California* [38 Cal. 2d 718 (1952)].

The basic provisions of California's alien land law read as follows:

> Chap. 113. Section 1. All aliens eligible to citizenship under the laws of the United States may acquire, possess, enjoy, transmit and inherit real property, or any interest therein, in this state, in the same manner and to the same extent as citizens of the United States, except as otherwise provided by the laws of this state.
>
> Sec. 2. All aliens other than those mentioned in section one of this act may acquire, possess, enjoy and transfer real property, or any interest therein, in this state, in the manner and to the extent and for the purposes prescribed by any treaty now existing between the government of the United States and the nation or country of which such alien is a citizen or subject, and not otherwise, and may in addition thereto lease lands in this state for agricultural purposes for a term not exceeding three years.

ALIEN REGISTRATION RECEIPT CARD The alien registration receipt card, commonly referred to as the *green card*, is the credit-card-size document that is issued to **lawful permanent resident**

aliens in the United States. "I-551" is the INS designation for the card and appears on the card. Three versions of the I-551 are currently in circulation. One is a white card issued from 1977 to 1989, the second is a pink card issued from 1989 to 1997, and the third is the permanent resident card that has been issued since 1997. The first two are labeled "Resident Alien" in the front, and "Alien Registration Receipt Card" on the back. The newest I-551 is labeled "Permanent Resident Card" on the front and the back. An even earlier version, Form I-151, is bluish in tinge and has not been acceptable for employment purposes since March 1996.

The white I-551 card does not bear an expiration date. The other I-551 cards are valid for either a two-year period [see **conditional permanent residence**] or ten-year (permanent resident) period. However, the expiration date means only that the card must be replaced by a new card (the idea being to allow the INS to maintain a high standard of card technology and security). The person's permanent residence status has not expired even though the card may have.

Some features of I-551 resident alien cards that are shared by all three versions include: (1) A color photograph with the individual's right ear exposed, which serves as an "earprint," much like a fingerprint, for identification purposes. The surface is flat, the photograph is embedded in the card, and the edges are not raised to the touch. (2) Alignment, with the first letters or digits in the cardholder's date of birth, alien number beginning with the letter *A*, card expiration date, country of birth, and other information located in each card to the right of the photograph, in vertical alignment and printed over an official seal. (3) High-quality printing with clear and distinct lettering, and with all information, except the signature, printed in an identical font (style and intensity). (4) Distinctive punctuation of double family names; Spanish names are treated by the INS as father's surname separated by a hyphen from mother's surname, followed by a comma, then the first name (e.g., Garcia-Lopez, Rosa).

AMBASSADOR   An ambassador is the highest-ranking diplomatic agent of one government who is stationed as a representative in another country. The United States has ambassadors to most foreign countries. The position is a political appointment by the president. The ambassador technically has no authority to issue visas, but can have influence over refugee matters and discretionary visa decisions by the **consulate general.**

AMERASIAN CHILDREN   An Amerasian child is an alien who was born after 1950 and prior to October 1, 1982, in Korea, Vietnam, Laos, Kampuchea, or Thailand, and who was fathered by a U.S.

citizen. The immigration laws allow an Amerasian child to file or have filed on his or her behalf an immigrant **visa petition** to become a **lawful permanent resident alien** of the United States. The impetus behind this law is the fact that many U.S. soldiers stationed in Asian countries during the period in question had relationships with women in those countries who gave birth to their children. In determining whether an alien was born under the circumstances described, immigration officials consult with government and private voluntary agency officials in the alien's country of birth, and consider the alien's physical appearance and any evidence presented. This includes birth and baptismal records, local civil records, testimony of witnesses, photographs of the U.S. citizen father, and letters of financial support from the father. [8 U.S.C. §1154(g); 8 C.F.R. §204.4(f)]

AMERICAN BAPTIST CHURCHES V. THORNBURGH
See **ABC Asylum Class.**

AMERICAN BAR ASSOCIATION IMMIGRATION PRO BONO DEVELOPMENT PROJECT
The American Bar Association (ABA) Immigration Pro Bono Development Project began in late 1990 with a grant from the Ford Foundation. The goal of the project has been to focus the organized bar on the often neglected legal needs of immigrants, refugees, and newcomers. Although the organized bar has long been involved in stimulating pro bono participation in addressing the legal needs of the poor, in most instances the legal needs of newcomers have not been incorporated into these pro bono delivery systems. As the national representative of the organized bar, the ABA plays a leadership role for bar associations throughout the country designing systems to deliver pro bono services to the poor. Prior to the project's inception, no entity in the ABA sought to incorporate the legal needs of newcomers into these systems.

Language and cultural barriers often isolate immigrants from available pro bono services. Many private bar involvement programs view the legal needs of immigrants as part of a specialty area of law to be handled by experienced immigration practitioners. Restrictions on Legal Service Corporation funding further marginalize immigrants from mainstream delivery systems, leaving many unable to turn to neighborhood legal services offices where other poor people go to resolve legal problems. Church-based and nonprofit organizations, as well as specialized immigration practitioners, have attempted to fill the void. Although the immigration bar is committed to providing pro bono services to newcomers, the 4,000 members the **American Immigration Lawyers Association** (AILA) cannot possibly meet the demand for services. With more than 20 million foreign-born residents in the United States, many of whom are working poor, the non-immigration bar must step forward to fill this need for legal assistance. The organized bar has the ability to harness the talent, energy, and skill of lawyers to participate in filling the need for legal services for newcomers. This has been the mission of the ABA's Immigration Pro Bono Development Project.

The project has worked to institutionalize the legal needs of newcomers in state and local bar associations by awarding mini-grants (of up to $5,000) on an annual basis to bar associations to create or expand pro bono projects for newcomers. The project has funded sixty-three bar-sponsored projects in twenty-five states. In many cases these projects have not only assisted immigrants with legal problems but have had a positive impact on public policy and served as a catalyst in reshaping the debate about immigration. Evaluation of mini-grant–funded projects has shown that more than 80 percent of these projects continue to provide services to newcomers after the mini-grant funding is spent, indicating the bar's ongoing commitment to, and expansion of, services to newcomers. In this way, the mini-grants have institutionalized the concerns of immigrants within the organized bar's delivery systems.

The Immigration Pro Bono Development Project is assisted by an Advisory Committee appointed by the ABA president and composed of ABA leaders as well as immigration practitioners. The chair and committee members have been extremely active in shepherding this project, ensuring that it receives visibility within the ABA and that ABA leadership is educated about the importance of these issues. In an association of over 380,000 members, with hundreds of entities and sections placing demands on its resources, the role the Advisory Committee plays in garnering and sustaining support for the project is critically important to the project's success. The project is represented at a wide variety of bar leadership forums, makes regular presentations to the National Conference of Bar Presidents, conducts workshops at the ABA Annual Pro Bono Conference, and publishes articles about its work, highlighting projects it has funded. The project also responds to requests for assistance from bar leaders interested in developing or expanding pro bono programs to serve newcomers. The number of requests for technical assistance increases yearly. The project serves as a clearinghouse for materials related to training attorneys to represent newcomers.

AMERICAN CONSUL   See **Consulate General.**

AMERICAN EMBASSY   The American embassy is the official residence and offices of the U.S. **ambassador** to a foreign country. The embassy generally houses the visa issuance offices of the **consulate general** as well.

AMERICAN IMMIGRATION LAWYERS ASSOCIATION
The American Immigration Lawyers Association (AILA) is a national bar association of nearly 6,000 attorneys who practice immigration law. AILA member attorneys represent tens of thousands of U.S. families who have applied for permanent residence status for their spouses, children, and other close relatives. AILA members also represent thousands of U.S. businesses and industries who sponsor highly skilled foreign workers seeking to enter the United States on a temporary or—having proved the unavailability of U.S. workers—permanent basis. AILA members also represent foreign students, entertainers, athletes, and asylum seekers, often on a pro bono basis.

Founded in 1946, AILA is a nonpartisan, nonprofit organization that provides its members with continuing legal education, information, professional services, and expertise through its thirty-five chapters and over seventy-five national committees. AILA is an Affiliated Organization of the American Bar Association and is represented in the ABA House of Delegates.

AMERICANIZATION   See **Assimilation.**

AMNESTY   This is the common term for legalization programs that were created by the **Immigration Reform and Control Act of 1986** (IRCA) that granted legal immigration status to certain **undocumented aliens.** IRCA made it possible for two groups of undocumented persons to apply for legal status. One group included persons who had lived in the United States since before January 1, 1982, without legal status. The other group's members were farmworkers who had done agricultural work between May 1, 1985, and May 1, 1986. Farmworkers who applied for amnesty under IRCA were known as **special agricultural workers** (SAWs).

Those who would commonly fall under the first program either entered by crossing the border surreptitiously [see **entry without inspection**] prior to January 1, 1982, or entered on a visitor's visa or nonimmigrant **foreign student** visa and worked without permission or overstayed the permitted length of stay prior to that date. Ultimately, 1.7 million applicants filed under the pre-1982 program and 1.2 million applied as SAWs.

ANGEL ISLAND   Located in the middle of San Francisco Bay, Angel Island was used as an **inspection** station for several decades. Between 1910 and 1940, about 175,000 Chinese were processed and confined—often for months and years at a time—in Angel Island's wooden barracks, where inspectors would conduct grueling interrogations to determine whether the prospective Chinese immigrants were admissible. While popularly called the "**Ellis Island** of the West," the immigration process on Angel Island was far more rigorous than what occurred on the East Coast. The confinement and interrogation on Angel Island were defended on the grounds that the **Chinese Exclusion Act of 1882** was in effect, and there was fear that many Chinese were making false claims to U.S. citizenship, such as through **paper son** documents or through other fraudulent means. It was not unusual for individuals to be sent back to China after months of confinement on Angel Island if inspectors were not convinced that claims were valid.

The facilities on Angel Island were gloomy. The barracks windows were enclosed with iron bars. Detainees were allowed outside only at mealtimes, when they were escorted by armed guards to the dining hall. Families were separated. All Chinese male applicants were housed in one large room with bunk beds arranged in double or triple rows around the walls. A small recreation yard was adjacent to the barracks, but no educational or recreational program was provided. Most of the immigrants, young men in their teens, were deprived of education, recreation, and health care.

Most of the immigration station on Angel Island was destroyed by fire in 1940. Efforts are currently under way to construct a historical immigration museum on the island.

ANKER, DEBORAH E. (B. 1948)   One of the leading scholars and practitioners in the asylum and refugee field, Deborah E. Anker has been practicing, writing, and teaching in immigration and refugee law for twenty years. She taught at Harvard Law School for many years. She now directs the immigration and refugee clinic located at Greater Boston Legal Services, and supervises students for the human rights program as well.

Anker is a cofounder of the Women Refugees Project (WRP), the first organization in the United States specifically established to advocate for the gender-specific claims to political asylum protection of women refugees. In the spring of 1995, in coalition with human rights, women's rights, and refugee organizations, the WRP succeeded in convincing the INS to adopt guidelines for adjudicators in determining women's gender-based asylum claims. The project has also engaged in human rights education and litigation on behalf of women refugees. The WRP participated as a certified nongovernmental organization at the Fourth World Conference on Women in Beijing in September 1995, where it successfully advocated for the inclusion of a number of important protections for women refugees in the conference's final Platform for Action.

Anker has litigated refugee cases before asylum adjudicators at all administrative levels and in the federal courts, and has filed amicus curiae briefs in the U.S. Supreme Court in every major refugee case in the past fifteen years. She serves on the Legal Advisor's Council to the United Nations High Commissioner for Refugees, and has developed training programs for immigration judges and asylum officers on U.S. asylum law. She has written extensively on the subject of U.S. asylum law and authored a leading treatise in the field, *The Law of Asylum in the United States*, which has just been published in its third, most comprehensive edition. Her articles on the **Refugee Act of 1980** and the use of discretion in asylum cases have been cited and relied upon by federal courts, including the U.S. Supreme Court. In 1989, she authored the first empirical study of the process of asylum adjudication in the immigration court. In 1991–1993, she served as the research director for the Ford Foundation–funded National Asylum Study Project, which conducted the first comprehensive study of the INS asylum process. From 1997 to October 1998, she served as codirector of another Ford Foundation study of **expedited removal proceedings,** a new procedure related to the admission of refugees and others into the United States.

In 1982, Anker was named by the *National Law Journal* as one of the twenty leading immigration lawyers in the United States. In 1991, she received the Edith Lowenstein Award from the **American Immigration Lawyers Association** for outstanding contributions to the field of immigration law. In 1993, she was a corecipient of the annual attorney award from the Massachusetts Chapter of the National Lawyers Guild. In 1994, she and her cofounders received the Founders Award of the American Immigration Lawyers Association for the work of the Women Refugees Project. Anker received her J.D. from Northeastern University in 1975, and an LL.M. from Harvard Law School in 1984.

▥ ANTI-TERRORISM AND EFFECTIVE DEATH PENALTY ACT OF 1996

The Anti-terrorism and Effective Death Penalty Act of 1996 is one of a number of laws enacted by Congress in the 1990s that aimed to more efficiently remove dangerous aliens from the United States. This law streamlined and accelerated the removal of aliens with criminal records by severely restricting or eliminating judicial review of administrative removal orders. Forms of relief from deportation were also substantially limited. In order to deter the arrival of aliens without proper documents, the law established provisions for **expedited removal proceedings** that largely eliminated the role of **immigration judge**s in such expulsion proceedings. Concerns with terrorism led to two new categories of barred aliens: representatives of foreign terrorist organizations and members of foreign terrorist organizations. [Pub. L. 104–132, 110 Stat. 1214]

▥ ASIAN AMERICAN LEGAL DEFENSE AND EDUCATION FUND

The Asian American Legal Defense and Education Fund (AALDEF) is the oldest not-for-profit organization on the East Coast dedicated to protecting and promoting the legal rights of Asian Americans. Founded in 1974, AALDEF addresses the critical legal issues facing Asian Americans on the national and local levels through litigation, legal advocacy, community education, leadership training, and the provision of free legal services to low-income Asian Americans and recent immigrants. Program priorities include immigrant rights, voting rights, the elimination of anti-Asian violence, workers' rights, and redress for Japanese Americans incarcerated during World War II.

AALDEF serves the Chinese, Filipino, Japanese, Korean, South Asian, and Vietnamese communities in the New York metropolitan area, which number over 700,000 Asian Americans citywide. Because their needs are the greatest, the largest proportion of its clients are immigrants, the working poor, and persons not proficient in English.

AALDEF is recognized for its local and national efforts to champion the legal rights of the largely immigrant, multiethnic Asian American population. AALDEF is a founding member of the Public Interest Law Center, located in New York City, which consists of the legal arms of the nation's leading civil rights groups, including the legal defense funds of the NAACP and the National Organization for Women, the Puerto Rican Legal Defense and Education Fund, and the Lawyers' Alliance for New York. It is AALDEF's mission to provide Asian Americans with the skills and education they need to become full participants in the civic life of the United States. AALDEF engages in litigation that will have major impact on broad segments of the Asian American community or bring about institutional changes, calls for reform of governmental policies, and comments on proposed legislation that affects Asian Americans. On a more local level, it educates the community about legal rights and the American legal system; acts as a legal resource for community-based organizations serving Asian Americans; trains student interns in public interest law and encourages them to use their legal skills to serve Asian American community needs; and conducts free, multilingual legal advice clinics that provide counseling to thousands of poor Asian Americans and recent immigrants each year.

AALDEF's recent achievements in New York City include securing political asylum in 1995 for a Chinese refugee aboard the *Golden Venture* freighter, which ran aground on Rockaway Beach, Queens; reaching a $400,000 settlement on behalf of the family of a Chinese American teenager fatally shot in the head by a police officer in Brooklyn; prompting a landmark environmental ruling that requires the city to conduct environmental review of new developments that may displace low-income residents and small businesses; successfully appealing a redress claim on behalf of a Japanese American dismissed from his job at the U.S. General Accounting Office during World War II; and successfully advocating the provision of fully translated bilingual ballots under the federal Voting Rights Act for over 54,000 Chinese American voters in Manhattan, Brooklyn, and Queens.

AALDEF has a nine-person staff, including five attorneys, who are assisted by over 120 volunteers, including pro bono attorneys, translators, paralegals, and other committed individuals. AALDEF works in cooperation with community organizations serving Asian Americans and civil rights groups to maximize the impact of its programs. Many of its community education activities are collaborative efforts, with community associates such as the Asian American Federation of New York, the Chinatown Voter Education Alliance, the Chinese Staff and Workers Association, the Coalition for Korean American Voters, Japanese American Social Services, Inc., and the Young Korean American Service and Education Center. AALDEF, however, is the only organization focusing on the legal needs of the community, and as such, provides training workshops and forums for community associates as a way to increase their effectiveness in providing social services to Asian Americans.

ASIAN LAW CAUCUS

The Asian Law Caucus (ALC) was founded in 1972 as the first Asian Pacific American civil rights and legal services organization in the country. Located in San Francisco, the mission of the Asian Law Caucus is to promote, advise on, and represent the legal and civil rights of the Asian Pacific Islander communities.

Recognizing that social, economic, political, and racial inequalities continue to exist in the United States, ALC is committed to the pursuit of equality and justice for all sectors of society, with an emphasis on the needs of low-income Asian Pacific Americans as well as elderly and refugee populations. Since the vast majority of Asians and Pacific Islanders in the United States are immigrants and refugees, ALC strives to create an informed and educated community empowered to assert its rights and to participate in American society. This perspective is reflected in ALC's broad strategy, which integrates the provision of legal services, educational programs, community organizing initiatives, and advocacy. ALC staff provide culturally appropriate services in five Asian languages: Cantonese, Mandarin, Vietnamese, Tagalog, and Cebuano. Areas of emphasis include immigration and naturalization, employment/labor, housing, elder law, and civil rights.

Most of ALC's current clients are either recent immigrants, refugees, or people with limited English-speaking ability. Over 75 percent are at or below Supplemental Security Income (SSI) levels; 64 percent are monolingual in an Asian language, while an additional 22 percent are limited-English speakers.

Information and Referral

ALC provides multilingual information and referral in several Asian languages. Target languages include Cantonese, Mandarin, Vietnamese, and other Southeast Asian languages. To address the large volume of telephone inquiries, ALC has expanded its telephone capacity and is employing several access points to provide basic information and referral about welfare reform and naturalization. This service is particularly needed for many seniors and disabled individuals who are homebound or who have difficulties with mobility.

Most of the information and referral is provided by legal staff, but to better serve homebound seniors, ALC also provides a senior telephone hotline staffed by twelve trained volunteer seniors to provide basic information and referrals about naturalization and welfare reform, and to encourage others to become citizens. At present, the volunteers provide services in English and five Chinese dialects (Cantonese, Mandarin, Toisanese, Fukienese, and Shanghainese).

ALC also supervises a semimonthly evening clinic with the Lawyers Committee for Civil Rights of the San Francisco Bay Area. Individuals who cannot attend workshops can receive information and assistance with their naturalization applications at the clinic. They may be referred to other workshops or to ALC's attorneys for more assistance. An average of ten to fifteen people seek help at each clinic.

Community Education

Through community education, ALC reaches out to senior and disabled centers with whom it has established relationships, including North and South of Market Adult Day Health, the San Francisco Senior Center, Self-Help for the Elderly, and Canon Kip, to explain the importance of becoming a citizen and to describe and demystify the naturalization process. The importance of voting is stressed and individuals are given information on the benefits of citizenship.

Workshops

ALC provides three different types of workshops: naturalization application assistance workshops, where trained paralegals and volunteers help individuals fill out naturalization applications, and two interview preparation workshops. In each naturalization workshop, an average of twenty to twenty-five persons are assisted, with the capacity to provide more individual assistance especially for the elderly and disabled. A significant number of immigrants qualify for language waivers under the law.

ALC collaborates with San Francisco Bay area community groups such as Filipinos for Affirmative Action, the Korean Community Center of the East Bay, and the Chinatown Resource Center, which help provide volunteers, equipment, and translation (when necessary) in exchange for training on methods, law, and community needs. ALC staff also train volunteers before the workshops on the naturalization process. At the workshop, individuals are given information on the importance of voting and encouraged to vote. This aspect of the program is nonpartisan.

ASIAN PACIFIC AMERICAN LEGAL CENTER The Asian Pacific American Legal Center (APALC) is the leading organization in Southern California dedicated to providing the growing Asian Pacific American community with multilingual, culturally sensitive legal services, education, and civil rights support. It was founded in 1983 with broad community-based support. APALC's services include legal counseling, education, and representation in the areas of family law and domestic violence, consumer law, employment, immigration, government benefits, and housing.

While open to everyone, APALC focuses on serving the diverse Asian Pacific American community. It has the capacity to facilitate in numerous Asian Pacific languages including Cambodian, Cantonese, Japanese, Korean, Mandarin, Tagalog, Thai, and Vietnamese. The organization is also involved in a wide range of civil rights issues, including hate crimes monitoring, language rights, police-community relations, immigrant rights, and voting rights. In addition, APALC has taken a leadership role in promoting collaboration with other ethnic groups, advocacy groups, and social service providers on a range of issues concerning the Los Angeles community at large.

APALC has become the largest Asian American legal services and civil rights organization in the United States. It provides services to over 15,000 individuals each year, including those who seek to become U.S. citizens and who seek relief from domestic violence or cutoffs from government benefits. APALC has represented victims of hate violence and exploitation by sweatshops, including the Thai workers who were enslaved in El Monte, California, for several years. APALC has pioneered the development of programs, coalitions, and projects that build bridges with other racial groups. For example, APALC has partnered with the Southern Christian Leadership Conference and the Central American Resource Center to create the Leadership Development in Interethnic Relations program, which has trained hundreds of participants in skills to improve human relations. The core of the program is a six-month voluntary training and work experience format that brings thirty participants together at one time to go through the course and project.

ASIAN-PACIFIC TRIANGLE See McCarran-Walter Act of 1952.

ASIATIC BARRED ZONE In the early 1900s, the number of Chinese and Japanese immigrants was reduced dramatically through the **Chinese Exclusion Act of 1882** and the **Gentlemen's Agreement.** Nativists, however, continued to clamor for more restrictions. They insisted that Asians were racially inferior to whites and should be completely barred.

Congress responded to the anti-Asian clamor, as well as the renewed xenophobia aroused by the influx of southern and eastern Europeans, by passing the Act of February 5, 1917. The constant influx of Italians, Russians, and Hungarians, which peaked in the first decade of the century, fueled racial nativism and anti-Catholicism, culminating in a controversial requirement that excluded aliens "who cannot read and understand some language or dialect." But the act also created the Asiatic barred zone by extending Chinese exclusion laws to all other Asians. The zone covered South Asia from Arabia to Indochina, as well as the adjacent islands. It included India, Burma, Thailand, the Malay States, the East Indian islands, Asiatic Russia, the Polynesian islands, and parts of Arabia and Afghanistan. China and Japan did not have to be included because of the Chinese exclusion laws and the Gentlemen's Agreement. But together these provisions declared inadmissible all Asians except teachers, merchants, and students. Only Filipinos and Guamanians, under U.S. jurisdiction at the time, were not included.

ASSIMILATION   At its most basic level, assimilation is the process of making differing racial and ethnic groups similar. In the United States, many refer to this process as "Americanization." Anglo-conformity, melting pot, and cultural pluralism constitute the three main conceptual models of assimilation in the United States. These categories may provide a mere description of the process, or an ideal, or both. The Anglo-conformity model assumes the "desirability of maintaining English institutions (as modified by the American Revolution), the English language, and English-oriented cultural patterns as dominant and standard in American life." [Milton M. Gordon, "Assimilation in America: Theory and Reality," *Daedalus*, vol. 90 (1961), pp. 263–265] The melting pot model is based on the belief that immigrants of all cultures together form a new national character.

Philosopher Horace Kallen coined the term *cultural pluralism* in the 1920s. In proposing cultural pluralism, Kallen argued that the nation should consciously allow and encourage its groups to develop democratically, each emphasizing its particular cultural heritage.

The traditional strict assimilationist sentiment merged racial and non-racial issues and embodied racial and cultural prejudices. **Restrictionist**s, who adamantly opposed the melting pot idea, embraced Anglo-conformity. Their Anglo-conformity aimed to strip the immigrant of his or her homeland culture and make the person over into an American along Anglo-Saxon lines.

ASYLEE   An asylee is an individual who has successfully applied for **asylum** after reaching the United States. In contrast, a **refugee** has applied for refugee status from abroad. Both an asylee and a refugee must establish a **well-founded fear of persecution.**

ASYLUM   Asylum can be granted to an **alien** who has a **well-founded fear of persecution** on account of race, religion, nationality, **membership in a particular social group,** or **political opinion.** Even if the applicant does not hold a particular view, if a particular opinion is imputed [see **imputed political opinion**] or attributed to the person by the persecutor, an asylum claim may still be valid. In theory, an asylum applicant can come from any country and can seek asylum status after reaching the shores of the United States. In contrast, a person applying for **refugee** status does so from abroad, and only if he or she is from a particular geographic region of the world. Once granted asylum, the person, often referred to as an **asylee,** is permitted to reside and work in the United States and, after one year, is eligible to apply for **lawful permanent resident alien** status. [8 U.S.C. §1101(a)(42), 1158]

Certain classes of individuals are not eligible for asylum:

- persons who themselves are persecutors, i.e., any person who ordered, incited, assisted, or otherwise participated in the persecution of any person on account of race, religion, nationality, membership in a particular social group, or political opinion
- persons who have been convicted of a particularly serious crime and constitute a danger to the community of the United States
- persons who committed a serious nonpolitical crime outside the United States
- persons who are a danger to the security of the United States
- persons who engage in terrorist activities
- persons who have firmly resettled in another country

Legislation in 1996 amended the definition of refugee to specifically provide that a person who has been forced to abort a pregnancy or to undergo involuntary sterilization, or who has been persecuted for resistance to coercive population control programs, is deemed to have been persecuted on account of political opinion, and to have a well-founded fear of persecution. See *In re X—P—T—.*

In *Immigration and Naturalization Service v. Aguirre-Aguirre* (1999), the Supreme Court unanimously deferred to the attorney general's interpretation of the "serious nonpolitical crime" preclusion. The case involved efforts to deport a former student leader in Guatemala who had led demonstrations that included forcing passengers off buses and then burning the empty buses to protest rising fares. The **Board of Immigration Appeals** had denied asylum to Aguirre, finding that although his actions and those of his fellow students were politically motivated, those goals were outweighed by their criminal strategy. The Court felt that it should not second-guess this judgment as to whether a crime was political or nonpolitical, because such decisions had diplomatic repercussions that the judiciary is not well positioned to reevaluate.

Homosexuality has been recognized as a social group for purposes of asylum [see *Matter of Toboso-Alfonso*]. Sexual abuse or rape is often regarded by immigration authorities as personal rather than political, even when perpetrated by government officials. See *Campos-Guardado v. INS*.

Claims by women on behalf of their daughters who will be forced to undergo female genital mutilation have received mixed results. Some immigration courts have recognized the claim, while others have not. However, the Board of Immigration Appeals held that a young woman being forced to undergo female genital mutilation (FGM) would suffer persecution on account of membership in the particular social group of "young women of the Tchamba-Kunsuntu Tribe who have not had FGM, as practiced by the tribe, and who oppose the practice." See *In re Kasinga* [Int. Dec. No. 3278 (BIA 1996)]. In that case, the BIA held that a subjective "punitive" or "malignant" intent was not required for harm to constitute persecution.

Because international law is relevant to United States asylum application, the **Handbook on Procedures and Criteria for Determining Refugee Status** of the **United Nations High Commissioner for Refugees** is an important tool in determining asylum eligibility.

ASYLUM OFFICER   An alien, not in **removal proceedings,** who is seeking **asylum** in the United States submits an application for asylum to the INS. The application is then reviewed and the applicant is interviewed by an asylum officer, who has received special training and is part of a corps of professional asylum evaluators. Often referred to as the "asylum adjudication corps," these officers are employed by the INS and fall under the direction of the assistant commissioner, Office of Refugees, Asylum, and Parole, and the director of the Asylum Policy and Review Unit. Adverse decisions by asylum officers are reviewable by **immigration judge**s in removal proceedings.

ATTORNEY GENERAL   The attorney general of the United States is a member of the president's cabinet and heads the **Department of Justice.** The attorney general has executive authority over the INS as well as over the **Executive Office of Immigration Review.** As such, the attorney general can review the decisions of these agencies. The attorney general and the president establish the philosophy and priorities of the INS in accordance with their own political beliefs and goals. Whether border or deportation enforcement is emphasized—for example, through budgeting shifts—may vary from administration to administration. Policy shifts can also be influenced by congressional pressures and the economic and social situation in the country. [8 U.S.C. §1103(a)]

AU PAIR   Many young aliens from their teens through their twenties look for an opportunity to reside in the United States, and perhaps to learn English, by doing domestic work or child care for a U.S. family in return for room and board. The term *au pair* is often used for this type of domestic worker, nanny, or child care provider.

An au pair program for child care providers has been established by the United States Information Agency. The program allows foreign students, ages 18 to 25, to provide child care for U.S. host families while receiving room, board, some salary, and tuition for their courses. Foreign students participating in this program use J-1 **exchange visitor** visas. The student must be attending classes at an institution of higher education for at least six hours of academic credit. The au pair may not provide more than ten hours of child care on any given day or more than forty-five hours of child care in any given week. Participants are covered by labor laws and must receive at least federal minimum wage. Participants who will care for children under the age of two must have no less than 200 hours of infant child care experience, involving the direct care and supervision of infant children. All au pairs receive not less than eight hours of child safety instruction and not less than twenty-four hours of child development instruction.

Although some young foreign visitors or students make these arrangements informally with United States families, without a proper visa the visitor or student may become subject to **removal** for engaging in unauthorized employment. The family also may be fined for knowingly hiring an **unauthorized alien** in violation of **employer sanctions** laws. Some foreign students on valid **foreign student** (F-1 or M-1) visas may be able to obtain permission to work off campus and make similar domestic work arrangements without violating the terms of their visas.

AUTHORIZED ALIEN   Under **employer sanctions,** employers can be penalized for hiring **unauthorized alien**s, those who do not have permission to work in the United States. Aliens who are authorized to work in the United States include **lawful permanent resident alien**s, **lawful temporary resident**s, persons granted **temporary protected status,** persons granted **deferred enforced departure,** persons granted **suspension of deportation,** persons granted **withholding of deportation (restric-**

tion on removal), asylees, refugees, and persons paroled into the United States as refugees. Other aliens who are granted employment authorization are also permitted to work.

B

BARK V. INS The 1975 case of *Bark v. INS* [511 F.2d 1200 (9th Cir. 1975)] established the principle that the intent at the time of marriage determines whether or not the union is a **sham marriage** for purposes of immigration.

Sang Chul Bark and his wife had been sweethearts for several years while they were living in their native Korea. She immigrated to the United States and became a lawful permanent resident. Bark subsequently entered the United States as a **business visitor** and then as a **foreign student.** They renewed their acquaintance and were married in Hawaii. Bark's wife filed a **visa petition** on his behalf, and he later sought **adjustment of status** to lawful permanent residence status based on the marriage.

At a hearing before an **immigration judge,** Bark and his wife testified that they married for love and not for the purpose of circumventing the immigration laws; they admitted quarreling and separating. The immigration judge discredited their testimony and held that the marriage was a sham, relying primarily on the evidence of their separation.

The court of appeals held that the marriage was a sham if the bride and groom did not intend to establish a life together at the time they were married. The concept of establishing a life as marital partners contains no federal dictate about the kind of life that the partners may choose to lead. Any attempt to regulate their lifestyles, such as prescribing the amount of time they must spend together or designating the manner in which either partner elects to spend his or her time, in the guise of specifying the requirements of a bona fide marriage, would raise serious constitutional questions. Aliens cannot be required to have more conventional or more successful marriages than citizens.

Conduct of the parties after marriage is relevant only to the extent that it bears upon their subjective state of mind at the time they were married. Evidence that the parties separated after their wedding is relevant in ascertaining whether they intended to establish a life together when they exchanged marriage vows. But evidence of separation, standing alone, cannot support a finding that a marriage was not bona fide when it was entered. The inference that the parties never intended a bona fide marriage from

65

proof of separation is arbitrary unless there is reasonable assurance that it is more probable than not that couples who separate after marriage never intended to live together; common experience is directly to the contrary. Couples separate, temporarily and permanently, for all kinds of reasons that have nothing to do with any preconceived intent not to share their lives, such as calls to military service, educational needs, employment opportunities, illness, poverty, and domestic difficulties.

BLANKET DETERMINATIONS   For large companies that frequently use the L-1 **intracompany transferee** nonimmigrant category (for executives, managers, and those with specialized company knowledge), the blanket determination procedure expedites and streamlines the application process.

Under the rules, any company that has used the L classification to transfer at least ten managerial or executive employees to the United States in the preceding twelve months can file blanket petitions that, upon approval, will permit the company to issue its own petition approval notices to prospective transferees. For example, a large company that rotates many employees throughout its international organization does not have to make repetitive showings of L category eligibility.

Once approved, a blanket petition is valid for three years. At the end of the three-year period, an extension can be obtained. The blanket arrangement can be revoked if the interrelationship among the affiliated offices is altered, the blanket approval has not been used for three years, or if the relationship of the employee to the business changes or is terminated. [8 C.F.R. §214.2(l)]

BOARD OF ALIEN LABOR CERTIFICATION APPEALS   This administrative appellate body reviews denials of **alien employment certification** (labor certification) applications by the **Department of Labor.** Those types of cases are heard by the entire body; individual members of the board, however, may be assigned cases involving labor certifications for **temporary worker**s such as H-1B professionals.

BOARD OF IMMIGRATION APPEALS   The appellate body of the **Executive Office of Immigration Review.** This administrative agency is comprised of fifteen members who, under the auspices of the U.S. attorney general, review removal orders and denials of petitions made by immigration judges and administrative adjudicators. Matters considered by the board include decisions to exclude or deport (see **removal**), denials of family petitions, bonds, **parole,** detention, imposition of fines and penalties on carriers, and recession of **adjustment of status.**

BONA FIDE RELIGIOUS ORGANIZATION   A person
seeking to enter the United States as a **special immigrant** religious worker must be a member of a religious denomination that is a *bona fide nonprofit, religious organization* in the United States. This term is defined in the regulations:

> Bona fide nonprofit religious organization in the United States means an organization exempt from taxation as described in section 501(c)(3) of the Internal Revenue Code of 1986 as it relates to religious organizations, or one that has never sought such exemption but establishes to the satisfaction of the [Immigration and Naturalization] Service that it would be eligible therefor if it had applied for tax exempt status. [8 C.F.R. §204.5(m)(3)]

BORDER CROSSING IDENTIFICATION CARD   This is
an identity document issued to an alien who is lawfully admitted for permanent residence, or to an alien who is a resident of Mexico or Canada. It is issued by a consular officer or an immigration officer for the purpose of crossing over the border to the United States for such things as shopping or visiting relatives. These documents include a biometric identifier (such as the fingerprint or handprint of the alien) that is machine readable. [8 U.S.C. §1101(a)(6)]

BORDER PATROL   The Border Patrol is the mobile and uni-
formed enforcement arm of the INS that is responsible for protecting more than 8,000 miles of international land and watery boundary. Although the INS is divided into three regions—eastern, central, and western—within these regions are twenty-one sectors of the Border Patrol, including nine southwestern border sectors, sectors on the northern border, and those headquartered in Livermore, California; Miami, Florida; New Orleans, Louisiana; and Mayaguez, Puerto Rico.

The Border Patrol is engaged in a variety of activities, including a boat patrol operation, anti-smuggling operations, **employer sanctions,** and intelligence work. The patrol also has desert-area rescue teams, emergency response teams, canine units, drug awareness programs for schools, scouting activities for youth, and is involved in the detection of aliens with criminal backgrounds. The Border Patrol is of course best known for border surveillance, or "linewatching," transportation and traffic checks, and interior enforcement. Patrolling the 2,000-mile southern border is the Border Patrol's primary task.

The purpose of transportation and traffic checks is to apprehend undocumented aliens who have penetrated the border area. Agents are assigned to "high traffic" areas such as bus and train terminals, as well as special highway checkpoint stations. Although agents in a roving patrol unit cannot constitutionally search a vehicle for undocumented aliens simply for being in the general vicinity of the border, they can stop such motorists for brief inquiry into their residence status. Border Patrol interior enforcement focuses on undocumented farm and ranch workers. Farm or ranch raids are usually based on tips that undocumented workers are at particular worksites.

🏛 BRACERO PROGRAM   When the **national origins quota system** of the 1920s reduced European immigration and closed the door to Japanese, Mexicans and other Western Hemisphere immigrants were exempt. Mexicans became the major source for agricultural labor and, in a very cynical way, increased flexibility because they could be deported easily as well. As the U.S. economy expanded due to war production in the 1940s, a series of bilateral agreements between Mexico and the United States established the Bracero program to provide Mexican agricultural workers in the Southwest. Under the agreements, even undocumented workers who were in the United States were to be given preference. Many were escorted to the Mexican border by the **Border Patrol,** who then allowed them back in as legal braceros. From 1947 to 1949, more than 142,000 undocumented workers were legalized in this way.

In the midst of the program, undocumented migration from Mexico also increased. Allegations that undocumented migration was depressing wages and displacing U.S. workers led to the roundup and deportation of hundreds of thousands of Mexicans and Latinos as part of **Operation Wetback.**

Growers were generally happy with the Bracero program because Mexicans provided a source of cheap, unorganized labor. But the braceros themselves were subjected to low wages, no schooling for their children, and deplorable living conditions. Congress eventually terminated the program in 1964.

🏛 BRADY, KATHERINE (B. 1952)   A staff attorney with the **Immigrant Legal Resource Center** (ILRC), Kathy Brady is one of the top experts in the United States on the intersections between immigration and criminal law and immigration and dependency law.

Brady has become a national resource in the area of criminal law because of her work at the ILRC, as well as with the **National Immigration Project of the National Lawyers Guild.** Under her guidance, both programs provide technical assistance, policy guidance, litigation support, and training and materials.

The ILRC's work has had a particular impact in the state of California. In the 1980s, very little material on crimes and immigrants was available to state public defenders. In 1987 Brady wrote *The Public Defender's Guide to Immigration Law* (1987), which was distributed to public defenders across the state. That short booklet grew into the full-scale book *California Criminal Law and Immigration,* which the ILRC has published and updated throughout the 1990s. Both immigration and criminal law practitioners often refer to this book as "the Bible" for California practice. Brady also took over writing the chapter on defending noncitizens in the basic California continuing education manual (*California Criminal Law: Procedure and Practice*), expanding and reorganizing it and bringing in an immigration judge and a noted criminal defense attorney as coauthors. She has also published articles in the statewide journal of the California Attorneys for Criminal Justice. Through these periodicals, plus her annual seminars, frequent speeches to the California Bar Association, and individual training sessions with numerous public defender offices, Brady and the ILRC have raised the standard of required practice for criminal defense attorneys in the state.

Brady and other ILRC attorneys consult daily on immigration and criminal law issues with immigration agencies, other nonprofit and government agencies, and immigration attorneys. Agencies have desperately needed advice about the impact of criminal record during two of the great recent mass applications—the amnesty program in the late 1980s and the push for naturalization in the 1990s. Agencies have needed guidance particularly on the complex matter of criminal records. This is especially true since Congress amended the Immigration and Nationality Act eight times from 1988 to 1996, including more and more minor offenses as having severe immigration consequences, imposing these penalties retroactively regardless of date of conviction, and in general making these rules extraordinarily complex.

Brady has consulted with INS detention center representation staffs across the country and has provided national and regional training, including speaking at **American Immigration Lawyers Association** and National Lawyers Guild events. She is a consultant to the American Bar Association's project on educating criminal court judges, and contributed a major article on aggravated felonies in a book by the American Immigration Law Foundation. Brady has consulted frequently with the American Civil Liberties Union, legislators, and other groups analyzing legislation or litigating cases. She was co-counsel in the Ninth Circuit Court case *Roldan* *v. INS*, and coauthored the amicus brief in the case before the U.S. attorney general, *Matter of Luviano/Marroquin*, both suits defending the use of expungement and other state rehabilitative relief to eliminate convictions of minor offenses for immigration purposes.

Brady's work on children's issues and dependency is also exemplary. In 1990 Congress passed the **special immigrant juvenile** statute (SIJS), groundbreaking legislation that offered abused immigrant children in county dependency proceedings the opportunity to become lawful permanent residents. Since then Brady and the ILRC have led the effort from the immigration side in providing technical assistance, policy guidance, and training and materials. As she had done earlier in the criminal law area, Brady developed expertise on dependency law, speaking with attorneys, judges, and social workers. She was able to determine how the ILRC could most effectively reach the parties within that system and offer technical assistance, while spotting what problems were most pressing. In the early 1990s Brady founded the Bay Area Task Force on Immigrant Children, a group of children's rights attorneys, social workers, county counsel, probation officers, and immigration specialists assembled to discuss policy issues and answer each other's questions. That group was responsible for several national and regional policy improvements.

Working with representatives of county governments and children's rights groups, Brady helped form a national coalition to analyze and respond to significant amendments to the SIJS law passed in 1997. The 1997 amendments led several INS offices to take the position that the INS should participate in dependency hearings or review confidential juvenile court documents to confirm that the dependency judge acted appropriately. Brady has consulted with the INS, judges, and attorneys across the country on how to deal with the many policy questions raised by the amendments.

Another critical issue in this area is that most dependency court systems, attorneys, and social workers do not know about the SIJS program and fail to apply on behalf of the children in their care. Brady has placed articles in national periodicals for juvenile court judges, attorneys, social workers, and volunteers; has spoken nationally; and has initiated a national volunteer outreach and training project in which immigration attorneys speak to local dependency courts to inform them about the program.

Brady also works with a third group, district attorneys who act against immigration service providers who commit fraud against immigrants. She has been a major resource in California on this issue since the early 1990s. She authored a manual on the topic that was republished in the California District Attorney Association law journal, and has consulted on several cases and acted as an expert witness. There are now far more prosecutions of bad providers than five years ago, at least partly due to the ILRC's work—

either directly or by providing materials and "changing the culture" of the state's district attorneys. Los Angeles had no convictions of bad providers as of a few years ago; by 1998, there were twenty-seven misdemeanor and three felony convictions. Brady directly advised a community group and the district attorney's office in Santa Rosa, California, on a case, which in May 1999 resulted in a five-year prison sentence for a large-scale operator.

Prior to joining the ILRC staff in 1987, Brady practiced with the immigration law firm Park and Associates. She also served as the interim legal director of Proyecto Libertad in 1991, and has taught immigration law at Santa Clara University Law School. Brady received her J.D. from Boalt Hall School of Law, University of California at Berkeley, in 1983.

BUSINESS VISITOR   There are two types of **nonimmigrant visas** that are issued to visitors: business visitors visas, and visas for a **visitor for pleasure.** The business visitors visa, often referred to as a B-1 visa, is issued for aliens entering the United States temporarily for business. Although most visitors enter the United States with either a B-1 or a B-2 (visitor for pleasure) visa, if a nonimmigrant is entering partly for business and partly for pleasure, the U.S. consulate will issue a combined B-1/B-2 visa.

Business visitors are permitted to enter the United States in order to do business for foreign employers or for themselves if they are business owners abroad. To qualify, (1) the person must not intend to abandon a foreign residence, (2) the principal place of business must be in a foreign country, and (3) each entry into the United States must be for a temporary period of time, although the business activity itself need not be of a temporary nature.

The B-1 is generally one of the easiest visas to obtain if the requirements are met. It requires no prior approval by the INS. Since "business" encompasses a wide variety of activities, the category is quite flexible. The classification permits negotiating contracts, consulting with business associates, attending meetings or conventions, looking for investments or real estate, litigating, or engaging in any commercial transaction. The business visitor can work as long as he or she does not receive a salary or remuneration from a U.S. source; the company abroad must pay any salary. [8 U.S.C. §1101(a)(15)(B); *Matter of B- and K-,* 6 I. & N. Dec. 827 (BIA 1955)] The B-1 cannot be issued to nonimmigrants entering to perform skilled or unskilled labor; see *International Union of Bricklayers and Allied Craftsmen v. Meese.*

C

CABLE ACT Beginning in 1907, female U.S. citizens were divested of citizenship if they married an **alien.** Thereafter, they would be regarded as **national**s of their husband's native country. The Cable Act repealed most of this rule in 1922. However, the automatic divestiture of U.S. citizenship among women continued to apply to any woman who married an "alien ineligible to citizenship" until 1931. This group consisted primarily of Asian immigrants.

The critical language of the Cable Act read as follows:

> Sec. 3 That a woman citizen of the United States shall not cease to be a citizen of the United States by reason of her marriage after the passage of this Act, unless she makes a formal renunciation of her citizenship before a court having jurisdiction over naturalization of aliens: *Provided,* That any woman citizen who marries an alien ineligible to citizenship shall cease to be a citizen of the United States.

CAMPOS-GUARDADO V. INS An **asylum** applicant from El Salvador was forced to watch the brutal, politically motivated murder of her relatives and was raped while attackers shouted political slogans. Reviewing her case [809 F.2d 285 (5th Cir. 1987)], the court refused to find grounds for asylum in these events, determining that the rape was not on account of her **political opinion** and threats of reprisal were "personally motivated."

In early 1984, Sofia Campos-Guardado took a two-hour bus trip to her uncle's home in El Salvador to repay a debt owed by her father. Her uncle was the chairman of a local agricultural cooperative, one formed as a result of the controversial agrarian land reform movement initiated several years earlier. When she arrived, she found her uncle apprehensive; he explained that the day before, two men had demanded money he held for the cooperative and he had refused. Although frightened, she remained to visit with her cousins. Later, an older woman and two young men with rifles arrived and knocked down the door. They dragged Campos, her uncle, a male cousin, and three female cousins to the rim of the farm's waste pit. They tied all the victims' hands and feet and gagged the women. Forcing the women to watch, they hacked the flesh from the men's bodies with machetes, finally shooting them to death. The male attackers then raped the women, including Campos, while the woman who accompanied the attackers shouted political slogans. The assailants cut the victims loose, threatening to kill them unless they fled immediately. Campos suffered a nervous breakdown and had to remain in the hospital for fifteen days.

The court of appeals refused to reverse the decision of the **Board of Immigration Appeals** denying Campos asylum. In its view, nothing was wrong with the BIA's approach in finding that the record did not establish that Campos was persecuted on account of any political opinion she herself possessed or was believed by the attackers to possess.

CANCELLATION OF REMOVAL   Some aliens who are deportable [see **deportation grounds**] and subject to **removal** from the United States may be eligible for a form of relief from removal called cancellation of removal. If granted the relief, the person can remain in the United States as a **lawful permanent resident alien.** The three main categories of cancellation of removal are for (1) certain **undocumented alien**s, (2) certain spouses and children who are victims of abuse, and (3) certain longtime lawful permanent resident aliens who have committed criminal offenses.

In order for an undocumented alien to be eligible for cancellation of removal, the following requirements must be met: (1) the person has been physically present in the United States for a continuous period of not less than ten years; (2) during the period of physical presence, the person was and is of **good moral character;** (3) the person has not been convicted of certain crimes involving narcotics, prostitution, moral turpitude [see **crime involving moral turpitude**], firearms, **document fraud,** or an **aggravated felon**y; (4) removal would result in exceptional and extremely unusual hardship to the alien's spouse, parent, or child who is a U.S. citizen or lawful permanent resident. Even if these requirements are met, the **immigration judge** must believe that the individual is worthy of favorable discretion.

Distinct and less rigorous requirements for cancellation of removal apply to deportable or inadmissible aliens who are the victims of spousal or parental abuse. To qualify, the following requirements must be met: (1) the alien has been battered or subjected to extreme cruelty in the United States by a spouse or parent who is a U.S. citizen or lawful permanent resident, or is the parent of a child of a U.S. citizen or lawful permanent resident and the child has been battered or subjected to extreme cruelty in the United States by the citizen or permanent resident parent; (2) the alien has been physically present in the United States for a continuous period of not less than three years immediately preceding the date of the application; (3) the alien has been a person of good moral character during this period; (4) the alien is not inadmissible on any ground related to security reasons or crimes involving narcotics, prostitution, or moral turpitude, or deportable for reasons related to a **sham marriage,** aggravated felony, firearms, or document fraud; (5) removal would result in extreme hardship to the alien, the alien's child, or (in the case of an alien who is a child) to the alien's parent.

A lawful permanent resident alien who commits a crime may be deportable. Those who are deportable for having two convictions involving moral turpitude or firearms may be eligible for cancellation of removal. The immigration court may cancel removal of such a person if he or she (1) has been a lawful permanent resident for at least five years; (2) has resided in the United States continuously for seven years; and (3) has not been convicted of an aggravated felony. It is important that since committing the crime that triggered removal proceedings, the person has been rehabilitated and is not likely to commit another crime. [8 U.S.C. §1229b]

CATHOLIC LEGAL IMMIGRATION NETWORK, INC.
The Catholic Legal Immigration Network, Inc. (CLINIC) was established in 1988 as a subsidiary of the United States Catholic Conference. Its mission is to enhance, extend, and support the legal immigration work of the Catholic Church in the United States. Its efforts consist of: (1) administering multiagency immigrant legal service programs; (2) managing full-service diocesan programs on a time-limited basis; (3) conducting more than 100 on-site training sessions per year plus monthly telephonic training sessions; (4) issuing a monthly newsletter; (5) producing manuals and legal publications; (6) staffing a toll-free 800 number for consultations; (7) assisting agencies and staff in the **Board of Immigration Appeals** recognition and accreditation process; (8) advocating on issues affecting poor immigrants, with a focus on the reunification of families and the protection of those fleeing persecution or civil unrest; and (9) providing direct client representation to particularly vulnerable immigrants such as detainees and asylum seekers. With offices throughout the United States, CLINIC is one of the primary service providers to immigrant communities in the nation.

CHAE CHAN PING V. UNITED STATES   This case [130 U.S.
581 (1889)], also known as the Chinese Exclusion Case, represents the Supreme Court's recognition of Congress's vast or **plenary power** over who can immigrate to the United States. The case involved a challenge to

the **Chinese Exclusion Act of 1882,** which prohibited Chinese laborers from entering the United States.

In upholding this power to exclude based on race and country of origin, the Court noted that Chinese laborers were aliens, not citizens of the United States. The government of the United States, through the action of the legislative department, can exclude aliens from its territory. This is a proposition that was not open to controversy. Jurisdiction over its own territory to that extent is an incident of every independent nation. It is a part of independence. If it could not exclude aliens, it would be to that extent subject to the control of another power.

> To preserve its independence, and give security against foreign aggression and encroachment, is the highest duty of every nation, and to attain these ends nearly all other considerations are to be subordinated. It matters not in what form such aggression and encroachment come, whether from the foreign nation acting in its national character or from vast hordes of its people crowding in upon us. The government, possessing the powers that are to be exercised for protection and security, is clothed with authority to determine the occasion on which the powers shall be called forth; and its determination, so far as the subjects affected are concerned, are necessarily conclusive upon all its departments and officers. If therefore, the government of the United States, through its legislative department, considers the presence of foreigners of a different race in this country, who will not assimilate with us, to be dangerous to its peace and security, their exclusion is not to be stayed because at the time there are no actual hostilities with the nation of which the foreigners are subject.

CHANGE OF NONIMMIGRANT STATUS   After arrival, **nonimmigrant**s often have the desire to change to a different nonimmigrant category. For example, a tourist who has taken a course part-time may want to remain and become a full-time student. Similarly, after graduating from college, a foreign student may want to work temporarily in the United States. To be eligible for a change of status, applicants must continue to maintain their prior nonimmigrant status and their **Form I-94** must not have expired. Of course, the applicant must be eligible for the new classification.

A grant of change of status is discretionary and may be denied when there are negative factors, such as visa abuse. For example, a tourist entering with the intent of actually going to school or working can be denied change of status as a matter of discretion. An alien in the United States who has failed to maintain status (such as by working without permission or overstaying the visa) and who wishes to qualify for another nonimmigrant category cannot change status in the United States. He or she must leave the country in order to apply for a visa in the new category abroad. [8 U.S.C. §1258]

CHILD   The term *child* has a special, technical meaning in the immigration laws. For example, in the **immediate relative** immigration category, the child of a United States citizen can immigrate, unrestrained by any quotas or numerical limitations. But the term *child* does not include an offspring who is 25 years old, or a son who was adopted at the age of 17.

The general definition of child is an unmarried person under the age of 21. A person who is divorced or widowed is considered unmarried for these purposes. Furthermore, the law requires that the child be legitimate unless the relationship being used for immigration purposes is with the natural mother or with the natural father who has had a "bona fide parent-child relationship with the person." This means that the parties lived together at some point, that the father acknowledged the child as his own, that he provided for some or all of the child's needs, or that in general the father's behavior indicated genuine concern for and interest in the child. At a minimum, some showing of emotional and/or financial ties or an active concern by the father for the child's support, instruction, and general welfare must be demonstrated. See *Matter of Vizcaino* [Int. Dec. No. 3061 (BIA 1988)].

The parent-child relationship can be valid under certain conditions when there has been adoption or a step relationship. Adoptive relationships are recognized if the son or daughter has been adopted while under the age of 16. Furthermore, the child must have resided with and been in the legal custody of the adopting parent for two years. Stepparent-stepchild relationships are also recognized; however, the statute requires that the child be under the age of 18 at the time of the marriage creating the step relationship. The **Board of Immigration Appeals** does not require a close family unit or active interest in order to sustain a step relationship for immigration purposes. See *Matter of McMillan* [17 I. & N. Dec. 605 (BIA 1981)].

In general, a child is considered illegitimate for immigration purposes when born out of wedlock. However, legitimacy is determined by the law of the place of the child's birth. Thus, if the particular jurisdiction has eliminated legal distinctions between children born in wedlock and those born out of wedlock, all children born in the jurisdiction will be deemed legitimate. Countries where the legal distinctions between children born in and out of wedlock have been eliminated include China, Panama, Honduras, Yugoslavia, Bolivia, Ecuador, Barbados, Haiti, Republic of Trinidad and Tobago, and Colombia. The state of New Jersey has also removed the distinction between legitimate and illegitimate children. [8 U.S.C. §1101(b)]

CHINESE EXCLUSION ACT OF 1882   Responding to anti-Chinese sentiment (based on economic and social complaints) in California and the West, the Forty-seventh Congress enacted the Chinese Exclusion Act of May 6, 1882. The law, which represented the first of many immigration control laws based on race or national origin, excluded Chinese laborers for ten years (later extended indefinitely) and effectively slammed the door on all Chinese immigration. It did permit the entry of teachers, students, and merchants, but their quota was quite small. The act crippled the development of the Chinese American community because Chinese women were defined as laborers. Chinese laborers who had already immigrated therefore had no way to bring wives and families left behind in China.

A major provision of the 1882 act read as follows:

> Chap. 126. In the opinion of the Government of the United States the coming of Chinese laborers to this country endangers the good order of certain localities within the territory thereof. . . .
>
> That from and after the expiration of ninety days next after the passage of this act, and until the expiration of ten years next after the passage of this act, the coming of Chinese laborers to the United States be, and the same is hereby suspended; and during such suspension it shall not be lawful for any Chinese laborer to come, or, having so come after the expiration of said ninety days, to remain within the United States.

The 1882 act was extended in 1892 and 1902, and then it was extended indefinitely in 1904. These laws were not repealed until 1943, when China became an ally during World War II.

The Chinese exclusion laws were upheld by the Supreme Court in *Chae Chan Ping v. United States.*

CHINESE EXCLUSION CASE   See *Chae Chan Ping v. United States.*

CHISHTI, MUZAFFAR A. (B. 1951)   Muzaffar A. Chishti is a nationally regarded spokesman for immigrant rights, particularly for the rights of working-class immigrants and refugees. Chishti is a lawyer and director of the Immigration Project of the Union of Needletrades, Industrial & Textile Employees (UNITE). UNITE represents apparel and textile workers in the United States and Canada. The Immigration Project provides immigration legal services to members of the union and their families.

Chishti is a member and former chair of the board of directors of the National Immigration Forum; secretary of the National Coalition for Haitian Rights; treasurer of the U.S. Committee for Refugees; a member of the board of directors of the **National Immigration Law Center** and of the **New York Immigration Coalition.** He has served as a member of the Coordinating Committee on Immigration of the American Bar Association. He has testified extensively on immigration and refugee legislation before various congressional committees and is a frequent speaker on immigration, labor, and related issues. In 1992, as part of a U.S. team, he helped the Russian parliament draft its legislation on forced migrants and refugees. He is a 1994 recipient of the New York State Governor's Award for Outstanding Asian Americans, and a 1995 recipient of the Ellis Island Medal of Honor. Chishti was educated at St. Stephens College, Delhi, India; University of Delhi; Cornell Law School; and Columbia School of International Affairs.

CITIZEN   A citizen of the United States is a person born in the United States or in certain territories of the United States, such as Puerto Rico and Guam. Certain persons born abroad enjoy **acquisition of citizenship** at birth through a citizen parent or parents. In essence, the United States follows both the **jus soli** and **jus sanguinis** rules of acquiring citizenship and nationality. Others obtain citizenship through **naturalization** after periods of lawful permanent residence and satisfaction of civics and English literacy requirements.

The right to vote and to hold certain jobs such as federal civil service jobs is conditioned on U.S. citizenship. Citizens cannot be subjected to **removal** (deportation) from the United States; under the immigration laws, citizens can file immigration applications for a wider range of relatives than can **lawful permanent resident aliens**.

CITIZENSHIP DISCRIMINATION   Under the immigration laws, treating an employee or prospective employee differently because of his or her citizenship or immigration status can be unlawful. Citizenship discrimination occurs when an employer disfavors a worker because of the individual's citizenship or immigration status. One blatant form of illegal citizenship discrimination is when a private employer requires that all job applicants be U.S. citizens. The main exceptions are when the employer has fewer than four employees and when the discrimination is required or essential for an employer to do business with a federal government agency; some agencies restrict who can be hired for certain jobs because of national security reasons. Also, it is not an unfair immigration-related employment practice for an employer to hire a citizen over a qualified alien if the two individuals are equally qualified or if the citizen is more qualified. [8 U.S.C. §1324b]

CLEAR PROBABILITY OF PERSECUTION   An applicant for **asylum** under 8 U.S.C. §1158 must establish only a **well-founded fear of persecution.** However, in order to qualify for the related relief of **restriction on removal,** the applicant must establish a clear probability of persecution. Simply put, the withholding applicant must establish that persecution is more likely to occur than not. If the applicant fails to establish a clear probability of persecution for purposes of withholding, the person in theory may still be granted asylum if the less rigorous standard of well-founded fear of persecution is shown.

The clear probability of persecution standard is synonymous with the preponderance of evidence standard that traditionally applies in civil cases. See *Immigration and Naturalization Service v. Cardoza-Fonseca; Immigration and Naturalization Service v. Stevic* [467 U.S. 407 (1984)].

COALITION FOR HUMANE IMMIGRANT RIGHTS OF LOS ANGELES   The Coalition for Humane Immigrant Rights of Los Angeles (CHIRLA) is a multiethnic coalition of individuals and organizations in Southern California that provide services to immigrants and refugees, sharing the common goals of educating and empowering immigrants and promoting a positive environment of race and human relations. Southern California boasts the largest concentration of immigrants and refugees of any region in the country, and contains newcomer communities from throughout the world. CHIRLA's mission is to advance the human and civil rights of immigrants and refugees and to foster an environment of positive human and community relations. CHIRLA's membership reflects this tremendous diversity. Among its member organizations are groups such as the **Asian Pacific American Legal Center,** the African Community and Resource Center, the Central American Resource Center, the Korean Immigrant Workers Advocates, the **Mexican American Legal Defense and Educational Fund** (MALDEF), and Search to Involve Filipino Americans.

CHIRLA was founded in late 1986 in response to the passage of the **Immigration Reform and Control Act of 1986** (IRCA). With an initial mandate to coordinate services dealing with IRCA's legalization program and to protect the rights of immigrants adversely affected by IRCA, CHIRLA has expanded its organizational mission to provide a broad range of services to assist the immigrant and refugee communities of Southern California. At the present time, CHIRLA provides services through three distinct project areas: immigration and citizenship, workers' rights, and human relations. Each of these areas is led by CHIRLA staff and by coalition members who chair committees composed of organizations and individuals that work in each of these areas. The immigration and citizenship project focuses on improving the service delivery systems of both the INS and nongovernmental community organizations. The workers' rights project focuses on the rights of immigrants and refugees in the workplace. The human relations project focuses on promoting positive relations among the various racial and ethnic groups in Southern California.

Within each project, direct services are provided to members and to other organizations and individuals. The services include: (1) acting as a resource center and maintaining a materials clearinghouse and library; (2) providing training and technical assistance to members and the public at large; (3) providing community outreach and education, particularly in the area of employment rights; (4) coordinating the delivery of services among legal, community-based, and governmental organizations; (5) offering media outreach and public relations assistance; (6) supporting a speakers' bureau on immigrant and refugee rights and services; (7) coordinating public policy research among academic and community organizations; (8) providing leadership to promote the self-empowerment of immigrants and refugees.

CHIRLA has moved beyond its original mandate to become a pivotal agent in the coordination of community responses to the myriad issues affecting immigrants and refugees. Toward this end, the member and affiliate organizations moved to institutionalize CHIRLA as an independent nonprofit organization in the summer of 1993. In October and November 1993, CHIRLA completed its transition from a United Way fiscal agency to independent status, including moving to a new site that is centrally located and more accessible to its membership. Support from local and national foundations has been instrumental in this organizational development process.

COHEN, ERIC (B. 1960)   Eric Cohen is a pioneer in collaborative lawyering and group processing approaches to the field of immigration law, while developing innovative models of partnering with grassroots immigrant communities and civic participation. He is currently a staff attorney with the **Immigrant Legal Resource Center** (ILRC).

Cohen grew up in Los Angeles witnessing the unjust treatment of immigrants in a city that has become the Ellis Island of the West. He often heard Spanish being spoken, and had a keen interest in the language and the people. In elementary school, many of his friends were Latinos, and it was there that he was first introduced to their culture and language. As a Jew growing up in Los Angeles, he identified somewhat with other minority groups; although there were millions of Jews in Los Angeles, he still knew he was different from many people with whom he went to school. While attending college in Colorado in the early 1980s, he did canvassing and grassroots political lobbying and organizing around issues of nuclear weapons, the dramatically increasing military budget, and U.S. intervention in Central America.

After attending Stanford Law School, he traveled to Guatemala to learn Spanish. Upon his return, he worked with organized labor. Specifically, he worked with the Los Angeles County Labor Immigrant Assistance Project of the AFL-CIO. This was a project of several international unions and the AFL-CIO to help union members and prospective union members legalize their status under the Immigration Reform and Control Act amnesty programs during the late 1980s. While working with the unions, he pioneered the concept of group processing of immigration applications in the context of legalization applications. Group processing was an efficient and effective way of helping groups of people apply for amnesty (and later phase II of amnesty, family petitions, and naturalization) at one time. The best aspect of group processing is that it can be an empowering experience for the applicants, as well as the advocate, because the applicants complete their own applications and organize their own evidence to submit to the INS, but only after having become very familiar with the legal requirements and procedures involved in the legalization program. Applicants who go through a group processing experience become more prepared for their INS interviews and thus are more likely to win their cases. Additionally, applicants who apply through a group processing program develop valuable life skills such as filling out forms, interviewing, organizing documents and evidence, and keeping important records.

Another important aspect of Cohen's work with the unions involved learning more about organizing campaigns. The unions saw his legal office as an important carrot to their members and to those workers the union wanted to organize. The union could help its members obtain legal status in the United States, something for which union members would be grateful. Plus, during the course of their work, they could help people apply for legalization who were not in a union but wanted to be. The local unions would use these people as leaders in organizing campaigns. The legalization work helped the existing unions become stronger and helped the workers in other factories form unions.

At the end of 1988, Cohen joined the staff of the ILRC. He quickly helped convert group processing into a way to process phase II amnesty applications, then visa petitions (I-130s), and recently naturalization applications (N-400s). He also spent considerable time encouraging (and often pleading with) other organizations to conduct group processing. He coauthored packets and manuals on the subject and gave presentations on the best ways to be involved in group processing. As a result, he became the leading expert in the country on group processing and one of the leading experts on alternative ways of service delivery in immigration cases.

In addition to group processing, Cohen helped immigrants author and then perform skits—the "Know Your Rights" campaign—on legal rights during an immigration raid. These skits have been performed throughout the San Francisco Bay Area and in other areas of the United States. He has become one of the foremost experts on immigrant leadership training, having conducted sessions and authored a manual on the subject. He has worked extensively with grassroots, immigrant-run community organizations and has helped them become viable forces in their communities. Cohen has become one of the country's foremost experts on how to involve immigrants in building their own cases. Such a vision of law practice helps immigrants learn how to excel in North American culture while maintaining their own cultural identities. Examples of how he involves immigrants in their cases include:

- having them complete forms in their native language
- making sure they understand the legal requirements and procedures that govern their cases
- producing video, oral, and written materials that explain all aspects of the legal process that the clients will be embarking upon so as to minimize the unknowns in the application process
- teaching about what the interview or court hearing will be like through role-playing exercises, moot courts, and peer teaching by former clients
- taking advantage of the small and big moments in relationships with clients to exchange information and knowledge, work in partnership, and teach each other how to excel in the other's culture while maintaining one's own cultural identity

Cohen received his J.D. from Stanford Law School in 1986.

COMMISSION ON IMMIGRATION REFORM   In 1990 Congress created the Commission on Immigration Reform, tasked with reviewing and evaluating the impact and implementation of U.S. immigration policy. The commission's work indicated that implementation

of immigration policies is beset with problems. In 1994, the commission reported that **undocumented alien**s were entering the United States too easily, many unlawful resident aliens were not being removed, and legal immigrants encountered too much difficulty in gaining entry to the United States. In its final report in 1997, the commission recommended dismantling the INS and distributing its current functions to other agencies such as the **Department of Labor** for immigration-related employment standards, the **State Department** for other immigrant and refugee/asylum-related applications, a new bureau of immigration enforcement within the **Department of Justice** for border and interior enforcement, and a special agency for **removal proceedings.**

COMMISSIONER   The commissioner is the head of the **Immigration and Naturalization Service,** and is appointed by the president and reports to the U.S. **attorney general.** He or she is charged with all responsibilities and authority in the administration of the INS and of the Immigration and Nationality Act. As such, the commissioner overseas the entire day-to-day enforcement, service, and administrative functions of the INS. The commissioner also helps to set enforcement and INS immigration policies for the entire country. The Border Patrol, regional commissioners, and district directors report to the commissioner. The office of the commissioner, known as the "central office," is located in Washington, D.C. [8 U.S.C. §1103(c)]

In essence, the attorney general has delegated most statutory authority over immigration enforcement to the commissioner. The attorney general does, however, have the authority to review actions of the commissioner and the INS.

COMMUNISM INADMISSIBILITY GROUND   Members of the Communist Party or any totalitarian political party are denied admission to the United States on security grounds, unless membership was involuntary, terminated at least two years prior to application, and the person is not a threat to the United States, or if admitting the alien is in the public interest or in the interest of family.

This **inadmissibility ground** does not apply to an alien who establishes that the membership or affiliation in the Communist organization is or was involuntary, or is or was solely when under sixteen years of age, by operation of law, or for purposes of obtaining employment, food rations, or other essentials of living.

This ground of inadmissibility can be waived in the case of an immigrant who is the parent, spouse, son, daughter, brother, or sister of a U.S.

citizen or a lawful permanent resident for humanitarian purposes, to ensure family unity, or when it is otherwise in the public interest and the immigrant is not a threat to the security of the United States.

COMMUTER ALIEN   The law provides for a class of **lawful permanent resident alien**s from Canada and Mexico who have homes in Canada or Mexico and commute daily, or on a seasonal basis, to places of employment in the United States, without actually establishing a permanent residence in the United States. Such aliens are originally admitted as immigrants, and thereafter cross the borders upon presentation of their resident alien cards. See *Saxbe v. Bustos* [419 U.S. 65 (1974)].

There are two categories of commuter aliens: daily and seasonal. An alien lawfully admitted for permanent residence or a **special agricultural worker** admitted for temporary residence may commence or continue to reside in foreign contiguous territory and commute as a special immigrant to a place of employment in the United States. The commuting can be daily or seasonal for employment that, on the whole, is regular and stable. [8 U.S.C. §1101(a)(27)(A); 8 C.F.R. §211.5]

An alien commuter engaged in seasonal work will be presumed to have taken up residence in the United States if he or she is present in the country for more than six months, in the aggregate, during any continuous twelve-month period. On the other hand, an alien commuter who has been out of regular employment for a continuous period of six months shall be deemed to have lost residence status, notwithstanding temporary entries in the interim for other than employment purposes, unless employment in the United States was interrupted for reasons beyond his or her control other than lack of a job opportunity, or he or she can demonstrate that he or she worked ninety days in the United States in the aggregate during the twelve-month period preceding application for admission into the United States.

Until the person has taken up residence in the United States, an alien commuter cannot satisfy the residence requirements of the **naturalization** laws and cannot qualify for any benefits under the immigration laws on his or her own behalf or on behalf of relatives.

CONDITIONAL PERMANENT RESIDENCE   In two important situations, the **lawful permanent resident alien** immigration status of individuals is considered to be conditional for a two-year period. In other words, a particular status must be maintained for two years until the permanent residence is actually permanent.

Aliens who seek to immigrate based on marriages to U.S. citizens or lawful permanent residents are granted permanent resident status initially on a conditional basis. In essence, final approval is conditioned on the viability of the marriage for two years. During the ninety-day period preceding the second anniversary of conditional status, the couple is required to jointly petition the district director to remove the conditional status. The couple will be interviewed and must establish that the marriage was legal, that it has not been terminated, that it was not entered into solely for immigration purposes (i.e., not a **sham marriage**), and that no fee was given for filing the immigration petition. Conditional status may also be removed when the alien's **removal** would result in extreme hardship or when the marriage was entered into in good faith by the alien spouse, but the marriage has been terminated and the alien was not at fault in failing to meet the requirements. A waiver of the requirements may also be granted if, during the marriage, the alien spouse or child was battered by or was the subject of extreme cruelty perpetrated by the spouse or citizen or permanent resident parent. [8 U.S.C. §1186a]

An alien who is granted immigrant investor's status under the employment-based fifth preference is considered, at the time of obtaining the status of lawful permanent residence, to have obtained such status on a conditional basis for a two-year period. The investor can lose his or her status during the two-year period if it is determined that the commercial enterprise was intended solely as a means of evading immigration laws, a commercial enterprise was not established by the person, the requisite capital was not invested, or the investment has not been continued. The person has a right to a hearing before investor's status is terminated. [8 U.S.C. §1186b]

CONSULATE GENERAL   A consulate general or U.S. consul is generally located in the various U.S. embassies throughout the world. U.S. citizens who work in the office of the consulate general are part of the foreign service of the United States, although many nationals of the foreign country are also employed in the consulate. U.S. consuls throughout the world are authorized to issue or refuse **visas** to aliens seeking entry into the United States. Some consulates, however, have no authority to issue visas; some may issue only **nonimmigrant visas**; and some may issue all types of visas, including immigration visas. Although a U.S. consul issues a visa, an immigration officer at the port of entry can still deny admission if the officer believes that the person is not eligible for the visa.

Decisions to deny visas by consular officers are theoretically final and unreviewable, although consuls receive instructions and directions from superiors in the Visa Office of the Bureau of Security and Consular Affairs of the **State Department** in Washington, D.C. Thus an informal review procedure can be requested from the Visa Office if a visa has been denied.

There are over a hundred consular offices of the United States located in foreign countries throughout the world. [22 C.F.R. §42; *Li Hing of Hong Kong, Inc. v. Levin,* 800 F.2d 970 (9th Cir. 1986); *Rivera de Gomez v. Kissinger,* 534 F.2d 518 (2d Cir. 1976)]

CONTROLLED SUBSTANCE EXCLUSION   Aliens convicted of violating any law or regulation related to controlled substances, such as marijuana, heroin, cocaine, drug paraphernalia, and synthetic drugs such as PCP or LSD are excluded from admission to the United States. Also, aliens who are drug addicts or drug abusers are excluded. Hospital records, doctors' reports, the person's own admission, and participation in drug rehabilitation programs may be used to determine if the alien is an addict. *Drug abuse* is the nonmedical use of a controlled substance, but is more than experimentation with the substance, for example as in the single use of marijuana or amphetamines.

In the case of marijuana offenders who have committed a single offense involving simple possession of not more than thirty grams, immigration authorities have the discretion to grant a **waiver of inadmissibility** if the offense took place more than fifteen years ago and the person is now rehabilitated, or the person is the spouse, parent, son, or daughter of a U.S. citizen or lawful permanent resident and exclusion would result in extreme hardship to that relative. [8 U.S.C. §§1182(a)(2), 1182(h); 42 U.S.C. §201(k)]

CONTROLLED SUBSTANCE TRAFFICKING   A person whom the INS or an American consul knows or has reason to believe is or has been a narcotics trafficker is excluded from admission to the United States. A conviction is not necessary. Thus, an arrest for a controlled substance offense that does not result in a conviction may form the basis for a reasonable belief that the person was a trafficker. [8 U.S.C. §1182(a)(2); *Nunez-Payan v. INS,* 815 F.2d 384 (5th Cir. 1987)] Furthermore, a conviction for trafficking is classified as an **aggravated felon**y. [8 U.S.C. §1101(a)(43)(B)]

CONVENTION RELATING TO THE STATUS OF REFUGEES OF 1951   The United Nations established this international agreement out of concern for refugees and "to assure refugees the widest possible exercise" of "fundamental rights and freedoms without discrimination." Although the United States did not join in this agreement in the 1950s, by becoming a party to the **United Nations Protocol Relating to the Status of Refugees** in 1968, the United States became obligated to follow the definition and treatment of refugees as set forth in the 1951 convention. Some of the important provisions include the following:

Article 1. Definition of the term "Refugee"

For the purposes of the present Convention, the term "refugee" shall apply to any person who:

. . .

(2) . . . owing to well-founded fear of being persecuted for reasons of race, religion, nationality, membership of a particular social group or political opinion, is outside the country of his nationality and is unable or, owing to such fear, is unwilling to avail himself of the protection of that country; or who, not having a nationality and being outside the country of his former habitual residence as a result of such events, is unable or, owing to such fear, is unwilling to return to it.

. . .

A. This Convention shall cease to apply to any person falling under the terms of Section A if:

(1) He has voluntarily re-availed himself of the protection of the country of his nationality; . . .

. . .

F. The provisions of this Convention shall not apply to any person with respect to whom there are serious reasons for considering that

(a) he has committed a crime against peace, a war crime, or a crime against humanity, as defined in the international instruments drawn up to make provision in respect of such crimes;

(b) he has committed a serious non-political crime outside the country of refuge prior to his admission to that country as a refugee;

(c) he has been guilty of acts contrary to the purposes and principles of the United Nations

. . .

Article 3. Non-discrimination

The Contracting States shall apply the provisions of this Convention to refugees without discrimination as to race, religion or country of origin.

. . .

Article 16 Access to courts

1. A refugee shall have free access to the courts of law on the territory of all Contracting States.

2. A refugee shall enjoy in the Contracting State in which he has his habitual residence the same treatment as a national in matters pertaining to access to the courts, including legal assistance. . . .

Article 17. Wage-earning employment

1. The Contracting State shall accord to refugees lawfully staying in its territory the most favourable treatment accorded to nationals of a foreign country in the same circumstances, as regards the right to engage in wage-earning employment.

2. In any case, restrictive measures imposed on aliens or the employment of aliens for the protection of the national labour market shall not be applied to a refugee who was already exempt from them at the date of entry into force of this Convention for the Contracting States concerned, or who fulfills one of the following conditions:

(a) He has completed three years' residence in the country;

(b) He has a spouse possessing the nationality of the country of residence. A refugee may not invoke the benefits of this provision if he has abandoned his spouse;

(c) He has one or more children possessing the nationality of the country of residence.

. . .

Article 22. Public education

1. The Contracting States shall accord to refugees the same treatment as is accorded to nationals with respect to elementary education.

. . .

Article 23. Public relief

The Contracting States shall accord to refugees lawfully staying in their territory the same treatment with respect to public relief and assistance as is accorded to their nationals.

. . .

Article 31. Refugees unlawfully in the country of refuge

1. The Contracting States shall not impose penalties, on account of their illegal entry or presence, on refugees who, coming directly from a territory where their life or freedom was threatened in the sense of Article 1, enter or are present in their territory without authorization, provided they present themselves without delay to the authorities and show good cause for their illegal entry or presence.

. . .

Article 32. Expulsion

1. The Contracting States shall not expel a refugee lawfully in their territory save on grounds of national security or public order.

2. The expulsion of such refugee shall be only in pursuance of a decision reached in accordance with due process of law. . . .

. . . .

Article 33. Prohibition of expulsion or return ("*refoulement*")

1. No Contracting State shall expel or return ("*refouler*") a refugee in any manner whatsoever to the frontiers of territories where his life or

freedom would be threatened on account of his race, religion, nationality, membership of a particular social group or political opinion.

2. The benefit of the present provision may not, however, be claimed by a refugee whom there are reasonable grounds for regarding as a danger to the security of the country in which he is, or who, having been convicted by a final judgment of a particularly serious crime, constitutes a danger to the community of that country.

COUNCIL OF JEWISH FEDERATIONS (CJF) The American Jewish community has always advocated for the right of Jews everywhere to live free of persecution. Too often, the exercise of that right has resulted in mass migrations of Jews from countries in which not only their freedom but their very existence was at risk. The United States has become home to millions of Jews who have proudly taken the oath of American citizenship in order to exercise the economic, religious, and political rights denied them in their countries of origin.

Assisting refugees and legal immigrants was one of the primary missions that spurred the creation of the Jewish federation movement across America in the late nineteenth century. Although the early immigrants found few institutions to assist them, they helped each other and soon formed more formal structures to aid those who came after them. During the late 1800s and early 1900s, the Settlement House movement spread rapidly across the country, helping many immigrants make their way in their new land.

As family service agencies, vocational services, homes for the aged, and other organizations were established to assist new Americans, along with the native-born, the need became apparent to create a communal structure that would collect more efficiently and allocate philanthropic dollars to support these institutions. The pioneer communities were Boston and Cincinnati, which established federations in 1895 and 1896, respectively.

By 1932 there were seventy-two Jewish federations across North America. The Council of Jewish Federations (CJF) was created that year to be the national association providing coordination on joint needs and responsibilities, serving as an information exchange, sharing program models and "best practices" among the federations, providing national and international leadership, and conducting research and needs assessments to guide federations in their planning for the future. Among the early tasks CJF undertook, at the request of the member federations, was the restructuring of four national organizations that all helped immigrants by providing services more efficiently across the country. The **New York Association for New Americans** (NYANA) was established as a result of a CJF study on resettlement needs in New York City, where most Jewish newcomers arrived. Today, CJF and its 174 member federations work closely in a collaborative partnership that draws on the strength of local, community-controlled, service-oriented federations and the expertise and leadership of a CJF national organization that offers planning and coordination, financial resource development, fiscal management services, education and training, and national and international advocacy for the federation system. As the central planning, allocations, and fund-raising organizations in their communities, local federations work with their affiliated agencies to assess needs, develop resources, and provide direct financial support to their agencies. These include, among others, family service agencies, vocational services, community centers, elderly housing, and nursing homes.

COUNTRY AND TERRITORIAL NUMERICAL LIMITATIONS

Persons who seek to immigrate to the United States under the **preference system** are subject to two types of numerical limitations: **worldwide numerical limitations** and country or territorial numerical limitations. In addition to the worldwide numerical cap, the rules provide an annual limitation of immigrant visas per country of 7 percent of the worldwide quotas. Thus, assuming a 226,000 worldwide family visa numerical limitation (the minimum) and 140,000 for employment visas, 7 percent of the total (366,000) is 25,620 for each country. But 75 percent of the visas issued for spouses and children of lawful permanent residents (family second preference 2-A) are not counted against the country's quota.

Generally, immigrant visas are issued in the chronological order in which aliens apply for them each fiscal year. However, if the total number of family and employment immigrant visas will exceed a particular country's quota, visa numbers are to be allocated in a manner in which each preference category receives a portion of the visas for that country in an amount equal to the ratio of the total number of visas made available under the worldwide level. [8 U.S.C. §1152] See **visa bulletin.**

The visa of any immigrant born in a colony or other dependent area of a country is charged to that country's quota.

CREDIBLE FEAR OF PERSECUTION   An **alien** who arrives at the U.S. border or a **port of entry** without proper travel documents is subject to **expedited removal proceedings.** However, those persons who are seeking asylum or who express a credible fear of persecution are exempted from expedited procedures. This critical determination is placed in the hands of an immigration officer at the port of entry who

prescreens such persons. If the officer finds that the alien does not have an intent to seek asylum or does not have a credible fear of persecution, the alien can be summarily removed from the United States. What constitutes a credible fear of persecution depends on the officer's determination of whether the person is honest; whether the facts asserted suggest a likelihood of persecution on account of race, religion, political opinion, nationality, or membership in a particular social group; and whether the person is believable. If a credible fear is established, the person then gets the opportunity to apply for asylum.

CREW MEMBERS   Flight attendants and crew members on ships usually may be admitted to the United States as **nonimmigrants** for a 29-day period. The crew member's passport is generally retained by the master or agent of the vessel or aircraft as some assurance that the crew member will return to the ship. The laws and regulations place severe restrictions on alien crew members. For example, they are ineligible for **change of nonimmigrant status.** Similarly, a crew member who falls into an immigrant category cannot obtain **lawful permanent resident alien** status without first departing the United States. They also cannot perform certain longshore work and will not be admitted during a strike or lockout involving the bargaining unit of the employer for which the crew member intends to work. [8 U.S.C. §§1101(a)(15)(D), 1184(f), 1258, 1288]

CRIME INVOLVING MORAL TURPITUDE   An alien who has been convicted of a crime involving moral turpitude may be inadmissible for immigration purposes or perhaps removable [see **inadmissibility grounds** and **deportation grounds**]. Moral turpitude crimes are those that involve activity that is morally and inherently wrong, involving depravity and baseness, generally as judged by the common conscience of the community. The determination is not based upon whether the crime is a felony or a misdemeanor. Neither the seriousness of the offense nor the severity of the sentence imposed is determinative of whether a crime involves moral turpitude. The question involves the offender's evil intent or corruption of the mind. Crimes that have been determined to involve moral turpitude include murder, voluntary manslaughter, aggravated assault, rape, kidnapping, theft, lewd conduct, bigamy, counterfeiting, bribery, willful tax evasion, extortion, perjury, grand theft, fraud, and other crimes having as an element the intent to defraud. On the other hand, crimes such as involuntary manslaughter, joyriding, draft evasion, passing bad checks, breaking and entering without intent to commit a moral turpitude offense, escape from prison, and simple assault have been held not to involve moral turpitude. [8 U.S.C. §§1182(a)(2), 1227(a)(2)]

The question of when the outcome of a criminal case is actually a conviction for purposes of deportability is the subject of dispute. The **Board of Immigration Appeals** has gradually moved toward finding that even expunged crimes remain convictions for immigration purposes. See **expungement,** *In re Roldan,* and *Matter of Ozkok.*

 **CUBAN REFUGEE ACT OF 1966** Many Cubans fled to the United States after the 1959 revolution in Cuba, which resulted in Fidel Castro taking control and installing a Communist government. These Cubans were in **parole** status until Congress authorized their **adjustment of status** to **lawful permanent resident alien** status in 1966. The primary requirement was that the applicant must have been physically present in the United States for at least one year. The **inadmissibility ground** of being or likely to become a **public charge** was not imposed on these applicants because the statute was designed to aid Cuban refugees to become reestablished in the United States. This policy of waiving the public charge ground of inadmissibility for refugees seeking permanent resident status was continued in the **Refugee Act of 1980** for all refugees eligible for adjustment of status.

CULTURAL PLURALISM   See **Assimilation.**

D

DEFERRED ACTION   Although an alien may be subject to **removal** from the United States, the district director of the local INS **district offices** has the power to allow the person to remain in the country even if the immigration laws do not provide a clear defense to removal. If the district director exercises that power on behalf of the alien, this is referred to as deferred action. For example, a nonimmigrant with a serious illness, or a longtime undocumented alien who has committed a minor narcotics offense but who has a U.S. citizen child, may be placed in the deferred action category. Deferred action allows the individual to remain in the country indefinitely.

Internal INS policy provides that the following factors should be considered by the district director when deferred action is requested:

- the likelihood of ultimately removing the alien, including physical ability to travel, or available relief
- the presence of sympathetic factors that might lead to protracted deportation proceedings or bad precedent from the INS perspective
- the likelihood that publicity adverse to the INS will be generated because of sympathetic facts
- whether the person is a member of a class whose removal is given high priority (dangerous criminals, large-scale alien smugglers, narcotic drug traffickers, terrorists, war criminals, habitual immigration violators)

The idea of deferred action is that the district director may consider it when particularly strong equities exist in the case. However, the decision is pretty much up to the district director, and courts are unlikely to disagree with the director's decision. [*Velasco-Gutierrez v. Crossland*, 732 F.2d 792 (10th Cir. 1984)]

DEFERRED ENFORCED DEPARTURE (DED)   Deferred enforced departure (DED) was a legal immigration status granted to certain categories of aliens who previously had **temporary protected**

95

status (TPS). DED allowed a person to live and work legally in the United States. TPS for nationals of El Salvador expired on June 30, 1992. Salvadorans who were initially granted TPS were then granted DED by an executive order. DED for Salvadorans expired on December 31, 1994. Employment authorization for Salvadorans under the DED program was automatically extended to April 30, 1996, when it expired.

DEFERRED INSPECTION   See **secondary inspection.**

DEPARTMENT OF JUSTICE   This department of the executive branch is headed by the U.S. **attorney general** of the United States, and includes the INS and the **Executive Office of Immigration Review.** As the chief enforcement officer, the attorney general enforces the immigration policy of the United States. The attorney general also has the authority to review and reverse all decisions of the INS and the Executive Office of Immigration Review.

DEPARTMENT OF LABOR   The U.S. Department of Labor (DOL) is part of the executive branch of the federal government. It plays a critical role in the entry of persons who seek to immigrate in employment categories that require labor certifications or **alien employment certifications.** In theory, the DOL's role is to protect the rights of U.S. workers and ensure that U.S. employers are not using foreign workers when U.S. workers are available for the prevailing wage for the particular occupation. Generally, the DOL must certify that there is a shortage of workers in the particular job classification sought. A similar certification is sought for certain temporary worker nonimmigrant categories.

Issuance of a labor certification by the department is not, however, positive assurance that an **immigrant** or **nonimmigrant visa** will be issued. For nonimmigrant visas, the certification is merely advisory, and for immigrant visas, the INS has the authority to review job requirements and applicant qualifications.

DEPORTATION   The term *deportation* is generally used to describe the forced departure of an alien from the United States. In 1996, Congress changed the terminology of the laws and the term *removal* is now used to describe the forced departure of an alien from the United States. See **removal.**

DEPORTATION GROUNDS   Congress has established a list of categories of deportable aliens. An alien falling into any one of these categories is subject to **removal proceedings (deportation)** and banned from the country. The most common classes of deportable aliens include the following:

- aliens who at the time of entry or **adjustment of status** were inadmissible [see **inadmissibility grounds**]
- **nonimmigrant**s (e.g., students and tourists) who have failed to maintain the nonimmigrant status, such as by working without authorization, or who have violated their status, such as by staying longer than permitted
- aliens who have, within five years of any entry, assisted in or encouraged the **smuggling of aliens** into the United States
- aliens who were parties to **sham marriages**
- aliens who have committed a **crime involving moral turpitude**
- aliens who have committed an **aggravated felony**
- aliens convicted of narcotics offenses [see **controlled substance exclusion**]
- drug addicts
- aliens who have been convicted of an offense relating to firearms or destructive devices [see **firearms and explosive devices**]
- aliens convicted of a crime of domestic violence, stalking, child abuse, child neglect, or child abandonment
- aliens who have committed **document fraud**
- aliens who have engaged in terrorist activity, sabotage, espionage, or criminal activity that endangers public safety or national security
- aliens who, within five years of entry, have become a **public charge** from causes not shown to have arisen since entry
- aliens who have voted in violation of any federal, state, or local laws

Some grounds of deportation can be waived, while relief such as **cancellation of removal** or **asylum** may be afforded in other situations. In general, however, the most serious grounds of deportation are those related to aggravated felonies and narcotics offenses. Individuals falling within those grounds generally have few options in removal proceedings.

DERIVATIVE BENEFICIARY   The law provides that the spouses and children of **preference system** immigrants are entitled to the same immigration status as the primary immigrant if "accompanying or following to join" the primary immigrant. These spouses and children are often referred to as derivative beneficiaries. For example, if a U.S.

citizen petitions for her married son under the family third preference, the son as well as the daughter-in-law will be able to immigrate when visas are available. Similarly, their minor, unmarried children will also be able to immigrate as derivatives. [8 U.S.C. §1153(d)]

The *accompanying* requirement is met when the derivative is traveling in the physical company of the primary immigrant. Otherwise, the requirement must be met within four months of the issuance of the visa to the principal alien or within four months of the **adjustment of status** in the United States of the primary immigrant. The *following to join* requirement is met anytime after the primary immigrant has immigrated so long as the derivative is still a spouse or child.

The derivative's visa is not valid unless the primary immigrant is traveling with the derivative or has preceded the derivative. See *Santiago v. INS*. If the primary immigrant dies before being able to immigrate, the derivative beneficiaries lose their status.

When a son or daughter obtains derivative status through a parent who is immigrating as a second-preference spouse [see **second preference for relatives**] or as a fiancé [see **fiancé visa**] of a U.S. citizen, **lawful permanent resident alien** status is granted on a conditional basis [see **conditional permanent residence**]. The conditional status can be made permanent in two years if the parent and the parent's spouse demonstrate that the marriage has not been terminated, that it was not entered into solely for immigration purposes (a **sham marriage**), and that no fee was given for filing the immigration petition.

DISABILITY WAIVER OR ACCOMMODATIONS FOR NATURALIZATION REQUIREMENTS

A person who is unable to comply with the English literacy requirement and/or the history and government requirement for **naturalization** due to a physical or developmental disability or mental impairment may apply to have the requirement(s) waived so long as the disability will last at least twelve months and was not the result of illegal drug use. To apply for the waiver, the applicant must submit supporting evidence showing the exact connection between the disability and the inability to learn English and/or U.S. civics. A doctor or licensed psychologist who has experience diagnosing disabilities and knows about the applicant's physical or mental condition must complete the waiver form.

For example, to qualify for waiver of English literacy, an applicant must show that he or she is unable to fulfill the English language requirements even with reasonable modifications in the testing process due to a medically determinable physical or mental impairment, or combination of impairments, that has lasted or is expected to last at least twelve months, and that was not the direct effect of illegal drug use. The applicant must demonstrate how the disability prevents him or her from meeting the requirement by showing a connection between the disability and the inability to learn.

Section 504 of the Rehabilitation Act of 1973 requires that the INS make reasonable accommodations or modifications to the naturalization process to make it possible for applicants who have disabilities to get through the process. The INS must make these accommodations whether or not the applicant is applying for a disability waiver. The INS need not make accommodations or modifications that would substantially interfere with the naturalization program. If an accommodation is sought, the applicant must specify the type of accommodation required (e.g., that an applicant needs to have a family member present at the interview so that the applicant does not get too frightened). Although no formal medical certification is required, supporting information from a physician is helpful.

DISPLACED PERSONS ACT   In 1948, Congress enacted the Displaced Persons Act (DPA) to enable European refuges driven from their homelands during World War II to emigrate to the United States without regard to traditional immigration quotas. The law enabled 400,000 refugees to enter the United States.

The DPA established an elaborate system for determining eligibility for displaced person status. Applicants were first interviewed by representatives of the International Refugee Organization of the United Nations, who ascertained whether they were **refugee**s or displaced persons. Applicants were then interviewed by an official of the Displaced Persons Commission, who made a preliminary determination about their eligibility under the DPA. The final decision was made by one of several **State Department** vice consuls, who were specially trained for the task and sent to Europe to administer the DPA. Thereafter, applications were reviewed by INS officials to make sure that the applicant was admissible into the United States under the standard immigration laws.

DISTRICT DIRECTOR   Each of the INS **district offices** is headed by a district director. The district director oversees the various functions of district offices, including **naturalization, adjustment of status,** investigations, and **removal** functions.

DISTRICT OFFICES   The Immigration and Naturalization Service district offices are located in thirty-three different cities around the United States, with three district offices outside the country in Bangkok, Mexico City, and Rome. **Regional INS offices** also provide support to the local district offices. Each district office is headed by a district director, who has vast authority over setting the tone for local employees in terms of service to customers and enforcement of immigration laws. While more and more adjudication of applications is handled by the **regional service centers,** the district offices still handle many visa applications and have tremendous authority over the decision to initiate **removal proceedings** against deportable aliens. **Naturalization** processing is another major function that is handled at local district offices.

Each office is generally divided into different departments such as deportation, investigations, and adjudications or examinations.

DIVERSITY VISAS   Aliens from low-immigration countries who have at least a high school education or two years of work experience are eligible for one of the 55,000 diversity-based preference visas, which are distributed by a lottery system. Which countries are low immigration is determined by the rate of immigration from that country for the past five years. Under a complicated formula that weights countries and regions of the world and uses relative populations as well, the **State Department** determines the distribution of visas. For example, **national**s of all countries of Africa, and most countries of Europe (including Northern Ireland, but not the rest of Great Britain) and Latin America (except Mexico, Jamaica, El Salvador, Dominican Republic, and Colombia) are eligible to apply for these lottery-type diversity visas. Natives of mainland China, Taiwan, India, the Philippines, Vietnam, and South Korea are not eligible to apply. [8 U.S.C. §1153(c)]

To qualify for these diversity visas, the applicant must have a high school education (or its equivalent), or within the five years preceding the application have at least two years of work experience in an occupation that requires at least two years of training or experience.

The application period for the lottery diversity visa usually runs from January 31 through March 1 each year. A particular application format for these visas must be followed and mailed to a particular site, usually the Diversity Visa program at the National Visa Center in Portsmouth, New Hampshire. Information on the diversity visa application can be obtained from the Bureau of Consular Affairs of the State Department.

Until October 1, 1994, a transition diversity program was in effect, providing 40,000 visas per year. These visas were made available to countries "adversely affected" by the **Immigration Amendments of 1965,** except that 40 percent of the visas were effectively designated for immigrants from Ireland.

🏛 **DOCUMENT ABUSE**   Employers who hire new workers must not hire unauthorized workers and they must also complete a Form I-9 [see Appendix], which entails examining certain documents related to employment permission and identity. If employers fail to follow these rules, they are subject to penalties under **employer sanctions** laws. In the course of the **I-9 process,** however, employers also must not be unreasonable in their demands to see certain documents of new workers or job applicants. In fact, the employer cannot request a specific document to satisfy the I-9 process. Requesting a specific document when the employee has already presented sufficient documentation can constitute employment discrimination. This is referred to as document abuse. The employer must be satisfied, as long as the individual provides a document or combination of documents that reasonably appear to be genuine and that are sufficient to meet the requirements. [8 U.S.C. §1324a]

🏛 **DOCUMENT FRAUD**   A person who is involved with using false immigration documents can be subject to civil and criminal penalties for document fraud. For example, civil penalties ranging from $250 to $2,000 can be imposed on any person who knowingly forges or counterfeits any document for immigration purposes or who uses another person's immigration documents. As for criminal penalties, a person who, for a fee, helps someone with a false application for benefits under the immigration laws can be imprisoned for up to five years. This includes forms filed with the INS, the **Executive Office of Immigration Review,** the **State Department,** or the **Department of Labor.** Also, criminal penalties apply for fraud and misuse of visas, permits, and other immigration documents. [8 U.S.C. §1324c; 18 U.S.C. §1546(a)]

An alien who is the subject of a final order for violation of document fraud restrictions is also inadmissible [see **inadmissibility grounds**] and is therefore barred from reentering the United States. [8 U.S.C. §1182(a)(6)]

🏛 **DRAKE, SUSAN (B. 1945)**   Susan Drake is one of the nation's leading experts on public benefits and employment rights for immigrants. She has been on the staff of the **National Immigration Law Center** (NILC) since 1986, and has served as NILC's executive director since

1996. Her policy analyses, reports, articles, and testimony before Congress and state legislatures have had a tremendous impact on the public policies affecting the lives of immigrants.

Drake has also served as co-counsel in several important immigrants' rights cases: *Gillen v. Belshe*, a statewide class-action challenge to California's implementation of the provisions of Proposition 187 imposing alien restrictions on AFDC, food stamps, and Medicaid in violation of federal law; *Ruiz v. Kizer*, a statewide class action that enjoined California's violation of federal law requirement that Medicaid benefits not be denied because of INS delays in checking immigration status through the SAVE computer verification program; *Crespin v. Coye*, a challenge to California's failure to cover medical emergencies and long-term care for immigrants in the Medi-Cal program; and *California Rural Legal Assistance Foundation v. Legal Services Corporation*, a nationwide class action that enjoined the Legal Services Corporation from implementing a regulation denying amnesty immigrants eligibility for legal services.

Prior to joining the staff of NILC, Drake worked for Terris and Sunderland, a private public-interest firm in Washington, D.C., specializing in environmental and civil rights law; the Land of Lincoln Legal Assistance Foundation in Champaign, Illinois, as an energy specialist; and as the project coordinator of the Hispanic Children's Law Project at the University of San Diego School of Law. She received her J.D. with honors from the University of Illinois College of Law in 1978.

E

EAD See **employment authorization document.**

 EASTERN HEMISPHERE IMMIGRANTS Immigrants from outside the Western Hemisphere, including Europe and Asia. See **Western Hemisphere immigrants.**

ELLIS ISLAND Located in New York Harbor, Ellis Island became the primary inspection site for Europeans immigrating to the United States. In 1891, Congress enacted legislation that laid the foundation for federal control of immigration. The federal government, aggravated by the lax ways that New York's immigration officials were handling immigration screening, assumed sole authority over immigration at the port of New York, and constructed the inspection depot on Ellis Island.

The main building at Ellis Island was the primary immigrant processing center, receiving about 70 percent of the more than 12 million arrivals to the United States during the peak immigration years of 1892 to 1924, part of the largest human migration in history. Not all immigrants had to pass through Ellis Island. Officials believed that those who could afford a first- or second-class ticket necessarily had a good education and good health care in their former country. These immigrants were given a cursory examination aboard the ship (avoiding the more stringent exams on Ellis Island), quickly processed, and allowed to leave the ship in Manhattan. About 20 percent of those who went through Ellis Island were detained for medical or legal reasons, and some were kept until friends or relatives could pick them up or until they were given money or directions to a final destination. Ultimately, only about 2 percent, or 250,000 of those processed during the peak years, were excluded from admission. But even those who went through Ellis Island (mostly Europeans) spent only a few hours or at most a few days at the island depot; in contrast, Asians, and particularly Chinese, who had to go through **Angel**

103

Island in San Francisco Bay, counted their detention time in weeks, months, and even years.

Opened in 1892, destroyed by fire in 1897 and reopened in late 1900, Ellis Island processed an average of 5,000 people a day. The busiest day—April 17, 1907—saw 11,747 immigrants pass through, part of the 1,004,756 arrivals during that record year. Almost half of Americans today can claim a family member who came through Ellis Island.

The Ellis Island Immigration Museum, which opened in 1990, is now a popular tourist attraction. The museum includes historic photos, priceless family possessions the immigrants brought to America, recorded voices of immigrants, and two movie theaters showing a documentary film. A Wall of Honor outside lists hundreds of thousands of immigrants whose descendants contributed $100 to have their names engraved there.

EMPLOYER SANCTIONS The **Immigration Reform and Control Act of 1986** (IRCA) imposed employer sanctions on persons who knowingly "hire, recruit or refer for a fee for employment" an alien who is not a lawful permanent resident or not authorized to work. Employer sanctions make it unlawful for an employer to knowingly hire an **undocumented alien** or an **unauthorized alien**. Employers must also complete a Form I-9 [see Appendix] for each new employee hired, including U.S. citizens, and check documents proving the employment eligibility of every new employee. There are two types of employer sanctions: one for knowingly hiring undocumented workers, and the other for not following the **I-9 process** paperwork requirements. Civil penalties range from $250 to $10,000 for hiring a person who is not authorized to work, and $100 to $1,000 for failing to meet the paperwork requirements. Criminal penalties of six months in prison and additional fines can be imposed if a "pattern and practice" of violations are established.

Within three business days of the first day of work, the employee must present the employer with original documents that establish the employee's identity and employment eligibility. A U.S. passport or an alien registration card (green card) can establish both identity and employment eligibility. Instead of one of those documents, an employee could present a social security card that does not have an employment prohibition stamp to establish employment eligibility, plus a driver's license to establish identity.

The law requires the following of all employers:

- verification of employment eligibility of all persons employed after November 6, 1986

- completion of INS Form I-9 for each new hire within three days of the date of hire (if the worker is being hired for three days or less, the form must be completed by the end of the first workday)
- checking documents proving employment eligibility and identity of each new employee at the commencement of employment

The requirements of the law apply to the following:

- all employers, including agricultural associations, agricultural employers, or farm labor contractors who employ workers or recruit or refer workers for a fee
- anyone who hires someone for domestic work in a private home on a regular basis, such as every week
- employees transferred to the United States from an overseas branch or affiliate of the U.S. company, regardless of the fact that they may remain on the foreign payroll

An employer does not have to complete an I-9 if self-employed, or if the person is also an employee of a business entity, such as a corporation or partnership, in which case the business entity is required to complete a Form I-9 for the person. No verification is necessary for temporary personnel provided by temporary agencies.

If a person is hired to do work infrequently, the person may be considered a *casual hire*, for whom the I-9 process does not need to be followed. For example, a person hired casually and infrequently to perform domestic jobs around the house or yard can be considered a casual hire. Hiring such a person once a month would probably be considered infrequent. But someone who is hired to work regularly once a week would probably not qualify as a casual hire; for that worker an I-9 form would be necessary.

No verification is required of an **independent contractor.** An employer may wish to avoid presenting or reviewing documents by characterizing a worker performing services as an independent contractor rather than an employee. The idea is that persons who have their own business and hire out their services are not considered employees.

Employers who have committed technical or procedural violations are excused from the paperwork penalties if there was a good-faith attempt to comply with the requirements. See **good faith compliance.** A technical or procedural violation would be such things as neglecting to have the employee provide a maiden name, alien registration number, address, or birth date. However, if the INS gives notice of the violation and the employer does not correct the violation within ten days, the employer can be penalized. [8 U.S.C. §1324a]

EMPLOYMENT AUTHORIZATION DOCUMENT   Issued by the INS, the employment authorization document (EAD) indicates that the holder is entitled to work in the United States. Many individuals applying for **adjustment of status** and **undocumented aliens** who are seeking some form of relief can be issued EADs as a matter of discretion by the **district director.**

EMPLOYMENT-BASED PREFERENCES   The immigration **preference system** has set aside 140,000 immigrant **visas** based on the employment skills of prospective immigrants. For example, people with extraordinary ability in science, arts, education, business, or athletics get first-priority status. Professionals with advanced degrees who have proof of a job offer get second-priority status [see **second preference employment category**]. Professionals with baccalaureate degrees and skilled workers in short supply get third-priority status. Religious workers and former U.S. government employees get **fourth preference.** Investors who will create at least ten United States jobs are given fifth preference [see **investor visa**]. Each preference category is subject to a separate numerical limitation, although unused visas in the higher preference category roll over to the lower preference categories.

ENGLISH-ONLY MOVEMENT   One manifestation of the sentiments of strong supporters of an Anglo-conformity model of **assimilation** is the English-only movement. While its supporters may argue that theirs is not an anti-immigrant movement, efforts to make English the official language of the United States or to support employers' efforts to demand that only English be spoken on business premises obviously affect the lives of immigrants.

Making English the official language of the United States is one of the main goals of the English-only movement. Dozens of states have enacted such legislation or made symbolic proclamations to that effect. In *Yniguez v. Arizonans for Official English* [69 F.3d 920 (9th Cir. En banc 1995)], the court of appeals, by a vote of 6–5, struck down an Arizona referendum that made English the state's official language on the ground that it violated the First Amendment rights of both state employees and private individuals who sought information from state employees. The court rejected the state's arguments that the choice of language is conduct rather than speech, and that employees' speech in the course of their employment is not entitled to First Amendment protection. The Supreme Court granted certiorari but ultimately vacated the Ninth Circuit Court's decision as moot, without deciding on its merits.

ENTRY   Physical presence in the United States after **inspection** and **admission** without further restraint, or after crossing the border without inspection. Until the terminology was changed in 1996, an alien who gained *entry* had to be deported and go through deportation proceedings, whereas an alien who had not entered could simply be expelled through a process called *exclusion,* which offered less protection. The term *entry* was removed from the statute by the **Illegal Immigration Reform and Immigrant Responsibility Act of 1996** (IIRAIRA), and the term **admission** is now used.

ENTRY WITHOUT INSPECTION   Prior to the **Illegal Immigration Reform and Immigrant Responsibility Act of 1996** (IIRAIRA), a person who entered surreptitiously along a border or who made a false claim of U.S. citizenship to get into the United States was said to have *entered without inspection* (EWI). As such the person was deportable. After IIRAIRA, a person who enters without inspection (most commonly along the Mexican and Canadian borders) falls within the **inadmissibility grounds** that cover aliens who are present in the United States without being admitted or paroled, or who arrive at a place other than a designated **port of entry.** As such, the person falls within the class of deportable aliens who were inadmissible at time of entry [8 U.S.C. §§1182(a)(6)(A); 1227]. These individuals are not only subject to **removal** from the United States, but they are very likely to be subject to a three- or ten-year bar from returning to the United States if they sustain an **unlawful presence** of six months or more in the country.

EXCHANGE VISITOR   An exchange visitor is a **nonimmigrant** scholar or student holding a J-1 nonimmigrant visa, entering the United States on a program sponsored by the United States or a foreign government. The exchange visitor program is designed to foster cultural and international relations. For example, recipients of Fulbright grants are J-1 exchange visitors.

Students, scholars, trainees, teachers, professors, research assistants, specialists, and leaders in their fields are included in the exchange visitor category. They must be entering temporarily to participate in a program recognized by the secretary of state for the purpose of teaching, studying, observing, conducting research, consulting, or receiving training. Some exchange students whose programs are paid for from government sources must return to their home country upon completion of their programs and live there for at least two years before they can return to the United States. [8 U.S.C. §§1101(a)(15)(J), 1182(e)]

EXCLUSION   This is the concept of barring an alien from entering the United States because the person falls within one or more of the **inadmissibility grounds.**

EXECUTIVE OFFICE OF IMMIGRATION REVIEW   The Executive Office of Immigration Review (EOIR) is an agency of the **Department of Justice,** independent of the INS, that oversees the **Board of Immigration Appeals** (BIA) and **immigration judge**s. The EOIR includes the Office of the Chief Immigration Judge, the BIA, and the **Office of the Chief Administrative Hearing Officer.** The chief immigration judge supervises the judges who hear deportation and exclusion (**removal**) cases in immigration courts. The BIA hears appeals of decisions made by immigration judges, who hear removal (deportation and exclusion) cases in immigration courts. The chief administrative hearing officer supervises the **administrative law judge**s, who hear cases involving **employer sanctions, document fraud,** and immigration-related employment discrimination claims.

EXPATRIATION   The voluntary relinquishment of citizenship for either a **natural born citizen** or a citizen by **naturalization** by combining intent to abandon citizenship with any of the following acts: becoming the natural citizen of a foreign country; taking an oath allying oneself with another country; serving in a foreign country's military; being employed by a foreign government; renouncing one's nationality before a consular officer in another country (see **renunciation of citizenship**); or committing an act of treason or subversion. In proving expatriation, an expatriating act and an intent to relinquish citizenship must be proved only by a preponderance of the evidence (e.g., more likely than not). When one of the statutory expatriating acts is proved, it is constitutional to presume it to have been a voluntary act until and unless proved otherwise by the actor. If he or she succeeds, there can be no expatriation. If he or she fails, the question remains whether on all the evidence the government has satisfied its burden of proof that the expatriating act was performed with the necessary intent to relinquish citizenship. [8 U.S.C. §1481(a)] See *Afroyim v. Rusk* and *Vance v. Terrazas.*

EXPEDITED REMOVAL PROCEEDINGS   Some persons do not have the right to regular **removal proceedings,** and may be subject to expedited removal proceedings. For example, persons who are apprehended at an airport without proper documents and those who are arrested at the border while crossing surreptitiously will be placed in expedited removal proceedings. The INS also has the option to put any person in expedited removal proceedings if they entered without **inspection** and have been in the United States for less than two years.

Many **asylum** seekers arrive at the border or **port of entry** without proper travel documents. But the law provides that aliens arriving at U.S. ports of entry who are found inadmissible for fraud, misrepresentation, or lack of valid travel documents are subject to expedited removal procedures [see **inadmissibility grounds**]. Those seeking asylum or who express a credible fear of persecution are exempted from expedited procedures. However, this determination is placed in the hands of an immigration officer at the port of entry who prescreens such persons as to whether the alien intends to apply for asylum or fears persecution. If the officer finds that the alien does not have such an intent or fear, the officer can order the alien summarily removed from the United States. [8 U.S.C. §1225(b)] See **credible fear of prosecution.**

EXPUNGEMENT   Most states have statutes that make it possible to expunge a criminal record. Until recently, the operation of certain statutes was extremely beneficial to **aliens** because they presented the possibility of eliminating convictions for **removal** and inadmissibility purposes [see **inadmissibility grounds**].

Expungement statutes vary. Some operate in a manner to seal records; others merely provide for the substitution of a not-guilty plea for a previous plea of guilty after the satisfaction of a probationary period. Generally, the theory is that the person has been rehabilitated and should not have to have a criminal conviction on his or her record.

For years, the **Board of Immigration Appeals** (BIA) struggled with the increasing numbers of state rehabilitative statutes and the varying methods of avoiding the state consequences of a conviction by either deferring or erasing the recording of a judgment. Generally, aliens were allowed to escape the immigration consequences of their criminal misconduct once the conviction had been expunged. Because of the semantic differences among the various states' methods for erasing criminal records, aliens have not been considered convicted for immigration purposes where the state's action has been deemed tantamount to an expungement. The general rule was that a criminal conviction that had been expunged would not support an order of deportation.

In *Matter of A—F—* [8 I. & N. Dec. 429 (BIA, A.G. 1959)], the **attorney general** departed from what was already long-standing BIA precedent and ruled that a conviction for a drug offense would render an alien deportable, notwithstanding the expungement of that conviction under a state rehabilitative statute. The attorney general's reasoning was that an alien's deportability should not be controlled by the "vagaries of state law."

In 1988 the BIA announced a new approach that made it easier to determine that a conviction had occurred in *Matter of Ozkok,* and Congress went further in the **Illegal Immigration Reform and Immigrant Responsibility Act of 1996.** In 1999 the BIA announced in *In re Roldan* that expungements that purport to erase the record of guilt do not eliminate the underlying conviction for immigration purposes.

The *Roldan* decision does not address the situation where the alien has had his or her conviction vacated by a state court on direct appeal, wherein the court determines that vacation of the conviction is warranted on the merits, or on grounds relating to a violation of a fundamental statutory or constitutional right in the underlying criminal proceedings. Also, an expungement or record-sealing statute that treats the defendant as a juvenile or youthful offender may still be effective since there are special policy reasons that might justify leniency toward such defendants.

EXTENDED VOLUNTARY DEPARTURE   From time to time individuals flee to the United States from regions of the world that are in the midst of civil war. Generally speaking, these persons will not be granted **asylum** unless they can demonstrate that they have been singled out for persecution rather than simply fearing conditions that endanger the general population of the native country.

Prior to 1990, various administrations felt a need to provide at least limited protection for such individuals. Thus, a status that came to be known as extended voluntary departure (EVD) was established for these situations. EVD was essentially a blanket exercise of prosecutorial discretion to withhold enforced departure for a particular nationality group for a limited period of time. The relief was authorized by the U.S. **attorney general** in consultation with the secretary of state.

EVD was generally granted to **alien**s who reached the United States from countries that were experiencing internal strife such as civil war or rebellion. For example, EVD was in force at various times during the 1980s for **national**s of Afghanistan, Ethiopia, Nicaragua, Poland, and Uganda. However, since this relief involved discretionary decisions at high levels of the government, there was no "right" to the relief in the sense that a court could force the administration to grant EVD to nationals of a particular country, even if evidence of civil strife in that country was available.

In recent years, the equivalent of EVD has been accomplished under an administrative mechanism known as **deferred enforced departure** (DED), which has been used to defer the deportation of Chinese, Kuwaitis, Salvadorans, and others. DED was also extended to Haitians who had applied for asylum before December 1, 1995.

Given the provision of statutory authority for **temporary protected status** in 1990 legislation as well as the DED programs, EVD as a formal concept is likely to be curtailed.

EXTREME HARDSHIP   Many aliens who are inadmissible or deportable may be forgiven for past problems if they can demonstrate *extreme hardship* to a relative such as a parent or spouse who is a U.S. citizen or **lawful permanent resident alien.** The concept of extreme hardship can lead to waivers of three- and ten-year bars for **unlawful presence,** waivers of certain **inadmissibility grounds,** and certain **cancellation of removal** remedies.

Factors that are relevant to extreme hardship include length of residence in the United States, family ties, economic hardship, social adjustment, community ties, medical problems, age, the situation in the country to which the person would have to return, whether the applicant will ever be able to immigrate, and language abilities. Mere economic hardship, or a lessening in earning power alone, is generally not sufficient to establish extreme hardship. However, factors relevant to economics, such as education, health, medical care, and emotional adjustment, are important, and their cumulative effects may amount to extreme hardship.

Although the mere existence of citizen children is not decisive as to extreme hardship, they are of course important. In most cases, the citizen child will be forced to return to the applicant's place of birth if relief is not granted. The possible effects of uprooting a U.S. citizen child who is assimilated into American life are critical—especially if the child is already of school age:

> [T]here is ample authority for the proposition that imposing on grade school age citizen children who have lived their entire lives in the United States, the alternatives of either prolonged and geographically extensive separation from both parents or removal to a country of a vastly different culture where they do not speak the language is a matter which must normally be considered by the INS in its determination of whether extreme hardship has been shown. [*Ramos v. Immigration and Natural-*

ization Service, 695 F.2d 181, 186 (5th Cir. 1983)] [See also *Ravancho v. INS* and *Immigration and Naturalization Service v. Jong Ha Wang.*]

Whenever denial of relief will result in separation from a spouse, child, or parent who is a citizen or lawful permanent resident, extreme hardship is simpler to establish because of the severe emotional trauma involved. See *Mejia-Carrillo v. INS.*

F

FAIR See **Federation for American Immigration Reform.**

FAMILY REUNIFICATION Most immigrant visas to the United States are set aside for relatives of U.S. citizens or **lawful permanent resident aliens.** While 140,000 immigrant visas are reserved for employment-based categories, the law provides at least 226,000 family preference category visas annually on a worldwide basis. Although in theory the worldwide quota can be increased to 480,000 annually, the level likely will not be much more than 226,000. This is because the family preference category level is determined by subtracting the number of **immediate relative** entrants—generally well over 200,000 annually—from the maximum (480,000). Still, the concept of family reunification dominates the U.S. immigration system.

FAMILY-SPONSORED PREFERENCES Certain relatives of U.S. citizens and lawful permanent residents may immigrate in family immigration categories [see **preference system**]. For example, the adult unmarried sons and daughters of U.S. citizens get first preference status. Spouses, children, and unmarried sons and daughters of lawful permanent resident aliens get second preference [see **second preference for relatives**]. Married sons and daughters of U.S. citizens get third preference, and brothers and sisters of adult U.S. citizens get **fourth preference.** Each preference category is subject to separate **numerical limitations,** although unused visas in the higher preference categories can be allocated to the lower preference categories. To avoid breaking up nuclear families, immediate family members who could not otherwise gain admission may accompany or follow the admitted family member as a **derivative beneficiary.**

Unmarried children of U.S. citizens under the age of twenty-one, spouses of U.S. citizens, and parents of adult U.S. citizens may immigrate in an **immediate relative** category and are not subject to any numerical limitation.

113

FAMILY UNITY The *family unity* provisions of the **Immigration Act of 1990** allow the spouses and unmarried children (under age eighteen) of **amnesty** aliens to remain in the United States and receive work authorization. For the spouses and children of those aliens who were granted legalization or amnesty through the pre-1982 legalization program to be eligible, they must have entered the United States before May 5, 1988, and resided in the United States since that time. For the spouses and children of those aliens who were granted legalization through the **special agricultural worker** (SAW) program, they must have entered the United States and resided here as of December 1, 1988. Brief absences do not render an applicant ineligible for the family unity provisions. [8 C.F.R. §§236.10–236.18]

The major disqualifying grounds for family unity relate to criminal convictions. Any three misdemeanors or one felony conviction, drug offenses or narcotics addiction, and serious nonpolitical offenses committed outside the United States are disqualifying.

A major benefit of the family unity provisions is employment authorization. The person is able to work as soon as the family unity application is filed. The person does not have to wait for official employment authorization before being able to work. [8 C.F.R. §242.6(e)(6)]

Family unity is not a form of amnesty or legalization; important limitations apply. For example, persons granted family unity do not have the right to travel outside the United States. They must obtain **advanced parole** from the INS based on an emergency need to travel. Those who travel abroad without such permission will lose family unity status. Unlike legalization, a grant of family unity protection will not result in **lawful permanent resident alien** status. The relative who was legalized or granted amnesty must submit a **visa petition** for the person who has family unity status. Furthermore, unlike the legalization program, a family unity application is not confidential. If the INS denies a family unity application, **removal proceedings** may result. In practice, however, the INS has not placed denied family-unity applicants in removal proceedings.

FEDERAL TAX RESIDENCY Individuals who are considered residents of the United States for federal income tax purposes are taxable on worldwide income, regardless of type, including wages, dividends, royalties, and interest, and regardless of whether such income is received in the United States or abroad. An **alien** is a U.S. tax resident for a calendar year if he or she satisfies either of two tests or makes an election to be a resident.

Green Card Test. Possession of **lawful permanent resident alien** status at any time during the year makes the alien a U.S. tax resident. This test should not apply to nonimmigrant **business visitors** (B-1), **intracompany transferees** (L-1), or **H-1b workers** who are professionals.

Substantial Presence Test. An alien is a U.S. tax resident under the substantial presence test if he or she either (1) is present for 183 days or more during a single year, or (2) is present for 183 days during a three-year period calculated as a the sum of days present in the United States during the current year, one-third of the number of days present in the United States during the prior year, and one-sixth of the number of days present in the United States during the preceding year.

An alien who satisfies the substantial presence test will nevertheless be a nonresident if the alien (1) is present in the United States for less than 183 days during the tax year; (2) has a tax home, defined as the location of the alien's principal place of business, outside the United States; (3) has a closer connection with a foreign country than with the United States, as determined on a facts-and-circumstances basis; and (4) has not taken affirmative steps to be a permanent resident.

FEDERATION FOR AMERICAN IMMIGRATION REFORM

The Federation for American Immigration Reform (FAIR) is a national, nonprofit, public-interest organization of concerned citizens who share a common belief that our nation's immigration policies must be reformed to serve the national interest.

FAIR is uniformly regarded as the nation's main restrictionist lobbying group. Its positions are premised on the understanding that the United States is receiving more immigrants than at any time in its history. Immigration has become an important issue because it affects virtually every aspect of life in America. With more than a million legal and undocumented immigrants settling in the United States each year, immigration has an impact on education, health care, government budgets, employment, the environment, crime, and countless other areas of American life. FAIR feels that it is evident to most Americans that large-scale immigration is not serving the needs and interests of the country.

FAIR advocates a temporary moratorium on all immigration except spouses and minor children of U.S. citizens and a limited number of refugees. A moratorium would allow the country to hold a national debate and devise a comprehensive immigration reform strategy. A workable immigration policy is one that would allow the nation time to regain control of its borders and reduce overall levels of immigration to more traditional levels of about 300,000 a year.

Since it was founded in 1978, FAIR has been leading the call for immigration reform. Representatives of the organization are routinely interviewed by the major news networks, radio talk shows, and the print media about all aspects of the immigration debate. Academics and government officials involved in formulating immigration policy often rely on its research and publications. FAIR representatives testify regularly before Congress on all immigration-related legislation. With more than 70,000 members nationwide, FAIR is a nonpartisan group whose membership runs the gamut from liberal to conservative. It has headquarters in Washington, D.C., a satellite office in Los Angeles, and field representatives across the nation. FAIR activities include research, public education, media outreach, grassroots organizing, government relations, and litigation and advocacy at the national, state, and local levels.

FEDORENKO V. UNITED STATES　The Fedorenko case [449 U.S. 490 (1981)] is one of several **revocation of naturalization** cases involving former Nazi war criminals who somehow entered the United States after World War II and eventually became naturalized U.S. citizens.

Fedorenko was born in the Ukraine in 1907. He was drafted into the Russian army in June 1941, but was captured by the Germans shortly thereafter. After being held in a series of prisoner-of-war camps, he was selected to go to the German camp at Travnicki in Poland, where he received training as a concentration camp guard. In September 1942, he was assigned to the Nazi concentration camp at Treblinka in Poland, where he was issued a uniform and rifle and served as a guard during 1942 and 1943. The infamous Treblinka concentration camp was a human abattoir at which several hundred thousand Jewish civilians were murdered. After an armed uprising by inmates at Treblinka led to the closure of the camp in August 1943, Fedorenko was transferred to a German labor camp at Danzig and then to a German prisoner-of-war camp at Poelitz, where he continued to serve as an armed guard. He was eventually transferred to Hamburg where he served as a warehouse guard. Shortly before the British forces entered that city in 1945, he discarded his uniform and was able to pass as a civilian. For the next four years, he worked in Germany as a laborer.

In October 1949, Fedorenko applied for admission to the United States under the **Displaced Persons Act** (DPA). He falsified his visa application by lying about his wartime activities. He told investigators that he had been a farmer in Sarny, Poland, from 1937 until March 1942, and that he had been deported to Germany and forced to work in a factory in Poelitz until the end of the war, when he fled to Hamburg. He signed a sworn statement containing these false representations as part of his application. He was issued a visa and was admitted for **lawful permanent resident alien** status, taking up residence in Connecticut for three decades, where he led an uneventful and law-abiding life as a factory worker.

In 1969, Fedorenko applied for **naturalization,** not disclosing his wartime service as a concentration camp armed guard in his application. The INS examiners took his application at face value and he was granted naturalization and became a U.S. citizen on April 23, 1970.

Seven years later, the government filed this action in federal district court seeking to revoke Fedorenko's citizenship [see **revocation of naturalization**]. The action alleged that he should have been deemed ineligible for a DPA visa because he had served as an armed guard at Treblinka and had committed crimes or atrocities against inmates of the camp because they were Jewish. The government charged that he had willfully concealed this information both in applying for a DPA visa and in applying for citizenship, and that therefore he had procured his naturalization illegally or by willfully misrepresenting material facts.

The government's witnesses included six survivors of Treblinka who claimed that they had seen Fedorenko commit specific acts of violence against inmates of the camp. Each witness made a pretrial identification of Fedorenko from a photo array that included his 1949 visa photograph, and three of the witnesses made courtroom identifications.

Fedorenko took the stand in his own behalf. He admitted his service as an armed guard at Treblinka and that he had known that thousands of Jewish inmates were being murdered there. He claimed that he was forced to serve as a guard and denied any personal involvement in the atrocities committed at the camp; he insisted that he had merely been a perimeter guard. He admitted, however, following orders on one occasion and shooting in the general direction of escaping inmates during the 1943 camp uprising. He maintained that he was a prisoner of war at Treblinka, although the Russian armed guards significantly outnumbered the German soldiers at the camp, and he was paid and received a good service stripe from the Germans.

Based on this evidence, the Supreme Court ruled that revocation was in order. His citizenship was illegally procured; therefore he should be stripped of citizenship, paving his way to be removed from the United States. See also *Kungys v. United States* [485 U.S. 759 (1988)].

Inadmissibility grounds now explicitly include participants in Nazi persecutions [see **Nazi Persecution Participant and Genocide Inadmissibility Ground**].

▥ *Fiallo v. Bell*   The Supreme Court reaffirmed Congress's vast and **plenary power** over the immigration system in this case [430 U.S. 787 (1987)] by upholding immigration provisions that discriminate on the basis of gender as well as status based on out-of-wedlock birth.

The **Immigration and Nationality Act** grants preferential immigration status to aliens who qualify as the children or parents of U.S. citizens or lawful permanent residents. A *child* is defined as an unmarried person under twenty-one years of age who is a legitimate or legitimated child, stepchild, or adopted child, or an illegitimate child seeking preference by virtue of his or her relationship with the natural mother. The definition does not extend to an illegitimate child seeking preference by virtue of a relationship with the natural father. Also, a person qualifies as a parent for the purposes of the immigration laws solely on the basis of the person's relationship with a child. As a result, the natural father of an illegitimate child who is either a U.S. citizen or permanent resident alien is not entitled to preferential treatment as a parent.

The law was challenged by three sets of unwed natural fathers and their illegitimate offspring who sought, either as an alien father or an alien child, an immigration preference by virtue of a relationship to a citizen or resident alien child or parent. In each instance the applicant was informed that he was ineligible for an immigrant visa.

In upholding this discriminatory law, the Court noted that the distinction in the statute is just one of many drawn by Congress pursuant to its determination to provide some—but not all—families with relief from various immigration restrictions that would otherwise hinder reunification of the family in this country. While it could be argued that the line should have been drawn at a different point and that the statutory definitions deny preferential status to parents and children who share strong family ties, these are policy questions entrusted exclusively to the political branches of the federal government, and the courts have no judicial authority to substitute their political judgment for that of the Congress. Congress obviously determined that preferential status is not warranted for illegitimate children and their natural fathers, perhaps because of a perceived absence in most cases of close family ties as well as a concern with the serious problems of proof that usually lurk in paternity determinations. It is not the judicial role in cases of this sort to probe and test the justifications for legislative decisions.

▥ **Fiancé Visa**   An alien who is the fiancé or fiancée of a U.S. citizen may enter the United States on a K visa in order to marry the citizen petitioner within 90 days. In order for the visa petition to be approved, the couple must have met personally within two years before filing the petition. [8 U.S.C. § 1184(d)] After entry, the couple must marry within 90 days. If marriage does not occur within the 90-day period, the permission to remain as indicated in the **Form I-94** arrival-departure form will expire. Upon entry to the United States, the fiancé or fiancée and any accompanying minor children are granted permission to work.

FIFTH PREFERENCE   See **investor visa; preference system.**

FIREARMS AND EXPLOSIVE DEVICES   A conviction for possession, use, or carrying a firearm or destructive device constitutes grounds for **removal** from the United States. In order to apply, the use or possession of a firearm or destructive device must be an element of the offense. The fact that a sentence can be enhanced if a firearm was used in a crime does not in and of itself render the crime one that falls under the law. [8 U.S.C. §1227(a)(2)(C)]

FIRST PREFERENCE   See **preference system.**

FIXED CHECKPOINT   In its 1976 ruling, *United States v. Martinez-Fuerte* [428 U.S. 543 (1975)], the Supreme Court carved an exception to the Fourth Amendment's protection against unreasonable search and seizure by allowing the **Border Patrol** to set up fixed checkpoints located on major highways away from the Mexican border for purposes of stopping and questioning individuals suspected of being undocumented aliens.

One of the checkpoints in question in the case was located on Interstate 5 near San Clemente, California. Interstate 5 is the principal highway between San Diego and Los Angeles, and the checkpoint was sixty-six miles north of the Mexican border. The checkpoint operated in this manner. The "point" agent standing between the two lanes of traffic visually screened all northbound vehicles, which the checkpoint brought to a virtual, if not complete, halt. Most motorists were allowed to resume their progress without any oral inquiry or close visual examination. In a relatively small number of cases, the point agent would conclude that further inquiry was in order. He directed these vehicles to a **secondary inspection** area, where the occupants were asked about their citizenship and immigration status. The average length of an investigation at the secondary inspection area was three to five minutes. A direction to stop in the secondary inspection area could be based on something suspicious about a particular vehicle passing through the checkpoint.

Another checkpoint that was part of this case was on Highway 77 near Sarita, Texas, ninety miles north of Brownsville, Texas, and the Mexican border. This checkpoint operated differently than the San Clemente checkpoint in that the officers in Sarita customarily stopped all northbound motorists for a brief inquiry.

The Supreme Court held that the checkpoints were constitutional because of the minimal intrusion on motorists. Even selective referrals to secondary inspection, as at San Clemente, was lawful. In fact, even if such referrals were made largely on the basis of apparent Mexican ancestry, the court perceived no constitutional violation. Since the intrusion was sufficiently minimal that no particularized reason was needed to justify it, the Border Patrol officers had wide discretion in selecting the motorists to be diverted for the brief questioning involved.

FOLEY V. CONNELIE   The Supreme Court has consistently upheld a number of exclusions of **lawful permanent resident aliens** from state public employment by exercising deferential review rather than strict scrutiny. In this case [435 U.S. 291 (1978)], the Court held that New York could bar employment of aliens as state troopers.

> Police officers in the ranks do not formulate policy, per se, but they are clothed with authority to exercise an almost infinite variety of discretionary powers. [Clearly] the exercise of police authority calls for a very high degree of judgment and discretion. . . . In the enforcement and execution of the laws the police function is one where citizenship bears a rational relationship to the special demands of the particular position.

Another example of this type of deference is *Ambach v. Norwick* [441 U.S. 68 (1979)], where the court held that a state may refuse to employ as elementary and secondary school teachers aliens who are eligible for citizenship but who refuse to seek **naturalization.** A less demanding scrutiny is required when aliens are excluded from "state functions" that are "bound up with the operation of the State as a governmental entity," and that includes public school teachers.

FOREIGN MEDICAL GRADUATE Foreign medical graduates (FMGs) who are entering to perform services as a member of the medical profession are inadmissible [see **inadmissibility grounds**] unless they meet one of the following conditions: (1) they are entering as the beneficiary of a family **preference system** or **immediate relative** immigration category; (2) they have passed parts I and II of the National Board of Medical Examiners examination, or an examination deemed the equivalent by the Secretary of Health and Human Services, and who are competent in oral and written English; (3) they have graduated from certain accredited schools; or (4) they were licensed to practice medicine in a state on or before January 9, 1978. [8 U.S.C. §1182(a)(5)(B)] Generally, if a doctor meets the National Board exam requirements and is competent in English, an **alien employment certification** to work in the United States is very possible, especially if the work is in an area where there is a health care shortage.

Similar restrictions apply to other **health care workers.**

FOREIGN STUDENT Most **nonimmigrant** students enter the United States with F-1 visas for academic studies. In 1981, the M category was added to create a separate category for vocational and nonacademic students. Some foreign students also enter under the **exchange visitor** program with a J-1 visa.

Generally, entering F-1 students receive permission to remain for "duration of status" as symbolized by the notation "D/S" on their arrival-departure **Form I-94.** There is an eight-year limit on the duration of stay, however.

F-1 students enter the United States to attend college, university, seminary, conservatory, academic high school, elementary school, or other academic institutions or language training programs. The place of study must be approved by the Immigration and Naturalization Service after consultation with the Department of Education. Such institutions have agreed to abide by certain rules, including the reporting of termination of attendance of any nonimmigrant student. Approved schools issue a Form I-20, which indicates that the nonimmigrant student has been accepted for studies. [8 U.S.C. §1101(a)(15)(F); 8 C.F.R. §214.3]

The student must be entering to pursue a full course of study. For undergraduate study at a college or university, a full course of study means at least twelve hours of instruction per week or its equivalent. A designated school official (DSO), such as a foreign student advisor, is authorized to advise a student to engage in less than a full course of study. The

INS can disapprove this decision at a later date. However, if the DSO's decision was made in good faith, no action will be taken against the student or the school.

F-1 students are barred from attending public elementary schools or publicly funded adult education programs. Such students must attend private schools. Public secondary school attendance is available, but only for up to twelve months and only if the student has reimbursed local school officials for the full, unsubsidized cost of the education. The F-1 student visa will be voided if the student enters to pursue a course of study at a private elementary school, but transfers to a public elementary school or publicly funded adult education language training program. [8 U.S.C. §1184(l)]

The M category is for foreign students entering to attend a vocational, trade, or other nonacademic institution. Examples of such institutions include beauty and modeling schools, barber colleges, aviation academies, computer training schools, and stenographic programs. The school must be recognized by the attorney general, the course of study must be full-time, and the student must have sufficient funds and nonimmigrant intent to return home.

Nonimmigrant students are permitted to work up to twenty hours per week on campus without first obtaining INS permission. This would include not only employment in the school cafeteria or dormitory, for example, but also employment pursuant to the terms of a scholarship, fellowship, or assistantship.

A student is not permitted to engage in off-campus employment until after the first year in the United States, and permission needs to be obtained. The DSO can endorse the Form I-20 for employment authorization off campus for one year. INS must provide authorization after that. As a condition to off-campus employment, a student must make a good-faith effort to pursue employment authorization on campus.

FORM I-94   A document that is required of all **nonimmigrant**s, often referred to as the *arrival-departure form*. The I-94 is generally stapled into the passport of the nonimmigrant and indicates when the person arrived, by what date the person must depart from the United States, and what type of nonimmigrant status the holder has.

FOURTH PREFERENCE   The **preference system** contains a fourth preference for family immigrant visas and a fourth preference for employment-based visas. In the family system, fourth preference is reserved for the brothers and sisters of adult U.S. citizens. [8 U.S.C.

§1153(a)(4)] This is a very popular category, and the waiting list or backlog in this category is very lengthy. For natives of most countries, the waiting period for the sibling category is several years. For countries such as the Philippines and Mexico, the waiting period can be ten to twenty years.

The fourth preference for employment-based visas sets aside visa numbers for certain **special immigrant**s, with particular attention to religious workers. In the religious worker area, the prospective immigrant must have been a member of a religious denomination for at least two years immediately preceding the filing of the immigrant **visa petition.** [8 U.S.C. §1153(b)(4)] A religious denomination is "a religious group or community of believers having some form of ecclesiastical government, a creed or statement of faith, some form of worship, a formal or informal code of doctrine and discipline, religious services and ceremonies, established places of religious worship, religious congregations, or comparable indicia of a bona fide religious denomination."

The types of religious workers who may qualify for the benefits of this fourth preference classification are ministers, professionals in a religious occupation, and individuals in religious occupations or vocations.

A minister is "an individual duly authorized by a recognized religious denomination to conduct religious worship and to perform other duties usually performed by authorized members of the clergy of that religion." There must be a reasonable connection between the duties of the position offered and the religious calling of the minister; lay preachers are expressly disqualified. [8 C.F.R. §204.5(m)(2)]

Professionals in a religious occupation qualify if the duties of the position offered are for a religious vocation or occupation and a U.S. baccalaureate degree or a foreign equivalent degree is required as a minimum in order to perform the vocation satisfactorily. Other religious occupations that fall into this preference include liturgical workers, religious instructors, religious counselors, cantors, catechists, workers in religious hospitals or religious health care facilities, missionaries, religious translators, and religious broadcasters. Religious vocations such as nuns, monks, and religious brothers and sisters qualify. Expressly excluded are janitors, maintenance workers, clerks, fund-raisers, persons solely involved in the solicitation of donations. Unlike the minister-of-religion category that has no time constraints, the religious-worker category is due to expire on September 30, 2000. [8 U.S.C. §1101(a)(27)]

🏛 *FRAGANTE V. HONOLULU*   This case [888 F.2d 591 (9th Cir. 1989)] involving an immigrant job applicant illustrates the difficulty of establishing an employment discrimination case based on an accent discrimination claim.

In April 1981, at the age of sixty, Manuel Fragante emigrated from the Philippines to Hawaii. In response to a newspaper ad, he applied for an entry-level civil service clerk position for the City of Honolulu's Division of Motor Vehicles and Licensing. The clerk position involved such tasks as filing, processing mail, cashiering, orally providing routine information to the "sometimes contentious" public over the telephone and at an information counter, and obtaining supplies. Fragante scored the highest of 721 test takers on the written civil service examination, which tested, among other things, word usage, grammar, and spelling. Accordingly, he was ranked first on a certified list of those eligible for the two clerk positions.

Fragante was interviewed in the course of the selection process by George Kuwahara, the assistant licensing administrator, and Kalani McCandles, the division secretary. Both Kuwahara and McCandles were personally familiar with the demands of the position, and both had extensive experience interviewing job applicants. During the interview, Kuwahara stressed that the position involved constant public contact and that the ability to speak clearly was one of the most important skills required for the position.

Both Kuwahara and McCandles had difficulty understanding Fragante due to his pronounced Filipino accent, and they determined on the basis of the oral interview that he would be difficult to understand both at the information counter and over the telephone. Accordingly, both interviewers gave Fragante a negative recommendation. It was their judgment that his accent would interfere with his performance of certain aspects of the job. As a consequence, Fragante dropped from number one to number three on the list of those eligible for the position. The other two applicants who were judged more qualified than Fragante got the two available jobs.

Under relevant employment discrimination law, once a plaintiff succeeds in establishing a prima facie case of disparate treatment, the burden shifts to the employer to rebut the presumption of discrimination by articulating some legitimate, nondiscriminatory reason for the adverse action. The relevant approach of the Equal Employment Opportunity Commission is that a plaintiff who proves he has been discriminated against solely because of his accent does establish a prima facie case of **national origin discrimination.** But the court of appeals felt that since Fragante did not carry the ultimate burden of proving national origin discrimination, the issue of whether Fragante established a prima facie case of discrimination was not significant.

Preliminarily, the court did acknowledge that:

> [W]e do well to remember that this country was founded and has been built in large measure by people from other lands, many of whom came

here—especially after our early beginnings—with a limited knowledge of English. This flow of immigrants has continued and has been encouraged over the years. From its inception, the United States of America has been a dream to many around the world. We hold out promises of freedom, equality, and economic opportunity to many who only know these words as concepts. It would be more than ironic if we followed up our invitation to people such as Manuel Fragante with a closed economic door based on national origin discrimination.

However, to the court, the record disclosed that Fragante's third-place ranking was based on his "pronounced accent which is difficult to understand." He could point to no facts that indicated that his ranking was based on factors other than his inability to communicate effectively with the public. This was a legitimate reason for Fragante's nonselection. The process may not have been perfect, but it revealed no discriminatory motive or intent. The defendants appear to have been motivated exclusively by reasonable business necessity. In the court's view, there was simply no proof whatsoever of a pretext for invidious discrimination. Fragante was passed over because of the deleterious effect of his Filipino accent on his ability to communicate orally, not merely because he had such an accent.

G

GENTLEMEN'S AGREEMENT This informal agreement between Japan and the United States resulted in a severe reduction in the number of Japanese laborers who could enter the United States after 1908.

The first appreciable numbers of Japanese to enter the United States came at the height of the Chinese exclusion movement [see **Chinese Exclusion Act of 1882**]. Agricultural labor demands, particularly in Hawaii and California, led to increased efforts to attract Japanese workers after the Chinese exclusion acts. But by the 1890s, when economic xenophobia was gaining greater acceptance on the East Coast, nativists with the backing of organized labor in California formed the Japanese and Korean Exclusion League (later renamed the Asiatic Exclusion League). The league joined forces with smaller organizations such as the Anti-Jap Laundry League and the Anti-Japanese League of Alameda County. In those California cities and agricultural communities where competition was most intense and conspicuous, immigrants encountered violence from whites who claimed that California would be "overrun" by Japanese. Japanese students in San Francisco were ordered to segregated schools, and demands for limits on Japanese immigration became frequent.

Japanese laborers were eventually restricted, but not in conventional legislative fashion. Japan's emergence as a major world power meant that the United States could not restrict Japanese immigration in the heavy-handed fashion with which it had curtailed Chinese immigration. To minimize potential disharmony between the two nations while retaining the initiative to control immigration, the United States negotiated an informal agreement with Japan. Under the terms of the so-called Gentlemen's Agreement reached in 1907 and 1908, the Japanese government refrained from issuing travel documents to laborers destined for the United States. In exchange for this severe but voluntary limitation, Japanese wives and children could be reunited with their husbands and fathers in the United States, and the San Francisco school board would be pressured into rescinding its segregation order. The terms of the agreement remained in force until 1924, when it was superseded by the **national origins quota system.**

127

GOOD FAITH COMPLIANCE   Employers who are guilty of "technical or procedural" violations of the **employer sanctions** paperwork requirements [see **I-9 process**] are excused if there was a good-faith attempt to comply with the requirements. The exemption does not apply, however, if the INS has given notice of the violation and the employer has not corrected the violation within ten days. The exemption also does not apply to an employer who has engaged in a pattern and practice of employer sanction violations. In short, an employer who makes a good-faith effort to comply with the employment verification processing rules is considered to have complied regardless of a technical or procedural failure to meet one of the requirements. The exception for technical violations only applies to a Form I-9 completed on or after September 30, 1996, when the exception was enacted by Congress.

In order to benefit from the exception, the employer must have corrected the violation within ten business days after the employer has been informed of the problem by the INS or another inspection agency such as the Department of Labor. When an employer has not hired unauthorized workers, notice of any technical paperwork violations is generally given in a written warning notice from INS. If alleged hiring of unauthorized workers is involved, notice of any technical paperwork violations is generally included in a formal Notice of Intent to Fine (NIF).

The obvious benefit of this good-faith exception is that an employer can avoid fines for technical paperwork violations and I-9 requirements that have nothing to do with hiring unauthorized workers. The avoidance of fines can be significant, especially for employers with large numbers of employees.

What is considered "technical or procedural" is important. Certain things are definitely not "technical or procedural" and would be considered substantive failures. A failure to prepare or present the Form I-9 is a substantive violation. Also, in section 1 of the I-9, it is not simply a technical or procedural failure for the employer to fail to ensure that (1) the employee provides his or her printed name; (2) the individual checks the box attesting to whether he or she is a U.S. citizen or national, a permanent resident, or an alien authorized to work until a certain date; (3) the individual provides his or her A number in the appropriate places, but only if the A number is not provided in section 2 or 3 of the I-9; (4) the individual signs the attestation; or (5) the individual dates the I-9 at the time of hire if the hire occurred before September 30, 1996.

In section 2 of the I-9, it is a substantive (rather than a technical or procedural) violation if the employer fails to: (1) review and verify a proper List A document or the proper List B and C documents; (2) provide the document title, identification number, or expiration date of a proper List A, B, or

C document, unless a legible copy is retained and presented at the I-9 inspection; (3) sign the attestation; or (4) date section 2 of the I-9 within three business days of the hire. A substantive violation cannot be corrected to avoid penalties.

Likewise, in section 3 of the I-9, it is a substantive (rather than a technical or procedural) violation if the employer fails to: (1) review and verify a List A document or the proper List B and C documents; (2) provide the document title, identification number, or expiration date of a proper List A, B, or C document, unless a copy is retained and presented at the I-9 inspection; or (3) sign or date section 3, including dating section 3 not later than the date the work authorization for the individual expires. If noticed, a substantive violation cannot be corrected to avoid a penalty.

What are considered to be purely "technical or procedural" verification failures? In section 1 of the I-9, it will be deemed a technical or procedural violation if the employer fails to ensure that: (1) an individual provides her maiden name, address, or birth date; (2) the individual provides his or her A number in the appropriate places on the I-9, but only if the A number is provided in sections two or three of the form; (3) the individual dates section 1, including dating at the time of hire if the hiring occurred before September 30, 1996; or (4) the preparer or translator provides his or her name, address, or signature.

In section 2 of the I-9, the employer will be deemed to have made a technical or procedural violation if the employer fails to: (1) provide the document title, identification number, or expiration date of a proper List A, B, or C document, but only if a copy of the document is retained with the I-9 and presented at the I-9 inspection; (2) provide the title, business name, and business address; (3) provide the date of hire in the attestation portion; or (4) date section 2 in the appropriate places.

In section 3 of the I-9, an employer will be deemed to have made a technical or procedural violation if it fails to: (1) provide the document title, identification number, or expiration date of a proper List A, B, or C document, but only if a copy of the document is retained with the I-9 and presented at the I-9 inspection, or (2) provide the date of rehire.

The INS has also provided illustrations of when an employer's technical or procedural failure will not be deemed a "good faith" attempt to comply. These include instances where (1) the failure was committed with the intent to avoid a requirement of the **Immigration and Nationality Act** as shown by the totality of the circumstances (including a substantial presence of unauthorized aliens and a pattern or repeated failures in the completion of I-9s); (2) the failure was committed in anticipation that the failure would be forgiven; (3) the employer attempted to correct the failure with the knowledge or in reckless disregard of the fact that the correction contains a false, fictitious, or fraudulent statement or material misrepresentation, or has no basis in law or fact; (4) the employer prepared the I-9 with knowledge or in reckless disregard of the fact that the form contains a false, fictitious, or fraudulent statement or material misrepresentation, or has no basis in law or fact; or (5) the type of failure was previously the subject of a warning notice, a notice of findings, or a "notification of technical or procedural failures" letter.

Evidently, the INS will have little patience with employers who repeatedly violate technical paperwork requirements. For example, INS will not be forgiving of employers who stop complying with I-9 paperwork requirements in a pattern that indicates that the employer thinks that it can rely on the ability to correct technical or procedural mistakes within ten-day notice periods over and over again. If such a pattern is shown, INS is likely to assess a fine regardless of employer attempts to make corrections. Similarly, the discovery of similar types of technical mistakes in subsequent INS investigations may result in the INS not providing a ten-day correction opportunity for the subsequent violations.

The INS recognizes that in certain circumstances an employer cannot correct a technical violation within ten days. In those situations, the INS may provide the employer with more time to correct the violation, and perhaps even excuse the employer from making corrections. Such circumstances might be when:

- the employee is no longer working for the employer
- the employee is on an excused leave of absence such as for vacation, medical care, or personal business
- the person who prepared the I-9 or the translator cannot be found
- the violation involves timeliness, such as failing to date the form in section 1 or section 2 within three days of hiring

In these circumstances, the employer should provide a written explanation of the situation and request that correction be excused, or that reasonable additional time be granted in order to correct the violation. The employer should make every effort to correct technical paperwork violations when given the opportunity to do so by INS personnel.

Although one might surmise that the existence of the good-faith exception for paperwork violations could result in INS paying less attention to certain industries that might be regarded as "low-risk" in terms of finding substantial violations, that has not been the case. INS continues a random approach to I-9 enforcement in addition to following leads. Its random approach is designed to avoid allegations that the INS is engaging in discriminatory enforcement.

▥ GOOD MORAL CHARACTER Among the requirements for **naturalization** and **cancellation of removal,** an applicant must demonstrate good moral character. Good moral character is a concept generally interpreted to mean character that measures up to the standards of average citizens of the community in which the person resides. Although this standard appears to be quite elastic, the immigration laws provide some parameters. Persons falling within the following categories during the requisite time frame (e.g., five years for naturalization) are barred from establishing good moral character:

- a habitual drunkard
- a person who falls within the description of one or more of the **inadmissibility grounds** such as a **crime involving moral turpitude,** prostitution, or narcotics offenses (except for simple possession of thirty grams or less of marijuana)
- a person whose income is derived principally from illegal gambling activities, or who has been convicted of two or more gambling offenses
- a person who has given false testimony for purposes of obtaining immigration benefits
- a person who has been imprisoned as a result of a conviction for 180 days or more
- a person who has been convicted of an **aggravated felon**y [8 U.S.C. §1101(f)]

This list is not intended to represent the only categories of persons considered not of good moral character; such a finding may be made for other reasons. Some notable examples are:

- Failure to file state or federal tax returns has been held to be relevant to the question of good moral character. For example, in *Gambino v. Pomeroy* [562 F. Supp. 974 (D.N.J. 1982)], the federal district court found that the applicant failed to carry the burden of persuasion on the element of good moral character because he had failed to file federal and state tax returns for three years and was under investigation by the Internal Revenue Service.
- The INS has taken a strict position against the finding of good moral character when there has been a failure to provide spousal or child support. Extenuating circumstances will be taken into account in assessing this failure. For example, if the spouse is self-supporting or receiving support from other sources, the children are no longer minors, or the person meets the burden of support to a reasonable extent, good moral character can still be established.

- Prior to a change in the law in 1981, the law provided for a mandatory preclusion of good moral character if the applicant had committed adultery during the relevant statutory period. Although adultery is no longer a mandatory bar to establishing good moral character, the INS continues to take a position that adultery, under certain conditions, can bar such a finding:

> [W]here civil or criminal adultery comes to the attention of the designated examiner which destroys a viable marriage, is grossly incestuous, as between parent and child, or brother and sister; or if it is commercialized, as where the petitioner prostitutes herself; or if it is flaunted openly with a willful disregard for proprieties, causing publicized notoriety and public scandal; or if it is committed in the home under circumstances contributing to the delinquency of minor children; or if illegitimate children are begotten, and become public charges supported by public funds, or if the frequency of the adulterous acts, and the number of illegitimate children born and other circumstances are such as to collectively indicate the petitioner's disregard for any standard of sexual morality, a finding of lack of good moral character shall be advanced.

- Related to adultery is the area of fornication and cohabitation. The INS takes the position that neither fornication alone nor fornication with cohabitation during the statutory period should automatically preclude a finding of good moral character, even though the sexual acts may be frequent in number. However, the INS will oppose a finding of good moral character when extramarital intercourse or an act of fornication with a lawfully married person tends to destroy an existing marriage, or when the act of fornication is grossly incestuous, scandalous, or commercialized.
- The law does not bar naturalization of recipients of public assistance per se. But if the applicant obtained public assistance through fraud or misrepresentation, good moral character may be difficult to establish. This may be the case, for example, when the applicant fails to fully disclose facts to the welfare authorities, such as true assets and income or actual marital status.
- The fact that the person is or has been practicing private homosexual acts with consenting adults is not, in itself, a sufficient basis for finding that the person is not of good moral character, as long as the homosexual conduct is not a criminal offense under the law of the jurisdiction. However, in the interest of uniformity, the INS will not oppose a finding of good moral character even if the applicant admits homosexual acts in a jurisdiction where such conduct is a crimi-

nal offense. The INS will oppose a finding of good moral character when the homosexual practices have "adverse public effects," such as the involvement of minors, the use of threat or fraud, the use of a public place, or violation of marital vows. But the fact that homosexuality has been removed as an inadmissibility ground suggests that good moral character issues are not automatically triggered when the applicant is gay or lesbian.

- INS offices have a policy of denying naturalization to men who knowingly and willfully do not register with the Selective Service when they are required to do so. Men between ages 18 and 26 who have not registered are given the opportunity to register before naturalization is denied. Men age 26 and over who should have registered but did not may be denied naturalization if the failure to register was with knowledge and willful. This is, however, a temporary bar. After five years has passed since the act of failing to register, the failure to register should no longer be an issue on the question of good moral character.

GORDON, CHARLES (1905–1999) As the primary author of the treatise *Immigration Law and Procedure*, Charles Gordon shaped the practice of immigration law for decades, influencing practitioners, policy makers, and courts. The son of immigrants from Eastern Europe, he was a seminal figure in modern immigration law. His treatise first appeared as a single-volume work in 1959, and eventually grew to twenty volumes. For years, the common understanding in the immigration bar was that no one could practice immigration law without having access to Gordon's treatise. The text has been widely cited in court opinions and scholarly articles.

Gordon was first admitted to the New York bar in 1929. After ten years of private practice he joined the INS, where he contributed thirty-five years of distinguished service. He joined the INS General Counsel's Office in 1948 and served as general counsel of the INS from 1966 to 1974. He thereafter returned to private practice until retiring in 1987.

Gordon was involved in the major immigration cases of his time. While with the INS, Gordon was primarily responsible for writing briefs and arguing cases on behalf of the government. He argued eight cases before the U.S. Supreme Court, including *Afroyim v. Rusk*, the seminal case regarding the loss of citizenship, and *Woodby v. INS*, a leading case on the government's burden of proof in deportation proceedings. After returning to private practice, he argued a number of other major cases, including *Slyger v. Attorney General*, challenging the legality of U.S. Information

Agency **exchange visitor** procedures; *Haitian Refugee Center v. Gracey,* challenging the interdiction of Haitian refugees on the high seas; *Narenji v. Civiletti,* challenging harsh measures instituted against Iranians in the United States during the Tehran hostage crisis; and *Joshi v. District Director,* challenging INS restrictions on the rights of people granted advanced parole to leave the country and return. He was famous for the generous assistance he gave to his opposing counsels, and was known as "the nicest man in government" when he worked for INS.

Gordon received various honors and awards acknowledging his contributions in the field of immigration law. The **American Immigration Lawyers Association** and the Federal Bar Association honored him for his zeal as an advocate and his skill as an author. He was the first attorney to be honored by the National Center for Immigrant Rights, and was also honored as its outstanding adjunct professor by Georgetown University Law Center, where for more than twenty years he taught an advanced course on immigration law. He was past chairman of American Bar Association's committees on immigration and nationality. Gordon received his law degree from New York University Law School in 1927.

GRAHAM V. RICHARDSON   In this case [403 U.S. 365 (1971)], the Supreme Court began using strict scrutiny in cases where states discriminated on the basis of alienage. Here, the court held that states could not deny welfare benefits to **lawful permanent resident alien**s.

> [The] Court's decisions have established that classifications based on alienage, like those based on nationality or race, are inherently suspect and subject to close judicial scrutiny. Aliens as a class are a prime example of a "discrete and insular" minority . . . for whom such heightened judicial solicitude is appropriate. Accordingly . . . the power of a state to apply its laws exclusively to its alien inhabitants as a class is confined within narrow limits.

The Court has applied strict scrutiny fairly consistently when states attempt to restrict the rights of lawful permanent residents, unless a public policy type of job is involved. See *Foley v. Connelie.*

GREEN CARD   The term *green card* is a popular expression used to describe the **alien registration receipt card** that is issued to **immigrant**s who have been granted **lawful permanent resident alien** status. Generations ago, these credit-card-size cards were actually green colored. Today the cards that are issued have a pink shade and bear the notation "Form I-551," and are labeled "Permanent Resident Card."

GUTTENTAG, LUCAS (B. 1951) Lucas Guttentag is one of the country's most outstanding litigators in the field of immigrant and refugee rights. He is the founder and director of the Immigrants' Rights Project of the National Office of the American Civil Liberties Union (ACLU) Foundation. The project has six lawyers and offices in New York and San Francisco. Since 1987, it has litigated landmark class-action and individual suits and worked collaboratively with community coalitions and national advocacy organizations nationwide.

Guttentag has worked in coalitions or independently as counsel in most of the major legal battles over immigrants' rights since the mid-1980s. He brought constitutional challenges to the 1986 Immigration Marriage Fraud Amendments in district and circuit courts around the country until Congress repealed certain provisions. He was one of the lead counsel in representing 240,000 Salvadoran and Guatemalan refugees in the historic *American Baptist Churches* case [see **ABC asylum class**]; he challenged construction of a remote immigration detention center in Oakdale, Louisiana, and the transfer of refugees to that isolated area away from their urban counsel; he obtained the first grant of **asylum** to a South African draft resister based on the illegality of apartheid under international law; and he was one of the lead trial counsel in the successful challenge to the indefinite detention of Haitian refugees at Guantanamo Naval Base.

Since 1996, Lucas has devised and directed the Immigrants' Rights Project's legal strategy for challenging the "court-stripping" provisions of the 1996 antiterrorism and immigration laws that deny judicial review to immigrants facing deportation. He and project lawyers have litigated the constitutionality of the new law in courts of appeals nationwide and have scored resounding victories in the First, Second, and Ninth Circuits.

Some of his other important cases are *Haitian Centers Council v. McNary* [823 F. Supp. 1028 (E.D.N.Y. 1993)], which held the indefinite detention and the conditions of confinement of Haitian refugees at Guantanamo Naval Base unconstitutional; *Mendez v. Thornburgh* [No. 88–04995-TJH (C.D. Cal. 1989)], a class-action preliminary injunction invalidating 30,000 asylum adjudications on due process grounds; *Velasquez v. Nelson* [No. 86–1262-CIV-Ryskamp (S.D. Fla. 1987)], a class-action preliminary and permanent injunction prohibiting transfer of detained aliens to a remote detention facility; and *Roshan v. Smith* [615 F. Supp. 981 (D.D.C. 1985)], a class-action challenge to construction of a remote detention facility on due process and environmental grounds.

Guttentag is a three-time winner of the Jack Wasserman Award for Excellence in Litigation from the **American Immigration Lawyers Association,** and is a two-time recipient of the Carol King Award for Outstanding Contribution to Immigration Law from the **National Immigration Project of the National Lawyers Guild.** He has served or currently serves on the National Advisory Committee of the Asylum Study Project of Harvard Law School, the Immigration Law Committee of the American Bar Association, the Advisory Group of the Columbia University Center for the Study of Human Rights, the Advisory Board of the American Friends Service Committee Immigration Law Enforcement Monitoring Project, and the board of the **National Immigration Forum.** He has taught several generations of law students, first at Columbia Law School and now at Boat Hall, University of California at Berkeley, in annual seminars on the civil and constitutional rights of immigrants.

Prior to joining the staff of the ACLU, Guttentag clerked for the Honorable William Wayne, justice of the U.S. District Court for the eastern district of Texas, then was a staff attorney for the Center for Law in the Public Interest in Los Angeles. Guttentag received his J.D. with honors from Harvard Law School in 1978.

H

 H-1B WORKER   The H-1B category is for nonimmigrants entering the United States for a temporary period to perform certain specialty occupations such as software engineering, accounting, or other **professional** occupations. The specialty occupation requires the attainment of at least a bachelor's or higher degree, or its equivalent. An employer must file an application for the prospective H-1B visa holder. To gain approval, the employer must file a **labor condition application** with the **Department of Labor** stating (1) that the employer is offering the prevailing wage for the occupation, (2) that the working conditions are such that they will not adversely affect those of workers similarly employed, (3) that there is not a strike or lockout in the course of a labor dispute in the occupation at the place of employment, (4) that the employer has given notice of the H-1B application to the bargaining representative of the employer's employees in the occupational classification or, if none, has posted notice of the filing in conspicuous locations at the place of employment, and (5) the number of workers sought, the occupational classifications, and wage rates and conditions under which they will be employed. The H-1B category is limited to 65,000 visas annually (although this figure was increased to 115,000 annually for 1999 and 2000), but each visa is valid for up to six years. [8 U.S.C. §1101(a)(15)(H)(1)]

HAITIAN REFUGEE CENTER V. GRACEY   This case [600 F. Supp. (D.C. 1985)] supported efforts by the federal government to stop the flow of Haitian refugees into the United States by turning them away on the high seas before they reached U.S. shores to seek asylum. The flow came at a time when poverty and the infant mortality rate in Haiti ranked the highest in the Western Hemisphere.

On September 29, 1981, President Ronald Reagan authorized the interdiction of certain vessels containing migrants from Haiti on the high seas. The president based this action on the belief that these undocumented aliens posed a "serious national problem detrimental to the interests of the United States," and that international cooperation to intercept vessels trafficking in such migrants was a necessary and proper means of ensuring the effective enforcement of U.S. immigration laws. By executive order, the Coast Guard was directed "to return the vessel and its passengers to the country from which it came, when there is reason to believe that an offense is being committed against the United States immigration laws." The Coast Guard's interdiction was only allowed outside the territorial waters of the United States.

The plaintiffs in the case argued that the actions of the president violated the obligations of the United States under the **Refugee Act of 1980** as well as the country's obligations under the **United Nations Protocol Relating to the Status of Refugees.**

The federal court upheld the actions of the president, holding that the president has inherent authority to act to protect the United States from harmful undocumented immigration. Since the program was carried out pursuant to an agreement with Haiti, this was further indication that the action came within matters of foreign relations that should not be disturbed by the court.

HAITIAN REFUGEE CENTER V. SMITH   This class action case [676 F.2d 1023 (5th Cir. 1982)] successfully challenged a program by U.S. immigration officials to expedite deportation procedures against Haitian refugees, many of whom were seeking asylum in the United States.

The program of accelerated processing to which the plaintiff class was subjected (the "Haitian Program") embodied the government's response to a tremendous backlog of Haitian deportation cases that had accumulated in the INS Miami district office by the summer of 1978. By June of that year, between six and seven thousand unprocessed Haitian deportation cases were pending. The asylum process as it had been administered up to that point was the cause of the administrative delay and consequent backlog, so the INS decided to change the process.

Under immense pressure from the central office of the INS to achieve rigid numerical goals, the process changed. Prior to the changes, only between one and ten deportation hearings were conducted each day. After the changes, **immigration judges** held fifty-five hearings per day, or approximately eighteen per judge; at the program's peak the schedule of deportation hearings increased to as many as eighty per day. Failure to seek **withholding of deportation** in a timely manner effected automatic entry of a deportation order. Deportation hearings were not the only matter handled during the Haitian program. Asylum interviews also were scheduled at the rate of forty per day. Hearings on requests for withholding deportation also were being conducted simultaneously with asylum and deportation hearings at several different locations. It was not unusual for an attorney representing Haitians to have three hearings at the same hour in different buildings. The INS was fully aware that only about twelve attorneys were available to represent the thousands of Haitians being processed, and that scheduling made it impossible for counsel to attend the hearings. The results of the accelerated program adopted were revealing; none of the over 4,000 Haitians processed during this program were granted asylum.

The federal court of appeals struck down the accelerated program. It concluded that the INS had knowingly made it impossible for Haitians and their attorneys to prepare and file asylum applications in a timely fashion. The program violated principles of procedural due process that were constitutionally protected. The plaintiffs had an interest in proving their entitlement to political asylum under the conditions set by the **United Nationals Protocol Relating to the Status of Refugees** and in rebutting the government's general conclusion that Haitians are primarily economic refugees. When speed was combined with knowingly creating scheduling conflicts and unattainable filing deadlines, uninformed and unreliable decisions were almost assured. In sum, the government created conditions that negated the possibility that a Haitian's asylum hearing would be meaningful in either its timing or nature. Under such circumstances, the right to petition for political asylum was effectively denied.

The court ordered the government to submit a procedurally fair plan for the orderly reprocessing of the plaintiffs' asylum applications.

HAMPTON V. MOW SUNG WONG The Supreme Court invalidated a federal Civil Service Commission regulation barring **lawful permanent resident aliens** from employment in the federal competitive civil service—even while recognizing that "overriding national interest may provide a justification for a citizenship requirement in the federal service [although] an identical requirement may not be enforced by a state." The majority opinion in the case [426 U.S. 88 (1976)] found that the national interests offered in defense of the ban either (a) were not properly the concern of the Civil Service Commission and had not explicitly emanated from Congress or the president, or (b) to the extent that they were within the commission's competence, had not been evaluated fully.

Although there is great federal power over immigration and naturalization, the court rejected the position that federal **plenary power** over aliens can mean that any agent of the federal government may arbitrarily subject all resident aliens to different substantive rules than those applied to citizens. The majority was willing to assume that if Congress or the president had expressly imposed the citizenship requirement, it would be justified by the national interest in providing an incentive for aliens to become naturalized, or possibly even as providing the president with an expendable token for treaty negotiating purposes. But those were not interests that could be assumed to have influenced the Civil Service Commission.

A few days after this decision, President Gerald Ford issued an executive order paralleling the regulation that had been struck down, barring lawful permanent resident aliens from employment in the federal competitive civil service. Challenges to this order have been unsuccessful, so resident aliens are precluded from federal civil service jobs. [*Mow Sun Wong v. Campbell*, 626 F.2d 739 (9th Cir. 1980); *Vergara v. Hampton*, 581 F.2d 1281 (7th Cir. 1978)]

HANDBOOK ON PROCEDURES AND CRITERIA FOR DETERMINING REFUGEE STATUS Because the United States is a party to the **United Nations Protocol Relating to the Status of Refugees,** the *Handbook on Procedures and Criteria for Determining Refugee Status,* written by the **United Nations High Commissioner for Refugees,** is a useful tool for determining **asylum** eligibility. The Supreme Court has also stated its strong approval of the use of the *Handbook* as a source for interpreting U.S. asylum and **refugee** law. [*INS v. Cardoza-Fonseca*, 107 S.Ct. 1207, 1216, n. 22 (1987)] Important provisions of the *Handbook* include the following paragraphs:

> 51. There is no universally accepted definition of "persecution," and various attempts to formulate such a definition have met with little success. From Article 33 of the 1951 [**Convention Relating to the Status of Refugees**], it may be inferred, [however,] that a threat to life or freedom on account of race, religion, nationality, political opinion, or membership in a social group is always persecution.

> 52. Whether other prejudicial actions or threats would amount to persecution will depend on the circumstances of each case, including the subjective element. . . . The subjective character of fear of persecution requires an evaluation of the opinions and feelings of the person concerned. It is also in the light of such opinions and feelings that any actual or anticipated measures against him must necessarily be viewed. Due to variations in the psychological make-up of individuals and in the circumstances of each case, interpretations of what amounts to persecution are bound to vary.

53. [A]n applicant may have been subjected to various measures not in themselves amounting to persecution (e.g., discrimination in various forms). . . . In such situations, the various elements involved may, if taken together, produce an effect on the mind of the applicant that can reasonably justify a claim to well-founded fear of persecution on "cumulative grounds."

62. A migrant is a person who, for reasons other than those contained in the definition, voluntarily leaves his country in order to take up residence elsewhere. He may be moved by the desire for change or adventure, or by family or other reasons of a personal nature. If he is moved exclusively by economic considerations, he is an economic migrant and not a refugee.

65. Persecution is normally related to action by the authorities of a country. It may also emanate from sections of the population that do not respect the standards established by the laws of the country concerned. A case in point may be religious intolerance, amounting to persecution, in a country otherwise secular, but where sizable fractions of the population do not respect the religious beliefs of their neighbors. Where serious discriminatory or other offensive acts are committed by the local populace, they can be considered as persecution if they are knowingly tolerated by the authorities, or if the authorities refuse, or prove unable, to offer effective protection.

68. Race, in the present connexion, has to be understood in its widest sense to include all kinds of ethnic groups that are referred to as "races" in common usage. Frequently it will also entail membership of a specific social group of common descent forming a minority within a larger population. Discrimination for reasons of race has found world-wide condemnation as one of the most striking violations of human rights. Racial discrimination, therefore, represents an important element in determining the existence of persecution.

71. The Universal Declaration of Human Rights and the Human Rights Covenant proclaim the right to freedom of thought, conscience and religion, which right includes the freedom of a person to change his religion and his freedom to manifest it in public or private, in teaching, practice, worship and observance.

72. Persecution for "reasons of religion" may assume various forms, e.g., prohibition of membership of a religious community, or worship in private or in public, or religious instruction, or serious measures of discrimination imposed on persons because they practice their religion or belong to a particular religious community.

74. The term "nationality" in this context is not to be understood only as "citizenship." It refers also to membership of an ethnic or linguistic group and may occasionally overlap with the term "race." Persecution for reasons of nationality may consist of adverse attitudes and measures directed against a national (ethnic, linguistic) minority and in certain circumstances the fact of belonging to such a minority may in itself give rise to well-founded fear of persecution.

77. A "particular social group" normally comprises persons of similar background, habits or social status. A claim to fear of persecution under this heading may frequently overlap with a claim to fear of persecution on other grounds, i.e., race, religion or nationality.

78. Membership of such a particular social group may be at the root of persecution because there is no confidence in the group's loyalty to the Government or because the political outlook, antecedents or economic activity of its members, or the very existence of the social group as such, is held to be an obstacle to the Government's policies.

80. Holding political opinions different from those of the Government is not in itself a ground for claiming refugee status, and an applicant must show that he has a fear of persecution for holding such opinions. This . . . presupposes that such opinions have come to the notice of the authorities or are attributed by them to the applicant.

82. There may, however, also be situations in which the applicant has not given any expression to his opinions. Due to the strength of his convictions, however, it may be reasonable to assume that his opinions will sooner or later find expression and that the applicant will, as a result, come into conflict with the authorities. Where this can reasonably be assumed, the applicant can be considered to have fear of persecution for reasons of political opinion.

84. If the prosecution pertains to a punishable act committed out of political motives, and if the anticipated punishment is in conformity with the general law of the country concerned, fear of such prosecution will not in itself make the applicant a refugee.

91. The fear of being persecuted need not always extend to the whole territory of the refugee's country of nationality. Thus in ethnic clashes or in cases of grave disturbances involving civil war conditions, persecution of a specific ethnic or national group may occur in only one part of the country. In such situations, a person will not be excluded from refugee status merely because he could have sought refuge in another part of the same country, if under all the circumstances it would not have been reasonable to expect him to do so.

169. A deserter or draft-evader may also be considered a refugee if it can be shown that he would suffer disproportionately severe punishment for the military offence on account of his race, religion, nationality, membership of a particular social group or political opinion. The same would apply if it can be shown that he has well-founded fear of persecution on these grounds above and beyond the punishment for desertion.

HARBORING OF ALIENS
A person is guilty of a felony for concealing, harboring, or shielding an alien from detection, knowing or in reckless disregard of the fact that the person is an **undocumented alien.** Warning aliens of the presence of INS officers has been held to fall within this law, as has paying for an apartment for undocumented aliens and promising work papers. However, the first instance of hiring and even exploiting undocumented workers has been held not to be a crime, although a pattern and practice of hiring undocumented workers may constitute a crime under **employer sanctions** provisions. Prosecutions of religious layworkers who assisted in the provision of church sanctuary to undocumented El Salvadoran and Guatemalan refugees in the United States during the 1980s were brought under the harboring provision.

The offense is punishable by imprisonment of up to five years and a fine of $10,000. [8 U.S.C. §1324(a)(1); *United States v. Sanchez,* 927 F.2d 276 (8th Cir. 1991); *United States v. Aguilar,* 871 F.2d 1436 (9th Cir. 1989); *United States v. Merkt,* 794 F.2d 950 (5th Cir. 1986); *United States v. Rubio-Gonzales,* 674 F.2d 1067 (5th Cir. 1982); *United States v. Singh,* 628 F.2d 758 (2d Cir. 1980)]

HEALTH CARE WORKERS
An alien who seeks to enter the United States for the purpose of performing labor as a health care worker, other than a physician, is excludable unless the alien presents to immigration officials a certificate from the Commission on Graduates of Foreign Nursing Schools, or a certificate from an equivalent independent credentialing organization approved by the INS. That document must verify that the alien's education, training, license, and experience meet all applicable statutory and regulatory requirements for entry into the United States and are comparable to those required for a U.S. health care worker of the same type. Nonimmigrant health care workers have been granted a blanket waiver of this provision, but immigrant health care workers remain subject to the requirements. [8 U.S.C. §§1182(a)(5)(C); 1182(d)(3)(A)]

For purposes of the certificate requirement, health care workers include nurses, physical therapists, occupational therapists, speech language pathologists, medical technologists, medical technicians, and physician assistants. Chiropractors, dentists, dental technicians, dental assistants, acupuncturists, psychologists, and nutritionists are not subject to this provision.

HEARING IN ABSENTIA If an alien facing **removal proceedings** fails to appear at the removal hearing after receiving proper notification, the **immigration judge** can proceed with the hearing even though the alien is absent and an order of removal can be issued in absentia. To support such an order, the INS must establish by clear, unequivocal, and convincing evidence that written notice was provided and that the alien is removable. The alien must have received written notice of the time and place of the hearing in person. If personal service is not practicable, the notice must be given by certified mail to the alien or to the alien's attorney.

An entry of a removal order in absentia carries with it other severe consequences. A person against whom such an order is entered is not eligible for **voluntary departure, cancellation of removal, registry,** or **adjustment of status** for five years.

A removal order issued in absentia may be rescinded only if the alien demonstrates that the failure to appear was because of exceptional circumstances, that proper notice was not received, or that he or she was in federal or state custody and could not appear. Exceptional circumstances refers to circumstances such as serious illness of the alien or death of an immediate relative. For example, in *Matter of Singh* [Int. Dec. No. 3324 (BIA 1997)] the **Board of Immigration Appeals** found exceptional circumstances and was sympathetic to the alien. The alien was fifteen minutes late for the hearing because he did not want to leave his ill stepson unattended at home, while he waited for his wife to return from a trip to buy medication. But in *Matter of S—A—* [Int. Dec. No. 3331 (BIA 1997)], the Board of Immigration Appeals held that the alien's assertion that he was prevented from reaching his hearing on time by heavy traffic did not constitute reasonable cause that would warrant a reopening of his *in absentia* proceedings. [8 U.S.C. §1229a(b)(5)]

HEIBERGER, MURIEL (B. 1943) Muriel Heiberger is a major voice in the immigrant rights community in the United States. As the executive director of the **Massachusetts Immigrant and Refugee Advocacy Coalition** (MIRA) until the end of 1999, she set an example for other state coalition efforts on how to work with broad-based constituencies and allies to forge positive results on behalf of immigrants at local, state, and national levels. Prior to helping to found and direct MIRA, Heiberger was the director of programs for the International Institute of Boston. In 1991, Heiberger was honored by Women in Philanthropy as one of twenty-three women in the Greater Boston area working to improve the quality of life in the community. In 1993, the Massachusetts Chapter of the National Association of Social Workers named her their Public Citizen of the Year in recognition of her long-standing commitment to social justice. In 1997, she received the state's New American Appreciation Award for outstanding contributions to helping immigrants establish roots in Massachusetts.

Heiberger serves on the Governor's Advisory Council on Refugees and Immigrants and the board of directors of the National Immigration Forum. She obtained her doctorate in education from the Harvard Graduate School of Education in 1982.

HING, BILL ONG (B. 1949)   Bill Ong Hing is on the law faculty at the University of California at Davis, where he teaches and is the director of clinical programs. He also volunteers as the executive director of the **Immigrant Legal Resource Center**, which he founded in 1979, and is Of Counsel to the international law firm Baker & McKenzie. For over twenty-five years, Professor Hing has been a civil rights advocate on behalf of immigrants and other disadvantaged groups. His long list of accomplishments has been accrued in his various capacities as a writer, educator, lawyer, and community activist.

Professor Hing has handled several important cases as a lawyer. In 1987, he co-counseled the precedent-setting U.S. Supreme Court case *INS v. Cardoza-Fonseca*, which established that the asylum laws of the United States should be construed generously, and *INS v. Yueh-Shaio Yang*, a case involving a waiver of fraud committed by a Chinese immigrant in which the Supreme Court found no abuse of discretion by INS. He also assisted in Supreme Court litigation (*INS v. Pangilinan*) on behalf of Filipino veterans of World War II who had been denied naturalization rights, and in *United States v. Mendoza-Lopez*, where the Supreme Court agreed that waivers of hearing rights by a group of aliens in deportation proceedings violated due process.

Other important cases he has handled include *Wall v. INS*, 722 F.2d 1445 (9th Cir. 1984) (establishing that residence accrued during period of appeal was legal for purposes of establishing eligibility for relief); *McMullen v. INS*, 658 F.2d 1312 (9th Cir. 1981) (political asylum case involving former member of the Provisional Irish Republican Army, granted; it was the first case testing the **Refugee Act of 1980** that reached the Federal Court of Appeals and established evidentiary precedent); *Yassini v. Crosland*, 618 F.2d

1356 and 613 F.2d 219 (9th Cir. 1980) (due process and A.P.A. challenge to INS regulations denying reinstatement of Iranian students); *Cabral-Avila v. INS*, 589 F.2d 957 (9th Cir. 1978) (challenge to arrest procedures of INS agents in early-morning neighborhood raid alleging coercive and uniformed admissions of alienage); *Matter of Atanacio* (BIA 1979) (successful challenge to the exclusion of lawful permanent resident who had received public benefits). Even as a law student, he was involved in two extremely important cases on behalf of immigrants: *Lau v. Nichols*, the famous case that established equal educational opportunity rights for limited and non-English-speaking children, and *Hampton v. Mow Sun Wong*, a case seeking federal civil service jobs for lawful resident aliens.

Professor Hing is well known for his community work. He worked as a law clerk, then as a lawyer in the Chinatown-North Beach office of San Francisco Neighborhood Legal Assistance Foundation from 1972 to 1979. He has been a constant advisor to community-based organizations throughout the country on immigration matters, and has helped to turn back many legislative attacks on the immigrant community. He has worked with many members of Congress, and appears regularly on radio and television vigorously speaking out on behalf of immigrants. In 1979 he established the Immigrant Legal Resource Center, a nonprofit support program for community agencies, and continues to serve as the center's volunteer executive director. He served as a member of the first Citizens' Advisory Panel of the **Department of Justice,** which monitored **Border Patrol** misconduct, the Restructuring Committee of the INS, and was named to the Committee on Immigrant Children and Family Health of the National Research Council. He also serves as a consultant to the Emma Lazarus Fund of the Open Society Institute, on the Immigration Advisory Committee of **Asian American Legal Defense and Education Fund** of New York, on the National Advisory Council of the **National Asian Pacific Legal Consortium,** and on the board of the **National Immigration Forum.** He was the first chair of the Immigration and Nationality Law Advisory Commission of the California Bar of Legal Specialization, and cofounded the Asian American Bar Association of Northern California, Break the Silence Coalition, and Asian Americans for Quality Education. He is the recipient of two public-interest awards, one from the Bar Association of San Francisco in 1984, and the other from California Rural Legal Assistance in 1989. He is also a consultant to Los Angeles–based Leadership Education for Asian Pacifics, for whom he directed a major research project entitled *Reframing the Immigration Debate,* which was nominated for outstanding research promoting human rights by the Gustavus Myers Center for the Study of Human Rights in North America.

Professor Hing has written extensively in the immigration field. His books include *To Be an American: Cultural Pluralism and the Rhetoric of Assimilation* (NYU Press 1997) (selected for a 1997 Outstanding Academic Book Award by the librarians' journal *Choice*), *Making and Remaking Asian America through Immigration Policy* (Stanford University Press 1993), and *Handling Immigration Cases*, 2d ed. (Aspen Law Publishers 1999). He received his J.D. with honors from the University of San Francisco School of Law in 1974.

HOLLEY V. LAVINE This case [553 F.2d 845 (2d Cir. 1977)] involved the right of an **undocumented alien,** residing in the United States with the knowledge of immigration authorities, to obtain public assistance (welfare). Gayle Holley, an adult, was born in Canada and at the age of twelve entered the United States as a **nonimmigrant** student. She overstayed her visa and years later she married a United States citizen. Eventually she had six children, all of whom were U.S. citizens by virtue of birth in the United States. Holley eventually separated from her husband.

Because she was poor, Holley sought public assistance. Initially, the New York State Department of Social Services paid to Holley on her own behalf and each of her six children a separately calculated sum under Aid to Families with Dependent Children (AFDC), a program cooperatively operated by the state and federal governments. Subsequently, the state enacted a law that provided that every alien "unlawfully residing in the United States . . . is not eligible for aid to dependent children." Thus the state ceased to pay Holley anything on her own account as a parent, but continued to pay AFDC benefits for the six children.

Holley's attorneys argued that she was also eligible to continue receiving benefits on her own account because the federal rules allowed payments to those "permanently residing in the United States under color of law." In this case, immigration officials were aware of Holley's presence in the United States. They notified state social service officials that "deportation proceedings have not been instituted . . . for humanitarian reasons" and the INS "does not contemplate enforcing her departure from the United States at this time."

The federal court of appeals agreed that under these circumstances Holley was "permanently residing in the United States under color of law" (**PRUCOL**), and therefore was entitled to public benefits as long as she met other requirements for assistance.

I

I-9 PROCESS   In 1986, Congress enacted the **Immigration Reform and Control Act** (IRCA), which imposed penalties on employers for (1) knowingly hiring or continuing to employ persons who are not authorized to work in the United States, (2) failing to verify the employment eligibility of each new employee with Form I-9, and (3) failing to keep the I-9 forms on file for a certain period of time and making them available to federal agents on request. This law is often referred to as **employer sanctions.**

In order to implement the employer sanctions law, the federal government devised a form that all employers must use in order to verify the employment status of a new employee. The form is the Form I-9, Employment Eligibility Verification [see sample in the Appendix]. The form number appears at the bottom of the form. By properly completing the form, employers show that they have looked at documents presented by each new employee that establish the person's identity and employment eligibility.

The law requires the following of all employers:

- verification of employment eligibility of all persons employed after November 6, 1986
- completion of INS Form I-9 for each new hire within three days of the date of hire (unless the worker is being hired for three days or less, the form must be completed by the end of the first workday)
- checking documents proving the employment eligibility and the identity of each new employee at the commencement of employment

These requirements of the law apply to the following:

- all employers, including agricultural associations, agricultural employers, or farm labor contractors who employ workers, or recruit or refer workers for a fee
- anyone who hires someone for domestic work in a private home on a regular basis, such as every week

- employees transferred to the United States from an overseas branch or affiliate of the U.S. company, regardless of the fact that they may remain on the foreign payroll

An employer does not have to complete an I-9 if self-employed, or the person is also an employee of a business entity, such as a corporation or partnership, in which case the business entity is required to complete a Form I-9 for the person. No verification is necessary for temporary personnel provided by temporary agencies.

If a person is hired to do work infrequently, the person may be considered a *casual hire* for whom the I-9 process does not need to be followed. For example, a person hired casually and infrequently to perform domestic jobs around the house or yard can be considered a casual hire. Hiring such a person once a month would probably be considered infrequent. But someone who is hired to work regularly once a week would probably not qualify as a casual hire, and an I-9 form would be necessary for that worker.

No verification is required of an **independent contractor.** An employer may wish to avoid presenting or reviewing documents by characterizing a worker performing services as an independent contractor rather than an employee. The idea is that persons who have their own business and hire out their services are not considered employees.

Employers who make technical mistakes in the I-9 process may be forgiven under certain circumstances under a **good faith compliance** provision.

ILLEGAL IMMIGRATION   See undocumented alien.

ILLEGAL IMMIGRATION REFORM AND IMMIGRANT RESPONSIBILITY ACT OF 1996   The 1996 Illegal Immigration Reform and Immigrant Responsibility Act (IIRAIRA) provides for (1) improvements in border control through increased resources and enhanced use of technology, (2) provisions to help facilitate legal entry, (3) increased resources for investigators to perform interior enforcement activities, (4) enhanced enforcement and penalties against alien smuggling, (5) provisions to further deter the use of fraudulent documents, (6) revised procedures for **removal** of inadmissible and deportable aliens, (7) pilot programs for enforcement of restrictions against employment of **undocumented aliens**, and (8) restrictions on benefits for aliens. The goal of Congress in this law and with the **Anti-terrorism and Effective Death Penalty Act of 1996** was to streamline and accelerate the removal of aliens with criminal

records. The statute severely restricted and eliminated judicial review of administrative removal orders in many situations. Relief from deportation was severely limited. For the first time, asylum applicants faced deadlines for filing claims. The law also changed certain terminology, such as relabeling exclusion grounds as **inadmissibility grounds** and using the term **removal proceedings** to describe what had previously been considered exclusion or deportation hearings. [Pub. L. 104–208, 110 Stat. 3009]

ILLINOIS COALITION FOR IMMIGRANT AND REFUGEE PROTECTION
The Illinois Coalition for Immigrant and Refugee Protection (ICIRP) evolved out of an effort by the Mexican American Legal Defense and Educational Fund (MALDEF) and Travelers & Immigrants Aid (TIA) to develop a coordinated response to the service needs created by the **Immigration Reform and Control Act of 1986** (IRCA). Initially, ICIRP focused on issues related to IRCA implementation, including **employer sanctions,** discrimination, education, and legal rights. Today, ICIRP is a statewide coalition with a broad mission of promoting the full and equal participation of immigrants and **refugee**s in social, political, and economic life.

The coalition works in partnership with member organizations on a wide range of issues affecting immigrants and refugees, including citizenship, civic participation, leadership development, education, health, employment, public benefits, legal status, and international human rights. Its primary activities include outreach, education, training, technical assistance, and policy advocacy. The coalition also serves as a vehicle through which community groups, citywide and statewide institutions, religious organizations, and government agencies can come together to discuss and develop strategies and programs to address these issues.

ICIRP has a long track record of advocating for humane immigration policies, reaching out to newcomer communities, and building the capacity of immigrant service organizations. It is well regarded throughout Illinois for its expertise in immigrant-related public policy, and has successfully advocated for policy changes at all levels of government. Examples of its accomplishments include:

- In 1994 ICIRP assumed the lead role in lobbying Governor Jim Edgar to create the Illinois Refugee and Immigrant Citizenship Initiative. Most recently, ICIRP successfully pushed for the program's extension through June 1998. Through this program, the state committed over $4,350,000—more than any other state—to support citizenship services.

- In partnership with the Chicago Board of Elections and the Cook County Clerk's Office, ICIRP successfully pushed the Chicago District Office of the INS to include voter registration as part of its citizen swearing-in ceremonies in spring and summer 1996. As a result of ICIRP's efforts, more than 34,000 new citizens were registered to vote in 1996. To maximize their participation in upcoming elections, ICIRP also mailed out 3,000 postcards to remind new citizens to vote in the November 1996 elections and worked with the ethnic media to encourage electoral participation.
- In spring 1996, ICIRP, working in partnership with other advocacy groups, successfully advocated with the Illinois Department of Public Aid to continue supporting perinatal care services for undocumented women.
- In spring 1996, ICIRP mobilized 3,000 low-income Latinos in suburban Prospect Heights to voice their concerns about and opposition to the creation of a tax increment financing (TIF) district that would raze their residential community. The effort resulted in the founding of a grassroots organization that is now advocating on its community's own behalf regarding the TIF district and other issues of concern.

IMMEDIATE RELATIVE The immediate relative category of immigration is for the spouses, children (unmarried and under age twenty-one), and parents of U.S. citizens, who can immigrate immediately if proper applications are submitted and **inadmissibility grounds** are satisfied. Unlimited numbers of immigrants may immigrate to the United States each year in the immediate relative category.

In order to be a spouse, the marriage must be valid in the country where it took place, and must not have been entered into solely for immigration purposes (i.e., a **sham marriage**). The spousal category includes widows or widowers of U.S. citizens if the marriage lasted at least two years before the citizen died, as long as they were not legally separated at the time of death. The spousal category does not, however, include same-sex marriages. See *Adams v. Howerton.*

Children of citizens qualify as immediate relatives if the child is unmarried and under the age of twenty-one. An adopted child can qualify if the child was adopted while under the age of sixteen, has been in legal custody of the adopting parents for two years, and has resided with the parents for two years. A stepchild can qualify if the child was under the age of eighteen at the time of the marriage creating the step relationship.

U.S. citizens can petition for their parents if the citizen is at least twenty-one years old. Many aliens believe that giving birth to a child in the United States will gain immediate immigration rights for the parents. Although the child becomes a citizen at birth, the offspring cannot petition for the parent until the age of twenty-one. [8 U.S.C. §1151(b)]

IMMIGRANT   An immigrant is a person who is not a U.S. citizen who enters the United States with the intent of residing permanently. A **lawful permanent resident alien** is a person who has immigrated lawfully to the United States, generally as an **immediate relative** of a United States citizen, or through the **preference system**. An **undocumented alien** is a person who may have entered the country surreptitiously or who may have overstayed permission to remain pursuant to a **nonimmigrant visa**. **Refugee**s may eventually become immigrants, but when they first enter they may not meet the technical definition of immigrant because they may only be intending to remain until things have calmed down in their homelands.

IMMIGRANT LEGAL RESOURCE CENTER   The Immigrant Legal Resource Center (ILRC) is one of the premier immigrant support centers for legal services programs and community-based organizations in the country. The ILRC blends a many-pronged, multidisciplinary approach to lawyering that includes collaboration with grassroots organizations, community education, training, consultation, policy advocacy, and litigation.

The ILRC began in 1979 as a group of volunteer attorneys and law students who recognized the pressing need for legal support to agencies working with immigrants and refugees in northern California. Responding to the wave of refugees fleeing war and repression in Central America in the 1980s, the ILRC was instrumental in organizing legal services and providing vital expertise. During that decade the ILRC established national legal precedents in political asylum law (*Immigration and Naturalization Service v. Cardoza-Fonseca; McMullen v. INS*) and developed innovative projects that helped make the immigration amnesty program work for three million people.

In the 1990s, in the face of unprecedented hostility toward immigrants, the ILRC worked extensively with immigrant groups, the media, and policy makers to reframe the immigration debate. The ILRC expanded its work nationally and now offers a variety of services related to immigration policies and the lives of immigrants.

Legal Support

ILRC staff attorneys provide on-site and telephone consultation, training workshops and seminars, and educational curricula on immigration issues to pro bono attorneys and nonprofit agencies serving immigrants throughout the United States. The ILRC also offers litigation support in select cases, including representing clients, filing amicus briefs, serving as expert witnesses, and providing analysis of rules and laws, both proposed and enacted.

Citizenship and Civic Participation

The ILRC has responded to the crisis created by 1996 anti-immigration legislation that targeted elderly immigrants and those with disabilities. The ILRC provides technical assistance and training to service providers on how to help their clients become U.S. citizens. Staff attorneys conduct on-site workshops around the country. ILRC attorneys staff a telephone hotline and write and distribute materials on the naturalization process.

The ILRC provides technical assistance and information on the issues of naturalization, family unity, and the effects of recent laws to immigrant advocates and organizations throughout California. In the state's Central Valley, the ILRC is a partner in a collaborative effort that encourages citizenship and access to English language instruction. These projects promote civic participation and leadership development among California's immigrants.

Combating Provider Fraud

The ILRC works with immigration advocates and district attorneys across California to prosecute scam artists who offer fraudulent immigration services. The ILRC also published a manual for district attorneys on fraud against immigrants.

Training of Nonprofit Service Providers

The ILRC designed and coordinates an intensive national training program on basic immigration law and practice for nonlawyers who provide legal services to low-income immigrants. Staff attorneys conduct the training course in cities throughout the United States. They have written both a student and a trainer manual and have developed advanced training on deportation defense hearing skills.

Assisting Central American Refugees

The November 1997 enactment of the Nicaraguan Adjustment and Central American Relief Act (NACARA) created significant hope for hundreds of thousands of Central American refugees stranded in the United States without legal residency after fleeing their war-torn countries in the 1980s. The ILRC provides seminars, informational videos, phone, email and fax consultation, the manual *Winning NACARA Suspension Cases,* updates on policy and regulation changes, and sample pleadings to inform pro bono attorneys and legal service providers about this form of relief for Salvadorans and Guatemalans and to assist them in making use of it for their clients.

Advocating for Children

Through a unique project, the ILRC helps abused and abandoned immigrant children in foster care become permanent U.S. residents. ILRC consults with juvenile court judges, county workers, and children's advocates working on special immigrant juvenile petitions. The ILRC works regionally and nationally to promote humane treatment for all immigrant children.

The ILRC Mission

The ILRC works with immigrants and citizens to make critical legal assistance and social services accessible to all, regardless of income, and to build a society that values diversity and respects the dignity and rights of all people.
To further that goal, the ILRC:

- educates and inspires immigrants to advocate for justice for themselves and their communities
- promotes civic participation and mutual respect for all groups
- provides support, training, and information about immigration law and policy to immigrants and their advocates in an effort to increase the quantity and quality of legal assistance available to low-income persons
- collaborates with immigrants, community organizations, and government agencies to create innovative and constructive solutions to issues involving immigration policy
- promotes public awareness of the contributions new Americans make to our society and the challenges they face

As part of a litigation team representing refugees from Fujian Province in China, the ILRC shared the 1994 American Immigration Lawyers Association Award for Human Rights.

IMMIGRATION ACT OF 1990 This law was enacted on November 29, 1990, and made changes to many aspects of immigration law. The law expanded the number of immigration visas based on employment and also expanded the **diversity visa** program. Some of the changes strengthened the employment antidiscrimination provisions in the law; for example, it is now illegal for employers to retaliate against employees who file discrimination complaints. The 1990 act also made it a requirement for employers to accept any documents that appear on the official list of documents acceptable for proving an employee's employment eligibility or identity [see **document abuse**]. Other changes made it possible for more categories of immigrants to get legal permission to work in the United States. The law's **family unity** provisions allowed the unmarried children (under age eighteen) and spouses of **amnesty** aliens to remain in the United States and receive work authorization.

IMMIGRATION AMENDMENTS OF 1965 Although the **McCarran-Walter Act of 1952** brought about major changes to the immigration laws, the basic format of the discriminatory **national origins quota system** remained in force. Token quotas for countries from the Asia-Pacific region and favorable limits for western and northern Europeans over southern and eastern Europeans were the rule. This quota system exasperated many observers, including President Harry S. Truman, who vetoed the 1952 legislation due to its failure to repudiate the quota system. Many felt the system perpetuated the philosophy that "some people are more equal than others." Congress, however, overrode Truman's veto. Critics cited the law as an embarrassment that was inconsistent with the stature of the United States as the leader of the free world.

Truman and others did not relent. President Dwight D. Eisenhower embraced the findings of a report during his administration that strongly urged the abolition of the national origins system. After years of unsuccessful efforts by Truman and Eisenhower, President John F. Kennedy submitted a comprehensive program that provided the impetus for ultimate reform. He envisioned a system governed by the skills of the immigrant and family reunification. Even after Kennedy's assassination, his successor, President Lyndon B. Johnson, pushed hard for the legislation. Kennedy's brothers, Attorney General Robert Kennedy and Senator Edward Kennedy, managed much of the legislative battle.

President Kennedy's hopes for abolishing the quota system were realized when the 1965 amendments were enacted. But his vision of visas on a first-come, first-served basis gave way to a narrower and more historically parochial framework. The new law allowed 20,000 immigrant visas for every country not in the Western Hemisphere [see **Western Hemisphere immigrants**]. The allotment was made regardless of the size of the country, so that mainland China had the same quota as Tunisia. Of the 170,000 visas set aside for the Eastern Hemisphere, 75 percent were for specified "preference" relatives of citizens and lawful permanent residents (the basic structure of today's **preference system**), and an unlimited number were available to **immediate relatives** of U.S. citizens.

Two occupational preference categories and a nonpreference category were also established. The occupational categories helped professionals and other aliens who filled jobs for which qualified U.S. workers were not available. Under the nonpreference category, an alien who invested $40,000 in a business could qualify for immigration to the United States.

Over the years, the 1965 amendments have been credited with changing the racial character of immigration to the United States. Prior to 1965, most immigrants were from northern and western Europe. The makeup changed through the 1970s and especially the 1980s. Today, more than 80 percent of all immigrants are from Asia and Latin America.

IMMIGRATION AND NATIONALITY ACT The Immigration and Nationality Act (INA) is the basic law governing the immigration and nationality policies of the United States. Although the INA has changed many times in recent years, the law is sometimes still referred to as the Immigration and Nationality Act of 1952, or the **McCarran-Walter Act,** because the basic framework of today's laws was enacted under that title in 1952. The INA contains definitions, **inadmissibility grounds,** grounds of **removal, naturalization** requirements, **nonimmigrant** category descriptions, and descriptions of **immigrant** categories. A copy of the INA can be purchased from a variety of law publishers or the U.S. government bookstore. The INA is also contained in Title 8 of the United States Code.

IMMIGRATION AND NATURALIZATION SERVICE The Immigration and Naturalization Service (INS), an agency of the **Department of Justice,** is charged with the primary responsibility for administering the nation's immigration laws. The chief administrator of the agency is the **commissioner,** who is stationed in the central office in Washington, D.C. The INS is divided into three regions in the United States—western, central, and eastern—each with a regional INS office. Each region

is broken down into different districts, such as New York, Los Angeles, or Chicago, which have their own **district directors**. A few **district offices** are also located in foreign countries. In all, there are thirty-three district offices. Each region also has a **regional service center** where many applications, particularly **visa petitions** for an alien who will be immigrating from abroad, must be filed directly.

Each district office is divided into various sections. For example, a typical office could have the following branches: deportation, citizenship, examinations, legal officers, and investigations. Each division is responsible for different functions. For example, visa work might be handled by the examinations branch. The investigations branch might be divided further into a fraud division, an area control operations department, and so forth. There may be an **asylum** unit to handle political asylum applications. The marriage fraud unit would investigate suspected **sham marriages**. Some districts may also rotate officers to **ports of entry** within the district for the purpose of inspecting incoming aliens.

The **Border Patrol** is also part of the INS and reports to the respective regional commissioner, operating largely independently from the district offices. The Border Patrol has its own chiefs, and its twenty-one division sectors do not necessarily coincide with various districts. In addition to its primary border patrolling responsibilities, the Border Patrol oversees rural and agricultural areas. Thus, the Border Patrol may have stations hundreds of miles from any U.S. border. Congress has also extended authority to the Border Patrol to participate in drug interdiction, to arrest anyone committing a crime, and to use advanced weapons.

Immigration-related services of the Border Patrol include such activities as port-of-entry admissions and processing requests for **adjustment of status, naturalization,** and **employment authorization documents**. Enforcement responsibilities include such activities as border control, apprehension of **undocumented aliens** and workers, and detention and **removal** of criminal aliens.

▟▜ *Immigration and Naturalization Service v.*
▀▀ *Cardoza-Fonseca*   The requirement that an applicant demonstrate a **well-founded fear of persecution** in order to qualify for **asylum** does not require the alien to show that he or she is more likely than not to be subject to persecution. Indeed, given the legislative history of the asylum statute and guidance from the analysis of the relevant international standards by the **United Nations High Commissioner for Refugees,** the Supreme Court found in *Immigration and Naturalization Service v. Cardoza-Fonseca* [480 U.S. 421 (1987)] that an applicant with only a 10 percent chance

of being shot, tortured, or otherwise persecuted may very well have a well-founded fear of the event happening.

Luz Marina Cardoza-Fonseca was a thirty-eight-year-old woman from Nicaragua who applied for asylum, arguing that she had a well-founded fear of persecution based on her political views if she were to return to Nicaragua. She fled to the United States with her brother, who had been tortured and imprisoned in Nicaragua because of his political activities. Cardoza-Fonseca asserted that the Sandinistas knew that the two of them had fled together, and that even though she had not been politically active herself, she would be interrogated, her own political opposition to the Sandinistas would be brought to the government's attention, and she would be tortured.

The reference to "fear" in the well-founded fear of persecution standard makes the eligibility determination turn to some extent on the subjective mental state of the alien. That the fear must be "well-founded" does not alter the focus on the individual's subjective beliefs, nor does it transform the standard into one of "more likely than not." One can certainly have a well-founded fear of an event happening when there is less than a 50 percent chance of the occurrence taking place. So long as an objective situation is established by the evidence, it need not be shown that the situation will probably result in persecution; it is enough that persecution is a reasonable possibility.

Deportation is always a harsh measure; it is all the more replete with danger when the alien makes a claim that he or she will be subject to persecution or death if forced to return to his or her home country. In enacting the **Refugee Act of 1980,** Congress sought to give the U.S. government sufficient flexibility to respond to situations involving political or religious dissidents and detainees throughout the world. The holding in this case increased that flexibility by rejecting the government's contention that no one should be considered for asylum who fails to satisfy a more-likely-than-not standard. Whether or not an applicant is eventually granted asylum is a matter that Congress left for the **attorney general** to decide. But it is clear that Congress did not intend to restrict eligibility for that relief to those who could prove that it is more likely than not that they will be persecuted if deported.

IMMIGRATION AND NATURALIZATION SERVICE v. ELIAS-ZACARIAS

The Supreme Court held in this case [502 U.S. 478 (1992)] that a guerrilla organization's attempt to coerce a person into performing military service does not necessarily constitute persecution on account of political opinion for purposes of **asylum.**

Around the end of January 1987, two armed, uniformed guerrillas with handkerchiefs covering part of their faces came to the home of Elias-Zacarias, a native of Guatemala who was eighteen at the time. Only he and his parents were there, and they were asked by the guerrillas to join them, but all refused. The guerrillas told them that they would be back, and that they should reconsider their refusal. Elias-Zacarias did not want to join the anti-government guerrillas because he feared government retaliation against him and his family. He left Guatemala at the end of March because he was afraid that the guerrillas would return.

The Supreme Court ruled that Elias-Zacarias was not eligible for asylum, finding that a guerrilla organization's attempt to conscript a person into its military forces does not necessarily constitute persecution on account of **political opinion.** A person who supports a guerrilla movement might resist recruitment for a variety of reasons—fear of combat, a desire to remain with one's family and friends, a desire to earn a better living in civilian life. The record not only failed to show a political motive on Elias-Zacarias's part, it showed the opposite. Elias-Zacarias testified that he refused to join because he was afraid that the government would retaliate against him and his family if he did so. This is not a political motive. Nor did the record indicate that the guerrillas erroneously believed that his refusal was politically based. Besides, the ordinary meaning of the phrase "persecution on account of . . . political opinion" under the law of asylum is persecution on account of the *victim's* political opinion, not that of the persecutor. The mere existence of a generalized "political" motive underlying the guerrillas' forced recruitment is inadequate to establish the proposition that Elias-Zacarias feared persecution *on account of* political opinion.

Thus, Elias-Zacarias did not establish that he had a well-founded fear that the guerrillas would persecute him because of political opinion, rather than because of his refusal to fight with them. The court could not require an applicant to provide direct proof of the persecutors' motives, but since the law makes motive critical, the person must provide some evidence of it, direct or circumstantial.

IIIII IMMIGRATION AND NATURALIZATION SERVICE V. JONG HA WANG   This case [450 U.S. 139 (1981)] suggests a strict view toward **extreme hardship** by the Supreme Court when considering an alien's application for possible relief to remain in the United States.

The applicants, a husband and wife from Korea, first entered the United States as nonimmigrant **treaty traders.** They overstayed their visas and eventually sought an opportunity for relief that required a showing of **ex-**

treme hardship. They alleged that their two children, who were U.S. citizens by virtue of birth in the United States, would suffer extreme hardship because neither child spoke Korean and would lose educational opportunities if forced to leave the United States. They also claimed that the entire family would suffer economic hardship from the forced liquidation of their dry-cleaning business and the sale of their home.

The Supreme Court felt that the judgment of the **Board of Immigration Appeals** (BIA) in this matter was not unreasonable. The BIA held that a mere showing of economic detriment was insufficient, and in any event the family had significant financial resources; the applicants could also probably find suitable employment in Korea. As for the children, the BIA did not think they would suffer serious economic deprivation if they went to Korea with their parents. The BIA could not believe that the two young children of affluent, educated parents would be subject to such educational deprivations in Korea as to amount to extreme hardship.

IMMIGRATION AND NATURALIZATION SERVICE V. LOPEZ-MENDOZA In this case [468 U.S. 1032 (1984)] the Supreme Court held that the Fourth Amendment exclusionary rule does not apply in **deportation** hearings. In criminal cases when the police obtain a confession from a defendant subsequent to an unlawful arrest, the exclusionary rule precludes the admission into evidence of the confession because of the unlawful practices of the police. However, since deportation proceedings are civil rather than criminal, the Court ruled that the policies that underlie the exclusionary rule do not apply even though INS agents may have unlawfully arrested the deportable alien.

Lopez-Mendoza was arrested by INS agents at his place of employment, a transmission repair shop. Responding to a tip, INS investigators arrived at the shop shortly before 8 A.M. The agents had not sought a warrant to search the premises or to arrest any of its occupants. The proprietor of the shop firmly refused to allow the agents to interview his employees during working hours. Nevertheless, while one agent spoke with the proprietor, another entered the shop and approached Lopez-Mendoza. In response to the agent's questioning, Lopez-Mendoza gave his name and indicated that he was from Mexico with no close family ties in the United States. The agent then placed him under arrest. Lopez-Mendoza underwent further questioning at INS offices, where he admitted he was born in Mexico, was still a citizen of Mexico, and entered the United States without **inspection** by immigration authorities. Lopez-Mendoza's attorney objected to the use of this information at the deportation hearing on the grounds that the information was obtained as the result of an illegal arrest. The immigration judge overruled the objection and used the information to find that Lopez-Mendoza was deportable.

The Supreme Court agreed that the use of such evidence is proper, even if the arrest was unlawful. A deportation proceeding is a purely civil action to determine eligibility to remain in this country, not to punish an unlawful entry. One of the purposes of the exclusionary rule is to deter unlawful police practices. The likely deterrence value of the rule in deportation proceedings is difficult to assess, but the social costs of its application would be greater. The average INS agent arrests almost 500 undocumented aliens each year. Besides, the INS has its own comprehensive scheme for deterring Fourth Amendment violations by its officers, such as rules restricting stop, interrogation, and arrest practices. One of the unique social costs of the application of the exclusionary rule in this context is unique to continuing violations of the law. It would require the courts to close their eyes to ongoing violations of the law. Presumably no one would argue that the exclusionary rule should be invoked to prevent an agency from ordering corrective action at a leaking hazardous waste dump if the evidence underlying the order had been improperly obtained, or to compel police to return contraband explosives or drugs to their owner if the contraband had been unlawfully seized.

The Court warned, however, that its views might change if there was good reason to believe that Fourth Amendment violations by INS officers were widespread, or if it were dealing with egregious violations of Fourth Amendment or other liberties that might violate notions of fundamental fairness. Here the evidence was gathered in connection with peaceful arrests by INS officers.

IMMIGRATION AND REFUGEE SERVICES OF AMERICA

Immigration and Refugee Services of America (IRSA) and its network agencies exist solely for the purpose of helping newcomers to the United States to succeed in joining the mainstream of American society. For nearly eighty years, this focus has held together a dedicated network that, through good times and bad, has delivered professional services to a clientele marginalized by other service networks and providers. Today, the IRSA network consists of 36 local agencies operating at 129 sites that offer a wide variety of services to immigrants, refugees, and others in need.

Over the decades, IRSA and its partner agencies have struggled to meet newcomer needs. Seldom have there been significant revenue sources upon which to draw. This has often forced communities into a patchwork pattern of services. Often, they have had to rely on funding sources intended principally for other purposes, and they have had to shoehorn the special needs of newcomers into these programs.

At the heart of the IRSA network's efforts have been its programs "to assist the foreign-born and non-English speakers, especially immigrants, refugees and their descendants in their adjustment to the United States and to facilitate their becoming fully participating citizens." This goal of promoting and facilitating naturalization and full societal participation are the IRSA network's raison d'être.

IMMIGRATION COURT   The immigration court is the trial level of the **Executive Office of Immigration Review (EOIR)**. While the appellate level of the EOIR is located in Falls Church, Virginia, immigration courts are located throughout the United States, usually in the same cities as INS **district offices** can be found. **Immigration judges** preside in the immigration courts.

IMMIGRATION HOLD   When an alleged deportable alien is in the custody of criminal justice authorities (e.g., in state or federal prison for a criminal offense), immigration officials often request that the criminal justice authorities notify the INS when the person is to be released. Criminal justice authorities are generally informed by the filing of an official INS Form I-203, generally referred to as an immigration hold or detainer. The immigration hold means that INS must be kept informed as to the person's whereabouts and the completion of criminal incarceration. If detainees are serving a sentence for a criminal conviction, they often will not be permitted to participate in activities such as family reunions or work furlough programs if they are the subject of an immigration hold. [*Mohammed v. Sullivan*, 866 F.2d 258 (8th Cir. 1989); *Lopez-Mexia v. INS*, 798 F. Supp. 625 (C.D. Cal. 1992)]

IMMIGRATION JUDGE   The trial level of the **Executive Office of Immigration Review** is the **immigration court**. Immigration judges preside. They are administrative judges who conduct removal hearings. They are appointed by the **attorney general** and have the power to act as judge and prosecutor, although they rarely act in the latter capacity. They administer oaths, receive evidence, interrogate, examine and cross-examine aliens and witnesses, fact find, and issue final decisions. If statutory requirements are met, immigration judges have the authority to cancel removal, grant asylum, grant voluntary departure, and approve **adjustment of status** applications.

IMMIGRATION MARRIAGE FRAUD AMENDMENTS OF 1986

In response to allegations that many aliens were entering into **sham marriage**s in order to gain immigration benefits, Congress enacted the Immigration Marriage Fraud Amendments of 1986, which for the first time imposed a time requirement before the immigrant spouse could obtain the status of **lawful permanent resident alien.** The law also imposes a criminal penalty for marrying for the purpose of subverting immigration laws: imprisonment of up to five years and/or a fine of not more than $250,000. The penalties may be imposed on both spouses.

Aliens who seek to immigrate based on marriages to U.S. citizens or lawful permanent residents are granted permanent resident status initially on a conditional basis. Final approval is essentially conditioned on the viability of the marriage for two years. See *Matter of McKee.* Procedurally, the petitioning spouse files a **visa petition** for the prospective immigrant spouse. When the petition is approved and the immigrant spouse is allowed to immigrate or adjust status, the immigrant spouse is granted **conditional permanent residence.** Ninety days before the second anniversary of receiving the conditional status, the couple must jointly petition the INS **district director** to remove the conditional status. The couple is usually interviewed within ninety days of that petition in order to establish that the marriage was legal, that it has not been terminated, that it was not entered into solely for immigration purposes, and that no fee was given for filing the immigration petition.

Conditional status may also be removed, as a matter of discretion, when the alien's **removal** would result in **extreme hardship** or when the marriage was entered into in good faith by the alien spouse, but the marriage has been terminated (other than through the death of the spouse) and the alien was not at fault in failing to meet the requirements. The law was amended to provide a procedure that allows an alien who is the victim of spousal abuse at the hands of a U.S. citizen spouse to file a self-petition for immigrant status. [8 U.S.C. §§1154(a); 1186a(a)]

IMMIGRATION REFORM AND CONTROL ACT OF 1986

In 1986 Congress enacted the Immigration Reform and Control Act (IRCA) to reform certain aspects of existing immigration law and to reduce the number of **undocumented alien**s who come to the United States. The plan to reduce the number of undocumented workers was twofold: (1) grant

amnesty or legalization to many of the undocumented workers, and (2) make it unlawful for employers to hire undocumented workers in order to remove the incentive for unauthorized workers to come to the United States (**employer sanctions**). These two methods of controlling undocumented workers represented a political compromise. Because Congress was concerned that some employers might use the threat of sanctions to justify discriminating against "foreign-looking" workers, IRCA also added prohibitions against certain unfair immigration-related employment practices. Specifically, the law regards as unlawful an employer's actions when he or she discriminates against someone because of that person's national origin or because of his or her citizenship or immigration status (**citizenship discrimination**).

The legalization programs for undocumented aliens consisted of one for those who had resided in the United States since January 1, 1982, and the other for **special agricultural workers** (SAWs) who had performed agricultural work for at least ninety days between May 1, 1985, and May 1, 1986.

Ultimately, 1.7 million applicants filed under the pre-1982 program, and 1.2 million applied as SAWs. About 70 percent who ultimately applied under the pre-1982 program were Mexican; the next largest groups were El Salvadoran (8.1 percent) and Guatemalan (3 percent). Those qualifying under the farmworker program were also mostly Mexican. Mexicans filed 81.6 percent of the SAW applications, Haitians 3.4 percent, El Salvadorans 2 percent, and Guatemalans and Asian Indians 1.4 percent each.

The passage of IRCA represented the culmination of years of social, political, and congressional debate about the perceived lack of control over the country's southern border. The belief that something had to be done about the large numbers of undocumented workers who had entered the United States from Mexico in the 1970s was reinforced by the flood of Central Americans that began to arrive in the early 1980s. While the political turmoil of civil war in El Salvador, Guatemala, and Nicaragua drove many Central Americans from their homeland, they, along with the Mexicans who continued to arrive, were generally labeled economic migrants by the Reagan administration, the INS, and the courts. Beginning in 1971, legislative proposals featuring employer sanctions as a centerpiece were touted as solutions to the undocumented alien problem. By the end of the Carter administration in 1980, a Select Commission on Immigration and Refugee Policy portrayed legalization as a necessary balance to sanctions.

While strong congressional sentiment to respond to the perceived problem of undocumented aliens drove Congress to pass IRCA, congressional endorsement of the plan for balancing employer sanctions with legalization does not mean that there was strong support for legalization per se. Congress essentially concluded that with an unchecked flood of aliens crossing illegally, the southern border was out of control. It was widely believed that the nation shared this fear. Opposition to legalization was intense and the program narrowly survived the House of Representatives. In the eleventh hour, on October 10, 1986, Representative Bill McCollum introduced an amendment to completely delete legalization from IRCA. The House defeated the amendment—thereby saving the legalization program—by a vote of 199 to 192, with 41 absent. A swing of only four votes would have reversed the result.

IMPUTED POLITICAL OPINION   Imputed political opinion is a theory developed to support **asylum** applications for individuals who are seeking asylum based on a **well-founded fear of persecution** because of their political opinion. Although some applicants may not actually hold a particular political opinion, the homeland government or other persecuting entity (such as a paramilitary group or rebels) may attribute or impute a particular political opinion to the applicants because of their actions or inaction, situation in life, relatives, friends, or background. The theory is that when applicants establish a well-founded fear of persecution because of the persecutor's belief about their views or loyalties, the applicants' actual political conduct, be it silence or affirmative advocacy, and their actual political views, be they neutrality or partisanship, are irrelevant. Whatever the circumstances, the persecution should properly be categorized as being on account of political opinion. Although this theory has been accepted in some decisions, it appears contrary to the restrictive position of the **Board of Immigration Appeals,** which requires applicants to actually possess a belief or characteristic that the persecutor seeks to overcome by punishment. But even under the board's restrictive position, applicants do not bear the unreasonable burden of establishing the exact motivation of a persecutor when different reasons for actions are possible. [see *Matter of Acosta; Matter of Fuentes,* Int. Dec. No. 3065 (BIA 1988); *Hernandez-Ortiz v. INS,* 777 F.2d 509 (9th Cir. 1985)]

IN RE DE BELLIS   In this case [493 F. Supp. 534 (E.D. Pa. 1980)] a Jehovah's Witness who was seeking **naturalization** was denied citizenship because of issues over the oath of allegiance. De Bellis had agreed to take the modified oath regarding "work of national importance" only if the work was not a substitute for military service. Furthermore, she testified that she would make the determination of whether the work was a substitute for military service and was willing to obey only those laws consonant with her religious beliefs. The federal district court denied the petition because she would not take the modified oath "freely without any mental reservation." In contrast, in *In re Naturalization of Del Olmo* [682 F. Supp. 489 (D. Or. 1988)], a statement by a Jehovah's Witness that he would do work of national importance only if he could do it in good conscience did not disqualify him for naturalization.

IN RE ROLDAN In this decision [Int. Dec. No. 3377 (BIA 1999)], the **Board of Immigration Appeals** (BIA) decided that the **expungement** of a crime, where a state rehabilitative statute purports to erase the record of guilt, does not erase the conviction for purposes of **removal.**

Mauro Roldan was an adult native and citizen of Mexico who pleaded guilty to possession of more than three ounces of marijuana, a felony under Idaho law. The state court withheld adjudication of judgment, sentenced him to three years' probation, and imposed several monetary penalties. The terms of his probation included restrictions forbidding Roldan to use alcohol or to associate with any individuals not approved by the probation officer. Roldan was also subject to search of his residence, vehicles, and person at his probation officer's request. The court also ordered that Roldan serve ninety days' confinement at the discretion of the probation officer.

While removal proceedings were pending, Roldan made a motion in state court for early release from probation and dismissal of the charge in accordance with the withheld judgment. The motion was granted, and the court allowed the guilty plea to be vacated pursuant to state law. In spite of this process, the BIA ruled that this was still a conviction for deportation purposes under its decision in *Matter of Ozkok,* and statutory changes following that decision. [8 U.S.C. 1101(a)(48)(A)]

Although this case involved narcotics, the BIA decided to go further in this case to announce its disapproval of recognizing expungements to escape immigration consequences for crimes involving non-narcotics violations as well. The BIA felt that changes in the law made by Congress in the **Illegal Immigration Reform and Immigrant Responsibility Act of 1996** made it clear that it was not to look to various state rehabilitative statutes to determine whether a conviction exists for immigration purposes.

> Congress clearly does not intend that there be different immigration consequences accorded to criminals fortunate enough to violate the law in a state where rehabilitation is achieved through the expungement of records evidencing what would otherwise be considered a conviction under [the law], rather than in a state where the procedure achieves the same objective simply through deferral of judgment. . . .

If we were to continue to give effect to state expungements, we would be forced to examine the vagaries of each state's statute to determine if the original determination of guilt survived for some purposes, or whether it was a complete expungement. We do not believe that Congress intends for the existence of a "conviction" to depend on whether or not an individual state would give continuing effect to the original determination of guilt for such purposes as approval or revocation of business or professional licenses, weapons permits, etc. . . . The result of such an approach would be different treatment, based solely on where the offense occurred, of aliens guilty of the same misconduct.

The BIA's decision was limited to circumstances where an alien has been the beneficiary of a state rehabilitative statute that purports to erase the record of guilt. It does not address the situation where the alien has had his or her conviction vacated by a state court on direct appeal, wherein the court determines that vacation of the conviction is warranted on the merits, or on grounds relating to a violation of a fundamental statutory or constitutional right in the underlying criminal proceedings.

In re X—P—T—   Legislation in 1996 amended the definition of **refugee** to specifically provide that a person who has been forced to abort a pregnancy or to undergo involuntary sterilization, or who has been persecuted for resistance to coercive population control programs, is deemed to have been persecuted on account of **political opinion,** and to have a **well-founded fear of persecution.** The applicant, a native of the People's Republic of China, presented credible testimony and documentary evidence that she and her husband violated the "one couple, one child" population control policy of China by having three children, and that as a result, she was forcibly sterilized. Accordingly, the **Board of Immigration Appeals** granted asylum. [Int. Dec. No. 3299 (BIA 1996)]

INADMISSIBILITY GROUNDS   Although a **visa** may be available to aliens under one of the **immigrant** or **nonimmigrant** categories, the prospective entrant may still be denied the visa or denied admission into the United States if one of the grounds of inadmissibility is violated. Dozens of categories and subcategories of inadmissible aliens are included in the law—ranging from physical or mental disability grounds to those relating to crimes and terrorism. The grounds of inadmissibility were formerly referred to as exclusion grounds.

Examples of grounds of inadmissibility include aliens with communicable diseases (e.g., tuberculosis, venereal diseases, HIV), those who are likely to become a **public charge** (usually those below 125 percent of the **poverty guidelines**), those who have not met the **vaccination requirement,** those convicted of a **crime involving moral turpitude** or narcotics offenses [see **controlled substance exclusion**], those who made **entry without inspection,** those who by fraud or willful **material misrepresentation** have sought a **visa** or other immigration benefit, those who have made a false claim to U.S. citizenship to obtain an immigration benefit, those who were guilty of **unlawful presence** in the United States for at least one year and who have departed, and those who have committed **document fraud.**

Under certain conditions a **waiver of inadmissibility** is available for some grounds of inadmissibility, clearing the way for immigration.

INDEPENDENT CONTRACTOR   Under **employer sanctions** laws, an employer can be penalized for hiring **unauthorized aliens** and for failing to satisfy Form I-9 paperwork requirements [see **I-9 process** and Appendix]. However, no verification is required of an independent contractor who is contracted to perform work. Thus an employer may wish to avoid presenting or reviewing documents by characterizing a worker performing services as an independent contractor rather than an employee. The idea is that persons who have their own business and hire out their services are not considered employees.

Simply declaring a new hire an independent contractor is not sufficient to waive the requirement for completing and retaining a Form I-9. The worker must in fact be an independent contractor in order to be classified as such. Therefore, employers have to understand the technical difference between an employee and an independent contractor. The INS interprets the guidelines for distinguishing independent contractors from employees more strictly than does the Internal Revenue Service. That is, an independent contractor for federal tax purposes (e.g., whose wages are reported on Form 1099) in fact may be considered an employee for employment eligibility verification purposes by INS.

INS regulations define *employee* as any person who provides services or labor for an employer for wages or other remuneration. Although, in most cases, an individual whose wages are subject to income taxes, social security, Medicare, and unemployment taxes will be considered an employee, the actual determination is not always so simple.

The key factor is the amount of control reserved for the employer over the worker. In a relationship where the employer has the right to control the where, when, and how of performing services, an employment rather than contractual relationship will generally be found under IRCA. Also, if an independent contractor has workers who help him or her, the independent contractor is responsible for completing an I-9 for each of his or her own employees.

A number of factors are weighed in determining whether a person is an employee rather than an independent contractor. This is important, because the I-9 process does not apply when the employer retains an independent contractor. One single factor may not be determinative, but the following factors are relevant to finding that an employer-employee relationship exists:

- The employer has right to control how work results are achieved (when, where, how, etc.), and the person receives a level of supervision and direction received by other employees.
- The employer trains the individual to perform the work.
- The individual's services are integrated into the employer's business operations.
- The individual renders services to the employer personally.
- The employer hires, fires, and pays other employees who work with and/or assist the individual.
- The individual has a continuing relationship with the employer, even though at recurring, irregular intervals.
- The employer establishes hours of work.
- The employer requires the individual to work full-time.
- The individual works on the employer's premises or at a location designated by the employer.
- The employer prescribes the order or sequence of the individual's duties.
- The individual is required to submit reports to the employer.
- The individual is paid by hour, week, month, etc., rather than by the job or on commission.
- The individual's business and travel expenses are paid or reimbursed by the employer.
- The employer furnishes tools, equipment, materials, etc. required to do the work.
- The individual has no significant investment in facilities or equipment used to perform services.
- The individual is not subject to profit or losses from services rendered to the employer.
- The individual is not free to perform services for more than one unrelated employer at the same time.

- The individual's services are not generally available to the public except through the employer.
- The individual's services can be terminated by the employer.
- The individual can terminate his/her employment for the employer without regard for breach of contract.

INSPECTION   The procedure that is used by an INS officer at a **port of entry** to determine whether an alien is admissible to the United States [see **inadmissibility grounds**]. The port of entry can be along the border, at an entry point where ships arrive, or at an airport. Even an airport such as one located in Denver, Colorado, may be regarded as a port of entry for inspection purposes if it is the first place that an airplane from abroad arrives. At some airports abroad, such as in Canada and the Bahamas, passengers are inspected by U.S. INS officers prior to departure to the United States. The inspection by the INS officer can include questioning the alien, questioning traveling companions, examining travel documents, and even examining the contents of baggage to determine whether the person is entitled to enter.

Inspection is important for a variety of reasons. **Entry without inspection** renders the person inadmissible and subject to **removal** from the country. An alien who enters without inspection is also not eligible for basic **adjustment of status** in the United States to **lawful permanent resident alien** status, even if the person subsequently qualifies for immigrant status in one of the lawful immigration categories. Such a person would have to process an application for an immigrant visa abroad.

Only aliens are subject to INS inspection. Although U.S. citizens are technically not subject to INS inspection, if a U.S. citizen does not have proof of citizenship at the time of attempted admission at the port of entry, the INS has the right to demand such proof, and a major delay in the citizen's admission can follow. Since only aliens are subject to inspection, an alien who is admitted using a false claim to U.S. citizenship is not regarded to have entered with inspection. [*Reid v. INS*, 420 U.S. 619 (1975)]

Every year thousands of aliens claiming to have valid **nonimmigrant visas** are turned away by INS inspectors at the ports of entry—even at airports. Generally this occurs when INS inspectors suspect that the visas are fraudulent and confront the bearer with the suspicions, and the persons decide to turn around rather than pursue a claim to admission. If an alien with questionable documents insists on pursuing admission, or if the INS inspector is simply not ready to make an admission determination based on what has been presented at the port of entry, the alien can be referred to a **secondary inspection** area at the port of entry. If an immediate decision cannot be made, but it appears that a determination as to admissibility can be made within two weeks, the person can be paroled into the United States for secondary inspection at a local INS office. At that point, the matter is given greater attention in a different setting away from the port of entry.

The names of many aliens who have previously been in the United States, but who, for example, have undergone **removal** for serious offenses, may appear in the INS or the Visa Office's "lookout book." The posting of lookouts is limited to the names of those who are outside the United States, are prima facie inadmissible, and are likely to seek admission to the United States. The INS lookout book is now computerized and updated regularly.

INTERNATIONAL RESCUE COMMITTEE The International Rescue Committee (IRC) was established by Albert Einstein in 1933 to help opponents of Adolf Hitler escape Nazi Germany. Since that time, the IRC has helped victims of racial, religious, and ethnic persecution, as well as people uprooted by war, violence, and famine worldwide. Today, it is the largest private nonsectarian **refugee** resettlement and relief agency in the United States. With an international headquarters in New York City, the IRC operates twenty-seven overseas and sixteen domestic offices. The IRC currently provides emergency relief to refugees in twenty countries, helps to resettle refugees in the United States, advocates for the rights of refugees under U.S. and international law, and informs the U.S. public and policy makers about refugee issues.

In the field of humanitarian assistance, the IRC is widely recognized for its flexibility, innovation, leadership, and courage. It is also known for its cost-effectiveness, consistently spending more than 92 percent of its revenues directly on program services. In its 1995 Guide to Giving, *U.S. News and World Report* selected the IRC as one of only five "Standout Good Guys."

The IRC operates two major program components: emergency relief and assistance overseas, and resettlement assistance to refugees entering the United States. While most U.S. refugee resettlement agencies have strong religious or ethnic affiliations, the IRC serves refugees from any country and any religious background. Its resettlement offices in the United States resettle more than 10,000 refugees each year who have been legally admitted to the United States.

The IRC provides the following services to newly arriving refugees:

• temporary financial assistance
• cultural orientation
• help in locating housing
• classes in English as a second language
• help in securing social security cards

- job search and placement
- information and referral regarding health, education, and social services
- immigration assistance

The IRC currently employs 120 full- and part-time staff in its U.S. resettlement offices. Staff are representative of the refugee population served and in many instances are refugees themselves. They currently include native speakers of English, Russian, Arabic, Amharic, Somali, French, Chinese, Vietnamese, Lao, Polish, Farsi, and Serbo-Croatian. Resettlement services are geared toward enabling refugees to become self-sufficient as soon as possible.

INTERNATIONAL UNION OF BRICKLAYERS AND ALLIED CRAFTSMEN V. MEESE A California corporation, Homestake Mining Company of California, began construction of a project in order to open a new gold mine. Due to problems in the region, Homestake concluded that it was necessary to employ technology not used previously in the gold mining industry. Its construction manager agreed to purchase a newly designed gold ore processing system from the West German manufacturing company Didier. The purchase agreement was make contingent upon Didier's West German employees' completing the work on the system at the California project site. Didier submitted B-1 **business visitor** petitions on behalf of ten of its West German employees to come to the United States to complete the work. Relying on an INS **operations instruction** that allowed business visitor visas for those "coming to install, service, or repair commercial or industrial equipment or machinery purchased from a company outside the U.S.," U.S. consular officials approved the petitions. However, the plaintiff unions brought this action [616 F. Supp. 1387 (N.D. Cal. 1985)], arguing that the practice of issuing business visitor visas under these circumstances violated the language in the immigration laws that prohibits the issuance of business visitor visas for those coming to perform "skilled or unskilled labor." The federal district court agreed, and ruled that the particular operations instruction was inconsistent with the immigration laws, and could not be followed. The visas issued had to be canceled. [8 U.S.C. §1101(a)(15)(b)]

INTRACOMPANY TRANSFEREE The intracompany transferee **nonimmigrant** classification (L-1) was added in 1970 to facilitate the transfer of personnel of multinational corporations. This category is important for large companies and international businesspersons.

It is a common visa for foreign businesspersons who are opening an affiliate or subsidiary company in the United States. The intracompany transferee visa has no educational requirements.

The L-1 intracompany transferee is an alien who (1) within the three years preceding the time of application for admission to the United States has worked for a company continuously for one year in a managerial or executive position or a position requiring specialized knowledge, and (2) will be entering the United States to work for that same company, its affiliate, or its subsidiary in a similar position. The L-1 nonimmigrant who is a manager or executive can remain in the United States for up to seven years; an intracompany transferee with specialized knowledge can remain for five years.

A managerial employee is one who manages the enterprise or a recognized department, regularly directs the work of other employees, has the authority to hire and fire other employees, and customarily and regularly exercises discretionary powers. An executive employee performs nonmanual work related to management policies or business operations, exercises independent judgment and discretion, and makes final decisions and executes special assignments under only general supervision. Applicants who claim specialized knowledge will qualify if they have either specialized knowledge of the company product and its application in international markets or an advanced level of knowledge of processes and procedures of the company. [8 U.S.C. §§1101(a)(15)(L), 1184(c)(2)]

INVESTOR VISA The immigration laws provide for two different types of investor visas: one for **nonimmigrants** (which does not lead to **lawful permanent resident alien** status), and the other for **immigrant**s. The nonimmigrant investor visa is often referred to as an *E-2 treaty investor,* and is for those who are entering the United States solely to develop and direct the operations of an enterprise in which they have invested or is in the process of investing a substantial amount of capital. The law does not define "substantial" in monetary terms, but the rules provide that a "substantial amount of capital" constitutes an amount that is: (1) substantial in the proportional sense (i.e., in relation to the total cost of either purchasing an established enterprise or creating the type of enterprise under consideration); (2) sufficient to ensure the treaty investor's financial commitment to the successful operation of the enterprise; and (3) of a magnitude to support the likelihood that the treaty investor will successfully develop and direct the enterprise. In general, the lower the cost of the enterprise, the higher, proportionately, the investment must be in order to be considered a substantial amount of capital. [8 C.F.R. §214.2(e)(14), 22 C.F.R. §41.51(n)]

In order to qualify for a nonimmigrant treaty investor visa, the person must be a **national** of a country with which the United States has a treaty or agreement related to commerce. Those countries include Argentina, Armenia, Austria, Bangladesh, Belgium, Bulgaria, Cameroon, China, Colombia, the Congo, Costa Rica, the Czech Republic, Ecuador, Egypt, Estonia, Georgia, Grenada, Jamaica, Kazakhstan, Korea, Kyrgyzstan, Latvia, Liberia, Luxembourg, Moldova, Mongolia, Morocco, the Netherlands, Nicaragua, Norway, Pakistan, Panama, Poland, Romania, Senegal, Slovakia, Sri Lanka, Thailand, Togo, Trinidad and Tobago, Tunisia, Turkey, the United Kingdom, Ukraine, Vietnam, Yugoslavia, and Zaire. Treaty investor visas are renewable as long as the person maintains the terms of admission. [8 U.S.C. §1101(a)(15)(E)]

The immigrant investor category, sometimes referred to as the "employment creation" category, is for those immigrants seeking to enter for the purpose of engaging in a new commercial enterprise. The statute requires that the investment be at least $1 million, although the amount may be adjusted down to a low of $500,000 if the enterprise is located in a rural area or any area that has experienced high unemployment of at least 150 percent of the national average. The enterprise must create ten new jobs for citizens and lawful residents of the United States. [8 U.S.C. §1153(b)(5)]

A **pilot investor program** has also been created to facilitate the issuance of investor visas in certain regions of the country.

J

🏛 *JANG MAN CHO v. INS*   This case [669 F.2d 936 (4th Cir. 1982)] illustrates the rule that a person issued an **alien employment certification** must enter the United States with the intent to work for the sponsoring employer. However, if things do not work out with that employer, the person can find other work and retain status as a **lawful permanent resident alien.**

Cho, age 37, was a native of Korea who entered the United States after being issued a labor certification (alien employment certification) authorizing employment as an auto body repairman for the Mt. Ranier Auto Body Shop in Mt. Ranier, Maryland. After his arrival, Cho went to the auto body shop. He had a conversation with an unidentified male who made it clear that he was not the owner. Cho asked if any jobs were open at the auto body shop, and he was told that none was available. Cho did not ask to speak to the owner, although he asked the unidentified male if he was the owner. The conversation was brief because Cho spoke little English and no interpreter was present. Cho left the shop and never returned or called to inquire further of the owner about a job. Cho did not meet the owner until five years later when he returned to the shop for a visit.

Cho did not seek other employment as an auto body repairman because two friends advised that he could not find a job as a mechanic or repairman until he learned to speak English well and had his own tools. About a month after his inquiry at the auto body shop, Cho obtained employment in a grocery store. Eventually he opened his own store and brought his family to the United States to join him. When he sought to be naturalized, his application generated an inquiry into the circumstances of his entry into the United States; the INS eventually attempted to remove him from the United States for never having worked at the auto repair shop.

The court of appeals ruled that to deport Cho, there must be a finding (1) that he entered the United States without the intent to take the certified job, or (2) that when he obtained the labor certification or visa for entry, or when he entered the United States, he fraudulently represented that he would take the certified job. The court intimated that at a new hearing, if

Cho came forward with additional evidence supporting his version of the story, the INS would be hard-pressed to establish his deportability.

JOAQUIN, LINTON (B. 1950) One of the top immigrant rights litigators in the country, Linton Joaquin is director of litigation at the **National Immigration Law Center** (NILC) in Los Angeles, where he has been a member of the staff since 1990. The NILC is a national support center that provides technical assistance to legal services and other nonprofit legal organizations serving low-income immigrants. It also conducts impact litigation, policy analysis, and training, and publishes legal reference materials concerning the areas of law that affect immigrants.

Joaquin has made enormous contributions to the field of immigrant and refugee rights. From 1984 to 1988, he was the founding executive director and directing attorney of the Central American Refugee Center (CARECEN) in Los Angeles. Responsible for the direction and promotion of the organization, from its beginnings as a purely volunteer organization to a staff of more than a dozen individuals. He led or participated in human rights delegations to El Salvador in 1980, 1984, 1986, 1989, and 1994, and to Honduras in 1985. He served on the Steering Committee of the **National Immigration Project of the National Lawyers Guild** (1981–1985); was the coordinator for the Los Angeles Mayor's Advisory Committee on Central American Refugees (1986–1990); and helped with the Americas' Watch Report, *Brutality Unchecked: Human Rights Abuses along the U.S. Border with Mexico* (1991). Joaquin has also worked as a staff attorney for the United Farm Workers of America and the AFL-CIO; as director of the People's Legal Clinic of the People's College of Law; and as staff attorney for the National Center for Immigrants' Rights.

Joaquin has served as lead or principal counsel in numerous class actions regarding the rights of immigrants, including *Walters v. Reno* [145 F.3d 1032 (9th Cir. 1998)], a nationwide permanent injunction of INS policies and practices in bringing civil **document fraud** cases; *Gorbach v. Reno* [No. C98–0278R (W.D. Wash.)], a nationwide permanent injunction of INS administrative denaturalization procedures; *Orantes-Hernandez v. Meese* [685 F. Supp. 1488 (C.D. Cal. 1988)], *aff'd. sub nom Orantes-Hernandez v. Thornburgh* [99 F.2d 549 (9th Cir. 1990)], a permanent injunction on behalf of a nationwide class of all Salvadorans detained by the INS; *Perez-Funez v. District Director* [619 F. Supp. 656 (C.D. Cal. 1985)], a permanent injunction on behalf of a nationwide class of all unaccompanied minors detained by INS; *Mendez v. Thornburgh* [No. CV 88–4995 TJH (C.D. Cal.)], a preliminary injunction on behalf of a class of all asylum applicants in the Los Angeles INS

District, issued in 1989; *El Rescate Legal Services, Inc. v. Executive Office of Immigration Review* [No. CV 88-1201 KN (C.D. Cal.)], a class action challenging policies and practices regarding interpretation in the immigration courts of Southern California; *Espindola v. INS* [No. CIV-S-92-1871 EJG/GGH (E.D. Cal.)], a nationwide permanent injunction enjoining the INS "green card" replacement program, issued May 1993; *Turcios v. Reno* [No. CV 94-5220 JSL (C.D. Cal.)], an action challenging INS failure to process work authorization requests in a timely fashion on behalf of a class of asylum applicants in Los Angeles; and *Maca-Alvarez v. INS* [No. CIV-S-1824 EJH/PAN (E.D. Cal.)], a nationwide class action challenging INS policies and practices regarding the adjudication of **family unity** applications. Joaquin received his J.D. from Boalt Hall, University of California at Berkeley, in 1976.

JOB SERVICE OFFICE   See **state employment office.**

JOHNSON, KEVIN (B. 1958)   Kevin R. Johnson, a law professor and associate dean at the University of California School of Law, Davis, California, is one of the most prolific immigration law scholars in the country, and one of the few who recognize the intersection of race with immigration policy and enforcement. His influential articles range from insightful analysis of provisions of the **Immigration and Nationality Act** to important essays on the impact of immigration laws and policies on racial identity, discrimination, and civil rights. Recent or forthcoming immigration-related books include *How Did You Get to Be Mexican?: A White/Brown Man's Search for Identity* (Temple University Press 1999); *Immigration and Citizenship Law and Policy for the Twenty-first Century: A Modern Approach* (LEXIS Law Publishing 2000), coauthored with Bill Piatt, Janet Calvo, and George A. Martinez; and *Perspectives on Race and the Law: A Multiracial Approach* (Carolina Academic Press 2000), coauthored with Timothy Davis and George A. Martinez. In addition to his scholarship, Johnson has been an active litigator. His cases include *American Immigration Lawyers Association v. Reno* [18 F. Supp. 2d 38 (1998)], a challenge to the lawfulness of changes to immigration laws expediting the removal of asylum applications from the country; *Barapind v. Rogers* [1997 U.S. App. LEXIS 11532 (9th Cir. May 15, 1997)], which reversed the denial of an asylum claim by a Sikh applicant; *Ceballos-Castillo v. INS* [904 F.2d 519 (9th Cir. 1990)], a challenge to the denial of asylum claims by Guatemalan applicants based on adverse credibility findings; and *Committee of Central American Refugees v. INS* [807 F.2d 769 (9th Cir. 1987)], challenging the lawfulness of the INS policy of transferring asylum applicants for detention in remote locations where it was virtually impossible for them to secure legal representation. He has also filed "friend of the court" briefs in Supreme Court cases such as *Immigration and Naturalization Service v. Elias-Zacarias* [502 U.S. 478 (1992)], where he argued that deference to the agency's denial of asylum to a Guatemalan teenager was unwarranted; *Immigration and Naturalization Service v. Doherty* [502 U.S. 314 (1992)], contending that the attorney general could not permissibly consider foreign policy in denying the asylum claim of a former Provisional Irish Republican Army member; and *Immigration and Naturalization Service v. Elramly* [518 U.S. 1051 (1996)], seeking Supreme Court review in a case involving the deportation of an alien convicted of a crime.

Professor Johnson began his legal career in 1984 as an associate with the San Francisco law firm of Heller, Ehrman, White & McAuliffe, and volunteered at the Pro Bono Asylum Project of the San Francisco Lawyers' Committee for Civil Rights. He began his teaching career in 1989. Johnson has served as a board member or advisory committee member of a number of organizations including the Coordinating Committee on Immigration Law of the American Bar Association, Legal Services of Northern California, American Civil Liberties Union of Yolo County, and the Milton L. Schwartz American Inn of Court. He graduated magna cum laude from Harvard Law School in 1983, where he was articles editor of the *Harvard Law Review.*

JUDICIAL REVIEW Judicial review is the process whereby a federal court, such as the federal district court, the federal court of appeals, or the U.S. Supreme Court, reviews an administrative decision of the INS or of the **Executive Office of Immigration Review** (EOIR). In recent years, Congress has attempted to narrow the types of administrative decisions that can be reviewed by federal courts. In general, review of removal orders by the EOIR's **Board of Immigration Appeals** is considered by the federal court of appeals. However, the **Illegal Immigration Reform and Immigrant Responsibility Act of 1996** (IIRAIRA) eliminated or limited the courts from hearing cases in several different areas: persons in **expedited removal proceedings** do not get judicial review, except in limited circumstances (e.g., **asylum** claims), persons with certain criminal offenses, denials of **voluntary departure,** certain waivers, and bond and detention issues. [8 U.S.C. §1252]

🏛 JUS SANGUINIS
The two most common principles of **acquisition of citizenship** at birth are **jus soli,** which confers citizenship or nationality based on the place (land or ground) where the individual was born, and jus sanguinis, which confers citizenship based on descent (through blood). With some exceptions, the United States follows the jus soli concept, but also follows the jus sanguinis rule to a certain extent.

Under certain conditions, a person can acquire U.S. citizenship at birth even though the birth place is outside the United States. The basis for such a citizenship claim is generally one of transmission from a parent who is a U.S. citizen. The rules have changed many times. For a person born outside the United States after 1952, if both parents were U.S. citizens at the time, and one of the parents had a residence in the United States, the person is automatically a U.S. citizen at birth. If the child had one parent who was an alien and one who was a U.S. citizen, transmission of citizenship could occur if the citizen parent was physically present in the United States or outlying possession for a total of five years prior to the child's birth. At least two of the five years must have been accrued after attaining the age of 14. Different requirements apply if the child was born out of wedlock. [8 U.S.C. §§1401, 1408, 1409]

🏛 JUS SOLI
The two most common principles of **acquisition of citizenship** at birth are jus soli, which confers citizenship or nationality based on the place (land or ground) where the individual was born, and **jus sanguinis,** which confers citizenship based on descent (through blood). With some exceptions, the United States follows the jus soli concept, but also follows the jus sanguinis rule to a certain extent.

The Fourteenth Amendment to the U.S. Constitution provides, in pertinent part, that "all persons born or naturalized in the United States, and subject to the jurisdiction thereof, are citizens of the United States and of the State wherein they reside." This means that, in general, all persons born in the United States, even of alien parents, acquire U.S. citizenship. This interpretation has been followed since the Supreme Court's decision in *United States v. Wong Kim Ark.* Because foreign diplomats are not subject to the jurisdiction of the United States, their children born here do not acquire citizenship. Their children are treated as **lawful permanent resident alien**s. [8 U.S.C. §1401(a); 8 C.F.R. §101.3(a)(1)]

In addition to the fifty states and the District of Columbia, persons born in Puerto Rico, the Virgin Islands, and Guam are citizens of the United States at birth. Birth in the United States includes birth in its ports, harbors, bays, and a marginal belt of the sea extending three miles from the coastline. [8 U.S.C. §1403]

K

KESSELBRENNER, DAN (B. 1953) Dan Kesselbrenner has been the executive director of the **National Immigration Project of the National Lawyers Guild** since 1986. In that capacity, he has become a national expert on the intersection of immigration law and criminal law and all aspects of deportation defense.

Kesselbrenner's accomplishments are varied. He was a member of the legal team in *American Baptist Churches v. Thornburgh*, which affected the lives of thousands of Central American refugees in the United States, and is the coauthor of *Immigration Law and Crimes*, a comprehensive and highly regarded publication on the subject. He has lectured throughout the country, helping to train hundreds of pro bono attorneys and community-based organization paralegals. In 1993, he was a member of the Department of Justice Cluster for President Bill Clinton's transition team.

Kesselbrenner was the corecipient of the American Immigration Lawyers Association's Jack Wasserman Award for Litigation in 1991, and was also awarded the National Immigration Project's Carol King Award. Prior to assuming his current position, he was the codirector of Centro Presente in Boston, where he acted as liaison to state departments, human rights groups, and other Central American refugee centers, while training and supervising a staff of fifty.

KNOW-NOTHING PARTY Organized in the 1850s, this secretive political organization was formed to push for the exclusion of all foreign-born citizens from office, to discourage immigration, and to "keep America pure." The organization also demanded a twenty-one-year **naturalization** period. On the East Coast it fought against Irish Catholic immigration, while on the West Coast the target was usually the Chinese. Members fostered the attitude that these immigrants were subversive influences, and induced the federal government to pass restrictive regulations governing the entry of foreign workers. If asked about the members or program of the party, which eventually adopted the name American Party, its members were instructed to answer, "I know nothing about it." A

183

division within the party over the question of slavery, and the voluntary enlistment of hundreds of thousands of immigrants (principally on the East Coast) into the Union armies during the Civil War, led to the demise of the Know-Nothings in the 1860s.

KWOH, STEWART (B. 1948) Stewart Kwoh is the president and executive director of the **Asian Pacific American Legal Center** of Southern California (APALC). He is a preeminent national civil rights activist who has devoted much of his energy to the rights of immigrants, and a builder of bridges between people of diverse racial backgrounds. Under Kwoh's leadership, the APALC has become the largest and most diverse legal assistance and civil rights organization targeting Asian Pacific Americans in the United States. APALC provides services for over 15,000 individuals per year, ranging from those seeking U.S. citizenship to others seeking relief from domestic violence or cutoffs of government benefits. APALC has represented victims of hate violence and exploitation from sweatshops, including the workers who were enslaved in El Monte, California, for several years. APALC has pioneered the development of programs, coalitions, and projects that build bridges with other racial groups. He is also vice-chair of the board of directors for the **National Asian Pacific American Legal Consortium** (NAPALC), the country's first national pan-Asian civil rights organization.

After the civil unrest in Los Angeles in 1992, Kwoh helped to initiate the Multicultural Collaborative, a committee of eleven minority organizations dedicated to developing a comprehensive plan for human relations improvements in Los Angeles. He also assisted the development of the joint dispute resolution program between the Martin Luther King Dispute Resolution Center and the Asian Pacific American Dispute Resolution Center. This program attempts to resolve interethnic conflicts by teaming African American, Korean American, and other mediators. Finally, APALC has partnered with the Southern Christian Leadership Conference and the Central American Resource Center to develop the Leadership Development in Interethnic Relations (LDIR) program, which has trained hundreds of participants in skills to improve human relations. The core of the program is a six-month voluntary training and work experience project that brings thirty participants together at one time.

In recognition of his dedication and achievements, Kwoh was named a MacArthur Foundation fellow in 1998. He is the first Asian American attorney and human rights activist to receive this highly prestigious "genius award." His other honors include the Mayor's Award, Los Angeles City Human Relations Commission, 1996; an honorary doctor of law degree from Williams College in 1996; the President's Award from the Southern Christian Leadership Conference of Greater Los Angeles and the Martin Luther King Legacy Association (King Week Festival) in 1994; the Faith and Freedom Award from the University Religious Conference at the University of California, Los Angeles, in 1993; the CORO Public Affairs Award in 1993; the Asian Pacific Heritage Month Award in 1993; the American Civil Liberties Union Award in 1993; the Professional Award from the Los Angeles County Human Relations Commission in 1992; and the "Individual Award" from the Public Counsel in 1991.

Currently, Kwoh is a board member of the City of Los Angeles Charter Reform Commission, El Pueblo Historical Monument Authority Commissioners, the Southern California Association for Philanthropy, and a member of the Council on Foreign Relations. He is an active member of AT&T's Consumer Advisory Panel. He is a trustee of the Methodist Urban Foundation, California Consumer Protection Foundation, the California Endowment, and the California Wellness Foundation. Kwoh received his J.D. from University of California, Los Angeles, Law School.

L

 LABOR CERTIFICATION See alien employment certification.

 LABOR CONDITION APPLICATION The **H-1B worker** category for **nonimmigrant** specialty occupation workers is very popular among employers seeking to hire recent college graduates who are aliens. To gain approval for the H-1B visa, the employer must file a labor condition application (LCA) with the **Department of Labor** stating: (1) that the employer is offering the prevailing wage for the occupation; (2) that the working conditions are such that they will not adversely affect those of workers similarly employed; (3) that there is not a strike or lockout in the course of a labor dispute in the occupation at the place of employment; (4) that the employer has given notice of the H-1B application to the bargaining representative of the employer's employees in the occupational classification or, if none, has posted notice of filing in conspicuous locations at the place of employment; and (5) the number of workers sought, the occupational classifications, and wage rates and conditions under which they will be employed. Employers of H-1B nonimmigrant workers are required to retain and make available for public inspection LCAs filed for the workers. The employer must retain LCAs at either the principal place of business or the place of employment.

 LAU V. NICHOLS Although this case [414 U.S. 563 (1974)] is often regarded as providing bilingual education rights to immigrant children, the Supreme Court in fact did not order bilingual education strategies, but sought to ensure that Chinese immigrant children were afforded equal educational opportunities.

In 1971, a federal district court in San Francisco, California, found that there were 2,856 students of Chinese ancestry in the San Francisco school system who did not speak English. Of those, about 1,000 were given supplemental courses in the English language, but about 1,800 did not receive

187

that instruction. This case was a class action on behalf of the non-English-speaking Chinese students seeking relief from the unequal educational opportunities; no specific remedy was urged by the plaintiffs. Teaching English to the students who did not speak the language was one choice; giving instructions to this group in Chinese was another; and there may have been others.

Under state-imposed standards for graduation from high school, the Supreme Court found that there was no equality of treatment merely by providing students with the same facilities, textbooks, teachers, and curriculum; students who did not understand English were effectively foreclosed from any meaningful education. The Court noted:

> Basic English skills are at the very core of what these public schools teach. Imposition of a requirement that, before a child can effectively participate in the educational program, he must already have acquired these basic skills is to make a mockery of public education. We know that those who do not understand English are certain to find the classroom experiences wholly incomprehensible and in no way meaningful....
>
> It seems obvious that the Chinese-speaking minority receive fewer benefits than the English-speaking majority from respondents' school system which denies them a meaningful opportunity to participate in the educational program—all the earmarks of the discrimination banned by the regulations. [Federal regulations require:] "Where inability to speak and understand the English language excludes national origin–minority group children from effective participation in the educational program offered by the school district, the district must take affirmative steps to rectify the language deficiency in order to open its instructional program to these students."

As a result, the court remanded the case to lower officials to fashion an appropriate remedy.

LAWFUL PERMANENT RESIDENT ALIEN   A lawful permanent resident alien is a person who has immigrated lawfully to the United States, generally as an **immediate relative** of a U.S. citizen or through the **preference system.** The terms *lawful permanent resident, permanent resident, lawful resident, resident alien, green card holder, immigrant,* and *LPR* are often used to describe persons in this category. A lawful permanent resident alien is issued an **alien registration receipt card** (Form I-551), often referred to as a *green card.* These cards, which were once green colored, are actually of a pink tinge and labeled "Permanent Resident Card."

Lawful permanent residents are subject to the **removal** and inadmissibility provisions of the immigration laws [see **deportation grounds** and **inadmissibility grounds**]. They do not have the right to vote, to file immigration applications for certain relatives, or to hold federal civil service jobs or certain state public function jobs; nor do they have full First Amendment rights. Lawful permanent resident aliens must have the intent to reside in the United States permanently. See *Foley v. Connelie.*

LAWFUL TEMPORARY RESIDENT   Under the legalization (**amnesty**) provisions of the **Immigration Reform and Control Act of 1986,** a person who qualified first became a lawful temporary resident. After a qualifying period of time (eighteen months for general legalization, and one or two years under the agricultural worker program), the temporary resident could then apply for lawful permanent resident status. [8 U.S.C. §§1160, 1255a]

LAWYERS' COMMITTEE FOR CIVIL RIGHTS UNDER LAW OF TEXAS, IMMIGRANT AND REFUGEE RIGHTS PROJECT
The Lawyers' Committee for Civil Rights under Law of Texas, Immigrant and Refugee Rights Project, known as the Lawyers' Committee, is the only statewide nonprofit project in Texas dedicated solely to defending the civil and constitutional rights of lawful immigrants and refugees. In recent years, the Lawyers' Committee has:

- secured a monetary settlement for a 13-year-old girl, a legal permanent resident, who was pulled naked from the shower by a male Border Patrol agent after he illegally entered her home without a warrant or consent
- successfully co-counseled a class action against the U.S. Department of Education over a policy that denied financial aid to students lawfully present in the United States pursuant to family unity applications
- defended a community where legal permanent residents and other lawful immigrants were randomly detained and questioned about their citizenship status by local police, in violation of their Fourth Amendment rights, not because they were suspected of criminal activity but simply because they appeared Mexican
- co-counseled a class action that resulted in asylum applicants receiving the work authorization that they were entitled to under the law
- represented seventeen high school students and faculty in a class action against the INS and Border Patrol where the judge held that "the

INS has repeatedly and illegally stopped, questioned, detained, frisked, arrested, and searched ... students from the Bowie High School District. El Paso Border Patrol agents have subjected [community members] to indecent comments, obscene gestures, and humiliation in the presence of their coworkers, friends, family, and relevant community." [*Murillo v. Musegades*, 809 F. Supp. 487 (W.D. Tex. 1992)]

- sued the INS over a policy that illegally prevented refugees, all of whom have been admitted to the United States because of persecution in their home countries, from bringing their spouses and minor children to join them in the United States
- filed amicus briefs in cases in the U.S. Supreme Court, the Fifth Circuit Court of Appeals, and the Board of Immigration Appeals, each of which involved significant constitutional or statutory rights of legal permanent residents
- negotiated a monetary settlement for a legal permanent resident after Border Patrol agents illegally jailed him with his children and threatened to rape his 13-year-old stepdaughter
- sued the INS and local law enforcement officials for indiscriminate, reckless immigration operations resulting in the unlawful arrest and detention of U.S. citizens, legal permanent residents, and their children
- represented U.S. citizens who have been wrongfully arrested, jailed, and even "deported" by INS or Border Patrol agents, simply because they are Latin in appearance
- sued the INS and the Social Security Administration over both agencies' failure to provide work authorization to foreign-born U.S. citizens while their applications for a certificate of citizenship were pending
- educated thousands of immigrants who are lawful residents of Texas about their rights under the Constitution and laws of the United States
- assisted dozens of pro bono and nonprofit attorneys around the state with cases involving immigrants and refugees

While still continuing to address Border Patrol and INS abuse, the Lawyers' Committee has expanded its litigation to address other issues identified as compelling by community organizations throughout Texas. Thus, for example, the Lawyers' Committee sued the city of Katy, Texas, to prevent police officers from stopping individuals solely because they appeared Latin and questioning them about citizenship. In a far-reaching settlement, the city agreed that its police officers have no authority to question individuals about their immigration status when there is no suspicion of criminal activity.

The Lawyers' Committee also filed a suit to protect the constitutional right to work of foreign-born citizens who acquired their citizenship through a parent. The committee sued the INS and the Department of State on behalf of refugees whose spouses and children cannot join them in the United States due to a misapplication of the law. The INS changed its policy as the result of this suit, and notified all refugees whose family reunification petitions were previously denied of the refugees' right to file new petitions.

The need for nonlitigation advocacy and education on behalf of immigrants is also tremendous and is a second major focus of the Lawyers' Committee's work. Each year, the Lawyers' Committee speaks with over 1,000 immigrants in conjunction with approximately thirty "Know Your Rights" seminars held in immigrant communities in Texas that have little or no access to legal services. In San Antonio, the Lawyers' Committee spearheaded a coalition of individuals and organizations interested in defending the rights of immigrants and Latinos. This group successfully convinced the city council to pass resolutions in opposition to both California's **Proposition 187** and **English-only movement,** and in support of affirmative action. The same coalition, with the support of the Lawyers' Committee's Community Outreach Coordinator, began a citizenship education project that has provided information on the process to over 1,000 individuals. This project has been expanded to include outreach and education on the impact of the new welfare bill.

Finally, the Lawyers' Committee addresses the great need for immigration legal services in Texas by providing supportive services to the staff of the state's many nonprofit organizations that represent immigrants, as well as to the numerous private attorneys who handle the cases of low-income immigrants on a pro bono basis. The committee provides counsel and advice in response to their immigration questions on a daily basis, organizes training in various aspects of immigration law, and cocounsels significant cases with them.

LEGALIZATION   See **amnesty; Immigration Reform and Control Act of 1986.**

LEGITIMATED CHILD   As a general rule, children born out of wedlock (e.g., illegitimate children) cannot obtain any benefits of the immigration laws of the United States. In order to qualify for such benefits—especially through a U.S. citizen father—the child has to be legitimated. See **child.**

▥ *LENNON V. INS*   In this case [527 F.2d 187 (2d Cir. 1975)], the court of appeals was called upon to decide whether former Beatles star John Lennon was inadmissible [see **inadmissibility grounds**] to the United States because of a 1968 British conviction for possession of cannabis resin (a marijuana derivative). The court held that the conviction should not bar his immigration to the United States.

On October 18, 1968, detectives from the Scotland Yard drug squad conducted a warrantless search of Lennon's apartment in London. There, the officers found one-half ounce of hashish inside a binocular case and thereupon placed Lennon under arrest. Lennon pleaded guilty to possession of cannabis resin in court on November 28, 1968, and paid a small fine.

On August 13, 1971, Lennon and his wife Yoko Ono arrived in New York. They had come to this country to seek custody of Ono's daughter by a previous marriage to a U.S. citizen. In the opinion of immigration officials, Lennon's British conviction made him inadmissible under an existing exclusion ground that applied to one who had been convicted of any law relating to the illicit possession of marijuana. However, the officials allowed Lennon to enter, granting him a waiver for a temporary visa.

The day after his visa expired, immigration officials informed Lennon that he had to leave or face deportation proceedings. A few days later, Lennon filed permanent immigration applications based on his musical talents. In response, the INS instituted deportation proceedings, initially ignoring Lennon's immigration application. Eventually, while the INS acknowledged Lennon's artistic standing, the government argued that he was inadmissible because of the British conviction. The **immigration judge** agreed with the INS, and ordered Lennon deported. The **Board of Immigration Appeals** affirmed the deportation order.

The Court of Appeals reversed the administrative decisions and ruled in Lennon's favor based on a strict reading of the immigration laws and the exact nature of Lennon's British conviction. The court felt that since the immigration laws referred to a conviction for the "illicit" possession of marijuana, this meant that a person had to have "knowledge" of the substance in possession in order to fall under the immigration prohibition. However, the British law that Lennon was convicted under made guilty knowledge irrelevant. A person found with tablets that he or she reasonably believed were aspirin would be convicted if the tablets proved to contain heroin. Thus, the British statute under which Lennon was convicted was not specific enough to trigger exclusion or deportation under U.S. immigration laws.

The court closed its majority opinion on a philosophical tone:

> The excludable aliens statute is but an exception, albeit necessary, to the traditional tolerance of a nation founded and built by immigrants.

If, in our two hundred years of independence, we have in some measure realized our ideals, it is in large part because we have always found a place for those committed to the spirit of liberty and willing to help implement it. Lennon's four-year battle to remain in our country is testimony to his faith in this American dream.

 **LITTLE, CHERYL (B. 1947)**   Since 1996, Cheryl Little has been the executive director of the Florida Immigrant Advocacy Center, a legal agency that protects and promotes the basic human rights of immigrants of all nationalities. From 1992 to 1995, she was a staff attorney with Florida Rural Legal Services, and was the staff and supervising attorney for the Haitian Refugee Center in Miami from 1985 to 1992. During her career, she has distinguished herself as one of the nation's leading advocates of the rights of Haitian refugees. She has been so effective in her work that she has been called one of the "six most unstoppable women under the sun" by *South Florida Magazine.*

Little has served as co-counsel in several major class-action lawsuits filed on behalf of refugees and immigrants. She coordinated efforts among various agencies assisting Haitian refugees held in the Guantanamo Bay detention camp, served as chair of the **American Immigration Lawyers Association**'s Haitian Task Force, and served as co-counsel in a class-action lawsuit to ensure that detainees at the Krome Detention Facility had meaningful access to lawyers and legal assistance. Reports written by Little about the treatment of Haitian refugees held at Krome and Guantanamo Bay led to the release of children from these camps. She also produced and hosted two cable television series, "South Florida's Immigrants: Hope for the Future" and "Immigration and Beyond." She has testified before many governmental entities, including Congress and the U.S. Commission on Civil Rights.

Little has received awards and recognition from the Dade County Commission on the Status of Women, the University of Miami School of Law, the Organization of Chinese Americans, ABC Television, the American Civil Liberties Union, Amnesty International, the American Immigration Lawyers Association, the Haitian Refugee Center, the Association of Haitian Educators of Dade County, and the Young Lawyers Division of the Florida Bar; she also received the Mickey Leland Award for Service to Refugees. She has authored dozens of articles and publications on immigrants and refugees. Little received her J.D. with honors from the University of Miami School of Law in 1985.

LOOKOUT BOOK   See inspection.

LOTTERY PROGRAM   See diversity visas.

LUTHERAN IMMIGRATION AND REFUGEE SERVICE

Lutherans have a long-standing history in the United States as an immigrant church that has actively cared for newcomers, a tradition dating from the eighteenth century. The Lutheran Immigration and Refugee Service (LIRS), the U.S. Lutheran Church's agency for service to uprooted people, was organized in 1939 to resettle refugees fleeing from the Nazis. Since then, LIRS has become a broad multiservice and advocacy agency that addresses the needs and rights of uprooted people at local, regional, national, and international levels. LIRS provides technical assistance to Lutheran church bodies and thirteen affiliate offices that provide direct services to uprooted people. These affiliates, all recognized by the Board of Immigration Appeals, offer a variety of services, such as naturalization, family visa petitions, and religious worker petitions. Thus, LIRS helps uprooted people by strengthening service providers rather than by providing direct services itself.

The LIRS Asylum Concerns Program seeks to uphold the basic rights and dignity of vulnerable immigrant populations—particularly those who are fleeing persecution in their home countries. This program, the only one of its kind nationwide, offers grants and technical assistance to local asylum and immigration projects, and advocates at a national level for immigrant rights and access to services.

The goals of LIRS include the following:

- to uphold safety, freedom, and human rights; to work in the best interests of those served, and to treat people with dignity, compassion, and respect
- to mobilize action on behalf of uprooted people; to see that they receive fair and equal treatment, regardless of national origin, race, religion, culture, or legal status
- to speak out for just and humane solutions to migration crises and their root causes, both national and international; to work with Lutherans and others to turn solutions into reality; and to encourage citizens to take part in shaping just and fair public policies, practices, and laws
- to reconnect uprooted people with society; to foster healing, economic independence, and realization of new potential
- to build community between newcomers and more established neighbors, believing that everyone holds a key to each other's revitalization, enrichment, and growth as world citizens

- to provide cost-effective, quality service and advocacy while seeking creative and durable solutions to the challenges faced

LYDON, SUSAN M. (B. 1955) Susan M. Lydon is one of the nation's leading immigration experts on asylum, appeals, procedural due process, arrest, detention, and practice issues. She is the assistant director of the **Immigrant Legal Resource Center** (ILRC) in San Francisco. As coordinator of the ILRC's National Immigration Paralegal Training Program, she has overseen the training of more than 3,000 immigration paralegals of nonprofit organizations across the country, thereby improving the delivery of legal services to poor and working-class immigrants and their relatives.

Lydon has also been involved in critical cases before the U.S. Supreme Court. She was co-counsel in *Immigration and Naturalization Service v. Cardoza-Fonseca* [480 U.S. 421 (1987)], a precedent-setting case setting the standard of proof in asylum cases at a more generous level, and *INS v. Pangilinan* [486 U.S. 875], a challenge to the denial of citizenship opportunities for Filipino World War II veterans that eventually led to favorable congressional action. She also helped to direct the litigation and write a friend of the court brief in *United States v. Mendoza-Lopez* [481 U.S. 828 (1987)], establishing that one can collaterally attack in a criminal proceeding an underlying deportation order entered in violation of due process. Lydon's representation of incarcerated refugees from Fujian Province, China, who reached the United States on ships earned the ILRC a share of the **American Immigration Lawyers Association** Human Rights Award in 1994.

Lydon is the primary editor of most publications of the ILRC. The major publications include *A Guide for Immigration Advocates* and its corresponding *Trainer's Manual,* which are comprehensive manuals for advocates on immigration law and practice; *Legalization: The Advocate's Guide to the New Immigration Law* and the subsequent *Legalization Phase II,* which were the seminal reference books on the law and procedure of the amnesty provisions of the **Immigration Reform and Control Act of 1986**; and *Immigrant Advocates' News,* a quarterly publication by the ILRC for the staff of community-based immigrant service organizations on professional issues and updates on immigration law and procedure.

Besides her impact on thousands of immigrant rights paralegals, Lydon has taught scores of law students in immigration and refugee courses at Golden Gate University School of Law, New College of California School of Law, and Stanford Law School. Lydon received her J.D. with high honors from Boalt Hall School of Law, University of California at Berkeley, in 1983.

M

MARIEL BOATLIFT   This began as a small-boat exodus of several thousand Cubans who were welcomed in the United States as **refugee**s from the regime of Fidel Castro in 1980. After President Jimmy Carter offered an "open arms" welcome to the initial group, the numbers swelled to 125,000, including individuals that Castro had released from Cuba's prisons and mental institutions. Americans became increasingly upset at the numbers. Some 2,500 criminals and mental patients were estimated to fall within this group. All of the refugees were called "Marielitos" for the Mariel port of Cuba from which most were launched to sea.

Initially, the exodus was called a "freedom flotilla," but it was downgraded to "boatlift" when criminals and others that Castro called "misfits" turned up among the masses of refugees. Many of the refugees were forced to leave spouses and children behind. Many who were criminals or who have become criminals have been held in detention for many years. Others have been subjected to racial discrimination because they are black.

Cubans who entered as part of the Mariel boatlift differ in many ways from the two waves of Cuban exiles who came to the United States in the 1950s and 1960s. In the first wave, 1959–1962, 200,000 Cubans came in an organized airlift. More than 90 percent were white, middle-aged, and well-educated. They had benefited from the system that preceded the Castro government and have established themselves in the social, business, and political life in the United States. For the most part they came in family units.

In the second wave, 1965–1970, 270,000 Cubans arrived, first by boat then in a more organized airlift. They were also mostly white, but 24 percent were black or mulatto. These were largely educated tradespeople, most of whom came with their families.

In the case of the Mariel refugees, the large majority were blue-collar workers, less educated, and mostly younger males. They had a higher level of divorce than those before them. About 20 percent were not allowed to bring their families, and 20,000 males were separated from their wives. Most of the Mariel refugees spoke only Spanish, and about half were black.

 MARIJUANA EXCLUSION   See **controlled substance exclusion.**

 MARRIAGE OF CONVENIENCE   See **sham marriage.**

MASSACHUSETTS IMMIGRANT AND REFUGEE AD-
VOCACY COALITION   The Massachusetts Immigrant and
Refugee Advocacy Coalition (MIRA) was established in 1987 after the passage of the **Immigration Reform and Control Act of 1986** in order to promote legalization among undocumented aliens who were eligible for
amnesty. MIRA is a broad-based network of community agencies, religious
groups, labor unions, human service organization, legal service providers,
and immigrant rights activists committed to protecting the rights and welfare
of immigrant and refugee communities in Massachusetts. MIRA is dedicated
to making the Commonwealth of Massachusetts a safe and welcoming place
for newcomers of all races and backgrounds. Its work includes:

- *Advocacy.* MIRA organizes to promote fair and humane policies toward immigrants and refugees and to oppose efforts to restrict newcomers' eligibility for essential services and benefits.
- *Training.* MIRA conducts workshops for human service providers, newcomer community leaders, and others concerning access to public benefits, job discrimination, changes in immigration law, and other issues
  of importance to newcomers and the communities that receive them.
- *Empowerment.* Through legislative forums, leadership training, and
  encouraging civic involvement, MIRA is committed to expanding
  newcomers' participation in the decision-making processes that affect their lives.
- *Public education.* MIRA works to promote respect and appreciation of
  racial, ethnic, and cultural differences and to combat bias against immigrants and refugees in the media and the public sphere.
- *National policy.* A respected voice on issues of national policy, MIRA
  has testified before Congress about the impact of current immigration law and has played a central and vital role in several national
  policy debates on immigration.

MATERIAL MISREPRESENTATION   An **alien** who by fraud
or by willfully misrepresenting a material fact seeks to obtain (or
has sought to procure or has procured) a **visa,** other documentation, or

admission into the United States or other immigration benefit is inadmissible [see **inadmissibility grounds**]. The idea is that anyone who has obtained immigration benefits through fraud or misrepresentation should not be admitted into the United States.

The U.S. attorney general has suggested a three-prong method of determining the materiality of a misrepresentation in *Matter of S— & B— C—* [9 I. & N. Dec. 436 (A.G. 1961)]:

1. Does the record establish that the alien is excludable on the true facts? If it does, then the misrepresentation was material; the inquiry ends. If it does not, then the second and third questions must be considered.
2. Did the misrepresentation tend to shut off a line of inquiry that is relevant to the alien's eligibility? A misrepresentation as to identity or place of past residence, for example, would almost necessarily have shut off an opportunity to investigate part or all of the alien's past history, and thus have shut off a relevant investigation. However, remote, tenuous, or fanciful connection between a misrepresentation and a line of inquiry that is relevant to the alien's eligibility is insufficient to satisfy this aspect of the test of materiality.
3. If a relevant line of inquiry has been cut off, might that inquiry have resulted in a proper determination that the alien be excluded? On this aspect of the question the alien bears the burden of persuasion and proof. Having made a willful misrepresentation that tends to cut off a relevant line of investigation, he or she cannot now try out his eligibility as if nothing had happened. One who, by an intentional and wrongful act, has prevented or restricted an inquiry into relevant facts bears the burden of establishing the true facts and the risk that any uncertainties resulting from the person's own obstruction of the inquiry may be resolved unfavorably.

Any alien who makes a false claim to U.S. citizenship for any federal or state law purpose is also inadmissible. [8 U.S.C. §1182(a)(6)(C)(ii)]

MATTER OF ACOSTA   An **asylum** applicatnt argued that the persecution he feared at the hands of the guerrillas was on account of his **membership in a particular social group** comprised of COTAXI drivers (a union-type cooperative of cab drivers) and persons engaged in the transportation industry of El Salvador. In reviewing his case [19 I. & N. Dec. 211 (BIA 1985)], however, the **Board of Immigration Appeals** first interpreted the term *social group* to require that its members share immutable characteristics, and then found that being a member of the taxicab cooperative was not an immutable characteristic. The social group basis for asylum was, therefore, not available. The BIA's reasoning follows:

> We find the well-established doctrine of ejusdem generis, meaning literally, "of the same kind," to be most helpful in construing the phrase "membership in a particular social group." That doctrine holds that general words used in an enumeration with specific words should be construed in a manner consistent with the specific words. The other grounds of persecution in the [**Immigration and Nationality Act** and the **United Nationals Protocol Relating to the Status of Refugees**] listed in association with "membership in a particular social group" are persecution on account of "race," "religion," "nationality," and "political opinion." Each of these grounds describes persecution aimed at an immutable characteristic: a characteristic that either is beyond the power of an individual to change or is so fundamental to individual identity or conscience that it ought not be required to be changed. Thus, the other four grounds of persecution enumerated . . . restrict refugee status to individuals who are either unable by their own actions, or as a matter of conscience should not be required, to avoid persecution.
>
> Applying the doctrine of ejusdem generis, we interpret the phrase "persecution on account of membership in a particular social group" to mean persecution that is directed toward an individual who is a member of a group of persons all of whom share a common, immutable characteristic. The shared characteristic might be an innate one such as sex, color, or kinship ties, or in some circumstances it might be a shared past experience such as former military leadership or land ownership. The particular kind of group characteristic that will qualify under this construction remains to be determined on a case-by-case basis. However, whatever the common characteristic that defines the group, it must be one that the members of the group either cannot change, or should not be required to change because it is fundamental to their individual identities or consciences.
>
> . . .
>
> In [Acosta's] case, the facts demonstrate that the guerrillas sought to harm the members of COTAXI, along with members of other taxi cooperatives in the city of San Salvador, because they refused to participate in work stoppages in that city. The characteristics defining the group of which [Acosta] was a member and subjecting that group to punishment were being a taxi driver in San Salvador and refusing to participate in guerrilla-sponsored work stoppages. Neither of these characteristics is immutable because the members of the group could avoid the threats of the guerrillas either by changing jobs or by cooperating in work stoppages. It may be unfortunate that [Acosta] either would have had to change his means of earning a living or cooperate

with the guerrillas in order to avoid their threats. However, the internationally accepted concept of a refugee simply does not guarantee an individual a right to work in the job of his choice.

The BIA used this notion of social group to affirm asylum for an individual claiming persecution on account of sexual orientation. See *Matter of Toboso-Alfonso.*

MATTER OF CONTRERAS   The holding in this case [18 I. & N. Dec. 30 (BIA 1982)] is a good example of when a **lawful permanent resident alien** is considered to be seeking **admission** to the United States after a brief absence abroad. This is important because an alien seeking admission must satisfy the **inadmissibility grounds** on entering the country.

Contreras was an adult married male, a native and citizen of Mexico. He was admitted to the United States as a lawful permanent resident on October 18, 1978. On May 6, 1979, he left the United States and drove to Mexico, where he remained for three hours. He then attempted to reenter the United States with a man concealed in the back of his car, but the man was discovered at the border. After being advised of his rights, Contreras admitted to the immigration inspector that he had gone to Mexico to bring a man into the United States for a friend who was going to pay him $100. On May 7, 1979, Contreras was convicted of attempted **smuggling of aliens,** placed on probation for two years, and fined $150.

The INS subsequently pursued **removal proceedings** against Contreras on the grounds that under the grounds of exclusion (inadmissibility) in force at the time, any alien who "knowingly and for gain, encouraged, induced, assisted, abetted, or aided any alien to enter or to try to enter the United States in violation of law" was excludable. The **Board of Immigration Appeals** ruled that because of his smuggling actions, Contreras was attempting a new entry for admission purposes; his departure was not innocent, brief, and casual in nature [see *Rosenberg v. Fleuti*] even though he was absent for only three hours.

MATTER OF KANE   This case [15 I. & N. Dec. 258 (BIA 1975)] involves a person who was stripped of her **lawful permanent resident alien** status, because she was guilty of **abandonment of permanent residence** based on her extended absences from the United States.

Kane was a married female, 69 years of age, who was a native and citizen of Jamaica. She was lawfully admitted for permanent residence on

March 18, 1964. For two years thereafter, she lived with her husband in New York, then separated from him and moved to Florida. She departed from the United States during 1967. After that departure, she was absent from the United States for eleven months of each year, during which time she was living in Jamaica in an eight-room house that she owned and operated as a lodging house. She supported herself from the rents she received from the lodgers. She stated at her hearing that the purpose of her annual trips to the United States was to maintain her legal resident status in the United States and for rest. While here, she rented a furnished room in Florida by the week.

Kane's last attempt to return to the United States was on July 31, 1972, in possession of her **alien registration receipt card.** She was traveling on a 21-day excursion round-trip airplane ticket, originating from and returning to Jamaica.

The **Board of Immigration Appeals** ruled that in order to retain her status, Kane's visits abroad had to be temporary and there must not have been a change in her status. In fact, her status changed after her 1967 departure; her trips abroad were not for a specified purpose of limited duration. She was living in Jamaica indefinitely. She left some belongings in Florida, but that was not sufficient evidence of intent to reside here, especially since her accommodations in Florida were on a temporary basis. Therefore, she was deemed to have abandoned her residence, and her alien registration card was no longer valid.

MATTER OF MCKEE   This case [17 I. & N. Dec. 332 (BIA 1980)] was decided prior to the **Immigration Marriage Fraud Amendments** of 1986 that impose a two-year viability requirement on marriages before an alien spouse can benefit permanently from marrying a U.S. citizen or permanent resident. However, the case is still good precedent for the proposition that a marriage that was not a **sham marriage** at inception does not prevent the alien spouse from enjoying permanent residence after all conditions of the immigration laws have been satisfied.

A 24-year-old U.S. citizen married McKee, a 25-year-old from Australia, on August 12, 1977, in Florida. On October 12, 1977, the citizen filed a **visa petition** on McKee's behalf. But because the couple had separated, the **district director** denied the petition. He based his denial of the petition on the sole basis that the parties were not residing together. Yet there was no evidence that they had obtained a legal separation or had dissolved the marriage.

The **Board of Immigration Appeals** ruled that it was erroneous to deny the petition solely on the basis of the separation of the parties. There was no evidence that at the time of the marriage there was any fraudulent intent to evade immigration laws.

MATTER OF OZKOK In this case [19 I. & N. Dec. 546 (BIA 1988)], the **Board of Immigration Appeals** (BIA) established some guidance to determine what constitutes a conviction for immigration purposes—a concept that is important for determining both **inadmissibility grounds** and **deportation grounds.**

Ozkok was an immigrant from Turkey who pleaded guilty to unlawful possession with intent to distribute cocaine in the Circuit Court for Baltimore County, Maryland, on August 20, 1981. On October 23, 1981, the court stayed judgment and placed Ozkok on probation for three years. The judge further ordered Ozkok to perform 100 hours of volunteer community service and to pay a fine of $1,500 plus court costs. The question was whether this constituted a conviction of a narcotics violation [see **controlled substance exclusion**] for purposes of **removal.** In answering this question, the BIA had to grapple with the fact that criminal procedures and even legal terminology vary from state to state.

The BIA determined that as a general rule, a conviction will be found for immigration purposes where all of the following elements are present:

1. A judge or jury has found the alien guilty or he or she has entered a plea of guilty or nolo contendere or has admitted sufficient facts to warrant a finding of guilty.
2. The judge has ordered some form of punishment, penalty, or restraint on the person's liberty to be imposed (including but not limited to incarceration, probation, a fine or restitution, or community-based sanctions such as a rehabilitation program, a work-release or study-release program, revocation or suspension of a driver's license, deprivation of nonessential activities or privileges, or community service).
3. A judgment or adjudication of guilt may be entered if the person violates the terms of his or her probation or fails to comply with the requirements of the court's order, without availability of further proceedings regarding the person's guilt or innocence of the original charge.

Applying this standard to Ozkok's case, the BIA noted that the first two parts of the test were met because he entered a plea of guilty and the judge imposed several forms of punishment. The third requirement was also met because the state law gave the court authority to enter judgment automatically without further review of the question of guilt and proceed with disposition of the person upon violation of probation. Ozkok was thus deemed to have been convicted for immigration purposes.

In the **Illegal Immigration Reform and Immigrant Responsibility Act of 1996,** Congress decided that this definition did not go far enough toward achieving a uniform federal approach and provided a statutory definition of conviction. See *In re Roldan.* The law now provides:

> The term *conviction* means, with respect to an alien, a formal judgment of guilty of the alien entered by a court or, if adjudication of guilt has been withheld, where—
> (i) a judge or jury has found the alien guilty or the alien has entered a plea of guilty or nolo contendere or has admitted sufficient facts to warrant a finding of guilt, and
> (ii) the judge has ordered some form of punishment, penalty, or restraint on the alien's liberty to be imposed. [8 U.S.C. §1101(a)(48)(A)]

In this new definition, Congress apparently excised the third prong of *Ozkok,* eliminating the need to refer to the vagaries of the states' ameliorative statutes in order to determine if an alien has been convicted. The legislative history of this change underscores the breadth of the legal definition:

> Ozkok . . . does not go far enough to address situations where a judgment of guilt or imposition of sentence is suspended, conditioned upon the alien's future good behavior. . . . In some States, adjudication may be "deferred" upon a finding or confession of guilt, and a final judgment of guilt may not be imposed if the alien violates probation until there is an additional proceeding regarding the alien's guilt or innocence. In such cases, the third prong of the Ozkok decision prevents the original finding or confession of guilt to be considered a conviction for deportation purposes. This new provision, by removing the third prong of Ozkok, clarifies Congressional intent that even in cases where adjudication is "deferred," the original finding or confession of guilt is sufficient to establish a conviction for purposes of the immigration laws. [H.R. Conf. Rep. No. 104-828, at 224 (1996) ("Joint Explanatory Statement")]

🏛 *MATTER OF TOBOSO-ALFONSO*   Toboso-Alfonso asserted that as a homosexual he had been persecuted in Cuba and would be persecuted again on account of that status should he return to his homeland. He had been systematically harassed, frequently jailed, sent to a forced labor camp, and threatened with long imprisonment because he was gay. In this case [20 I. & N. Dec. 819 (BIA 1990)], he successfully argued that homosexuals have **membership in a particular social group** in Cuba and suffer persecution by the government as a result of that status.

Toboso-Alfonso's testimony described an office in the Cuban government that registers and maintains files on all homosexuals. His file was opened in 1967, and every two or three months for thirteen years he received a notice to appear for a hearing. Each hearing consisted of a physical examination followed by questions concerning his sex life and sexual partners. On many occasions he would be detained in the police station for three or four days without being charged and for no apparent reason. On one occasion when he had missed work, he was sent to a forced labor camp for sixty days as punishment because he was a homosexual. During the **Mariel boatlift,** homosexuals were given the option of spending four years in the penitentiary for being a homosexual or leaving Cuba for the United States. He was given a week to make a decision, and decided to leave rather than be jailed. The day he left his town, the neighbors threw eggs and tomatoes at him.

The INS opposed Toboso-Alfonso's claim, arguing that "socially deviated behavior, i.e., homosexual activity is not a basis for finding a social group within the contemplation" of the law and that such a conclusion "would be tantamount to awarding discretionary relief to those involved in behavior that is not only socially deviant in nature, but in violation of the laws or regulations of the country as well."

The **Board of Immigratioon Appeals** was not moved by the government's arguments because the INS had not challenged the **immigration judge**'s finding that homosexuality is an "immutable" characteristic. Nor was there any evidence that once registered by the Cuban government as a homosexual, this characterization is subject to change.

Even before this decision, an immigration judge granted asylum to a Brazilian man on the basis that as a homosexual he was a member of a persecuted social group. The judge agreed that "homosexuality is an immutable characteristic, and that even if homosexuality were a voluntary condition, it is one so fundamental to a person's identity that a claimant ought not to be compelled to change it." Other asylum requests have been filed with U.S. officials by gay applicants from China, Romania, Colombia, Peru, Nicaragua, and Pakistan. At least nine other countries have recognized gays as members of a social group for asylum purposes: Australia, Austria, Canada, Denmark, Finland, Germany, the Netherlands, New Zealand, and Sweden.

 **MCCARRAN-WALTER ACT OF 1952**   The McCarran-Walter Act of 1952 is often labeled the basic immigration law in

effect today, but in truth, most of its provisions have been amended over the years. Certainly, it was the first comprehensive, single-statute **Immigration and Nationality Act**. It established three principles for immigration policy: (1) the reunification of families, (2) the protection of the domestic labor force, and (3) the immigration of persons with needed skills. Based on visa allocations, the family reunification concept was valued the most. However, the concept of the **national origins quota system** was retained, as well as unrestricted immigration from the Western Hemisphere. An important provision of the statute removed the bar to immigration and citizenship for races that had been denied those privileges prior to that time. Asian countries, nevertheless, were still discriminated against, for prospective immigrants whose ancestry was one-half of any Far Eastern race were chargeable to minimal quotas for that nation, regardless of the birth place of the immigrant.

Although the act abolished the 1917 act's **Asiatic barred zone,** the law created a new restrictive zone—the Asia-Pacific triangle—that consisted of countries from India to Japan and all Pacific islands north of Australia and New Zealand. A maximum of 2,000 Asians from this triangle were allowed to immigrate annually. Small quotas were set for each of the nineteen countries in the region.

MEISSNER, DORIS (B. 1942) Doris Meissner is the **commissioner** of the **Immigration and Naturalization Service.** She was appointed to the post by President Bill Clinton in 1993, after years of government experience in the immigration area as well as a stint with a policy think tank. From 1977 to 1980 during the Jimmy Carter administration, she served as deputy associate attorney general with the **Department of Justice,** holding line authority over the INS. She was the acting INS commissioner during the Ronald Reagan administration from 1981 to 1982, and was the executive associate commissioner of the INS from 1983 to 1986. From 1986 to 1993, Meissner was a senior associate and director of the Immigration Policy Project at the Carnegie Endowment for International Peace. Before she became commissioner, she authored numerous articles on a wide variety of immigration issues and testified before Congress on many legislative proposals, always noting that immigration is a complex issue that must be addressed with a view to the economic development of countries and general migration patterns.

Since becoming commissioner, Meissner has concentrated on beefing up enforcement along the Mexican border, implementing a streamlined **naturalization** process (which drew criticism from many quarters for being too lax), and restructuring the INS to improve customer service and make enforcement efforts more efficient and responsive to public needs. Combined with the high positions she held in the Carter and Reagan administrations, Meissner has probably had more influence on INS administrative policies than any other single individual over the past two decades.

Meissner is a founding member of the National Women's Political Caucus, and served as its executive director in 1971. She began her series of policy positions as a White House fellow at the Justice Department in 1973. Upon her nomination by President Clinton in 1993, she stated:

> The movement of people is emerging as one of the critical global issues that we face in a new age. I am proud to be able to return to the agency that plays such a key role in responding to the dilemmas we must anticipate and in carrying out this country's continuing commitment to our immigrant heritage. . . .
>
> And I want to pay special tribute to my parents, who are no longer with us. Both [German] immigrants, they taught me to cherish this country for the promise it represents and for the opportunity it gives to strangers. In the service I now have the chance to give, I pledge to preserve their faith in America by making it real for succeeding generations of immigrants.

MEJIA-CARRILLO V. INS   This case [656 F.2d 520 (9th Cir. 1981)] illustrates that separation of family is a critical factor in determining **extreme hardship** for various remedies under the immigration law.

Rosa Mejia-Carrillo was a forty-six-year-old woman from Mexico who had made **entry without inspection.** She had a fifth-grade education and worked as a maid for $75 a week. She lived with two young children, also undocumented aliens, and her seventeen-year-old son Juan, a **lawful permanent resident alien** who came to the United States at the age of thirteen. Juan was a high school senior at the time of the hearing. Mejia-Carrillo also had another son and daughter who were lawful permanent residents and six grandchildren who were U.S. citizens, all living in the United States. Her ex-husband, Juan's father, was also a lawful permanent resident of the United States.

At her hearing, Mejia-Carrillo testified that she would face unemployment or underemployment in Mexico, and that she could not support her two young children without Juan's help. She said she wanted Juan to remain in the United States to finish his education. Juan testified that he wanted to finish school and become a U.S. citizen. He also said that he would return to Mexico if his mother asked him, even though it would mean separation from his father, whom he visited often, and jeopardize his status due to **abandonment of permanent residence** issues.

In considering whether or not Mejia-Carrillo would face extreme hardship if forced to return to Mexico, the court of appeals noted that personal and emotional hardships that would result have to be considered. Included among these are the personal hardships that flow naturally from an economic loss—decreased health care, educational opportunities, and general material welfare. The most important single factor may be the separation of the alien from family living in the United States. Here, denial of the application would separate Mejia-Carrillo from relatives living in the United States. This would also place Juan in the worst of situations. If he remained in the United States, he would be separated from his mother, who depended upon him to help care for his young sisters. If he returned to Mexico to help his mother, he would be separated from his father, miss the chance to further his education, and possibly lose his permanent resident status. Taking all of these factors together, the court of appeals sent the matter back to the **Board of Immigration Appeals** for proper consideration.

MEMBERSHIP IN A PARTICULAR SOCIAL GROUP

One of the bases for obtaining **asylum** in the United States is **well-founded fear of persecution** on account of membership in a particular social group. A social group is a group of people who share or are defined by certain characteristics. Such characteristics might include gender, class background, family ties, shared past experience (e.g., former military leadership or residence in a refugee camp), and coming from a common geographic location.

The approach toward social group varies from court to court. For example, the **Board of Immigration Appeals** (BIA) uses a very narrow view of social group, requiring that the characteristics be immutable [see *Matter of Acosta*]. The *Handbook on Procedures and Criteria for Determining Refugee Status* of the **United Nations High Commissioner for Refugees** is a bit broader:

> 78. Membership of such a particular social group may be at the root of persecution because there is no confidence in the group's loyalty to the Government or because the political outlook, antecedents or economic activity of its members, or the very existence of the social group as such, is held to be an obstacle to the Government's policies.

Examples of decisions on social group cases are somewhat helpful.

- Members of a taxicab cooperative who refused to participate in a work stoppage called for by guerrillas were not considered a social group. [*Matter of Acosta*]

- Young males who feared being forcibly drafted into a guerrilla movement were not considered a social group. [*Sanchez-Trujillo v. INS*, 801 F.2d 1572 (9th Cir. 1986); *Immigragtion and Naturalization Service v. Elias-Zacarias*]
- Persecution on account of being gay was granted on a social group basis. [*Matter of Toboso-Alfonso*]
- An applicant was granted asylum based on membership in a particular social group because of the persecution he suffered based on his relationship with his brother. [*Gebremichael v. INS*, 10 F.3d 28 (1st Cir. 1993)]
- A young woman being forced to undergo female genital mutilation (FGM) was held by the BIA to be fleeing persecution on account of membership in the particular social group of "young women of the Tchamba-Kunsuntu Tribe who have not had FGM, as practiced by the tribe, and who oppose the practice." [*In re Kasinga*, Int. Dec. No. 3278 (BIA 1996)]

MEXICAN AMERICAN LEGAL DEFENSE AND EDUCATIONAL FUND
The Mexican American Legal Defense and Educational Fund (MALDEF) was founded in San Antonio, Texas, in 1968 in response to decades of discrimination and the violation of the civil rights of Mexican Americans. The organization was the fulfillment of the dream of many dedicated individuals who determined that the discriminatory treatment of Latinos should no longer be tolerated.

Today, MALDEF is a national nonprofit organization whose mission is to protect and promote the civil rights of the over 26 million Latinos living in the United States. It is particularly dedicated to securing such rights in employment, education, immigration, political access, language, and leadership development. The organization achieves its objectives through litigation, advocacy, community education, collaboration with other groups and individuals, and scholarship awards.

Throughout the years, MALDEF has been at the forefront of civil rights litigation, setting precedent in many cases and establishing new systems to elect officials, hire and promote employees, and educate children. On the nonlitigation side, MALDEF has worked extensively on the issues of redistricting and census adjustment. Through its leadership programs, MALDEF has empowered and trained Latinos to join boards of directors and commissions in their communities and parents to become advocates for their children's education.

Headquartered in Los Angeles, MALDEF has regional offices in Los Angeles, San Francisco, Chicago, and Washington, D.C., with a satellite office in Sacramento, California, and program offices in Fresno and Santa Ana, California; Detroit, Michigan; and El Paso, Texas.

MINISTERS OF RELIGION See special immigrant; fourth preference.

MISREPRESENTATION See material misrepresentation.

MOTION TO REOPEN After **removal** has been ordered or relief has been denied, it is possible to file a motion with the **immigration court,** or with the INS if the **district director** has made the decision, to reopen the proceedings or to request reconsideration of the decision. If the decision has been appealed to the **Board of Immigration Appeals** (BIA), it has jurisdiction over such motions. If granted, the applicant gets a new opportunity to present evidence and arguments for the relief or benefit sought. The filing of a motion to reopen or for reconsideration does not automatically delay deportation; a separate request for a **stay of removal** must be made if removal is pending. [8 C.F.R. §§3.2, 3.23]

A motion to reopen to apply for discretionary relief will not be granted if the relief was available to the client at the first hearing and its availability was fully explained to him or her by the **immigration judge.** The motion to reopen should therefore explain why the relief now sought was not initially addressed. However, because a motion to reopen can be granted in light of new evidence, a motion to reopen is in order when information not available at the first hearing has been obtained.

The Supreme Court ruled in *Immigration and Naturalization Service v. Rios-Pineda* [471 U.S. 444 (1985)] that a motion to reopen can be denied, regardless of a preliminary showing of eligibility for the relief, if the relief would have been denied as a matter of discretion anyway. The Court made it quite clear that the BIA has substantial discretion in denying a motion to reopen based on the failure to establish a basic showing of eligibility, or if the person waived the opportunity to apply for the desired relief at an earlier time.

MUÑOZ, CECILIA (B. 1962) Cecilia Muñoz is vice-president of the Office of Research, Advocacy and Legislation of the **National Council of La Raza** (NCLR). Located in Washington, D.C., she is one of the nation's most influential spokespersons on behalf of immigrant rights and has been a constant resource on immigration policy for many years. A recent example of her impact was her leadership role in convincing Congress to restore many of the rights to public benefits and food stamps for immigrants and refugees that had been taken away under welfare reform legislation in 1996.

Muñoz joined the NCLR staff in 1988 as senior immigration policy analyst. In her current role at NCLR she supervises all legislative activities conducted by policy staff, who cover a variety of issues of importance to Latinos, including civil rights, employment, poverty, farmworker issues, education, housing, and foreign policy. Muñoz is the NCLR's principal spokesperson on immigration policy, and has represented its views to the media, Congress, and policy makers in Washington. She has testified numerous times before Congress, and appears regularly in the Spanish- and English-language media. Her media credits include "The Today Show," "Good Morning America," "The Newshour with Jim Lehrer," Dateline NBC," "The McLaughlin Group," CNN, and National Public Radio.

Before coming to Washington, Muñoz directed the Legalization Outreach Program for Catholic Charities in the Archdiocese of Chicago, a program that operated twelve offices throughout the Chicago area and assisted over 5,000 immigrants in becoming legal residents during the one-year amnesty program enacted by Congress in the mid-1980s. She is the daughter of immigrants from Bolivia, and was born in Detroit, Michigan. She received her undergraduate degree from the University of Michigan in Ann Arbor, and her master's degree from the University of California at Berkeley.

MUSALO, KAREN (B. 1952) Karen Musalo is resident scholar at the Center for Human Rights and International Justice at Hastings College of the Law, where she directs the Expedited Removal Study and the Center for Women Refugees. She is a nationally recognized expert on refugee law, and litigated the landmark **asylum** decision in *In re Kasinga*, which established that a successful claim to asylum may be based upon fear of female genital mutilation. Her work in the Ninth Circuit Court of Appeals expanded the criteria in two important decisions: *Canas-Segovia v. INS* upheld imputed political opinion as a basis for asylum, and *Ramirez-Rivas v. INS* held that measures considered legitimate punishment by a foreign government may be considered political persecution worthy of asylum by the United States.

Musalo has worked tirelessly to educate judges about the effects of cultural differences and psychological stresses in asylum cases. As a staff attorney with the Father Moriarty Central American Refugee Program early in her career, she pioneered efforts to convince U.S. courts that international law standards of justice and fairness should be applied in U.S.

asylum claims. Musalo is the coauthor of the law school casebook *Refugee Law and Policy*, published by Carolina Academic Press.

In 1997, the *American Lawyer* recognized Musalo as one of the 45 outstanding young public-sector lawyers. She is also the recipient of the **Immigrant Legal Resource Center**'s Philip Burton Immigration and Civil Rights Award for Outstanding Lawyering (1997), the Political Asylum and Immigration Representation Project's Outstanding Achievement Award (1998), and the New York Central American Refugee Center's Annual Award for Dedication to the Struggle for Human Rights and in Defense of Immigrants (1998). She is also a consulting professor at Stanford Law School, teaching courses in immigration and refugee law. Musalo received her J.D. in 1981 from Boalt Hall, University of California at Berkeley.

N

NACARA The Nicaraguan Adjustment and Central American Relief Act of 1997 (NACARA) established two programs. The first allows certain Nicaraguans and Cubans in the United States to adjust their status to **lawful permanent resident alien.** The second gives certain Salvadorans, Guatemalans, and nationals of several former Soviet bloc and Eastern European nations the opportunity to apply for suspension of deportation.

Those Cubans and Nicaraguans who are physically present in the United States may adjust to lawful permanent residence if they have been physically present in the United States for a continuous period beginning not later than December 1, 1995, and file an application by April 1, 2000. In general, Guatemalans, Salvadorans, and Eastern bloc nations must meet more rigorous standards. They must have entered by 1990 and must have filed for **asylum** in 1990 or 1991. They must also demonstrate (1) continuous physical presence in the United States for seven years, (2) good moral character, (3) extreme hardship to themselves or to a child or parent who is a U.S. citizen or lawful permanent resident, and (4) facts that demonstrate that they are deserving of favorable discretion.

NARASAKI, KAREN (B. 1958) As the executive director of the **National Asian Pacific American Legal Consortium** (NAPALC), a nonprofit, nonpartisan organization, Karen Narasaki has become one of the most influential voices in immigration policy circles, advocating for fair and just treatment of immigrants in the United States and for immigration policies that remain fair to deserving refugees and prospective immigrants. Headquartered in Washington, D.C., the consortium's mission is to advance the legal and civil rights of Asian Pacific Americans through litigation, advocacy, public education, and public policy development. Narasaki also serves on the Executive Committee of the Leadership Conference on Civil Rights as the chairperson of its Compliance/Enforcement Committee, and is chairperson of the National Network against Anti-Asian Violence.

Before joining the consortium, Narasaki was the Washington, D.C., representative for the Japanese American Citizens League (JACL), the nation's largest membership-based Asian American civil rights organization. She directed JACL's national advocacy program. Prior to that she was a corporate attorney at Perkins Coie in Seattle, Washington. Before joining Perkins Coie, she served as a law clerk to Judge Harry Pregerson on the U.S. Court of Appeals for the Ninth Circuit in Los Angeles.

She currently serves on the board of the **National Immigration Law Center** and has served on the boards of the National Asian Pacific American Bar Association, the Asian Bar Association of Washington, the **Asian Pacific American Legal Center** of Southern California, and the Organization of Pan Asian American Women. She is a graduate, magna cum laude, of Yale University, and, Order of the Coif, of the University of California at Los Angeles School of Law.

Narasaki has appeared on ABC, CBS, PBS, and Fox news programs; "America with Dennis Wholey"; and several National Public Radio shows, including "Talk of the Nation" and "Powerpoint." She has also been quoted by the *New York Times*, the *Washington Post*, the *Wall Street Journal*, and *USA Today*, as well as numerous regional newspapers, including the *Chicago Tribune*, the *Houston Chronicle*, the *Seattle Post-Intelligencer*, and the *Los Angeles Times*.

 **NARCOTICS AND MARIJUANA EXCLUSION**   See con-trolled substance exclusion.

 **NARCOTICS TRAFFICKING**   See **controlled substance trafficking.**

 **NATIONAL**   A national of the United States is someone who owes permanent allegiance to the United States. The term includes citizens of the United States and certain noncitizen nationals of the United States. At present, the only noncitizen nationals of the United States are persons born in American Samoa or the Swains Islands. Since they are not aliens, nationals are not subject to inadmissibility or deportation provisions of the immigration laws. Noncitizen nationals also enjoy relaxed requirements for obtaining full citizenship through **naturalization.**

NATIONAL ASIAN PACIFIC AMERICAN LEGAL CONSORTIUM   The National Asian Pacific American Legal

Consortium (NAPALC) was founded in 1992 by its affiliates, the **Asian Law Caucus**, the **Asian Pacific American Legal Center**, and the **Asian American Legal Defense and Education Fund** (AALDEF). The NAPALC office opened in Washington, D.C., in 1994. By 1999, the staff in Washington had grown from two to ten persons and the annual budget had grown from $200,000 to $1,600,000. The consortium contracts with its affiliates, who provide over a dozen of their attorneys to work on various projects, cases, research, and policy development.

NAPALC also works closely with the National Asian Pacific American Bar Association and its forty-five affiliates. In addition, its Community Partners Network now has as members sixty-six Asian Pacific American community-based organizations from thirty-eight cities in twenty-three states.

NAPALC focuses its work in eight areas:

- *Affirmative action.* NAPALC continues its work in defending affirmative action policies at the state and federal levels, continuing its work with Americans for a Fair Chance (AFC), a coalition of six of America's leading civil rights organizations. AFC has produced several resource materials and organized conferences on affirmative action. In addition, NAPALC has assisted in fighting anti–affirmative action ballot initiative in Washington State and filed an amicus brief with AALDEF and other affiliates, in a case challenging Department of Defense affirmative action programs. The consortium continues to monitor affirmative action ballot initiatives and litigation, and filing or participating in amicus briefs where appropriate.

- *Anti-Asian violence.* NAPALC produces annual audits of anti-Asian violence in America. These audits receive national media coverage and have helped communities fight for tougher laws and enforcement. The consortium was a presenter at the 1997 White House Conference on Hate Crimes and has provided assistance to victims of anti-Asian violence and technical assistance to U.S. attorneys and the Federal Bureau of Investigation. The consortium also works on race relations issues and has participated in a series of meetings with the president and members of the Race Advisory Board on the President's Race Initiative project. Recently, NAPALC joined with other civil rights leaders to bring national and local attention to the issue of police brutality. Responding to the call, President Bill Clinton outlined a five-step plan to restore faith in law enforcement.

- *Census.* NAPALC has launched an education and outreach effort to inform Asian Pacific Americans about the year 2000 census. The efforts will include education guides, instructional videos, media kits, posters, and fliers. The consortium has also monitored legislation and policy issues surrounding the census—specifically, the tabulation of multiple race responses, the Census Bureau's plans to reach Asian Pacific American communities through an advertising campaign and language assistance, the issue of confidentiality of census responses, and the hiring of noncitizens. NAPALC supports the use of statistical sampling methods in the census and has advocated against the use of nonsampled data by states in the redistricting process.

- *Immigration.* NAPALC has been active in efforts to fight anti-immigrant measures and soften some of the harsh provisions of the 1996 immigration laws. It recently worked with local advocacy groups to end a county school board's practice of requiring documentation of citizenship and visa status from students and their parents. In response to the INS's failure to deliver adequate services to the Asian Pacific American community, NAPALC recently released a paper based on data collected from over forty community-based organizations. Geared toward members of Congress and administration officials, this policy paper lays out guiding principles to restructure the INS. The consortium continues to disseminate community education materials on the 1996 changes in the law and has completed coordination of a series of briefing papers on immigration-related concerns translated into eleven Asian languages.

- *Language rights.* NAPALC has continued to monitor legislation, on local and national levels, that seeks to limit the rights of immigrants to basic government services. It has focused on countering efforts to establish English-only laws and to end bilingual education [see **English-only movement**]. The consortium provided technical assistance to community organizations in Utah who successfully advocated against the passage of a restrictive English-only law. It has also recently developed an education handbook about English-only laws, entitled *The Politics of Language: Your Guide to English-only Laws and Policies.* On bilingual education, NAPALC advocated against a bill entitled "The English Fluency Act," which passed in the House of Representatives in 1998; the legislation would have reduced federal funding for language assistance programs and would have arbitrarily set time limits on learning English. NAPALC has also provided technical assistance to community groups in Arizona, where there is a move to place an anti–bilingual education initiative on the ballot. It is also monitoring efforts to reauthorize the Elementary and Secondary Education Act (ESEA), which provides federal funding for language assistance programs to limited-English-proficient children.

- *Naturalization.* NAPALC launched a citizenship education and training program in 1995 and completed it in early 1999. This program has provided training, technical assistance, and education materials (and Asian language translations) to over 1,000 community organizations and assistance to over 8,167 immigrants. The consortium has continued to work on regulations and legislative proposals to make the **naturalization** and citizenship process more accessible to immigrants.

- *Voting rights.* NAPALC continues to defend the rights of legal immigrants and citizens to participate in the political process. Last year, it advocated against legislation attached to the campaign finance reform bill that would have banned legal permanent residents from making campaign contributions, would have required voter verification and photo identification, and would have repealed the motor-voter law. The organization has also embarked on a redistricting project by organizing a training session of affiliate and consortium staff and developing a redistricting handbook that will aid Asian Pacific American communities interested in redistricting after the 2000 census.

- *Welfare reform.* In summer 1998, NAPALC led a national grassroots effort to restore food stamp eligibility to certain categories of legal immigrants. The consortium developed a food stamp outreach packet in eight different Asian languages to notify the community of the restoration, which became effective on November 1, 1998. NAPALC also worked with the media and policy makers to illustrate the continuing inhumane and unfair impact of the 1996 welfare law on Asian Pacific American families. The consortium also continues to provide legislative updates, technical assistance, and community education materials regarding immigrant eligibility for benefits.

NATIONAL ASSOCIATION OF LATINO ELECTED OFFICIALS EDUCATIONAL FUND

The National Association of Latino Elected Officials (NALEO) Educational Fund is the nation's leading organization devoted to empowering Latinos to participate fully in the American political process, from citizenship to public service. Since it was established in 1981, the NALEO Educational Fund has made numerous contributions to the political and social progress of the nation's 30 million Latinos.

- The NALEO Educational Fund pioneered the naturalization group processing model, which has been replicated by scores of organizations nationwide. Since 1987, the fund has directly helped more than 83,000 individuals to become U.S. citizens.
- The fund conducts leadership development seminars for candidates and newly elected officials nationwide. In 1998, the fund conducted

training seminars in the Midwest and Southern California for community leaders, candidates, and elected officials. The fund also held a national institute for newly elected officials in Washington, D.C., on November 19–22, 1998.

- The NALEO Educational Fund holds an annual conference in June that is the largest annual gathering of Latino elected and appointed officials. Over 600 participants attended the 15th Annual Conference held June 18–20, 1998, in Houston.
- The NALEO Educational Fund's Summer Legislative Internship Program provides leadership development opportunities for fourteen Latino college students. This program is designed to inspire young Latinos to pursue careers in public service, including elected and appointed office.
- In 1997, the NALEO Educational Fund established its newest initiative, Nuestra Comunidad/Our Community, a comprehensive community education effort to increase the civic participation of Latinos, with an emphasis on Latino youth and newly naturalized citizens.
- The fund publishes an annual directory of the nation's Latino elected officials. The 1998 edition lists 4,989 Latinos in elected office nationwide.
- The fund publishes analyses of the political and electoral behavior of Latinos, including an analysis of every general election held since 1982.
- The fund conducts periodic research on varying issues of importance to Latino community leaders. Most recently, it published groundbreaking research on the demographics and public policy needs of Dominicans and Colombians in New York, and Guatemalans and Salvadorans in Los Angeles.

The NALEO Educational Fund is headquartered in Los Angeles, and maintains project offices in Chicago, Houston, New York, and Washington, D.C. It has a full-time staff of twenty-nine and an annual budget of $2.2 million.

NATIONAL COUNCIL OF LA RAZA   The National Council of La Raza (NCLR) is a private, nonprofit, nonpartisan, tax-exempt organization established in 1968 to reduce poverty and discrimination and improve life opportunities for Hispanic Americans. Headquartered in Washington, D.C., NCLR has chosen to work toward this goal through two primary, complementary approaches:

- Capacity-building assistance to support and strengthen Hispanic community-based organizations. NCLR provides organizational assistance in management, governance, program operations, and re-source development to local Hispanic organizations in urban and rural areas nationwide, especially those that serve low-income and disadvantaged Hispanics.

* Applied research, policy analysis, and advocacy. NCLR provides a Hispanic perspective on issues such as education, immigration, housing, health, employment and training, and civil rights enforcement to increase policy maker and public understanding of Hispanic needs, and to encourage the adoption of programs and policies that equitably serve Hispanics.

NCLR strengthens these efforts with public information and media activities and special international projects. These include innovative projects, catalytic efforts, formation of and participation in coalitions, and other special activities that use the NCLR structure and credibility to create other entities or projects that are important to the Hispanic community, and can sometimes be "spun off' as independent entities.

NCLR is the largest constituency-based national Hispanic organization, serving all Hispanic nationality groups in all regions of the country. NCLR has over 220 formal affiliates who together serve 37 states, Puerto Rico, and the District of Columbia—and a broader network of more than 20,000 groups and individuals nationwide—reaching more than 3 million Hispanics annually. Capacity-building assistance to support and strengthen local Hispanic groups—provided from NCLR's Washington, D.C., headquarters and its field offices in Los Angeles, Phoenix, Chicago, and San Antonio—focuses on resource development, program operations, management, and governance. NCLR provides services not only to its own affiliates, but also to other local Hispanic organizations; NCLR welcomes affiliation from independent Hispanic groups that share NCLR's goals and self-help philosophy. NCLR also assists Hispanic groups that are not formal affiliates through issue networks on HIV/AIDS, health, elderly, education, leadership, and other issue areas.

NCLR's Policy Analysis Center is the preeminent Hispanic "think tank," serving as a voice for Hispanic Americans in Washington. The *Albuquerque Tribune* has called NCLR "the leading Hispanic think tank in the country," and the *Baltimore Sun* routinely refers to NCLR as "the principal" Latino advocacy group. Its unique capacity to provide timely policy analyses, combined with its considerable advocacy expertise, a reputation for political independence, and an identifiable constituency, permits NCLR to play an important role in policy and advocacy efforts. Its policy-related documents command extensive press and policy maker attention, and NCLR is consistently asked to testify and comment on public policy issues such as immigration and education, as well as other issues of broad concern, from free trade to affordable housing, health policy, and tax reform. The synergistic and complementary approach between NCLR's capacity-building efforts and its advocacy-related activities is exemplified by its Census Information Center, which serves as a clearinghouse on Hispanic Census data and other information, and has begun to establish local policy centers at six of its affiliated Hispanic community-based organizations.

NCLR has a strong and stable leadership. The NCLR's president, Raul Yzaguirre, has led the organization for 25 years, and is among the best-known and most respected national Hispanic leaders; he serves on the boards of such entities as the Enterprise Foundation, the National Democratic Institute, the National Hispanic Leadership Agenda, and the National Alliance of Business. He was founding chairperson of the National Neighborhood Coalition, and was the first minority chairperson of the Independent Sector. He served as chairperson of President Bill Clinton's Advisory Commission on Educational Excellence for Hispanic Americans, and is currently president of the Mexican and American Solidarity Foundation.

NCLR works closely with the private sector and has a broad base of financial support. NCLR's credibility in the corporate sector is demonstrated by its active Corporate Board of Advisors, which includes senior executives from twenty-five major corporations and their liaison staff, who provide ongoing consultation and assistance on efforts ranging from education and community health projects to visibility and fund-raising. NCLR maintains a diverse revenue base; the organization receives two-thirds of its funding from corporations and foundations, and the remaining from government sources.

NCLR believes in cooperation and collaboration. Staff members belong to many issue-focused coalitions and associations, cooperating with other nonprofit organizations and private-sector entities on issues ranging from welfare reform to energy. All of NCLR's national-emphasis projects, which sometimes include pass-through funding—health, housing and community development, employment and training, education, elderly issues, volunteer programs, and leadership—include efforts to educate mainstream organizations, public and private, about Hispanic needs and help them develop partnerships with Hispanic community-based organizations. NCLR also carries out joint projects with other organizations; it is a partner with the National Urban League Project PRISM (Partners for Reform in Science and Mathematics), a national education reform project funded by the Annenberg/CPB Project.

NCLR's major reports include the third in a series of statistical analyses on *Latino Education Status and Prospects;* a comprehensive analysis of the Immigration Reform and Control Act's objective-related performance, *Rac-*

ing toward Big Brother; an analysis of the performance of the Equal Employment Opportunity Commission (EEOC) in serving Hispanics, *The Empty Promise;* a statistical "snapshot" of the status of the Hispanic population, *State of Hispanic America: 1991;* a report assessing the burden and fairness of federal, state, and local taxes for Hispanics, *Burden or Relief?;* a major analysis of Hispanic health status, *Hispanic Health Status;* a report providing an empirical basis for comparing the magnitude of the effects of alternative antipoverty strategies on Hispanics, *State of Hispanic America 1993;* and a report documenting the negative portrayal of Hispanics in the media and entertainment industry, and its effects on Hispanic and non-Hispanic public opinion, *Out of the Picture: Hispanics in the Media.*

NCLR also publishes a quarterly newsletter, *Agenda.* NCLR's extensive series of policy reports and training modules are briefly described in its *Publications Guide.*

NATIONAL IMMIGRATION FORUM   Based in Washington, D.C., the National Immigration Forum is a leader in the national effort to secure fair, generous immigration and refugee policies and to solidify public support for America's tradition as a nation of immigrants. The forum fights for policies that reunite families, rescue refugees, encourage immigrants to become citizens, and ensure that newcomers receive equal treatment under the law. The forum stands up to the anti-immigrant forces by countering what it regards as myths and misinformation with data gleaned from empirical studies and available statistics. The forum attempts to share this information by educating the public and public officials through media and through its highly regarded, informative publications and studies.

The National Immigration Forum joins allies from across the political spectrum and from across the country in support of fair and sensible policies affecting immigrants and refugees. It is at the forefront of the fight to preserve the American tradition as a nation of immigrants and a beacon of hope for those fleeing persecution. It believes that giving immigrants and refugees the chance to build a better life for themselves and their families gives the entire nation the chance to build a better America for all residents and their children.

The forum believes that the country's ability to integrate its diversity with a unity based on shared democratic principles has made America the most successful nation in history. Indeed, the genius and dynamism of America stem from its heritage and from its promise, which has drawn people from every corner of the globe to make common cause in the pursuit of political freedom, economic prosperity, and social peace.

NATIONAL IMMIGRATION LAW CENTER For nearly twenty years, the National Immigration Law Center (NILC) has provided litigation and other technical assistance to legal aid offices, pro bono attorneys, and community groups throughout California and the United States. NILC's constituency has sought assistance regarding a complex set of issues on which NILC has developed expertise: the interplay between an immigrant's status and his or her right to fair treatment under U.S. laws, from the Constitution to a local welfare office regulation. NILC staff specialize in immigration law and immigrants' rights to public benefits and employment. NILC's purpose is to protect and promote the rights of low-income immigrants and their family members.

The office that eventually grew into NILC was started in 1977 as a small, local project of the Legal Aid Foundation of Los Angeles (LAFLA). In addition to assisting individual clients, the project initiated several precedent-setting national class-action lawsuits addressing aliens' due process rights, access to counsel, and eligibility for public benefits. As the project found itself increasingly called upon to help address these issues in other parts of the country, it sought formal permission from the Legal Services Corporation (LSC) to be established as a legal services national support center. In 1979, LSC granted the request, and the project began its work as the National Center for Immigrants' Rights. In the 1980s and early 1990s, NILC added public benefits and employment expertise to the issues covered by its staff, and opened a Washington, D.C., policy office in 1994.

The NILC remained administratively tied to LAFLA until 1995, when Congress eliminated funding for LSC national support centers. By October 1995, when NILC became independent, the organization had changed its name to the National Immigration Law Center, and had grown to nine staff persons in the Los Angeles office and one policy analyst in the D.C. office. NILC began the next phase of its history inauspiciously—in addition to the loss of federal funding, NILC faced a state and national political climate increasingly hostile to immigrants.

NILC survived the loss of LSC funding and emerged as a resilient organization that has taken the lead in identifying and addressing issues stemming from the historic changes to U.S. immigration and welfare laws enacted in 1996. In the late 1990s, NILC grew from ten to twenty employees. In addition to its Los Angeles headquarters and D.C. policy office, NILC maintains offices in Oakland and operates a Sacramento office for the California Immigrant Welfare Collaborative. As a national support center, NILC does not assist individual clients, but instead focuses on impact litigation, policy advocacy, and providing publications, technical assistance, and training.

In bringing its impact litigation, NILC co-counsels with legal aid agencies, civil rights groups, and immigrants' rights agencies. Historically,

NILC's impact litigation has involved protecting refugees and the right to due process, and protecting immigrants' access to public benefits. In 1998, NILC secured a nationwide preliminary injunction prohibiting the INS from initiating new procedures to take away a person's citizenship without due process protections (*Gorbach v. Reno*), and won a nationwide class-action challenge to INS procedures for alleging that immigrants had used false documents without giving them adequate opportunity to contest the allegations (*Walters v. Reno*). NILC has also worked closely with other California advocates in litigation to preserve prenatal care for immigrant women.

NILC employs two policy analysts in the Washington, D.C., office and one policy analyst working in Sacramento on behalf of the California Immigrant Welfare Collaborative. They develop analyses of proposed legislative and regulatory action and work with numerous community groups in coordinating organized responses to these proposals. They also meet with elected and other government officials and provide them with information from the perspective of low-income immigrants. At the national level, NILC's policy analysts were instrumental in the successful effort to roll back some of the welfare law cuts by restoring $12 billion in Supplemental Security Income (SSI) benefits and more than $800 million in food stamp benefits to legal immigrants.

Because the impact of the changes to welfare laws would be felt greatest by California's immigrant communities, in late 1996 NILC joined the **Asian Pacific American Legal Center, the Coalition for Humane Immigrant Rights of Los Angeles,** and the **Northern California Coalition for Immigrant Rights** to form the California Immigrant Welfare Collaborative (CIWC). CIWC works in three program areas—policy analysis and advocacy, technical assistance and training to service providers, and community education and outreach—to help immigrant communities plan coordinated responses to the changes in welfare law and policy. Since its inception, CIWC has helped to persuade California establish state-funded nutrition and cash assistance programs for immigrants losing food stamps and SSI, and to provide full Medicaid and Temporary Assistance for Needy Families (TANF) services with state funds to newly entering legal immigrants during their first five years in the United States.

In an average month, NILC staff answer almost 500 requests (or "field requests") for assistance from legal services, pro bono attorneys, staff at health clinics, and other community agencies, government officials, and the media. About half of these requests relate to general immigration law issues, such as eligibility for visa processing, defenses to deportation, and changes resulting from the **Illegal Immigration Reform and Immigrant Responsibility Act of 1996.** The other half of the requests deal with public benefits issues and immigrants' rights to employment.

NILC publishes several leading manuals that help nonprofit agency staff working on immigration, employment, and public benefits issues. In addition, NILC produces the *Immigrants' Rights Update,* a newsletter published eight times a year that reports on current developments in immigration law, employment issues, and public benefits. Since 1997, NILC has been publishing *CIWC– California Update,* a companion to the *Immigrants' Rights Update* that examines the latest developments in California regarding immigrants and welfare. And more than 600 organizations subscribe to NILC's *Email Benefits Update,* an electronic bulletin disseminated by NILC's D.C. office containing analyses of proposed legislative and administrative changes to public benefits laws.

NILC staff conduct an average of sixty training sessions and conference presentations per year throughout California and the United States on topics such as the impact of welfare reform on immigrants, deportation defense, naturalization, and workers' rights.

NATIONAL IMMIGRATION PROJECT OF THE NATIONAL LAWYERS GUILD

The National Immigration Project is a network of immigration lawyers, law students, jailhouse lawyers, and legal workers who work to end unlawful immigration practices, to recognize the contributions of immigrants in the United States, to promote fair immigration practices, and to expand the civil and human rights of all immigrants, regardless of their status in the United States.

The National Lawyers Guild (NLG) was founded in 1937 as the first racially integrated bar association in the United States. Throughout its history, the National Lawyers Guild has fought for justice for immigrants. Since 1974, the National Immigration Project has worked hand in hand with the immigrant rights movement. The project provides technical assistance, advice, and resources to legal practitioner and community groups throughout the country. It sponsors seminars and produces publications on a variety of subjects to develop and improve legal and advocacy skills. It participates in impact litigation and develops new legal strategies for advancing the rights of immigrants.

Headquartered in Boston, the project sponsors substantive work groups (commissions) in the areas of immigrant women, border violence, HIV and immigrants, children in detention, incarcerated noncitizen criminal defendants, ideological visa denials, and INS raids.

NATIONAL INTEREST WAIVER

The national interest exemption provides an opportunity for individuals (usually professionals) to immigrate in the **second preference employment category** without a job offer and an **alien employment certification.** Seven factors are considered in determining whether a national interest waiver should be granted:

1. Improving the U.S. economy
2. Improving wages and working conditions of U.S. workers
3. Improving education and training programs for U.S. children and underqualified workers
4. Improving health care
5. Providing more affordable housing for young and/or older, poorer, U.S. residents
6. Improving the environment of the United States and making more productive use of natural resources
7. A request from an interested U.S. government agency

The existence of one or more of these factors providesthe possibility for an individual to obtain a national interest waiver.

NATIONAL ORIGIN DISCRIMINATION   Under the **Immigration Reform and Control Act of 1986** (IRCA), it is an unfair immigration-related employment practice for an employer to discriminate against a person who is authorized to work with respect to hiring the individual for employment or discharging the individual from employment on the basis of the individual's national origin, or the individual's citizenship status, as long as the person is a **protected individual.**

An employment discrimination provision was made part of IRCA for two basic reasons: (1) concern that some unsavory employers would use the law against hiring unauthorized workers (**employer sanctions**) as an excuse not to hire individuals "who look like aliens," and (2) some lazy employers will not learn the employer sanctions rules carefully, and simply "take the easy way out" by not hiring someone who "looks" foreign or who does not present a particular document.

National origin refers to the person's place of origin (or that of the person's ancestors) as well as those things (physical features, dress, language) that are identified specifically with the people of that place of origin. Employers cannot favor one nationality group or another in their workforce. Thus, the Equal Employment Opportunity Commission, which handles discrimination claims under Title VII of the Civil Rights Act of 1964, finds national origin discrimination when an individual is treated differently from others because of the "individual's, or his or her ancestor's, place of origin; or because an individual has the physical, cultural or linguistic characteristics of a national origin group."

An employer who is guilty of discrimination based on national origin may be subject to a claim under the IRCA employment discrimination laws or Title VII of the Civil Rights Act of 1964. The injured party must elect to choose only one of these routes. The main difference in the protections afforded by these two laws is that the immigration-related provision covers smaller employers, while Title VII covers most larger employers.

Specifically, Title VII covers employers with fifteen or more full- or part-time workers, for at least 20 out of 52 weeks during the year. In contrast, the IRCA employment discrimination provision covers employers employing four to fourteen part- or full-time workers, and larger employers not covered by Title VII. For example, seasonal employers who have more than fourteen workers, but who do not employ them for at least 20 weeks a year, are covered by the IRCA provision. Most states also have laws that protect against discrimination based on national origin.

The most common example of national origin discrimination is when an employer refuses to hire someone who is from a particular country. So if an employer does not want to hire people from Japan, or Mexico, or France, or Iran, that would constitute national origin discrimination. Similarly, if an employer does not want to hire a person who was born in the United States because that person's parents are from Iran, that too would be national origin discrimination.

An employer would also be in violation of the law if the job applicant in a sense represents a particular national origin. For example, if an applicant's spouse is from Mexico, many of the applicant's friends are of Mexican origin, and the employer refuses to hire the applicant due to those reasons, that would be problematic. Similarly, if one spouse has adopted the Japanese surname of the other spouse and the employer refuses employment because of the surname, discrimination has occurred.

English Proficiency

Some jobs require a higher level of English proficiency than others. If an employer requires a certain level of English proficiency for a particular position in a firm, the employer must be able to provide justification for the particular level of proficiency required. A secretary might be required to know more English than a janitor. An employer who requires more English than is reasonably required for a particular job may be charged with national origin discrimination. Such a practice is discrimination if the effect of the requirement is that some qualified workers are treated differently from other qualified workers solely on the basis of their ability to speak English.

When a specific level of English is required of a particular position, the employer should use specific methods of measuring proficiency. The goal of the law is to ferret out those employers who are simply using English proficiency as a pretext for not hiring applicants of particular national origins.

Accent Discrimination

Discriminating against an applicant because of what is perceived as an accent can also be problematic. Generally, the accent should be taken into account only if it interferes with the worker's ability to do the job. Again, the employer must not use a purported accent simply as a pretext for not hiring applicants from a particular country or region of the world. See *Fragante v. Honolulu.*

Requiring English-only on the Job

Depending on the location, employers may be committing unlawful discrimination if they impose a rule that requires workers to speak only English at certain times. Some courts allow English-only rules if the employer can show that the rule is required by a legitimate business necessity. For example, there may not be a legitimate business necessity for imposing a rule that workers cannot speak Spanish to each other during their breaks or at any time during work hours. But requiring that everyone helping on a surgical team in a hospital speak only English during surgery might be legitimate.

Some courts do not require employers to justify English-only rules by showing a business necessity unless the persons to whom the rule is applied have difficulty speaking English, or the rule is applied in such a way as to create a work environment that is hostile to workers from minority national origin or language groups. See **English-only movement.**

NATIONAL ORIGINS QUOTA SYSTEM   The national origins quota system for immigration was in force from 1924 to 1965. The reactionary, isolationist political climate that followed World War I, manifested in the Red Scare of 1919–1920, led to severe exclusionist demands. The landmark Immigration Act of 1924, opposed by only six senators, took direct aim at southern and eastern Europeans, whom the Protestant majority in the United States viewed with dogmatic disapproval. The arguments advanced in support of the bill stressed recurring themes: the racial superiority of Anglo-Saxons, the fact that immigrants caused the lowering of wages, and the unassimilability of foreigners, while citing the usual threats to the nation's social unity and order posed by immigrants.

The act restructured criteria for admission to respond to nativist demands and represented a general selection policy that remained in place until 1965. It provided that immigrants of any particular country be limited to 2 percent of their nationality in the United States population of 1890. The law struck most deeply at Jews, Italians, Slavs, and Greeks, who had immigrated in great numbers after 1890, and who would be most disfavored by such a quota system.

Though sponsors of the act were primarily concerned with limiting immigration from southern and eastern Europe, they simultaneously eliminated the few remaining categories for Asians whose immigration had been severely restricted by earlier **exclusion** laws. The act provided for the permanent exclusion of any alien "ineligible to citizenship." Since Asians were barred from naturalization under an 1870 statute, the possibility of their entry was cut off indefinitely. The prohibition even covered previously privileged merchants, teachers, and students. Asians were not allowed even under the 2 percent quota rule. The primary target were the Japanese, who had never before been totally barred by federal immigration laws.

Not until the **Immigration Amendments of 1965** was the national origins quota system removed from the immigration laws.

NATURAL BORN CITIZEN A person who acquires citizenship by virtue of being born in the United States or a U.S. territory such as Puerto Rico or Guam. But citizenship can also be obtained by a **child** born abroad to a U.S. citizen parent under certain circumstances. In essence, the United States follows both the **jus soli** and **jus sanguinis** rules of acquiring citizenship and nationality. [8 U.S.C. §§1401, 1403]

NATURALIZATION Naturalization is the process by which an **immigrant** or noncitizen **national** of the United States becomes a U.S. **citizen.** The general requirements for naturalization include **lawful permanent resident alien** status for five years; **good moral character;** physical presence in the United States for at least thirty months; the ability to read, write, and speak basic English; knowledge of basic U.S. history and civics; and an oath of allegiance to the United States. A naturalization applicant must be at least eighteen years old. However, immigrant children under age eighteen can obtain citizenship automatically if their parents become naturalized. Immigrants who are married to U.S. citizens or who are members of the U.S. armed forces have shorter residency requirements. Noncitizen nationals of the United States, such as American Samoans, need only reside in the United States for three months to be eligible to naturalize. [8 U.S.C. §§1423, 1427; 8 C.F.R. §337] A naturalization applicant must complete Form N-400. One is reproduced in the Appendix.

There are some exceptions to the English literacy requirement. If the applicant is over fifty years old, and has lived in the United States for at least twenty years since becoming a lawful permanent resident, or is over fifty-five years old and has lived here for at least fifteen years as a lawful permanent resident, the English literacy requirement is waived. Such applicants will, however, be tested on U.S. history and government in their native language. A waiver of the English literacy and civics requirements can be obtained by applicants who suffer from physical or developmental disabilities. Short of a waiver, at least reasonable accommodations have to be made for applicants with disabilities during the testing. See **disability waiver or accommodations for naturalization requirements.**

An applicant must understand the fundamentals of U.S. history and the principles of and form of government of the United States. The INS has published a list of the 100 questions that should be studied for this civics portion of the test. Usually, an applicant is only asked a few questions taken from this list. These questions and answers are reproduced in the Appendix.

The final step in the naturalization process requires the taking of an oath of allegiance. Applicants must demonstrate that they are "attached to the principles of the Constitution of the United States and well disposed to the good order and happiness of the United States." This oath is usually taken at a naturalization ceremony before a federal judge, magistrate, or INS official.

The text of the oath of loyalty reads as follows:

> I hereby declare, on oath, that I absolutely and entirely renounce and abjure all allegiance and fidelity to any foreign prince, potentate, state, or sovereignty, of whom or which I have heretofore been a subject or citizen; that I will support and defend the Constitution and laws of the United States of America against all enemies, foreign and domestic; that I will bear true faith and allegiance to the same; that I will bear arms on behalf of the United States when required by the law; that I will perform noncombatant service in the Armed Forces of the United States when required by law; that I will perform work of national importance under civilian direction when required by law; and that I take this obligation freely without any mental reservation or purpose of evasion; so help me God. [8 C.F.R. §337.1(a)]

Once the oath is administered, the applicant receives a Certificate of Naturalization.

There are some exceptions to the loyalty oath. A conscientious objector can take an amended version of the oath. Those who oppose bearing arms or all military service because of religious training or beliefs may take the oath, leaving out the words "I will bear arms" and "I will perform non-combatant services." This means that they accept the oath in every way but they will not bear arms or perform noncombatant services. Those who cannot use the words "on oath" and "so help me God" can have those words deleted. This includes applicants who may be Quakers, Jehovah's Witnesses, or other individuals opposed to oaths. But the allegiance statement must still be taken "freely without any mental reservation." See *In re De Bellis*.

NATURALIZATION CLAUSE Article I, §8, clause 4 of the U.S. Constitution enables Congress to establish a "uniform Rule of Naturalization." This clause and inherent powers of sovereignty have provided the basis for the Supreme Court consistently to hold that Congress has virtual **plenary power** to decide what categories of **alien**s can be admitted, excluded, and deported from the country.

NATURALIZED CITIZEN A person who acquires U.S. citizenship by meeting the **naturalization** requirements.

NAZI PERSECUTION PARTICIPANT AND GENOCIDE INADMISSIBILITY GROUND The **inadmissibility grounds** provide for the **exclusion** of participants in Nazi persecution. Any alien who, during the period beginning on March 23, 1933, and ending on May 8, 1945, under the direction of, or in association with (1) the Nazi government of Germany, (2) any government in any area occupied by the military forces of the Nazi government of Germany, (3) any government established with the assistance or cooperation of the Nazi government of Germany, or (4) any government that was an ally of the Nazi government of Germany, ordered, incited, assisted, or otherwise participated in the persecution of any person because of race, religion, national origin, or political opinion is inadmissible.

Furthermore, any alien who has engaged in conduct that is defined as genocide for purposes of the International Convention on the Prevention and Punishment of Genocide is inadmissible. [8 U.S.C. §1182(a)(3)(E)]

NEW YORK ASSOCIATION FOR NEW AMERICANS

The New York Association for New Americans, Inc. (NYANA) is the largest local refugee resettlement and immigrant services agency in the United States. Since its founding in 1949, NYANA has helped nearly 500,000 refugees and immigrants from more than 145 countries as diverse as the former Soviet Union, Iran, Cambodia, Vietnam, Syria, Ethiopia, Uganda, Afghanistan, Haiti, and Tibet to begin new lives in the United States.

The agency's mission is to assist the foreign-born in achieving economic self-sufficiency, social integration, and **naturalization** in the shortest possible time. As a result, NYANA uses one of the most innovative, multifaceted, full-service, multidiscipline approaches to immigration services among community-based-organizations in the country. NYANA provides the following direct services to newcomers.

- *Case management services.* From the moment of arrival, NYANA provides refugee clients with intensive case management services to ensure that families receive all the help they need to become self-sufficient as quickly as possible.
- *Income maintenance.* NYANA administers federal and private refugee funds to provide immediate financial assistance for food, rent, clothing, and other basic necessities for refugees for their first four months in the United States.
- *Employment services.* NYANA provides employment services including vocational skills training or retraining, integrated with occupationally specific English instruction, work-readiness skills instruction, counseling, job development, placement assistance, and short-term vocational follow-up.
- *English as a second language.* NYANA's English-as-a-second-language school provides intensive language instruction to help immigrants become socially integrated and prepare for the world of work.
- *Acculturation.* American acculturation is an aspect of all services delivered at NYANA. Specific programs available to assist immigrant families in understanding their rights and responsibilities and in functioning independently in the United States have included information on employment and taxation, home ownership, the public education system, the U.S. court and legal system, the electoral system, and the U.S. health care system.
- *Housing location assistance.* NYANA provides refugee clients with assistance in locating affordable and safe housing in New York City, based on the needs of the family and the resources available.

- *Citizenship services.* NYANA's citizenship courses, which combine English instruction with U.S. civics and history, help immigrants prepare for their INS interviews and written exams. The agency also assists new Americans in the completion of naturalization and citizenship applications.
- *Legal services.* NYANA provides a comprehensive array of immigration-related legal assistance, including preparing and filing applications for asylum, permanent residency, work authorization, replacement of lost documents, and family reunification.
- *Center for Women and Families.* The Center for Women and Families provides social service counseling, support groups, information and referral, and advocacy for women and children who are victims of domestic violence.
- *Business Center for New Americans.* NYANA's Business Center for New Americans is designed to help newcomers start their own enterprises by serving as a "one-stop shop" for information and technical assistance, and for microenterprise loans.
- *Immigrant Community Development.* This program offers emerging immigrant organizations technical assistance in a variety of areas, from basic service delivery to strategic planning, management training, and technical assistance with infrastructure-related areas such as resource development and financial systems management.
- *Health education and services.* In addition to refugee health assessments and medical referrals, NYANA provides health and safety programs that introduce immigrants to the complexities of the American health care system and help foster attitudes of responsibility toward personal and family safety.
- *Project RINA.* Through Project RINA (Rehabilitation Institute for New Americans), an outpatient treatment program for newcomers with alcohol and drug addictions, NYANA assists newcomers in their recovery efforts to achieve sobriety and live healthy and productive lives.
- *Technical assistance.* In addition to providing direct services to clients, NYANA provides technical assistance and resource materials on refugee and immigrant service operations to other national and international service providers.

NEW YORK IMMIGRATION COALITION The New York Immigration Coalition (NYIC) is an umbrella advocacy organization for over 120 groups in New York State that work with "newcomers" to our country—immigrants, refugees, asylees, and parolees. As the coordinating body for organizations serving one of the largest and most diverse newcomer populations in the United States, NYIC has become a

leading advocate for immigrant communities on both the local and national levels.

NYIC successfully brings together multiethnic, multiracial, and multisector constituencies to pursue common goals. These include improving access to services and public agencies, combating discrimination and ensuring civil rights protections, advocating for equitable immigration policies, educating both newcomer communities and the public at large about immigration issues, and fostering improved quality of life for New York's diverse newcomer and native-born communities. Member organizations regularly participate in and lead NYIC efforts via an active task force structure, which includes regular meetings and activities in the areas of legal services, education issues, citizenship, and community mobilization and public education. The NYIC's leadership role in these areas is of vital importance in addressing the serious impact of the immigration reforms and day-to-day policy changes.

For generations, New York has been the primary **port of entry** for immigrants to the United States. During the 1980s immigration to the state surged, with approximately 100,000 newcomers per year making New York their home, totaling over 1 million new immigrant residents in the course of that decade. This trend has intensified in the 1990s, with roughly 125,000 immigrants per year entering the state on a permanent basis. This sixteen-year surge of immigration to the state has been notable for both its size and diversity. Prior to the 1960s, most immigrants came to New York from Europe. Since then, the immigration flow has been primarily from the Caribbean, Latin America, Asia, and the former Soviet Union. The state of New York is now home to an estimated 3 million foreign-born persons, approximately 90 percent of whom live in New York City. At least one-third of the city's 8.5 million residents is estimated to be foreign-born. Immigrants and their children account for nearly 50 percent of the city's residents.

NONIMMIGRANT Nonimmigrants are persons who enter the United States on a **nonimmigrant visa**. This includes foreign students, **visitors for pleasure** or tourists, **business visitors**, foreign journalists, foreign officials, and **temporary workers**. Generally, nonimmigrants must be entering the United States for a temporary purpose with the intent of returning to their native country. [8 U.S.C. §1101(a)(15)]

NONIMMIGRANT VISA Visa issued to someone intending to reside for a limited period of time in the United States and who meets the requirements of a specific **nonimmigrant** class.

NONRESIDENT ALIEN   A nonresident alien is a person who is issued a **border crossing identification card** for purposes of visiting a local border area of the United States for a period of seventy-two hours or less. The cards are generally issued to citizens of Mexico or Canada and British subjects who reside in Canada. The cards can be valid for a number of years. The purpose is to facilitate common travel for those individuals who frequently visit relatives or shop on the U.S. side of the border. [8 C.F.R. §212.6]

NORTH AMERICAN FREE TRADE AGREEMENT (NAFTA)   Although the publicity surrounding the passage of the North American Free Trade Agreement during the early years of the Bill Clinton administration included little information on its impact on immigration laws, the agreement contained provisions that were eventually integrated into U.S. immigration laws. Legislation enacted on December 8, 1993, provided treaty (E visa) status (see **treaty traders** and **investor visas**) to citizens of Mexico and Canada. Canadian and Mexican professionals entering to engage in professional activities were facilitated (**TN professional** visas). However, individuals from Mexico and Canada seeking to enter on E, TN, or L-1 **intracompany transferee** visas can be barred from entering if their entry might adversely affect the settlement of a labor dispute at the location where the person will work or the employment of any person involved in the dispute. [8 U.S.C. §1184]

NORTHERN CALIFORNIA COALITION FOR IMMIGRANT RIGHTS   The Northern California Coalition for Immigrant Rights was founded in 1987 to coordinate services and advocacy in response to the **Immigration Reform and Control Act of 1986** (IRCA). Today the coalition advances immigrant rights through a comprehensive matrix of strategies, each supporting and enriching each other: public policy advocacy, grassroots organizing, information and referrals, coalition building, public education, and service coordination.

Since its founding, the coalition has launched dynamic and effective projects such as Mujeres Unidas y Activas, a 200-member Latina immigrant organizing project that is a national model and which is now working on a pivotal project with a group of immigrant Chinese women; the Immigrant Assistance Line; and VOICE (Voting and Organizing for Immigrant and Community Empowerment), which has registered over 20,000 new citizen voters in the past year.

The coalition is in a unique position as an advocate, historically and in this most challenging time. It serves as a critical link from service agencies and community-based constituencies to those who work solely in the state capital or Washington, D.C., ultimately bringing to the task an accountability to the immigrants served, listened to, and organized.

The coalition brings to the capital and administrative bodies an almost instantaneous sense of what is taking place "on the ground." Immigrants and service agencies know to call the coalition immediately if, for instance, a state or county agency is taking inappropriate measures to cut services or actions that make immigrants reluctant to seek needed help.

The coalition is able, perhaps uniquely, to translate the workings of distant decision-making bodies to hard-to-reach monolingual constituencies and beleaguered social services agencies who do not have the time to unravel the issues. It is able to involve these constituencies in the decision-making process.

In addition, the coalition brings to this new period an incredible infrastructure on which can be built a strong response to reforms that affect immigrants. It has a membership of approximately 100 social services agencies and advocates, an emergency broadcast fax network of 450, and a mailing list of over 2,000 advocates and organizers throughout Northern California. It has contacts in every Bay Area county ranging from government officials and administrators to social service agencies and grassroots immigrant groups.

The coalition's alerts (for advocates, service providers, and immigrant communities) are well known for being multilingual and for making complicated policy issues accessible. They are duplicated all over the country and often copied word-for-word in the ethnic press.

The Northern California Coalition for Immigrant Rights has played a leading role in bringing together several statewide advocacy networks:

- the New California Coalition, focused on immigrant advocacy
- the Interfaith Coalition for Immigrant Rights, focused on building religious community support for immigrants
- the Statewide Coalition for Ethical Welfare Reform (organized by the coalition's public policy director), focused on creating a united agenda by all sectors affected by welfare reform
- a statewide immigrant-focused collaboration involving the **National Immigration Law Center** (NILC), **Mexican American Legal Defense and Educational Fund** (MALDEF), the **Coalition for Humane Immigrant Rights of Los Angeles** (CHIRLA), the **Asian Pacific American Legal Center** (APALC) based in Southern California, and the New California Coalition

- a network in Sacramento in which the Northern California Coalition for Immigrant Rights, MALDEF, the New California Coalition, and the American Civil Liberties Union are the central members

The coalition's Citizenship Task Force, comprised of forty active members from throughout the region, has a three-year relationship advocating with the regional INS for fair and timely naturalization services. The Citizenship Task Force has also worked with immigration coalitions across the country to take their demands to the INS in Washington. Its history led to the coalition playing a key role in developing San Francisco's welfare reform naturalization collaborative and facilitating the formation of others in the remaining counties.

The coalition has ongoing and long relationships with immigrant rights coalitions in New York, Boston, Chicago, Texas, Los Angeles, New Jersey, the Northwest, and Washington, D.C. As coalitions based in geographic regions, they share strategies, information, and resources. The coalition's affiliation with the **National Immigration Forum** helps it bring its views to policy makers in Washington and strengthens national advocacy efforts by bringing strong California advocacy and on-the-ground experiences to the table.

In San Francisco, one of the U.S. counties most affected by welfare reform measures targeting permanent residents, the coalition's leadership is looked to by administrative agencies and elected officials. Coalition staff members have been on the Mayor's Task Force on Welfare Reform, as is the director of Mujeres Unidas y Activas, the only representative of a grassroots immigrant group. The coalition has received a city Community Development Block Grant to help coordinate service provision, and has also been consulting on advocacy strategies and developing trainings in Alameda and Santa Clara Counties.

The coalition receives approximately 45 calls a day on its welfare reform hotlines for immigrants, advocates, and service providers, precisely because it is recognized as an accurate and timely information source.

With this infrastructure the coalition has played a leading role in many important victories: the Northern California vote against **Proposition 187,** the passage of the **Violence Against Women Act** (with its provision to help battered immigrant women), the passage of strong legislation to punish fraud committed by immigration consultants, and the maintenance of perinatal health care in the state of California despite the former governor's direct attack on it for several consecutive years.

During the welfare reform crisis, for example, the coalition helped limit its damage. Most significantly, Senator Dianne Feinstein eventually voted against the bill, after weeks of pressure by the coalition and other allies.

The coalition's materials and the links made between the senator and immigrants found their way into the *Congressional Record*. During the debate on the immigration bill, the coalition organized over 3,000 Chinese immigrants to write letters to their representatives in Congress by working with the Chinese-language media.

Through this battle the coalition forged a network of advocates, grassroots organizers, and social service agencies that well positions it for the challenge posed by immigration reform generally.

NOTICE TO APPEAR   The notice to appear is the formal legal document that charges a person subject to **removal proceedings** (**exclusion** or **deportation**). In the notice to appear, the INS must state specific facts that show (1) that the person is not a U.S. citizen and what the person's home country is, (2) the acts or conduct that are in violation of the immigration laws, (3) the legal authority under which the INS is conducting the proceedings, and (4) the provision of the law that the person has violated. The INS must provide a copy of the notice to appear to the individual. This is generally done in person if the person is in INS custody. If the person is not in detention, the INS will serve the notice to appear through the mail. [8 U.S.C. §1229(a)(1)]

NUMERICAL LIMITATIONS   When a person wants to immigrate to the United States, he or she must fit into an immigration category and not be subject to an **inadmissibility ground.** Additionally, a visa must be available. Certain **immediate relatives** of U.S. citizens may immigrate to the United States without being subject to numerical limitations or quotas. Thus, visas are always available to immediate relatives of U.S. citizens as long as they are not inadmissible. However, other prospective immigrants who immigrate under the **preference system** are subject to two types of numerical limits: **worldwide numerical limitations** and **country and territorial numerical limitations.** The preference system provides separate systems for family immigration and for employment-related immigration.

Under the law, at least 226,000 family preference category visas are available annually on a worldwide basis. Although in theory the worldwide quota can be increased to 480,000 annually, the level likely will not be much more than 226,000. This is because the family preference category level is determined by subtracting the number of immediate relative entrants—generally well over 200,000 annually—from the maximum (480,000), with an absolute floor of 226,000. A separate worldwide numerical limitation of

140,000 is set aside for employment-based immigrants. Another 55,000 visas are set aside for **diversity visas** on a worldwide basis.

The law also provides an annual limitation of visas per country of 7 percent of the worldwide quotas. Thus, assuming a 226,000 worldwide family visa numerical limitation and 140,000 for employment visas, 7 percent of the total (366,000) is 25,620 for each country. But 75 percent of the visas issued for spouses and children of lawful permanent residents (**second preference for relatives** 2-A) are not counted against each country's quota.

Prospective immigrants from countries with great visa demands such as the Philippines and Mexico face long backlogs. Until a visa becomes available, these individuals cannot immigrate to the United States. [8 U.S.C. §1152] A **visa bulletin** that illustrates these backlogs is included in the Appendix.

O

OFFICE OF INTERNAL AUDIT The Office of Internal Audit (OIA) of the INS is responsible for handling complaints of abuse and rudeness lodged against INS employees by the public. The OIA also handles allegations of internal misconduct and dishonesty by INS employees.

Much of the jurisdiction over these matters is shared between the OIA and the **Office of the Inspector General** (OIG). If and when abuse cases get returned to the INS for consideration of administrative discipline, the OIA decides whether to investigate the matter itself with its own staff of special agents. Because it feels that its limited investigative resources are utilized most efficiently through oversight and quality control of locally conducted inquiries, the OIA actually conducts investigations on its own in a relatively small number of high-level, sensitive, controversial, or difficult cases. The OIA refers the majority of cases to local INS management for inquiry.

OFFICE OF THE CHIEF ADMINISTRATIVE HEARING OFFICER The Office of the Chief Administrative Hearing Officer (OCAHO) is the branch of the **Executive Office of Immigration Review** that supervises the work of **administrative law judge**s, who hear cases involving **employer sanctions,** immigration-related employment discrimination claims, and civil **document fraud** cases under the immigration laws. OCAHO was established following the passage of the **Immigration Reform and Control Act of 1986,** which enacted employer sanctions.

OFFICE OF THE INSPECTOR GENERAL When an individual has been abused by an INS or **Border Patrol** agent, the victim, a witness, or any other interested party can file a complaint against the agent. Complaints can be initiated with the Border Patrol itself, other INS personnel, the Civil Rights Division of the Department of Justice, local police authorities, or the Office of the Inspector General (OIG) of the **De-**

partment of Justice. Depending on the circumstances of the abuse, the matter could end at the OIG, be forwarded to the Civil Rights Division, or go to the INS's **Office of Internal Audit.**

The OIG has over 150 employees assigned to the investigations division. They are located in ten field offices across the country at thirteen different locations. Each field office is headed by a special agent.

OPERATION GATEKEEPER In 1994, the **Border Patrol** revised its deterrence strategy in El Paso, Texas, and San Diego, California, in part following the **Operation Hold-the-Line** experiment and the recommendations of a consulting firm. The INS recognized that most of the line-watching operations were focused on apprehending **undocumented aliens** once they had crossed the border or had traveled to various interior geographical locations. Researchers from Sandia National Laboratories were commissioned to come up with recommendations on how to prevent illicit entries in the first instance. They offered two suggestions: (1) multiple lighted barriers in urban border areas with patrol roads between barriers, and (2) enhanced checkpoint operations to prevent undocumented aliens who succeeded in crossing the border from leaving the border area.

As a result of these observations and recommendations, chief Border Patrol agents were brought together to discuss strategy for controlling the border. San Diego and El Paso were selected as the first sites for implementing the new strategy, Operation Gatekeeper, because those sectors historically represented the vast majority of apprehensions and attempted entries. Following the installation of substantial new fencing and lighting along several miles of the border near San Diego, apprehensions decreased 20 percent within two years as a result of the new deterrents. In El Paso, illicit border crossings dropped roughly 10,000 per day to 500. The anticipated effect of new barriers, lighting, and agents along the border was to discourage attempted illicit entries because the border terrain that is not guarded as closely is much more difficult and dangerous to traverse.

Unfortunately, many have not been discouraged from attempting to enter along areas of dangerous terrain that is not as closely guarded. Human rights critics of Operation Gatekeeper have counted about 400 individuals who have died trying to enter the United States in these desolate areas during 1994–1999.

OPERATION HOLD-THE-LINE This operation involved a highly concentrated enforcement strategy used by the **Border Patrol** in the El Paso, Texas, area for about a year beginning in September

1993, which purportedly severely reduced the number of undocumented immigrants coming across the border at that point. The idea was to discourage entry by increasing the number and visibility of agents at areas frequently subject to surreptitious entries. Apprehensions were reduced from 700 to about 200 per day. Studies demonstrated that the operation reduced local border-crossing activity by some types of unauthorized commuter migrants (street vendors, older female domestic workers) and juvenile delinquents. However, long-distance migrants simply were diverted to other border-crossing points in the state of Arizona, where apprehensions rose by more than 60 percent in the same period studied. Thus, the operation may have impacted a highly localized problem, but the larger phenomenon of illegal entry by migrants from the interior of Mexico merely was shifted. Since late 1994, the El Paso area has been part of a new enforcement effort dubbed **Operation Gatekeeper.**

OPERATION JOBS   Mexican immigrants are the victims of the most highly publicized INS raids. In what the INS labeled Operation Jobs (or Operation Cooperation) in April 1982, 5,000 people of primarily Latin appearance were arrested in nine metropolitan areas across the country. INS officials argued that they were arresting undocumented immigrants in order to free up jobs for native workers. Critics of the raids charged that the operation was directed at Mexicans, whipped up anti-alien hysteria, and caused much fear in the Latino community, while providing no jobs for citizens. Curiously, Operation Jobs was launched during the same week that restrictive legislation was being marked up in the U.S. Senate's subcommittee on immigration. The raids also coincided with Congress's consideration of additional funding for the INS.

Operation Jobs merely highlighted what had been going on for many years. A review of litigation initiated long before the 1982 operation indicates that the INS had long focused its sweeps on persons of Latino descent. Every year most of the aliens arrested in the United States and subjected to **removal** are Mexican, although demographers and INS officials acknowledge that most **undocumented aliens** in the United States are not Mexican.

OPERATION WETBACK   World War II created a labor shortage in the United States that shifted American attitudes toward immigration from Mexico, and for a short while Mexican nationals were welcomed. In fact, the **Bracero program** was implemented to provide a supply of thousands of low-wage workers in the Southwest during this era.

But by the 1950s, many Americans were alarmed by the number of immigrants from Mexico. In 1954, in the midst of a post–Korean War recession, the INS implemented Operation Wetback, a mass removal of Mexicans that was rationalized as a way to protect the labor market for citizens. Even U.S. citizens of Mexican descent were caught up in the expulsion frenzy. To ensure the effectiveness of the expulsion process, many of those apprehended were denied a hearing to assert their constitutional rights and to present evidence that could have prevented their deportation. More than a million persons of Mexican descent were expelled from the United States during Operation Wetback.

OPERATIONS INSTRUCTIONS   The Operations Instructions of the INS provide a very useful insight into the internal guidelines and procedures followed by INS personnel in implementing immigration laws. For example, instructions on what considerations to use in making certain decisions are included, along with restrictions and policy statements. The INS Operations Instructions can be found in government sections of major libraries and are often included in multivolume immigration law treatises.

ORPHANS   The immigration laws provide a special immigration process for orphans abroad under the age of sixteen. The **child** can qualify as an orphan if both parents have died, disappeared, or abandoned the child, or if the sole parent is incapable of providing proper care and has irrevocably released the child for emigration and adoption. The orphan must either have been adopted abroad or be coming to the United States to be adopted. If abroad, the adoption must have been by a U.S. citizen and spouse jointly, or by an unmarried U.S. citizen at least twenty-five years old who personally observed the child prior to or during the adoption proceedings. The orphan can be coming to the United States for adoption by such individuals who have complied with the adoption requirements of the proposed state of residence. Whether the orphan is adopted abroad or in the United States, a valid home study by an appropriate agency is required, along with other documentary evidence, such as proof of orphan status and proper forms.

P

PACKET III This term is used to describe the basic immigrant visa application forms that are used at U.S. consulates abroad.

PALMER RAIDS In 1918 a law was passed providing for the **deportation** of noncitizens who were members of organizations seeking to overthrow the government by force or violence. The law was a direct reaction to the Russian Revolution of 1917 and the increasingly effective efforts in the United States to organize workers through militant action. Under this law, 248 "radicals" were deported, including prominent labor organizers.

Acting on the initiative provided by the 1918 legislation, Attorney General A. Mitchell Palmer initiated the notorious "Palmer Raids." Over 5,000 activists were arrested for deportation over a three-month period. Federal agents invaded homes, schools, churches, and other buildings to seize militants in an attempt to halt their labor-organizing efforts. On one night alone, in January 1920, over 2,500 arrests were made in 31 cities across the country. Citizens as well as noncitizens were apprehended and released only on proof of citizenship or legal residence in the United States.

PAPER SON This is a term that was used to describe many male Chinese immigrants who entered the United States with fraudulent claims to U.S. citizenship in order to get around the restrictions of the **Chinese Exclusion Act of 1882.**

When this first Chinese exclusion law was enacted, the Chinese American population totaled more than 100,000, and most were male laborers. Because many had lived here for years and suffered from family separation and antimiscegenation laws, Chinese were given to undocumented migration more than any other group in that era. Their gambits were many. A legion entered after the enactment of the exclusion laws under false citizenship claims. A Chinese laborer might assert, for example, that he had been born in San Francisco and that his birth certificate had been destroyed in the 1906 earthquake that destroyed city hall. Then he would claim, after various trips to China, that his wife there had given birth to children (usually sons) who automatically derived U.S. citizenship through the father who had purportedly been born in San Francisco. In fact, the children were often fictitious, and the few immigration slots were given or sold to others in China; they came to be known as "paper sons." Some who had valid claims of entry would simply sell their identity to another.

PAROLE Some aliens who present themselves at the border or **port of entry** are not eligible for **admission** in the opinion of the immigration inspector. Generally, such individuals are turned away. However, in some circumstances, the person is granted *parole* and allowed to travel in the United States for limited purposes. Persons granted parole are not considered to have gained admission. [8 U.S.C. §1182(d)(5)] See **advanced parole.**

The concept of parole also has a relationship with **asylum.** Prior to the **Refugee Act of 1980,** the **attorney general** often used the parole authority to allow thousands of persons fleeing persecution to enter the United States. The **McCarran-Walter Act of 1952** granted the attorney general discretionary authority to parole into the United States any alien for "emergent reasons or for reasons deemed strictly in the public interest." Although the original intent was to apply this parole authority on an individual basis, the 1956 Hungarian refugee crisis led to its expanded use to accommodate those fleeing Communist oppression. The parole authority was also used to admit more than 15,000 Chinese who fled mainland China after the 1949 Communist takeover and more than 145,000 Cubans who sought refuge after Fidel Castro's 1959 coup. See **Cuban Refugee Act of 1966.**

Using that authority, the attorney general also permitted over 400,000 refugees from Southeast Asia to enter between 1975 and 1980. By 1980, 99.7 percent of the more than 1 million refugees admitted under the parole system were from countries under Communist rule.

PERMANENT RESIDENT CARD See **alien registration receipt card.**

PETTY OFFENSE Generally, a person who is convicted or formally admits the elements of a **crime involving moral turpitude** is excludable from **admission** to the United States. However, if this was the person's first crime involving moral turpitude, the maximum sentence for the offense was one year or less, and the actual sentence imposed was six months or less, the person can be admitted. [8 U.S.C. §1182(a)(2)(A)(ii)]

 **PICTURE BRIDE**   The term *picture bride* is used to describe a woman who entered the United States to marry a man whose decision to marry is based in large part on a photograph that he saw of the woman. While the term is derived from historical practices, in a real sense this practice continues today with certain conditions. Several "matchmaking" services in the United States offer men in the United States the opportunity to peruse photograph catalogues of women from places such as Russia and Asian Pacific countries who are interested in immigrating to the United States through marriage. However, current law does not allow a man in the United States to simply file a **fiancé visa** petition for a woman whose photograph he has seen in a catalogue. A fiancé visa cannot be issued unless the consular officer is satisfied that the parties have previously met in person within two years before the date of filing the petition and have a bona fide intention to marry. Therefore, these situations generally are not allowed until the man in the United States has traveled abroad to meet the prospective bride. [8 U.S.C. §§1101(a)(15)(K), 1184(d)]

Decades ago when a personal meeting was not necessary before the entry of a picture bride, many men sent for women to marry from their native countries after seeing photographs. Consider the Japanese. Although the 1907–1908 **Gentlemen's Agreement** curtailed the number of Japanese laborers who could emigrate to the United States, those who were already here, as well as any new immigrants, were allowed to bring or send for wives and children. A substantial share of the Japanese women immigrants during this period were picture brides, whose prospective husbands had seen only a picture before the marriage. Given antimiscegenation laws and the Japanese custom to arrange marriages, it is not surprising that many men sent back to Japan for brides. A Japanese immigrant who wished to marry but was unable to return to Japan had few other options. Picture brides caused an outrage in the United States, and part of the impetus for Japanese **exclusion** grew out of an aversion to the practice. The United States strongly protested Japan's issuing passports to picture brides. Japan stopped the practice in 1920 and established a new policy that permitted marriages between Japanese women and emigrés who returned to Japan for at least thirty days. The new brides were then issued passports.

 **PILOT INVESTOR PROGRAM**   A pilot investor program was created in 1993 in response to concerns that the normal immigrant

investor visa program was being underused. Only a few hundred alien investors were taking advantage of the fifth preference investors category. Congress sought alternative ways for aliens to obtain investor visas through the new pilot program by modifying the job creation requirements to allow alien investors to show that they created jobs indirectly. To take advantage of the pilot program, an alien investor must invest in a "regional center" designated by the INS. Three hundred visas are allocated annually.

Fourteen regional centers have been designated and are located in Greer, South Carolina; Blaine, Washington; New Orleans, Louisiana; Rouses Point, New York; Tukwila, Washington; Dallas, Texas; Atlanta, Georgia; Weston, Massachusetts; Charleston, South Carolina; Trenton, Michigan; Pueblo, Colorado; Golden Valley, Arizona; Las Vegas, Nevada; and Honolulu, Hawaii.

PLENARY POWER Congress is said to have vast or *plenary* power over the field of immigration. This is best illustrated by the Supreme Court's considerable deference to congressional judgment over what aliens should be admitted, excluded, or deported from the United States. Thus, immigration cases that involve racial **exclusion** (*Chae Chan Ping v. United States*), gender and illegitimacy (*Fiallo v. Bell*), and sexual orientation (*Adams v. Howerton*) receive limited review by the courts. In nonimmigration contexts, the constitutional scrutiny by the courts would be much more severe. In short, the Supreme Court has never ruled unconstitutional an immigration law enacted by Congress that deals with **admission,** exclusion, or deportation criteria.

PLYLER V. DOE The Supreme Court held that the Equal Protection Clause of the Fourteenth Amendment was violated by a Texas statute that withheld from local school districts any state funds for the education of children who were not "legally admitted" into the United States and that authorized schools to deny enrollment to such children. This case [457 U.S. 202 (1982)] was a class action filed on behalf of school-age children of Mexican origin residing in Smith County, Texas, who could not establish that they had been legally admitted into the United States. The Court ruled on their behalf, finding that the discrimination contained in the statute was not rational because it did not further a substantial goal of the state.

Although undocumented resident aliens cannot be treated as a "suspect class," and although education is not a "fundamental right," so as to require the state to justify the statute by showing that it serves a compelling governmental interest, nevertheless the statute imposed a lifetime hardship on a discrete class of children not accountable for their status. These children could neither affect their parents' conduct nor their own undocumented status.

> The deprivation of public education is not like the deprivation of some other governmental benefit. Public education has a pivotal role in maintaining the fabric of our society and in sustaining our political and cultural heritage. The deprivation of education takes an inestimable toll on the social, economic, intellectual, and psychological well-being of the individual, and poses an obstacle to individual achievement. The stigma of illiteracy would mark these children for the rest of their lives. By denying them a basic education, we would deny them the ability to live within the structure of our civic institutions, and foreclose any realistic possibility that they would contribute in even the smallest way to the progress of the Nation.

Texas's justification for the statute in the "preservation of the state's limited resources for the education of its lawful residents" was not sufficient. While the state might have an interest in mitigating the potentially harsh economic effects of an influx of undocumented immigrants, charging tuition to undocumented children constitutes an ineffectual attempt to stem the tide of undocumented immigration. The record also did not show that exclusion of undocumented children would likely improve the overall quality of education of the state.

 **POLICE CLEARANCE** When an alien applies for **immigrant** or **nonimmigrant** status, he or she must satisfy the **inadmissibility grounds,** which include several categories related to criminal activity. All such applicants must submit fingerprint cards, which are forwarded to the Federal Bureau of Investigation and international authorities to verify that the person does not fall within one of the criminal grounds of inadmissibility.

POLITICAL ASYLUM See **asylum.**

POLITICAL OPINION In order to be granted **asylum** in the United States, the applicant must establish a **well-founded fear of persecution** on one of five bases: nationality, race, religion, **membership in a particular social group,** or political opinion. Most asylum applicants base their claims on a fear of persecution based on their political opinion or views. In spite of the frequency of these claims, reported asylum cases have contained little discussion of what is and what is not political opinion for purposes of asylum. Instead, the attention of the courts has focused more on whether the alien can prove actual involvement in political groups, whether the foreign government is aware of the alien's political views, or whether a well-founded fear has been established.

Those courts and agencies that have considered the definition generally suggest that political opinions that are viable for asylum are those opinions not tolerated by the authorities that are critical. For applicants who have fled homelands suffering from great civil unrest and turmoil, their position actually may be one of neutrality, but merely holding a neutral opinion without revealing the neutrality does not qualify one for asylum. Although a few courts have indicated that asylum may be in order simply when the government attributes a particular view to the applicant (an **imputed political opinion**), many do not. Holding political opinions different from those of the government generally is not in itself a ground for claiming refugee status, and an applicant must show that he or she has a fear of persecution for holding such opinions. This presupposes that such opinions have come to the notice of the authorities or are attributed by them to the applicant.

Participation in political, student, peasant, union, or professional organizations is an example of activity that may qualify as expression of political opinion. Membership in a work cooperative may be an expression of political opinion, but merely attending meetings may not be sufficient. Once a reasonable possibility of persecution is established, it must be connected to the political belief or activity of the applicant, so the focus then turns to the persecutor's motive. [8 U.S.C. §§1101(a)(42), 1158; *Immigration and Naturalization Service v. Elias-Zacarias,* 112 S. Ct. 812 (1992); *Balazoski v. INS,* 932 F.2d 638 (7th Cir. 1991); Garcia-*Ramos v. INS,* 775 F.2d 1370 (9th Cir. 1985); *Bolanos-Hernandez v. INS,* 749 F.2d 1316 (9th Cir. 1984)]

PORT OF ENTRY   Officers of the INS conduct **inspection**s at ports of entry to determine whether aliens are admissible to the United States [see **admission**]. The port of entry can be along the border, at an entry point where ships arrive, or at an airport. Even an airport such as the one in Denver, Colorado, may be regarded as a port of entry for inspection purposes if it is the first place that an airplane arrives from abroad. At some airports abroad, such as in Canada and the Bahamas, passengers are inspected by U.S. INS officers prior to departure to the United States. The inspection by the INS officer can include questioning of the alien, questioning of traveling companions, examination of travel documents, and even examinations of the contents of baggage to determine whether the person is entitled to enter.

POVERTY GUIDELINES   A prospective immigrant who is likely to become a **public charge** can be denied an immigrant visa. In deciding whether a person is likely to become a public charge, officials generally refer to income poverty guidelines published each year by the Department of Health and Human Services. [45 C.F.R. §1060.2]

Any family-sponsored immigrant and some employment-based immigrants must submit an **affidavit of support** as part of the immigrant or **adjustment of status** application. A person petitioning for a family member must submit a legally binding affidavit of support on behalf of the prospective immigrant. The **sponsor** must agree to provide support to maintain the sponsored alien at an annual income that is not less than 125 percent of the federal poverty line. The affidavit of support must be enforceable by the alien, the federal government, and the state. The affidavit must continue to be enforceable until the alien has become a citizen of the United States or has worked forty qualifying quarters for purposes of Social Security coverage.

The key to applying the income poverty guidelines and satisfying the 125 percent rule is knowing which household members or dependents must be counted in determining family unit size, as well as whose income can be included. The sponsor must include the intending immigrant's accompanying family members, although separate sponsors for **derivative beneficiary** family members can be sought. All income generated by individuals living in the household can be considered, provided they have been living in the household for at least six months. [8 U.S.C. §§1182(a)(4), 1183a]

PREFERENCE SYSTEM   The immigration selection system is divided into two preference systems, one for family-based immigration [see **family-sponsored preferences**] and the other for employment-based immigration [see **employment-based preferences**], that are subject to worldwide and per-country **numerical limitations. Immediate relatives** of United States citizens are not part of either preference system and therefore are not subject to any numerical limitations.

The family-based preference system has four categories. First preference is reserved for the adult (age twenty-one or over) unmarried sons and daughters of United States citizens. The term *unmarried* includes persons who were previously married but who are presently not married. Second preference is the only category under which **lawful permanent resident**

aliens can petition for relatives. This category is further divided into two subcategories: 2-A for the spouses and children (unmarried and under twenty-one) of lawful permanent residents, and 2-B for unmarried sons and daughters (age twenty-one and over) of lawful permanent residents. As the only category available to lawful permanent resident petitioners, the popularity of second preference has resulted in significant waiting periods for prospective immigrants from countries such as Mexico and the Philippines. This is due to the demand for visas from these countries and the country numerical limitations that are imposed on immigrants from individual countries. [8 U.S.C. §1153(a)(2)] See **visa bulletin.**

Third preference is reserved for the married sons and daughters of U.S. citizens. Only U.S. citizens, not lawful permanent residents or noncitizen **nationals**, can petition for married sons and daughters. **Fourth preference** is for the brothers and sisters of adult (at least age twenty-one) United States citizens. The beneficiary brother or sister can be married or unmarried and can be an adult or a child. Fourth preference is possible even if the siblings are half brothers or half sisters. Stepbrothers and stepsisters can also qualify for fourth preference. [8 U.S.C. §1153(a)]

The employment-based preference system is divided into five categories. First preference is for immigrants with extraordinary ability (such as in the sciences, arts, education, business, or athletics), outstanding professors and researchers, and certain executives and managers of multinational companies. Second preference provides for two separate means of qualification: those who are individuals "of exceptional ability" or those "members of the professions holding advanced degrees." These categories were created in 1990 and significantly decreased the length of time required for **professionals** with advanced degrees to immigrate to the United States.

For those seeking exceptional ability classification, the law requires that the ability be in the sciences, arts, or business. Furthermore, it must be shown that the individual's immigration will substantially benefit the U.S. economy, cultural or educational interests, or welfare. Generally, the individual's services in the sciences, arts, professions, or business must be sought by an employer in the United States, but a **national interest waiver** provides an opportunity for some individuals to immigrate without a job offer or an **alien employment certification.**

Professionals with advanced degrees have long been able to immigrate to the United States. The term *profession* is defined to mean "any occupation for which a U.S. baccalaureate degree or its foreign equivalent is the minimum requirement for entry into the occupation," as well as any of the occupations listed in the statute: architects, engineers, lawyers, physicians, surgeons, and teachers in elementary or secondary schools, colleges, academies, or seminaries. The second preference immigrant classification is limited to professionals with advanced degrees. An "advanced degree" may be "any U.S. academic or professional degree or a foreign equivalent degree above that of baccalaureate." An individual is considered to hold the equivalent of a master's degree after the award of a U.S. baccalaureate degree or a foreign equivalent degree followed by at least five years of progressive experience in the specialty. [8 U.S.C. §1153(b)(2); 8 C.F.R. §204.5(k)]

Third preference is for skilled workers, professionals, and other workers. Fourth preference is for **special immigrants** (except returned lawful permanent residents and former citizens). Fifth preference is a category for investors whose investments create at least ten new jobs [see **investor visa**].

PREVAILING WAGE An **alien employment certification** (or labor certification) for individuals who are seeking to immigrate based on certain **employment-based preference** system categories will not be issued unless it can be shown that the employment of the alien will not adversely affect the wages of U.S. workers similarly situated. Thus the application for labor certification must offer the alien the prevailing rate of pay in the locality of intended employment. [20 C.F.R. §656] The offer must equal or exceed the prevailing wage rate; however, the standard will be deemed met if the offer is within 5 percent of the average rate or was negotiated between a union and the employer.

The Employment and Training Administration of the **Department of Labor** (DOL) has issued instructions effective January 1, 1998, on the new Occupational Employment Statistics (OES) system for determining prevailing wages. These procedures are used to set prevailing wages for nonagricultural immigration programs, including employment-based immigrant visas and **H-1B worker** and H-2B nonimmigrant programs.

For years, the labor certification system has been relying on prevailing wage determinations at the **state employment office** (SESA) level. That system produced numbers inconsistent from state to state. DOL examined alternatives and settled on the OES system of the Bureau of Labor Statistics, which is able to provide wage data for numerous jobs nationwide and also break down data according to geographic areas. Now the SESAs will have no role in producing prevailing wage determinations. Instead, SESAs will access the OES data. OES surveys will be based on the jobs listed in the Bureau of Labor Statistics' OES dictionary.

In determining prevailing wages for permanent and temporary labor certification programs, a regulatory scheme must be followed. [20 C.F.R. §656.40] When a wage determination has been issued under the Davis-Bacon Act or the Service Contract Act, or negotiated in a collective bargaining agreement, that wage controls. In the absence of such wage determinations, SESAs are to determine prevailing wage rates using wage surveys conducted under the wage component of the OES program. If the employer provides the SESA with a wage survey, whether public or private, that meets DOL requirements, that rate will be used by the SESA as the prevailing wage determination in response to that particular request. When no wage determination exists under any of these sources and the SESA is aware of alternative sources of wage information, the SESA may utilize that wage data for prevailing wage purposes as long as it meets DOL criteria.

The methodology in any type of survey must reflect the average rate of wages, that is, the rate of wages to be determined, to the extent feasible, by adding the wages paid to workers similarly employed in the area of intended employment and dividing the total by the number of such workers. This will usually require computing a weighted average. The wage offered by the employer will generally be considered as meeting the prevailing wage standard if it falls within 5 percent of the average rate of wages (except for some H-1B situations). In issuing wage determinations, the SESAs may be required to convert an hourly rate to a weekly, monthly, or annual rate, or to convert a weekly, monthly, or annual rate to an hourly rate.

PRIORITY DATE   Because **preference system** visa demand for several countries often surpasses the per-country **numerical limitations,** as reflected in the monthly **visa bulletin,** a system of priority dates is used to determine the order of processing family and **employment-based preference** category immigrants. A priority date is generally established on the date a **visa petition** is filed on behalf of the prospective immigrant. For **alien employment certification** (labor certification) cases, the priority date is established on the date the labor certification application is filed.

For example, if a first, second, third, or fourth preference family visa petition form is filed on February 20, 1999, that date becomes the beneficiary's priority date, even though the petition may not be approved until later. Similarly, when a person seeks to immigrate through the labor certification process under the third preference employment category, the date on which the application for labor certification is filed with labor officials establishes the priority date. If a labor certification is not needed, the date of the filing of the employer's visa petition establishes the priority date.

If the status of the beneficiary changes during a waiting period, the beneficiary can retain the same priority date so long as he or she still falls into an immigrant category. For example, if a third preference family beneficiary (married son or daughter of a U.S. citizen) becomes unmarried, the petition is automatically converted to first preference (or immediate relative if under the age of 21).

PROFESSIONAL   A professional is an individual immigrating to the United States in order to perform a job that requires at least a baccalaureate degree from a U.S. university or a foreign equivalent degree. The term *profession* is defined by statute to include, but is not limited to, architects, engineers, lawyers, physicians, surgeons, and teachers in elementary or secondary schools, colleges, academies, or seminaries. The statutory definition is expressly written in a nonexclusive manner and administrative decisions have further identified professional occupations. Furthermore, the standing of an occupation as a profession can evolve with time as the minimum educational requirements needed for entry into that occupation increase. The common denominator is that professions require specialized training that is normally obtained through higher education or for which a bachelor's degree can be obtained. Equivalent specialized instruction and experience may also suffice.

Accountants, engineers, biochemists, biologists, chemists, dentists, dietitians, veterinarians, zoologists, economists, mathematicians, sociologists, hotel managers, journalists, librarians, pharmacists, and social workers have been classified as professionals. Professional standing has been denied to translators, laboratory assistants, school counselors, and mechanical technologists. [8 U.S.C. §1101(a)(32)]

PROFESSIONAL ATHLETE   Professional athletes who do not qualify for employment first preference (exempt from labor certification due to extraordinary ability) can qualify for third preference through a labor certification (see **alien employment certification**). The term *professional athlete* means an individual who is employed as an athlete by a team that is a member of an association of six or more professional sports teams whose total combined revenues exceed $10 million per year, or any minor league team that is affiliated with such an association. The immigration laws recognize that professional athletes often get traded from one team to another. A labor certification for a professional athlete remains valid even if the athlete changes employers, if the new employer is a team in the same sport as the team that employed the athlete when the athlete first applied for certification. [8 U.S.C. §1182(a)(5)(A)(iii)]

PROPOSITION 187   In 1994, the voters of California passed an initiative directed at discouraging undocumented immigration to California. The sweeping language of Proposition 187 would deny public education benefits to **undocumented alien** children and the documented children of undocumented alien parents, and cut off their access to public benefits and health benefits. Proposition 187 has been ruled unconstitutional by a federal district court, and in 1999 an appeals court agreed to a mediated settlement that Proposition 187 would not be enforced. Before such an educational prohibition could go into effect, the Supreme Court would have to reverse its opinion in *Plyler v. Doe,* in which the court ruled unconstitutional a similar restriction in Texas that would have prevented undocumented alien children from attending public schools.

The major provisions of Proposition 187 were as follows:

Section 1. Findings and Declaration.

The People of California find and declare as follows:

That they have suffered and are suffering economic hardship caused by the presence of illegal aliens in the state.

That they have suffered and are suffering personal injury and damage by the criminal conduct of illegal aliens in this state.

That they have a right to the protection of their government from any person or persons entering this country unlawfully.

Therefore, the People of California declare their intention to provide for cooperation between their agencies of state and local government with the federal government, and to establish a system of required notification by and between such agencies to prevent illegal aliens in the United States from receiving benefits or public services of the State of California.

. . .

Section 5. Exclusion of Illegal Aliens from Public Social Services.

. . .

(a) In order to carry out the intention of the People of California that only citizens of the United States and aliens lawfully admitted to the United States may receive the benefits of public social services and to ensure that all persons employed in the providing of those services shall diligently protect public funds from misuse, the provisions of this section are adopted.

(b) A person shall not receive any public social services to which he or she may be otherwise entitled until the legal status of that person has been verified as one of the following:

(1) A citizen of the United States.

(2) An alien lawfully admitted as a permanent resident.

(3) An alien lawfully admitted for a temporary period of time.

(c) If any public entity of this state to whom a person has applied for public social services determines or reasonably suspects, based upon the information provided to it, that the person is an alien in the United States in violation of federal law, the following procedures shall be followed by the entity:

(1) The entity shall not provide the person with benefits or services.

(2) The entity shall, in writing, notify the person of his or her apparent illegal immigration status, and that the person must either obtain legal status or leave the United States.

(3) The entity shall also notify the State Director of Social Services, the Attorney General of California and the United States Immigration and Naturalization Service of the apparent illegal status, and shall provide any additional information that may be requested by any other public entity.

Section 6. Exclusion of Illegal Aliens from Publicly Funded Health Care

. . .

(a) In order to carry out the intention of the People of California that, excepting emergency medical care as required by federal law, only citizens of the United States and aliens lawfully admitted to the United States may receive the public benefits of publicly funded health care, and to ensure that all persons employed in the providing of those services shall diligently protect public funds from misuse, the provisions of this section are adopted.

(b) A person shall not receive any health care services from a publicly funded health care facility, to which he or she is otherwise entitled, until the legal status of that person has been verified as one of the following:

(1) A citizen of the United States.

(2) An alien lawfully admitted as a permanent resident.

(3) An alien lawfully admitted for a temporary period of time.

(c) If any publicly funded health care facility in this state from whom a person seeks health care services, other than emergency medical care as required by federal law, determines or reasonably suspects, based upon the information provided to it, that the person is an alien in the United States in violation of federal law, the following procedures shall be followed by the facility:

(1) The facility shall not provide the person with services.

(2) The facility shall, in writing, notify the person of his or her apparent illegal immigration status, and that the person must either obtain legal status or leave the United States.

(3) The facility shall also notify the State Director of Social Services, the Attorney General of California and the United States Immigration and Naturalization Service of the apparent illegal status, and shall provide any additional information that may be requested by any other public entity.

. . .

Section 7. Exclusion of Illegal Aliens from Public Elementary and Secondary Schools.

. . .

(a) No public elementary or secondary school shall admit, or permit the attendance of, any child who is not a citizen of the United States, an alien lawfully admitted as a permanent resident, or a person who is otherwise authorized under federal law to be present in the United States.

(b) Commencing January 1, 1995, each school district shall verify the legal status of each child enrolling in the school district for the first time in order to ensure the enrollment or attendance only of citizens, aliens lawfully admitted as permanent residents, or persons who are otherwise authorized to be present in the United States.

(c) By January 1, 1996, each school district shall have verified the legal status of each child already enrolled in attendance in the school district in order to ensure the enrollment or attendance only of citizens, aliens lawfully admitted as permanent residents, or persons who are otherwise authorized under federal law to be present in the United States.

(d) By January 1, 1996, each school district shall also have verified the legal status of each parent or guardian of each child referred to in subdivision (b) and (c) above, to determine whether such parent or guardian is one of the following:

(1) A citizen of the United States.

(2) An alien lawfully admitted as a permanent resident.

(3) An alien admitted lawfully for a temporary period of time.

(e) Each school district shall provide information to the State Superintendent of Public Instruction, the Attorney General of California and the United States Immigration and Naturalization Service regarding any enrollee or pupil, or parent or guardian, attending a public elementary or secondary school in the school district determined or reasonably suspected to be in violation of federal immigration laws within forty-five days after becoming aware of an apparent violation. The notice shall also be provided to the parent or legal guardian of the enrollee or pupil, and shall state that an existing pupil may not continue to attend the school after ninety calendar days from the date of the notice, unless legal status is established.

(f) For each child who cannot establish legal status in the United States, each school district shall continue to provide education for a period of ninety days from the date of the notice. Such ninety-day period shall be utilized to accomplish an orderly transition to a school in the child's country of origin. Each school district shall fully cooperate in this transition effort to ensure that the educational needs of the child are best served for that period of time.

PROTECTED INDIVIDUAL Under the **Immigration Reform and Control Act of 1986** (IRCA), it is an unfair immigration-related employment practice for an employer to discriminate against a person who is authorized to work with respect to hiring the individual for employment or discharging the individual from employment on the basis of the individual's national origin, or the individual's citizenship status, as long as the person is a protected citizen or alien. See **national origin discrimination.**

The term *protected individual* includes the following: (1) **citizen**s or non-citizen **nationals** of the United States, (2) **lawful permanent resident alien**s, (3) **lawful temporary resident** aliens, (4) **refugee**s, and (5) **asylee**s.

An alien ceases being a protected individual if (a) he or she fails to apply for **naturalization** within six months of the date of becoming eligible to apply for naturalization (usually after being a lawful permanent resident for five years), or (b) he or she has filed for naturalization in a timely fashion, but has not become naturalized as a citizen within two years of the application. This essentially covers applicants who fail to pursue their application after being called in for the naturalization exam or interview. Processing time consumed by the INS in handling the application does not count toward the two-year period.

PROXY MARRIAGE A proxy marriage is one during which the contracting parties are not physically in the presence of each other. Unless such a marriage is consummated, the marriage will not be recognized for U.S. immigration purposes. [8 U.S.C. §1101(a)(35)] Even in nonimmigrant **fiancé visa** situations, petitions will not be approved unless the parties have met personally.

PRUCOL The acronym PRUCOL stands for "permanently residing in the United States under color of law." This phrase is used as a standard for determining whether certain aliens, who may not yet be **lawful permanent resident alien**s, are eligible for certain public benefits or welfare. In general, an alien who is "permanently residing in the United States under color of law," with the knowledge of authorities and who has not been ordered deported, will be regarded as having met legal residence requirements for public benefits. See *Holley v. Lavine.*

PUBLIC CHARGE A prospective immigrant who is likely to become a public charge is not admissible to the United States. In general, this means that a person who is likely to need public assistance or welfare will not be allowed to immigrate. Immigration authorities define *public charge* as an **alien** who has become (for **removal** purposes) or is likely to become (for **admission** or **adjustment of status** purposes) "primarily dependent on the government for subsistence, as demonstrated by either the receipt of public cash assistance for income maintenance, or institutionalization for long-term care at government expense." This definition alone, however, cannot be used to determine if an alien is a public charge—other issues must be considered. Consular and INS officials have tremendous discretion in determining whether an alien is likely to become a public charge. In making this determination, officials consider the alien's health, age, family status, assets, resources, financial status, education, and skills. A healthy person in the prime of life should not ordinarily be considered likely to become a public charge.

In deciding whether a person is likely to become a public charge, officials generally refer to income **poverty guidelines** published each year by the Department of Health and Human Services. [45 C.F.R. §1060.2]

Any family-sponsored immigrant and some employment-based immigrants must submit an **affidavit of support** as part of the immigrant or adjustment-of-status application. The person petitioning for the family member must submit a legally binding affidavit of support on behalf of the prospective immigrant. The **sponsor** must agree to provide support to maintain the sponsored alien at an annual income that is not less than 125 percent of the federal poverty line. The affidavit of support must be enforceable by the alien, the federal government, and the state. The affidavit must continue to be enforceable until the alien has become a citizen of the United States or has worked forty qualifying quarters for purposes of Social Security coverage.

The key to applying the income poverty guidelines and satisfying the 125 percent rule is knowing which household members or dependents must be counted in determining family unit size and whose income can be included. The sponsor must include the intending immigrant's accompanying family members, although separate sponsors for **derivative beneficiary** family members can be sought. In determining the amount of household income that can be considered, income generated by individuals living in the household is allowed, provided that they have been living in the household for at least six months. [8 U.S.C. §§1182(a)(4), 1183a]

Certain immigrants who later become public charges may become deportable and subject to removal. An immigrant who becomes a public charge within five years of entry from a cause not affirmatively shown to have arisen since entry is deportable. This means that if the reason the person needs public assistance developed after entry, then removal is not appropriate. For example, if the person became disabled after immigrating and then needed public assistance, presumably this **deportation ground** would not apply. [8 U.S.C. §1227(a)(5); *Matter of B*, 3 I. & N. Dec. 323 (BIA 1948) (approved by Acting Att'y Gen. 1948)]

As for aliens who are in the United States, government officials have provided specific guidance as to particular programs. Examples of benefits that will not be considered for public charge purposes include Medicaid and other health insurance and health services (including public assistance for immunizations and for testing and treatment of symptoms of communicable diseases, use of health clinics, and prenatal care), other than support for institutionalization for long-term care; Children's Health Insurance Program (CHIP); nutrition programs, including Food Stamps, the Special Supplemental Nutrition Program for Women, Infants and Children (WIC), the National School Lunch and Breakfast programs, and other supplementary and emergency food assistance programs; housing assistance; child care services; energy assistance, such as the Low Income Home Energy Assistance Program; emergency disaster relief; foster care and adoption assistance; and educational assistance, including benefits under the Head Start Act and aid for elementary, secondary, or higher education, and job training programs. A public charge problem, however, does arise from cash assistance for income maintenance, including such programs as Supplemental Security Income (SSI), cash assistance from the Temporary Assistance for Needy Families (TANF) program, and state or local cash assistance programs.

PUBLIC HEALTH SERVICE The immigration laws provide a number of ways to prevent persons who are or have been afflicted with certain psychological and medical problems or contagious diseases from entering the United States. The U.S. Public Health Service under the Department of Health and Human Services has sole responsibility to make determinations regarding the medical and psychological conditions of these visa applicants. These determinations are only reviewable by a panel of doctors under the Public Health Service. [8 U.S.C. §1222]

Public Health Service doctors are often stationed in foreign countries and conduct examinations before visas are issued; others inspect incoming passengers at **ports of entry.**

The Public Health Service is headed by the surgeon general, who is responsible for designating doctors who can perform medical examinations of all applicants for visas and **adjustment of status.** Most of these examinations are in fact performed by private doctors who have been authorized to perform examinations. Local **district offices** of the INS provide lists of such authorized doctors to adjustment applicants.

Q

QUOTAS See **numerical limitations.**

R

RAVANCHO V. INS This case [658 F.2d 169 (3rd Cir. 1981)] illustrates the importance of having U.S. citizen children of school age to the issue of whether or not an applicant would suffer **extreme hardship** if relief is denied.

Zenaida and Alejandro Ravancho, husband and wife, were citizens of the Philippines who had an eight-year-old U.S. citizen daughter born in the United States. The Ravanchos were deportable and were seeking a form of relief from **deportation** that required a showing of **extreme hardship.** They proved that they had stable employment and that they had purchased a house. They also sought to establish hardship for their child, arguing that she knew no other life than that in the United States, was unable to speak the Philippine language, was a straight-A student in school, and that her life would be dramatically upset by being uprooted from her home, friends, and the only life she knew.

The court of appeals was receptive to these arguments, and urged the **Board of Immigration Appeals** to consider all of these factors. Having school-age children who were Americanized made all the difference.

REDUCTION IN RECRUITMENT In October 1996, the **Department of Labor** established the reduction in recruitment (RIR) procedure, which offered a streamlined, time-saving process for **alien employment certification,** an important step in becoming an immigrant based on specialized employment. Under the RIR procedure, the employer who wishes to hire an immigrant worker permanently gets credit for unsuccessful recruitment efforts to find available U.S. workers that were made prior to seeking the permanent hiring of the immigrant worker. The best RIR scenario is when the prior recruitment demonstrated that the **prevailing wage** rate and working conditions were advertised, a sustained pattern of recruitment efforts took place for six months, and no qualified applicants responded to the recruitment efforts. In such RIR situations, no further recruitment by the employer is necessary before seeking the labor certification on behalf of the immigrant worker from the Department of Labor.

During the unsuccessful recruitment period, the employer must show that all the advertised requirements for the job are normal for the particular job. To demonstrate that the job requirements are normal, the employer must show that other similarly situated employees also possess the same skill or knowledge, and that the employer's preexisting job descriptions and recruitment efforts delineated the need for the requirements or that changed conditions have mandated an upgrade in job requirements. Often the Department of Labor refers to the *Dictionary of Occupational Titles* to determine the requirements that are commonly used in the industry.

A successful RIR case means that conventional recruitment pursuant to the *Technical Assistance Guide* (e.g., internal notice to current employees for ten days in conspicuous locations, a thirty-day job order with the local unemployment office) is waived. However, to achieve this position, the employer must demonstrate that recruitment through sources normal to the occupation has occurred and that further recruitment will not be fruitful. Of course the demonstration is dependent on the type of job, location of the job, and the labor market of the region. Prior recruitment must be sustained or extensive, and the employer should consider going beyond newspaper advertisements to include such efforts as the Internet and college campus recruitment to show good faith.

REENTRY DOCTRINE   Exclusion and inadmissibility grounds are numerous and represent years of ad hoc congressional determinations as to which aliens are deemed unfit to be admitted into the United States. The grounds of inadmissibility and exclusion apply to all aliens, including **lawful permanent resident alien**s, not just new or first-time entering immigrants. Every attempted return to the United States could be the equivalent of an application for **admission.** The concept of the reentry doctrine provides that a lawful permanent resident alien may be subject to the grounds of inadmissibility when a new admission is attempted into the United States.

However, the law does provide that a lawful permanent resident who has been absent from the United States for 180 days or less is not considered an applicant for admission, unless special circumstances apply. In general, therefore, the grounds of inadmissibility do not apply to such returning immigrants. The special circumstances under which an immigrant will run into problems are when (1) the alien has abandoned or relinquished status [see **abandonment of permanent residence**]; (2) the alien has engaged in illegal activity since departing the United States; (3) the alien departed the United States under legal process seeking his or her **removal** from the United States; (4) the alien committed a crime; or (5) the alien is attempting to enter by avoiding **inspection**. See *Rosenberg v. Fleuti; Matter of Collado* [Int. Dec. No. 3333 (BIA 1997)].

REENTRY PERMIT Whenever a **lawful permanent resident alien** desires to leave the United States for more than a year, the person should obtain a reentry permit from the INS. In general, a lawful permanent resident alien who travels abroad for more than a year runs the risk of being deemed to have abandoned lawful permanent residence [see **abandonment of permanent residence**]. A reentry permit provides evidence that the person intends to travel out of the United States only temporarily.

The reentry permit is valid for a maximum of two years and cannot be extended. Possession does not guarantee readmission, especially if there is other evidence that the person actually intended to abandon permanent residence. Lawful permanent resident aliens who make trips of short duration out of the United States, for example for no more than a year, do not need a reentry permit if the type of trip is rare.

REFUGEE The immigration laws permit the president, in consultation with Congress, to admit refugees from abroad into the United States. A person who is outside the United States who has a **well-founded fear of persecution** on account of race, religion, nationality, **membership in a particular social group**, or **political opinion** may be eligible to apply for refugee status to enter the United States. In order to qualify, however, the person must originate from one of the geographic regions of the world designated by the president and Congress as areas from which refugees may enter. These areas generally include Africa, East Asia, Europe, Latin America and the Caribbean, the Near East, and South Asia. Special considerations exist for persons in Vietnam, Cuba, and the former Soviet Union. Individuals seeking refugee status and **asylum** status are similar in that they both must establish a well-founded fear of persecution. Asylum seekers, however, are those who have made it to the shores of the United States or inside its borders and theoretically can be from any country, while those seeking refugee status are applying from abroad and must be from one of the designated areas. [8 U.S.C. §§1101(a)(42), 1157, 1158]

The term *refugee* does not include any person who ordered, incited, assisted, or otherwise participated in the persecution of any person on account of race, religion, nationality, membership in a particular social group, or political opinion.

In response to mainland China's one-child-only policy, Congress has recognized that a person who has been forced to abort a pregnancy or to undergo involuntary sterilization, or who has been persecuted for failure or refusal to undergo such a procedure or for other resistance to a coercive population control program, shall be deemed to have been persecuted on account of political opinion, and a person who has a well-founded fear that he or she will be forced to undergo such a procedure or subject to persecution for such failure, refusal, or resistance shall be deemed to have a well-founded fear of persecution on account of political opinion. [8 U.S.C. §1101(a)(42)] See *In re X—P—T—*.

REFUGEE ACT OF 1980   The Refugee Act of 1980 amended the **Immigration and Nationality Act** by adding specific statutory provisions to establish categories and requirements for aliens who seek **asylum** or **refugee** status. The United States became a party to the **United Nations Protocol Relating to the Status of Refugees** in 1968. The protocol is a multilateral treaty that effectively incorporates the terms of the United Nations **Convention Relating to the Status of Refugees of 1951.** The legislative history of the 1980 act reveals that it was intended to bring U.S. law into conformity with the protocol. For example, the House of Representatives report accompanying the amendments declared that the "Committee Amendment conforms United States law to our obligations under Article 33 [of the Convention] in two of its provisions." And the conference report stated that the "conference substitute adopts the House provision with the understanding that it is based directly under the language of the Protocol and it is intended that the language be construed consistent with the Protocol." However, even prior to 1980, the United States was required to apply the provisions of the protocol by acceding to its terms in 1968.

Note that the **withholding of deportation** relief that existed prior to the enactment of the 1980 Refugee Act contains language similar to the asylum and refugee provisions. An alien in **removal proceedings** will apply for both asylum and withholding. Asylum is discretionary, but withholding was made mandatory by the Refugee Act if its requirements are met. See *INS v. Stevic* [467 U.S. 407 (1984)].

The Refugee Act of 1980 made several other important changes. The **parole** authority of the **attorney general** could no longer be used to admit groups of refugees; only individual refugees can be admitted under parole for compelling reasons of public interest. The law eliminated language in the law that gave special preference to those fleeing from Communist-dominated countries or countries of the Middle East. The statute also established the position of U.S. coordinator of refugee affairs, with the rank of ambassador-at-large, to be appointed by the president with the advice and consent of the Senate. However, a 1994 law eliminated the coordinator position.

REGIONAL INS OFFICES The **Immigration and Naturalization Service** is divided into three regions: Eastern, Central, and Western. Each regional office is headed by a regional director, who directs and supervises INS local **district offices**. The regional directors are responsible for fiscal management of the region and have authority over **regional service centers**. In truth, much of the authority of the regional directors has diminished over the years, with various associate commissioners in the Washington, D.C., central office assuming much more authority over issues such as appeals of decisions by local offices and the settlement of tort claims against local officials.

REGIONAL SERVICE CENTERS These offices were originally established in 1982 to centralize and expedite the processing and decisions of certain applications more efficiently. There are four such service centers, located in Laguna Niguel, California; Lincoln, Nebraska; St. Albans, Vermont; and Mesquite, Texas.

Each service center has its own character and processing procedures. But the idea is the same at all centers: process applications consistently and efficiently, and develop expertise among the staff in different types of immigration applications.

REGISTRY This term is often used to describe an amnesty type of procedure for **undocumented aliens** who have lived in the United States for many years. One form of registry is for those aliens who entered prior to July 1, 1924. In those cases, INS authorities establish a record of lawful admission for permanent residence for such individuals as of the actual date of entry, as long as the person is not inadmissible under provisions relating to criminals, subversives, narcotics, alien smuggling, or immoral activities.

Another form of registry is for those aliens who entered prior to January 1, 1972, who have maintained continuous residence in the United States since entry, and who are of **good moral character**. The good moral character requirement relates to a reasonable period of time preceding the application. The greater the gravity of an applicant's past misconduct, the longer the period of intervening good conduct must be. [8 U.S.C. §1259; *Matter of Sanchez-Linn*, Int. Dec. No. 3156 (BIA 1991)]

RELATIVE VISA PETITION See **visa petition**.

RELIGIOUS WORKER   See **fourth preference.**

REMOVAL   The process whereby an inadmissible or deportable alien is excluded or deported from the United States. The terminology of *deportation* and *exclusion* from the United States was changed to *removal* in the **Illegal Immigration Reform and Immigrant Responsibility Act of 1996** (IIRAIRA). In order to be removed from the United States, the person must fall within one of the **inadmissibility grounds** or one of the **deportation grounds.** Many persons who are removable have the right to **removal proceedings** before an **immigration judge.**

REMOVAL GROUNDS   See **deportation grounds.**

REMOVAL PROCEEDINGS   The administrative court process that determines whether someone will be subjected to **removal** (**deportation** or **exclusion**) from the United States. Removal proceedings against a person begin when the INS issues a **notice to appear,** files it with the **immigration court,** and provides a copy to the person. Often the INS arrests the person first, then issues the notice to appear. The notice to appear contains factual allegations that support the government's position that the person falls within one or more **deportation grounds.**

If the person is taken into custody, he or she may be entitled to a bond hearing to determine a bail amount. The next stage is a master calendar hearing, where the **immigration judge** begins a preliminary inquiry into whether the person is removable as charged by the INS and whether some form of relief or defense may be sought. If the person can apply for some form of relief (e.g., **adjustment of status, asylum,** or **cancellation of removal**), the judge will schedule another longer hearing to decide the application at a merits hearing or a regular calendar hearing. If the person cannot apply for any relief, the person may be afforded the privilege of **voluntary departure,** or may be ordered removed.

If the person has a defense or is seeking some type of relief, a merits hearing will be scheduled. The person has a right to an attorney, but not at government expense, at any stage of the process. [8 U.S.C. §1229a(b)(4)] See *Aguilera-Enriquez v. INS.* The government is represented at the merits hearing by an INS district counsel, and of course the immigration judge is present. A court reporter is present, and if the person subject to proceedings cannot speak English, an interpreter is provided at government expense.

In general, the hearings are formal and open to the public. Depending on the physical facilities, the immigration judge may limit the number of persons who may attend at any one time, giving priority to the press over the general public. For the protection of witnesses or charged aliens, or in consideration of the public interest, the judge may exclude the public or particular individuals from the hearing.

Some persons do not have the right to regular removal proceedings and may be subject to **expedited removal proceedings.** For example, persons who are apprehended at an airport without proper documents and those who are arrested at a border while crossing surreptitiously are placed in expedited removal proceedings.

RENUNCIATION OF CITIZENSHIP The process of signing a statement giving up U.S. citizenship. The law provides for **expatriation** for renunciation of U.S. citizenship upon the formal written renunciation before a diplomatic or consular officer of the United States abroad. [8 U.S.C. §1481(a)(5)] The following statement may be used for such renunciation:

> I desire to make a formal renunciation of my American nationality, as provided by [statute], and pursuant thereto I hereby absolutely and entirely renounce my nationality in the United States, and all rights and privileges thereunder pertaining, and abjure all allegiance and fidelity to the United States of America.

Renunciation is not contingent upon acquiring the nationality of another country; in such circumstances, statelessness can result. See *Jolley v. INS* [441 F.2d 1245 (5th Cir. 1971)]. The person becomes an alien for purposes of U.S. immigration law.

A finding of expatriation is not appropriate when the person can establish that renunciation was impelled by economic duress sufficient to negate free choice.

In *Davis v. District Director* [481 F. Supp. 1178 (D.D.C. 1979)], Garry Davis challenged his **exclusion** from the United States on the grounds that he did not have valid immigration documents on his attempt to be admitted. He was a native of the United States and served as a bomber pilot during World War II. In 1948, he voluntarily signed an oath of renunciation of U.S. nationality at the American embassy in Paris, France. As a result, the U.S. consul issued him a Certificate of Loss of Nationality of the United States.

After that, Davis devoted his time and energy toward the establishment of world government and the furtherance of world citizenship. He frequently traveled abroad to promote those principles and goals. At various times he had been allowed to enter the United States as a **lawful permanent resident alien** or on a visitor's visa.

On May 13, 1977, Davis attempted to enter the United States on a passport issued by the World Service Authority, an organization formed to promote world citizenship. However, the **immigration court** and eventually the **Board of Immigration Appeals** would not admit him because he lacked a valid entry document. The federal district court agreed. Since Davis's renunciation was intentional and voluntary, his expatriation was appropriate and he became an alien. Thereafter, he had to obtain a proper visa to be admitted to the United States.

RESTRICTION ON REMOVAL In **removal proceedings,** aliens must be afforded relief if their life or freedom would be threatened in their native country because of race, religion, nationality, **membership in a particular social group,** or **political opinion.** Prior to 1996, this relief was referred to as **withholding of deportation.** Restriction on removal or withholding of removal is very similar to obtaining **asylum.**

However, there are two technical, but critical, differences between these two remedies. One difference relates to the degree of proof that is necessary to establish eligibility. For restriction on removal, the applicant must demonstrate a **clear probability of persecution,** which, according to the Supreme Court, means showing that it is more likely than not that persecution will occur. In contrast, for asylum, the applicant need only show a **well-founded fear of persecution,** which means that if a reasonable person in the shoes of the applicant would fear persecution, the standard of proof is met. In asylum the person should be given the benefit of the doubt.

The second distinction is that if the respective standards of proof are met, restriction on removal is mandatory, while asylum is discretionary. This means that the **immigration judge** must grant restriction on removal if a clear probability of persecution is established. On the other hand, if a well-founded fear of persecution is established, the INS or the immigration judge can still deny asylum as a matter of discretion if negative factors exist, such as the fact that the person may have firmly resettled in a third country.

A person is not eligible for restriction on removal if he or she has (1) persecuted others, (2) been convicted of a particularly serious crime and is a danger to the community, (3) committed a serious nonpolitical crime outside the United States, or (4) become a danger to the security of the United

States. [8 U.S.C. §1231(b)(3); *Immigration and Naturalization Service v. Cardoza-Fonseca*, 107 S.Ct. 1207 (1987); *Stevic v. INS*, 104 S.Ct. 2489 (1984)]

In *Immigration and Naturalization Service v. Aguirre-Aguirre* (1999), the Supreme Court unanimously deferred to the attorney general's interpretation of the "serious nonpolitical crime" preclusion.

RESTRICTIONIST   Someone who advocates a policy or philosophy favoring restrictions on immigration. See **Federation for American Immigration Reform; Know-Nothing Party.**

REVOCATION OF NATURALIZATION   Revocation of **naturalization,** or denaturalization, is authorized under certain circumstances. For example, revocation may be sought when naturalization was illegally procured or procured by concealment of a material fact or by willful misrepresentation. Affiliation with a Communist or other proscribed organization within five years is also a ground of revocation. These types of revocation require federal court action initiated by federal prosecutors. [8 U.S.C. §1451] See *Fedorenko v. United States.*

The law also provides that the **attorney general** has the power to correct, reopen, alter, or vacate an order of naturalization. [8 U.S.C. §1451(h)] Thus, the INS may move to denaturalize when it discovers fraud or a mistake within two years of the naturalization order. [8 C.F.R. §340.1]

ROBERTS, MAURICE A. (B. 1910)   Often considered the "dean of immigration law," Maurice A. Roberts is known to recent generations of immigration lawyers as the editor-in-chief of *Interpreter Releases*, a loose-leaf publication of weekly updates on immigration law, and as the former chair of the **Board of Immigration Appeals.**

Roberts received his law degree summa cum laude from Rutgers University Law School in 1932. Admitted to the New Jersey bar that year, he practiced law in Newark, New Jersey, until March 1941, when he began working for the INS. In the approximately sixty years since then, he has been continuously involved in all aspects of immigration and nationality law. In the INS from 1941 to 1955, he was successively a naturalization examiner, special inspector, and chief of the Adjudications Division in the Philadelphia district office. In the INS central office in Washington, D.C., he was assistant chief of investigations and deputy general counsel. In the **Department of Justice**'s Criminal Division from 1955 to 1968, he was active in the Immigration Litigation Unit, which supervised the conduct of lower federal court litigation under the immigration and nationality laws, and was head of the unit from 1965 to 1968. Among the many Supreme Court cases in which he participated were *Shaughnessy v. Mezei* [345 U.S. 206 (1953)]; *Marcello v. Bonds* [349 U.S. 302 (1955)]; and *Rosenberg v. Fleuti* [374 U.S. 449 (1963)]. He argued for the government before the Supreme Court in *Hintopoulos v. Shaughnessy* [353 U.S. 72 (1957)] and *Chaunt v. United States* [364 U.S. 350 (1960)]. From 1968 until his retirement from government service in November 1974, Roberts was chair of the Board of Immigration Appeals. Upon his retirement from the board in November 1974, Roberts assumed chief editorship of *Interpreter Releases,* one of the leading immigration law publications in the United States, now in its 75th year of publication. It is published weekly by Federal Publications. He was formerly executive editor of the monthly *Immigration Briefings,* and is coauthor of *Understanding the 1986 Immigration Law* (1987). Active as a lecturer at law schools and symposiums on immigration law and procedure, Roberts's illustrious career also includes authorship of numerous law review articles and papers in the field. His many honors and awards include the Attorney General's Medallion (1974); the Founder's Award of the **American Immigration Lawyers Association** (AILA) (1975); the AILA Edith Lowenstein Award (1985); the Ivan Veit Award for Professional Excellence, awarded by the American Council for Nationalities Service (1988); and Honorary Fellow, American Immigration Law Foundation (1990). He has also received plaques from the immigration committees of the New Jersey State Bar Association (1983) and the Federal Bar Association (1988); the National Center for Immigrants' Rights, Inc. (1988); the Washington, D.C., chapter of the American Immigration Lawyers Association (1988); the American Immigration Law Foundation (1990); and the International Institute of Connecticut (1992). Following the 1992 presidential elections, he was a member of the presidential transition team covering the INS.

ROSENBERG V. FLEUTI This case [374 U.S. 449 (1963)] established the principle that a brief, innocent, and casual departure from the United States does not subject an alien to **inadmissibility grounds** once again under the **reentry doctrine.**

Fleuti was a Swiss national who was originally admitted to the United States for **lawful permanent resident alien** status in 1952, and had been in the country continuously since then except for a visit lasting "about a couple of hours" to Ensenada, Mexico, in August 1956. The INS sought to deport Fleuti in April 1959 on the ground that at the time of his return in 1956, he was within one or more of the classes of aliens excludable by law at the time of such entry. In particular, the INS alleged that Fleuti had been convicted of a **crime involving moral turpitude** before his 1956 return, and had for that reason been excludable when he came back from his brief trip to Mexico. Although that charge later proved unsustainable because the crime was a **petty offense,** he was eventually held excludable at the time of the 1956 return under a ground of inadmissibility that existed at the time directed at homosexuals who were deemed to be "afflicted with psychopathic personality."

The Supreme Court struck down Fleuti's deportation order by construing the definition of entry generously. To the Court, a returning lawful permanent resident should only be deemed to be making a new entry if the person intended to depart in a manner that could be regarded as meaningfully interruptive of the alien's permanent residence. One major factor relevant to whether such intent can be inferred is the length of time the alien is absent. Another is the purpose of the visit; if the purpose is to accomplish some object that is itself contrary to some policy reflected in the immigration laws, the interruption of residence thereby occurring would properly be regarded as meaningful. Still another is whether the alien has to procure any travel documents in order to make the trip, since the need to obtain such items might well cause the alien to consider more fully the implications of leaving the country. Thus, the Court remanded the case to a lower court for reconsideration, but noted that Fleuti was probably protected from the **reentry doctrine** by the facts in the record.

ROVING BORDER PATROL In 1975, the U.S. Supreme Court held in *United States v. Brignoni-Ponce* [422 U.S. 873 (1975)] that under certain circumstances, roving Border Patrol officers (traveling in cars) could stop motorists in the general area of the Mexican border for brief inquiry into their residence status if there was reasonable suspicion that passengers were undocumented. This decision represented a major concession to immigration enforcement officials on the part of the Court. Only two years earlier, in *Almeida-Sanchez v. United States* [413 U.S. 26 (1973)], the Supreme Court had held that aliens were protected by the Fourth Amendment's prohibition against unreasonable searches and seizures. There, the Court had struck down the ability of roving border patrols to conduct arrests and full-scale searches unless there was probable cause that unlawful activity was occurring. But in *Brignoni-Ponce*, the Court permitted at least brief stops of vehicles that looked suspicious to experienced immigration enforcement officers. At **fixed checkpoint**s, however, brief stops are allowed by the Court even without suspicion.

RUBIN, ROBERT (B. 1951)   Robert Rubin, an outstanding civil rights attorney for the past twenty years, is the director of litigation for the Lawyers' Committee for Civil Rights of the San Francisco Bay Area. He specializes in the areas of immigration and voting rights. Prior to coming to the Lawyers' Committee, he was the American Civil Liberties Union staff counsel in Jackson, Mississippi.

In the area of immigrant and refugee rights, Rubin has successfully litigated more than twenty class actions. He was co–lead counsel in the **Proposition 187** class action that successfully challenged the threatened expulsion of undocumented children from schools. He is also co–lead counsel in the challenge to the summary removal provision that was enacted as part of the 1996 federal immigration bill. That action seeks to ensure due process protections in a system that allows low-level INS officials to summarily remove fleeing refugees immediately upon their arrival at airports.

Rubin also directs the committee's voting rights project, and secured the first injunction in the nation ordering a state to comply with the National Voter Registration Act (the so-called motor-voter law), a case successfully litigated through the U.S. Supreme Court. In another action decided during the same 1996 Supreme Court term, Rubin was counsel to Latino voters in Monterey County who were opposed to at-large county judicial elections that diluted their voting power. In this action involving Section 5 of the Voting Rights Act, the Court unanimously ruled that the change from district elections to an at-large system violated the interests of Latino voters. After a subsequent dismissal upon remand, this same matter returned to the Supreme Court. On January 20, 1999, the Supreme Court issued its second ruling in favor of the Latino voters, rejecting the state's argument that the change to at-large elections was a product of state law and therefore immune from the Voting Rights Act.

Rubin has appeared on numerous occasions before the California legislature and the U.S. Congress, where he has testified regarding congressional proposals to reform the political asylum system. In 1992, Rubin served on then President-elect Bill Clinton's transition team.

Rubin has lectured extensively, including adjunct positions at Stanford Law School and at the University of California at Berkeley's Boalt Hall, and currently serves as an adjunct professor at the University of California's Hastings College of the Law, where he teaches a constitutional law seminar. He received his J.D. from the University of San Diego School of Law in 1978.

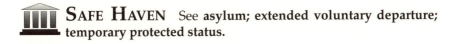

SAFE HAVEN See **asylum; extended voluntary departure; temporary protected status.**

SANCTIONS See **employer sanctions.**

SANTIAGO V. INS In this case [526 F.2d 488 (9th Cir. 1975)], **derivative beneficiary** status was denied to family members of the primary immigrants because the primary immigrants did not immigrate prior to or at the same time as the family members.

This decision involved four cases, each concerning the husband or child of a preference immigrant [see **preference system**]. In each case, the husband or child was issued an immigrant visa as a person who would be "accompanying, or following to join," the primary immigrant. Each husband or child traveled to the United States alone and was admitted by an immigration officer. Death or expiration of the visa of the primary immigrant prevented that person from later joining the husband or child in the United States.

In spite of the error made by immigration officers in admitting the derivative beneficiaries, the court of appeals held that the derivative beneficiary visas were not valid because the primary immigrant did not precede or accompany the derivative immigrants on their entry into the United States. They were deemed to have lost no rights to which they were entitled under the immigration laws. At the time of their **admission,** none had any right to enter. Therefore, since their visas were not valid, they in fact were subject to deportation (**removal**) proceedings.

SCHEDULE A The **Department of Labor** has promulgated a schedule listing occupations it has precertified as characterized by a shortage of available U.S. workers, and for which employment of immigrants will not adversely affect the wages and working conditions of others similarly employed. Prospective immigrant employees falling into these occupational categories can therefore obtain an automatic **alien employment certification**. This list is known as Schedule A. The procedures of the local job service office and the Department of Labor are therefore bypassed. The employer does not have to document efforts to recruit U.S. workers. The person's employer may directly file a petition with the INS. [20 C.F.R. §656.10]

There are four main groups of occupations in Schedule A. Group I is for occupations in short supply. This includes physical therapists who are qualified to take the physical therapist licensing examination in the state of intended practice. Nurses who have passed the Commission on Graduates of Foreign Nursing Schools examination, or who are fully licensed to practice nursing in the state of intended employment, also qualify under Group I.

Group II is comprised of aliens who have attained a level of exceptional ability in the sciences or arts. The category includes college teachers, but not aliens in the performing arts or sports. The term *science or art* means any field of knowledge and/or skill with respect to which colleges and universities commonly offer specialized courses leading to a degree in the knowledge and/or skill. It is helpful if the person has won prizes or awards, is a member in international associations requiring outstanding achievement, or has authored published articles. [20 C.F.R. §§22(d), 656.21(a)]

Group III provides blanket certification of religious preachers, teachers, and workers. Examples of persons admitted under this category include monks, nuns, Christian Science practitioners, cantors, and translators of religious texts. It is not necessary for ministers, rabbis, or priests to apply for Group III because they are eligible for a **special immigrant** classification. A prerequisite for Group III is documentary evidence of having been primarily engaged in the religious occupation or in working for the non-profit religious organization for two years before application. Group III does not include lay members of a religious organization who intend to engage in lay occupations such as housekeeping for a minister or selling religious literature. The religion and organization must meet the specific criteria for the applicants to qualify [see **bona fide religious organization**].

Group IV encompasses managerial or executive **intracompany transferee**s who have been employed abroad for at least one year in such capacity and who are coming to the United States to work in the same capacity for an affiliate or subsidiary of the company. The company must also have been doing business in the United States for at least one year prior to the alien's admission as a permanent resident. For Group IV purposes, acceptable corporations and organizations include affiliates, associations, firms, partnerships, joint ventures, joint stock companies, and subsidiaries. This category is a natural immigrant classification for aliens in the United States holding an L-1 intracompany transferee **nonimmigrant visa,** because the qualifications are similar. However, only L-1 aliens who entered as managers or executives can qualify for Group IV. [20 C.F.R. §656.10]

SCHEDULE B This is the **Department of Labor**'s list of occupations for which it has determined that there is a surplus of U.S. workers. This list of jobs presumably requiring lesser skills or little education or training (less than ninety days) is quite extensive. It includes such occupations as janitors, parking lot attendants, porters, receptionists, hotel clerks, guards, sales clerks, truck drivers, household domestic workers, and housekeepers. In general, an application for **alien employment certification** for an occupation that appears on Schedule B will be denied. However, waivers may be requested when all the advertising, recruitment, and **prevailing wage** requirements have been met. In such cases, the Labor Department requires exacting proof of job requirements and recruitment efforts and results. No **reduction in recruitment** will be granted on a request for waiver of a Schedule B occupation. [20 C.F.R. §656.11]

In order to avoid Schedule B situations, a job title and description may be carefully worded so as to bring the occupation outside Schedule B. However, some of the occupations listed in Schedule B are described in sufficiently broad terms to include several job titles listed in the *Dictionary of Occupational Titles* (DOT). It may be possible to remove a particular job from Schedule B, for example, by requiring one year of experience. However, such a tactic is limited to situations where the requirement is reasonable and the *specific vocational preparation* (SVP) ratings do not indicate that shorter periods of experience are sufficient. The SVP code is provided for each occupation in the companion volume to the DOT entitled *Selected Characteristics of Occupations Defined in the Dictionary of Occupational Titles.*

Supervisory responsibilities or foreign language requirements may also be used to take the job description out of Schedule B.

The complete list of noncertifiable occupations in Schedule B is included in the Appendix.

SCHEY, PETER A. (B. 1947) Peter A. Schey is one of the premier immigrant rights litigators in the country. He is the founder, president, and executive director of the Center for Human Rights and Constitutional Law Foundation in Los Angeles.

Schey has served as lead counsel or co-counsel in over 100 major civil rights cases in federal courts throughout the United States involving the constitutional rights of immigrants and refugees; access to education, health and welfare benefits; and the rights of children and indigenous people. His cases include *Plyler v. Doe,* a statewide class-action case in which the Supreme Court held unconstitutional a Texas statute that denied public education to undocumented children; *League of United Latin American Citizens v. Wilson,* a statewide class action challenging the constitutionality of California's **Proposition 187**; *Catholic Social Services v. Meese,* a nationwide class-action case seeking legalization for 200,000 immigrants who briefly traveled abroad during the **amnesty** program set up by the **Immigration Reform and Control Act of 1986; *Haitian Refugee Center v. Smith,*** a class action involving Haitian refugees who were denied due process in their applications for asylum; *Flores v. Meese,* a class action challenging INS release policy for minors, conditions of detention, and failure to provide minors probable cause hearings; *National Center for Immigrants' Rights v. INS,* a nationwide class action challenging INS regulations that prohibited immigrants in deportation proceedings from working as a condition of release on bail; *Orantes-Hernandez v. INS,* a nationwide preliminary injunction regarding the postarrest rights of Salvadoran asylum seekers by the INS; *Mendez v. INS,* a precedent-setting case holding that when an immigrant's deportation was accomplished in violation of due process, the immigrant may return to the United States for further proceedings; *American-Arab Anti-Discrimination Committee v. Meese,* which found sections of the **McCarran-Walter Act of 1952** unconstitutional as a violation of the First Amendment.

Schey has also engaged in significant international work, including advising Haitian president Jean-Bertrand Aristide on matters related to human rights and impunity; filing a human rights petition before the Inter-American Commission on Human Rights of the Organization of American States (OAS) challenging the U.S. government's program of interdicting Haitian refugee boat people; petitioning the OAS in challenging the Mexican government's human rights record in responding to the rebellion of the Zapatista National Liberation Army in Chiapas; and petitioning the OAS Inter-American Commission on Human Rights with a challenge to the excessive use of force by the U.S. **Border Patrol** along the U.S.-Mexico border.

Schey is also the founder and director of Safe Haven and Freedom House, licensed group homes for Los Angeles inner-city homeless minority youth; and founder of the Los Angeles Homeless Youth Legal Clinic, a program that offers homeless youth free legal services on matters relating to guardianships, emancipation, and juvenile justice and immigration issues.

Schey has written numerous immigration articles and contributed to several important immigration treatises. In 1982, he was a legal consultant to the Select Commission on Immigration and Refugee Policy. His work has been honored by the National Lawyers Guild (the Carol King Award), the **American Immigration Lawyers Association** (the Jack Wasserman Memorial Award), the State Bar of California (Pro Bono Services), and the Clarence Darrow Foundation. Schey received his J.D. with honors from California Western School of Law in 1973.

🏛 SECOND PREFERENCE EMPLOYMENT CATEGORY
Under the **preference system** for individuals wishing to immigrate through employment, second preference provides for two separate means of qualification: those who are individuals "of exceptional ability," and those "members of the professions holding advanced degrees." These categories were created in 1990 and significantly decreased the length of time required for professionals with advanced degrees to immigrate to the United States.

For those seeking an exceptional ability classification, the law requires that the ability be in the sciences, arts, or business. Furthermore, it must be shown that the individual's immigration will substantially benefit the U.S. economy, cultural or educational interests, or welfare. Generally, the individual's services in the sciences, arts, professions, or business must be sought by an employer in the United States, but a **national interest waiver** provides an opportunity for some individuals to immigrate without a job offer or an **alien employment certification.**

Professionals with advanced degrees have long been able to immigrate to the United States. The term *profession* is defined as "any occupation for which a U.S. baccalaureate degree or its foreign equivalent is the minimum requirement for entry into the occupation," as well as any of the occupations listed in the statute: architects, engineers, lawyers, physicians, surgeons, and teachers in elementary or secondary schools, colleges, academies, or seminaries. The second preference immigrant classification is limited to **professional**s with advanced degrees. An "advanced degree" may be "any U.S. academic or professional degree or a foreign equivalent degree above that of baccalaureate." An individual is considered to hold the equivalent of a master's degree after the award of a U.S. baccalaureate degree or a foreign equivalent degree followed by at least five years of progressive experience in the specialty. [8 U.S.C. §1153(b)(2); 8 C.F.R. §204.5(k)]

🏛 SECOND PREFERENCE FOR RELATIVES
In the immigration **preference system** for families and relatives, the second preference is the only category under which **lawful permanent resident alien**s can petition for relatives. This category is further divided into two subcategories: 2-A for the spouses and children (unmarried and under

twenty-one) of lawful permanent residents and 2-B for unmarried sons and daughters (age twenty-one and over) of lawful permanent residents. As the only category available to lawful permanent resident petitioners, the popularity of second preference has resulted in significant waiting periods for prospective immigrants from countries such as Mexico and the Philippines. This is due to the demand for visas from these countries and the **numerical limitations** imposed on immigrants from individual countries. [8 U.S.C. §1153(a)(2)] See **visa bulletin.**

SECONDARY INSPECTION   An alien who has not satisfied the INS officer at the **port of entry** during the **inspection** process that the alien is eligible for **admission** may be referred to a secondary inspection area at the port of entry. If an immediate decision cannot be made, but it appears that a determination as to admissibility can be made within two weeks, the person can be **parole**d into the United States for secondary inspection at a local INS office. At that point, the matter is given greater attention in a different setting away from the port of entry. At the port of entry, the person's documents are retained by the inspector and forwarded to the INS office nearest the person's intended destination. The person is given an appointment notice and allowed to proceed to the city of destination on the promise that he or she will appear a few days later for the additional inspection. This type of deferred inspection will not take place if the person is taken into custody on the belief that the person will abscond, for example, because the documents presented are believed to be false. Aliens can also be placed in the custody of the carrier.

If the person is a returning **lawful permanent resident alien,** the issue at secondary inspection often involves a question of whether the person is seeking a new admission for purposes of evaluating **inadmissibility grounds** (see **reentry doctrine**) or whether the person has abandoned lawful permanent residence status [see **abandonment of permanent residence**].

At secondary inspection, another INS inspector reviews the visa documents that have been forwarded from the primary inspector at the port of entry. Documents may even include nonofficial items, such as letters or books, that were found in the person's possession and from which inadmissibility may be inferred.

If the inspector and the **district director** conclude that the person is inadmissible and refuse to grant any applicable **waiver of inadmissibility,** the person can be afforded the opportunity to withdraw the application for admission and return to the foreign country, or to have a **removal** hearing before an **immigration judge.**

SHAM MARRIAGE A sham marriage or marriage of convenience is a marriage between a prospective immigrant and a U.S. citizen that has been entered into solely for immigration purposes. An alien who marries a U.S. citizen solely to obtain lawful permanent residence status would be entering into a sham marriage. If immigration authorities determine that the marriage is a sham, the immigration application will be denied. Often in such cases, the prospective immigrant is also deported. In theory, the citizen can also be criminally prosecuted, although in practice such prosecution is rare.

A marriage is a sham for immigration purposes if the bride and groom did not intend to establish a life together at the time of the marriage; intent at the time of marriage is the key element. See *Bark v. INS.* Conduct of the parties after the marriage, such as a separation, is relevant only to the extent that it bears upon their subjective state of mind at the time of the marriage. Presumably, a marriage between parties who marry for love, experience marital disharmony, and then separate is not a sham. For example, in *Matter of Tawfik* [Int. Dec. No. 3130 (BIA 1990)], the **Board of Immigration Appeals** agreed that the mere fact that, at the time of the **visa petition** denial, the petitioner was living separately from the beneficiary was not evidence of an attempt or conspiracy to enter into a sham marriage. However, in *Baria v. Leno* [849 F. Supp. 750 (D. Haw. 1994)], the marriage was deemed a sham when, immediately after entering the United States, the alien established the six-week residency required in Nevada for a divorce, petitioned for divorce from his wife of twenty-one years, traveled to Hawaii and met and married a U.S. citizen within a short period of time, then separated from her about a year after obtaining immigrant status.

The **Immigration Marriage Fraud Amendments of 1986** add a different slant on these issues. Under this provision, the marriage must remain viable for at least two years before the prospective immigrant can obtain lawful permanent residence. So even if the marriage was not a sham at inception, if the parties obtain a divorce or dissolution of marriage within two years, permanent immigrant status is not available in the absence of special circumstances such as spousal abuse. During the two-year period, the prospective immigrant is granted **conditional permanent residence.** After two years of viability and after the conditions on permanent residence are removed, a party to a sham marriage can still be subject to **removal** if there is evidence that the marriage was a sham from the beginning. On the other hand, after the conditions on permanent residence are removed from a real marriage, if a couple breaks up due to legitimate marital problems, there is no basis for bringing sham marriage charges. See *Matter of McKee.*

SHARRY, FRANK (B. 1956) Frank Sharry is the executive director of the **National Immigration Forum** and is one of the nation's leading spokespersons on behalf of immigrant rights. Based in Washington, D.C., the forum is one of the premier immigration advocacy organizations. Its mission is to embrace and uphold America's tradition as a nation of immigrants. It advocates and builds public support for public policies that welcome immigrants and refugees and that are fair and supportive to newcomers in the United States.

Since becoming the National Immigration Forum's executive director in 1990, Sharry has emerged as a national spokesperson for generous immigration policies in the United States. He is cited by major newspapers throughout the country on a regular basis, and has appeared on national television to speak on immigration policy on dozens of occasions. Sharry's other experience includes serving as the deputy campaign manager of Taxpayers Against Proposition 187, the effort opposing the California ballot initiative [see **Proposition 187**]. Prior to coming to the forum, Sharry was executive director of Centro Presente, a legal and social services center for Central American refugees in the greater Boston area. He also served as the director of Refugee Services and led efforts to resettle Cuban and Vietnamese refugees at the American Council for Nationalities Service.

SHAUGHNESSY V. UNITED STATES EX REL. MEZEI This case [345 U.S. 206 (1953)] extends the principle of *United States ex rel. Knauff v. Shaughnessy* that Congress can severely limit the due process rights of aliens seeking to enter the United States. The case involved an alien permanently excluded from the United States on security grounds but stranded in his temporary haven on Ellis Island because other countries would not take him back. The continued **exclusion** without a hearing did not amount to an unlawful detention.

Mezei was born in Gibraltar of Hungarian or Romanian parents and lived in the United States from 1923 to 1948. In May of that year he sailed for Europe, apparently to visit his dying mother in Romania. Denied entry there, he remained in Hungary for about nineteen months due to difficulty in securing an exit permit. Finally, armed with an immigration visa issued by the U.S. consul in Budapest, he proceeded to France and boarded a ship bound for New York. Upon arrival on February 9, 1950, he was temporarily excluded from the United States by an immigration inspector. On administrative review, the **attorney general** on May 10, 1950, ordered the temporary exclusion to be made permanent without a hearing, on the "basis of information of a confidential nature, the disclosure of which would be prejudicial to the public interest." That determination rested on a finding that Mezei's entry would be prejudicial to the public interest for security reasons. But attempts to enforce his departure failed. Twice he shipped out only to return; both France and Great Britain refused him permission to land. The **State Department** unsuccessfully negotiated with Hungary for his readmission. He applied for entry to about a dozen Latin American countries but all turned him down. In short, he sat on Ellis Island because this country shut him out and others were unwilling to take him in. He brought this action claiming that his confinement on Ellis Island was unlawful.

It is true that aliens who have once passed across U.S. borders, even illegally, may be expelled only after proceedings conforming to traditional standards of fairness encompassed in due process of law. But an alien on the threshold of initial entry stands on a different footing. Because the action of the executive officer under the authority to deny entry is final and conclusive, the attorney general cannot be compelled to disclose evidence underlying the determinations in an exclusion case. Neither Mezei's harborage on Ellis Island nor his prior residence here transformed this into something other than an exclusion proceeding.

Mezei's continued exclusion did not deprive him of any statutory or constitutional rights. His right to enter the United States depended on congressional will, and the courts cannot substitute their judgment for legislative mandate.

This case epitomizes the tremendous power that Congress has over the admission of aliens. But in *Barrera-Echavarria v. Rison* [21 F.3d 314 (9th Cir. 1994)], the Ninth Circuit Court of Appeals argued that there reaches a point when the detention can become excessive. The government should not lose sight of the sense of proportion that must inform any governmental intrusion of liberty. Thus a Cuban who sought entry during the **Mariel boatlift** who had been detained for over eight years was ordered released to a halfway house. The government had no authority to imprison indefinitely an inadmissible alien whom it could not remove, and whom it deemed presented no danger to society.

SILVA V. LEVI Between 1965 and 1976, while the rest of the world enjoyed an expansion of **numerical limitations** and a definite **preference system** as provided in the **Immigration Amendments of 1965,** Mexico and the Western Hemisphere were suddenly faced with numerical restrictions for the first time. Additionally, while the first-come, first-served basis for immigration in the Western Hemisphere sounded fair, applicants had to meet strict labor certification requirements. Of course, waivers of the labor certification requirement were obtainable for certain applicants, such as parents of U.S. citizen children. By 1976 the procedure resulted in a severe backlog of approximately three years and a waiting list of nearly 300,000 names.

During the 1965–1976 experience, two noteworthy things happened. First, Mexicans used about 40,000 of the Western Hemisphere's allocation of 120,000 visas annually. Second, during this eleven-year period, the **State Department** wrongfully subtracted about 150,000 visas from the Western Hemisphere quota and gave them to Cuban refugees.

In 1977, Congress imposed the preference system on Mexico and the Western Hemisphere along with a 20,000-visa-per-country numerical limitation. Thus, Mexico's annual visa usage rate was virtually cut in half overnight, and thousands were left stranded on the old system's waiting list. The eleven-year misallocation of visas to Cuba eventually led to a permanent injunction and a recapturing of the wrongfully issued visas in *Silva v. Levi* [(N.D. Ill. Oct. 10, 1978); see also *Silva v. Bell*, 605 F.2d 978 (7th Cir. 1979)]. However, Mexicans again received the short end of the stick when the State Department's formula for reallocation, which failed to provide sufficient visas for thousands of Mexicans on the *Silva* waiting list, was upheld. As a result, in February 1982, INS authorities began to round up those *Silva* class members who had not been accorded immigrant visa numbers in order to advise them of the termination of the *Silva* injunction against their deportation and the end of their work authorization derived from their *Silva* class status. The recipients were further informed that unless provisions of the existing immigration law qualified them to remain in the United States, they would have thirty days to depart voluntarily. Because of the public outrage, on August 20, 1982, the INS ceased to enforce departure in cases involving former *Silva* class members subject to deportation or exclusion proceedings. However, on February 1, 1983, the enforcement wing of the INS ordered that the processing of *Silva* class members be resumed.

To make matters worse, in the first year of the preference system and the 20,000 limitation on countries of the Western Hemisphere, Mexico lost 14,000 visas due to a congressional mistake. The effective date of the new law was January 1, 1977. Since the government's fiscal year runs from October 1 to September 30, by January 1 one full quarter of fiscal year 1977 had expired. During that first quarter, 14,203 visas were issued to Mexicans pursuant to the immigration system that prevailed in the Western Hemisphere before the new law became effective. The State Department nevertheless charged those visas against the newly imposed national quota of 20,000, leaving only 4,797 visas available for Mexican immigrants between January 1 and September 30, 1977. See *De Avila v. Civiletti* [643 F.2d 471 (7th Cir. 1981)].

SILVERMAN, MARK (B. 1946) Mark Silverman is one of the nation's leading experts on asylum law, is credited with setting up models for pro bono efforts throughout the country, and has established innovative lawyering strategies that intensely involve constant collaboration with grassroots immigrant and refugee groups. He is a staff attorney and director of asylum policy at the **Immigrant Legal Resource Center.** He has been a staff attorney with the ILRC since 1983, and from 1983 to 1985 he was also the first coordinator of the Political Asylum Emergency Representation Program of the San Francisco Lawyers' Committee for Urban Affairs. Silverman has served as national cochair of the **American Immigration Lawyers Association** pro bono committee.

A major focus of Silverman's work involves working with immigrant-based groups to educate their communities and organize and advocate for a more humane immigration policy. In particular, he works closely with El Comité de Padres Unidos in San Francisco, which launched a Justice for Families campaign in 1999. In the course of this advocacy work, Silverman has made hundreds of community presentations to immigrant communities, including dozens in Catholic churches throughout Northern California and the state's Central Valley. He has frequently appeared on Spanish television as part of this community education and advocacy work.

Silverman is the author or coauthor of more than eight manuals on various aspects of immigration law. These manuals include *Winning Asylum Cases, Winning Suspension Cases, A Guide for Immigration Advocates, Winning NACARA Suspension Cases,* as well as publications on **family unity, temporary protected status,** and establishing pro bono asylum programs. He has been a presenter at numerous seminars on immigration law, covering a variety of subjects, including but not limited to the topics of the manuals he has authored. He regularly provides technical assistance to attorneys and immigration advocates on a wide variety of cases.

Silverman was lead counsel in the successful *Maca-Alvarez* class-action case, which obtained a successful settlement on issues related to the family unity program. He was also counsel on the class-action challenge to **Proposition 187** in California and a challenge to administrative denaturalization proceedings.

Since April 1998, Silverman has directed technical assistance projects for attorneys and other legal workers on Section 203 of the Nicaraguan Adjustment and Central American Relief Act (**NACARA**). This section of NACARA permits certain Salvadorans, Guatemalans, and former Soviet bloc nationals to apply for suspension of deportation/special rule **cancellation of removal.** As part of this project, Silverman runs a free e-mail update service, has published three editions of a practitioner's manual, has written several articles, and has made numerous presentations at conferences, including the 1999 **American Immigration Lawyers Association** convention. In recognition of his consistent advocacy for justice on behalf of refugees from Central America, Silverman was honored by the Central American Refugee Center (CARECEN) in 1989. Silverman received his J.D. from New College School of Law in 1983.

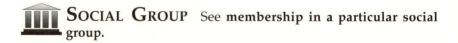 **SMUGGLING OF ALIENS** An alien who at any time has knowingly encouraged, induced, assisted, abetted, or aided any other alien to enter or try to enter the United States in violation of law is inadmissible [see **inadmissibility grounds**]. In 1990, the requirement that such smuggling be conducted "for gain" (e.g., for a fee) to be a violation of the law was eliminated. Thus, although the prior law was clearly aimed at punishing professional smugglers, the language of the current law covers anyone who helps or encourages another alien to try to cross the border without **inspection,** even when payment is not contemplated. [8 U.S.C. §1182(a)(6)(E)]

The smuggling provision does not apply to the spouse or child of a legalized alien who received **amnesty** under the **Immigration Reform and Control Act of 1986,** when the prospective immigrant is seeking admission as an **immediate relative** or family **preference system** second preference and the smuggling involved a spouse, parent, son, or daughter prior to May 5, 1988 (see **family unity** provision).

The smuggling provision may also be waived, but only for a **lawful permanent resident alien** who helped a spouse, parent, son, or daughter to enter illegally, or for an alien seeking **admission** or **adjustment of status** as an immediate relative or family preference immigrant (except for the sibling category).

An otherwise lawful alien who commits alien smuggling before, during, or within five years of any entry into the United States can be deported for the offense. [8 U.S.C. §1227(a)(1)(E)]

SOCIAL GROUP See **membership in a particular social group.**

SPECIAL AGRICULTURAL WORKER A special agricultural worker (SAW) is an **alien** who was granted **lawful temporary resident** status or **lawful permanent resident alien** status through the farmworker legalization (**amnesty**) program of the **Immigration Reform**

and Control Act of 1986 (IRCA). Two categories of farmworkers were eligible to apply for SAW status. Group 1 were those who showed they had done at least ninety days of qualifying agricultural work in each of three years between May 1, 1983, and May 1, 1986. They also had to prove that they lived in the United States for six months during each of those years. Group 2 were those who showed that they had done at least ninety days of qualifying work between May 1, 1985, and May 1, 1986. Group 1 could apply for lawful permanent resident status on December 1, 1989. Group 2 obtained lawful temporary resident status first, and could apply for permanent status on December 1, 1990. Many of the Group 2 members have yet to apply for permanent status.

SPECIAL IMMIGRANT   Several categories of special immigrants are contained in the immigration laws. For example, a person who is already a **lawful permanent resident alien** who is returning from a temporary visit abroad is considered a special immigrant, and is not subject to any **numerical limitations.** A visit abroad by a lawful permanent resident alien for up to 180 days will generally be regarded as a temporary visit.

Two limited groups of former U.S. citizens may qualify as special immigrants who are seeking reacquisition of citizenship. The first group includes women who lost their citizenship under prior laws as a result of marriage to aliens prior to September 22, 1922, or to aliens who were ineligible for citizenship on or after September 22, 1922. The second group includes persons who lost citizenship during World War II due to military service for another country, when that country fought on the same side as the United States.

Other special immigrant groups include ministers of religion (who have been ministers for at least two years); former employees of the U.S. government for at least fifteen years (such as with the **consulate general**); certain individuals who worked in the Panama Canal Zone; foreign medical graduates who are fully licensed to practice in one of the fifty states prior to January 9, 1978; and juvenile court dependents who have been adjudged eligible for long-term foster care. See **special immigrant juvenile.**

Besides ministers of religion, the special immigrant category provides special status for those who work for a religious organization at its request in a professional capacity in a religious vocation or occupation. The same opportunity applies to such workers for organizations that are affiliated with the religious denomination. For at least two years immediately preceding the application, the person must have been a member of the religious organization that has bona fide nonprofit status in the United States. The applicant must have also carried on the vocation or occupation for at least two years immediately preceding the application [see **fourth preference**]. Unlike the minister-of-religion category that has no time constraints, the religious worker category is due to expire on September 30, 2000. [8 U.S.C. §1101(a)(27)]

SPECIAL IMMIGRANT JUVENILE   A subcategory of **special immigrant,** special immigrant juveniles are eligible for visas to remain in the United States permanently. A special immigrant juvenile is one who has been declared dependent on a U.S. juvenile court or whom such a court has legally committed to, or placed under the custody of, an agency or department of a state and who has been deemed eligible by that court for long-term foster care due to abuse, neglect, or abandonment. There must be a determination in administrative or judicial proceedings that it would not be in the person's best interest to be returned to the person's or parent's previous country of nationality or country of last residence, and the **attorney general** must have granted consent to the dependency order.

SPONSOR   The term *sponsor* may be used to describe an individual or employer who files a **visa petition** on behalf of a relative or employer. The term may also be used to describe the person who signs an **affidavit of support** on behalf of a prospective immigrant.

SS ST. LOUIS   The plight of European Jews fleeing Nazi Germany aboard this ship in 1939 is a horrific example of the operation of the **national origins quota system** of the 1920s and the absence of fair and systematic treatment of refugees prior to international agreements on refugees [see **United Nations Protocol Relating to the Status of Refugees.**]

In a diabolical propaganda ploy in the spring of 1939, the Nazis had allowed this ship carrying destitute European Jewish refugees to leave Hamburg bound for Cuba, but had arranged for corrupt Cuban officials to deny them entry even after they had been granted visas. It was the objective of Nazi propaganda minister Joseph Goebbels to prove that no country wanted the Jews.

The *St. Louis* was not allowed to discharge its passengers in Cuba and was ordered out of Havana harbor. As it sailed north, it neared U.S. territorial waters; the U.S. Coast Guard warned it away. President Franklin D. Roosevelt said that the United States could not accept any more European refugees because of immigration quotas. Untold thousands had already fled the Nazi terror in central Europe, and many had come to the United States, still in the throes of depression.

Nearly two months after leaving Hamburg, and due to the efforts of U.S. Jewish refugee assistance groups, the ship was allowed to land in Holland. Four nations agreed to accept the refugees—Great Britain, Holland, Belgium, and France. Two months later, the Nazis invaded Poland and the Second World War began. Over 600 of the 937 passengers on the *St. Louis* were killed by the Nazis before the war was over. When the United States refused the *St. Louis* permission to land, many Americans were embarrassed; when the country found out after the war what had happened to the refugees, there was shame.

Maintaining a generally restrictive immigration policy during this era, the United States did accept an estimated 105,000 refugees from Nazi Germany in the 1930s, including such luminaries as Albert Einstein; But many more—primarily Jews—were refused entry, returning to Europe and oblivion. But during the war, the Roosevelt administration brought fewer than 1,000 Jewish refugees out of Europe.

The Roosevelt administration displayed near-total indifference to Adolf Hitler's Final Solution. Its initial reaction to evidence of genocide in Europe was denial. By June 1942, the State Department had reliable reports about the Nazis' systematic extermination of the Jews. Even then, after learning from U.S. officials in Switzerland that the Nazis were killing 6,000 Jews per day at one site in Poland alone, the State Department in February 1943 instructed the officials not to transmit any more information of this kind.

When news of Nazi death camps became public in late November 1942, civic and religious groups began urging President Roosevelt to rescue those Jews still alive, but he refused. Some speculate that he refused because he did not want to bring Jewish refugees to the United States for fear he would lose the votes of Jew-haters and immigration opponents in the 1944 election. He also supported the British government, which, under Winston Churchill, bitterly opposed rescuing Jews. The British were afraid that if Jewish refugees demanded entry into Palestine, it could precipitate an Arab rebellion.

STATE EMPLOYMENT OFFICE The state employment office plays an important role in the **alien employment certification** (labor certification) process. The employment certification application initially goes to the state office, even though the actual certification is issued by the federal **Department of Labor.** The state offices, often referred to as "state employment service agencies" (SESAs), help to assess **prevailing wage**s for the particular job in question, and also have expertise on the local job market.

STATE DEPARTMENT This part of the executive branch of the federal government has tremendous authority over the issuance of visas. Under the immigration laws, the secretary of state is charged with the responsibility of administering the immigration laws through consular offices abroad. Essentially this responsibility is discharged by conducting preliminary screenings and the issuance of documents in foreign countries for persons seeking to travel to the United States. Within the State Department there is a Passport Office and a Visa Office. U.S. **consulate general**s serving at embassies and consulates abroad are responsible for the issuance of immigrant and **nonimmigrant visa**s to aliens who are seeking admission to the United States. [8 U.S.C. §1104]

Significantly, adverse decisions on visa applications by U.S. consuls are not reviewable by federal courts. Thus, the tremendous discretion that is exercised by consular officials cannot be appealed to a court. The only recourse is to seek an advisory opinion from the Bureau of Consular Affairs, within the State Department, but these opinions are only advisory and not binding.

STAY OF REMOVAL An alien under a final order of **removal** may request a stay of removal from the **district director** in order to halt removal, at least temporarily. A stay is generally granted only for important health, family, or business needs. The decision to grant the stay request is an extremely discretionary one.

A stay of removal is sometimes requested when the alien is making a **motion to reopen removal proceedings** after a removal order has been entered. If the district director denies the stay request while the motion to reopen is pending, a similar request can be made to the **immigration court** and the **Board of Immigration Appeals.**

A stay of removal is also available for individuals who are **victims of torture.**

SUSPENSION OF DEPORTATION This was a form of relief from deportation that existed in the immigration laws prior to 1996. The primary beneficiaries of this relief generally were **undocumented aliens** or those who had overstayed their **nonimmigrant visas**. Suspension of deportation required that the deportable alien demonstrate seven years' continuous physical presence in the United States, **good moral character** during the seven years, and that deportation would result in **extreme hardship** to the applicant or to certain family members who were U.S. citizens or **lawful permanent resident aliens**. After the **Illegal Immigration Re-**

form and Immigrant Responsibility Act of 1996 (IIRAIRA), suspension of deportation was replaced with a more rigorous form of relief—**cancellation of removal**—that requires a showing of "exceptional and extremely unusual" hardship. **NACARA** applicants from Guatemala, El Salvador, and former Soviet bloc countries also have a suspension-like relief available.

T

TAMAYO, WILLIAM R. (B. 1953) William Tamayo is the regional attorney of the U.S. Equal Employment Opportunity Commission's San Francisco District Office. The EEOC is the federal agency charged with enforcing Title VII of the Civil Rights Act of 1964, the Americans with Disabilities Act, the Age Discrimination in Employment Act, and the Equal Pay Act. As the regional attorney for the EEOC, Tamayo oversees the commission's litigation and legal program in the San Francisco district, which includes Northern California, Hawaii, and U.S. territories and possessions in the Pacific. He is also the EEOC's leading immigration and employment law expert.

Prior to joining the EEOC in June 1995, he served for sixteen years as a staff attorney and managing attorney for the **Asian Law Caucus,** a San Francisco–based public-interest law office. While at the caucus he emphasized the practice of immigration and nationality law, as well as civil rights litigation and advocacy involving employment discrimination, affirmative action, immigrant rights, voting rights, and the census. He became one of the country's primary voices and experts on immigrant rights. He has testified on several occasions before the U.S. House of Representatives, the California legislature, and various local bodies on immigration policy, voting rights, and public policy issues affecting Asian Americans and other minorities. He was co-counsel for plaintiff-intervenor in *EEOC v. Tortilleria La Mejor* [758 F. Supp. 585 (E.C. Cal. 1991)], which held that undocumented workers are covered by Title VII of the Civil Rights Act of 1964. Tamayo also served as lead attorney for the Oakland City of Refuge Committee, which successfully obtained a resolution from the city of Oakland, California, barring the city's cooperation in the arrest, detention, and deportation of any individual.

Tamayo has received several awards for his work, including the 1990 Phillip Burton Award for Lawyering in Immigration from the **Immigrant Legal Resource Center;** the 1993 Judge John Wisdom Award from the American Bar Association, Section on Litigation; and the 1995 Carol King Award from the **National Immigration Project of the National Lawyers Guild.**

Tamayo is currently vice-president of the Asian Pacific Islander Health Forum. He previously served on the boards of the Poverty and Race Research Action Council, the American Civil Liberties Union of Northern California, Filipinos for Affirmative Action, and the Coalition for Immigrant and Refugee Rights and Services, and served as a national vice-president of the National Lawyers Guild. He received his J.D. from the University of California at Davis School of Law in 1978.

TAX RESIDENT   See federal tax residency.

TECHNICAL ASSISTANCE GUIDE   This publication contains detailed information on **alien employment certification** procedures and requirements, with the operations instructions of the **Department of Labor.** It is a publication of the Division of Labor Certification of the Office of Technical Support, United States Employment Service.

TEMPORARY PROTECTED STATUS   In 1990, Congress added a provision to the laws that essentially codified the practice of **extended voluntary departure.** Under the law, the **attorney general** may grant temporary protected status (TPS), designating for protection **nationals** of any foreign country where (1) an ongoing armed conflict posing a serious threat to the personal safety of its nationals exists; (2) there has been an earthquake, flood, drought, epidemic, or other environmental disaster, resulting in substantial, but temporary, disruption of living conditions and the foreign country is unable, temporarily, to adequately handle the return of its nationals; or (3) extraordinary and temporary conditions exist in the foreign country that prevent its nationals from returning in safety. The period of initial protection can range from six to eighteen months, with the possibility of renewal upon review. [8 U.S.C. §1254]

Nationals from the following countries have been granted TPS at various times since 1990: El Salvador, Somalia, Bosnia-Herzegovina, Liberia, Rwanda, Montserrat, Burundi, Sierra Leone, and Sudan.

TEMPORARY WORKER   This term is most often used to describe **nonimmigrant**s who are issued **H-1B worker** visas for professionals. However, the term could also describe other nonimmigrants who have been granted **work permit**s, such as students.

TERRORIST ACTIVITIES

TERRORIST ACTIVITIES A person who has been a member of a foreign terrorist organization or has engaged in terrorist activities is inadmissible [see **inadmissibility grounds**]. Terrorist activity means any activity involving highjacking or sabotage of any conveyance; seizing or detaining, and threatening to kill, injure, or continue to detain, another individual in order to compel a third person (including a governmental organization) to do or abstain from doing any act as an explicit or implicit condition for the release of the individual seized or detained; assassination; or the use of any biological agent, chemical agent, or nuclear weapon or device, or explosive or firearm with the intent to endanger the safety of one or more individuals or to cause substantial damage to property.

The **State Department** may designate an organization as a terrorist organization if the group (1) is a foreign organization, (2) engages in terrorist activity, and (3) threatens the security of United States nationals or the national security of the United States. [8 U.S.C. §§1182(a)(3)(B), 1189]

Thirty organizations are designated by the State Department as terrorist groups, including:

- Abu Sayyaf Group (also known as Al Harakat Al Islamiyya). Active in the Philippines.
- Armed Islamic Group (also known as GIA, Groupement Islamique Armée, AIG, Al-Jama'ah al-Islamiyah al-Musallah). Active in Algeria.
- Aum Shinrikyo (also known as Aum Supreme Truth, AIC Sogo Kenkyusho, AIC Comprehensive Research Institute). Active in Japan.
- Democratic Front for the Liberation of Palestine–Hawatmeh Faction (also known as Democratic Front for the Liberation of Palestine, DFLP, Red Star Forces, Red Star Battalions). Active in the Middle East.
- Euzkadi Ta Askatasuna (also known as Basque Fatherland and Liberty, ETA). Active in Spain.
- Gama'a al-Islamiyya (also known as Islamic Group, IG, al-Gama'at, Islamic Gama'at, Egyptian al-Gama'at al-Islamiyya). Active in the Middle East.
- Hamas (also known as Islamic Resistance Movement, Harakat al-Muqawama al-Islamiya, Students of Ayyash, Students of the Engineer, Yahya Ayyash Units, Izz Al-Din Al-Qassin Forces, Izz Al-Din Al Qassim Battalions, Izz al-Din Al Qassam Brigades, Izz al-Din Al Qassam Forces, Izz al-Din Al Qassam Battalions). Active in the Middle East.
- Harakat ul-Ansar (also known as HUA, al-Hadid, al-Hadith, al-Faran). Active in Pakistan.
- Hizballah (also known as Party of God, Islamic Jihad, Islamic Jihad Organization, Revolutionary Justice Organization, Organization of the

Oppressed on Earth, Islamic Jihad for the Liberation of Palestine, Organization of Right Against Wrong, Ansar Allah, Followers of the Prophet Muhammad). Active in the Middle East.

- Japanese Red Army (also known as Nippon Sekigun, Nihon Sekigun, Anti-Imperialist International Brigade, Holy War Brigade, Anti-War Democratic Front, JRA, AIIB). Active in Japan.
- al-Jihad (also known as Egyptian al-Jihad, Vanguards of Conquest, Vanguards of Victory, Talai'I al-Fath, Tala'ah al-Fatah, Tala'al al-Fatah, Tala' al-Fateh, Talaah al-Fatah, Tala'al al-Fateh, New Jihad, Egyptian Islamic Jihad, Jihad Group). Active in Egypt.
- Kach (also known as the Repression of Traitors, Dikuy Bogdim, DOV, State of Judea, Committee for the Safety of the Roads, Sword of David, Judea Police). Active in Israel.
- Kahane Chai (also known as Kahane Lives, Kfar Tapuah Fund, Judean Voice). Active in Israel.
- Khmer Rouge (also known as Party of Democratic Kampuchea, National Army of Democratic Kampuchea). Active in Cambodia.
- Kurdistan Workers' Party (also known as PDD, Partiya Karkeran Kurdistan). Active in Turkey.
- Liberation Tigers of Tamil Eelam (also known as LTTE, Tamil Tigers, Ellalan Force). Active in Sri Lanka.
- Manuel Rodriguez Patriotic Front Dissidents (also known as FPMR/D Frente Patriotico Manuel Rodriguez-Autonomos, FPMR/A, Manuel Rodriguez Patriotic Front, Frente Patriotico Manuel Rodriguez, FPMR). Active in Chile.
- Muhahedin-e Khalq Organization (also known as MEK, MKO, Muhahedin-e Khalq, People's Muhahedin Organization of Iran, PMOI, Organization of the People's Holy Warriors of Iran, Sazeman-e Muhahedin-e Khalq-e Iran). Active in Iran.
- National Liberation Army (also known as ELN, Ejercito de Liberacion Nacional). Active in Colombia.
- Palestine Islamic Jihad–Shaqaqi Faction (also known as PIJ-Shaqaqi Faction, PIJ, Islamic Jihad in Palistine, Islamic Jihad of Palestine, Abu Ghunaym Squad of the Hizballah Bayt Al-Magdis). Active in the Middle East.
- Palestine Liberation Front–Abu Abbas Faction (also known as Palestine Liberation Front, PLF, PLF-Abu Abbas). Active in the Middle East.
- Popular Front for the Liberation of Palestine (also known as PFLP, Red Eagles, Red Eagle Group, Red Eagle Gang, Halhul Gang, Halhul Squad). Active in the Middle East.
- Revolutionary Armed Forces of Colombia (also known as FARC, Fuerzas Armadas Revolucionarias de Colombia). Active in Colombia.

- Revolutionary Organization 17 November (also known as 17 November, Epanastatiki Organosi 17 Noemvri). Active in Greece.
- Revolutionary People's Liberation Party/Front (also known as Devrimci Halk Kurtulus Partisi-Cephesi, DHKP/C, Devrimci Sol, Revolutionary Left, Dev Sol, Dev Sol Silahli Devrimci Birlikleri, Dev Sol SDB, Dev Sol Armed Revolutionary Units). Active in Turkey.
- Revolutionary People's Struggle (also known as Epanastatikos Laikos Agonas, ELA, Revolutionary Popular Struggle, Popular Revolutionary Struggle). Active in Greece.
- Shining Path (also known as Sendero Luminoso, SL, Partido Comunista del Peru en el Sendero Luminoso de Jose Carlos Mariategui, Partido Comunista del Peru, PCP, Socorro Popular del Peru, SPP, Ejercito Guerrillero Popular, EGP, Ejericito Popular de Liberacion, EPL). Active in Peru.
- Tupac Amaru Revolutionary Movement (also known as Movimiento Revolucionario Tupac Amaru, MRTA). Active in Peru.

According to State Department officials, the Irish Republican Army (IRA) was not listed because of various cease-fire agreements and the fact that its political wing has begun peace talks on Northern Ireland. However, the IRA remains under active review by the department.

 TEXAS PROVISO This provision essentially provided a loophole for the employment of **undocumented alien** workers in the Southwest in the 1950s. In 1952, Congress enacted a law that made it a crime to "harbor, transport, or conceal illegal entrants." However, an amendment to the provision—the Texas Proviso—demanded by Texas growers excluded "employment" from the concept of "harboring." The provision was interpreted by all concerned, including the INS, as authority for the employment of undocumented workers.

 THIRD PREFERENCE See **preference system.**

 THREE- AND TEN-YEAR BARS See **unlawful presence.**

TN PROFESSIONAL The North American Free Trade Agreement (NAFTA) created a **nonimmigrant** TN temporary employment category for professionals that is available to Canadian and Mexican nationals. A person who belongs to one of sixty-three professions with corresponding educational requirements or alternative credentials may qualify. The TN category can be held indefinitely, as long as employment continues on a temporary basis. [8 C.F.R. §214.6; 22 C.F.R. §41] The **H-1B worker** visa, on the other hand, is valid for a maximum of six years.

Professional occupations that qualify for TN status include the following: accountant, architect, computer systems analyst, disaster relief insurance claims adjuster, economist, engineer, forester, graphic designer, hotel manager, industrial designer, interior designer, land surveyor, landscape architect, lawyer (including notary in the Province of Quebec), librarian, management consultant, mathematician (including statistician), range manager/range conservationist, research assistant (working in a post-secondary educational institution), scientific technician/technologist, social worker, sylviculturist (including forestry specialist), technical publications writer, urban planner (including geographer), vocational counselor, dentist, dietitian, medical laboratory technologist (Canada)/medical technologist (United States and Mexico), nutritionist, occupational therapist, pharmacist, physician (teaching and/or research only), physiotherapist/physical therapist, registered nurse, veterinarian, agriculturalist (including agronomist), animal breeder, animal scientist, apiculturist, astronomer, biochemist, biologist, chemist, dairy scientist, entomologist, epidemiologist, geneticist, geologist, geochemist, geophysicist (including oceanographer in Mexico and the United States), horticulturist, meteorologist, pharmacologist, physicist (including oceanographer in Canada), plant breeder, poultry scientist, soil scientist, zoologist, and teacher (college, seminary, and university).

TOMÁS RIVERA POLICY INSTITUTE   The Tomás Rivera Policy Institute (TRPI) works toward the fulfillment of its mission to improve the well-being of the Latino community in the United States by fostering sound public policies. To this end, TRPI conducts rigorous, objective, policy-relevant research and evaluates the effects of governmental and corporate practices on the nation's Latino community. TRPI serves as a timely source of information, analysis, and ideas on key Latino issues for policy makers, educators, academicians, activists, and the media.

Established as an independent nonprofit organization, TRPI is affiliated with the Claremont Graduate School in Claremont, California, and with the Department of Government at the University of Texas at Austin. The work of the institute is carried out by scholars located throughout the United States and by staff located at its offices in California and Texas. TRPI's headquarters are in Claremont and all of its administrative and development activities are conducted from that location.

The research agenda of the Tomás Rivera Policy Institute has expanded considerably over the past several years. In addition to its focus on education, employment, and other related issues, the institute's research agenda now includes programmatic public policy evaluation, the incorporation of Latino native citizens and immigrants into American society, the economic integration of Latinos, and the assessment of the role Latinos play in shaping U.S. foreign policy. Given the extensive expertise of TRPI's leadership in the areas of immigration, foreign policy, and politics, it has been a natural progression for TRPI to become involved in these areas, which are at the forefront of policy issues facing the nation's Latino community today.

TRPI's vast policy research capabilities are founded on its unique capacity to engage in primary and secondary research as well as its proficiency in conducting survey research. TRPI possesses extensive expertise in the design and implementation of survey instruments targeting native and foreign-born Latinos. In addition, TRPI's assessment experience, ranging from corporate to governmental programs, uniquely positions the institute to conduct its project.

TORTURE CONVENTION   Under certain circumstances, the INS will allow an alien to remain in the United States if the person falls within the Torture Convention. The Torture Convention is a multilateral United Nations treaty that was designed to prevent torture and to compensate and protect a **victim of torture.** A person who has experienced torture or fears being tortured is covered. Torture is defined as

> [a]ny act by which severe pain or suffering, whether physical or mental, is intentionally inflicted on a person for such purpose as obtaining from him or a third person information or a confession, punishing him for an act he or a third person has committed or is suspected of having committed, or intimidating or coercing him or a third person, or for any reason based on discrimination of any kind, when such pain or suffering is inflicted by or at the instigation of or with the consent or acquiescence of a public official or other person acting in an official capacity. It does not include pain or suffering arising only from, inherent in or incidental to lawful sanctions.

The INS has recognized that Article 3 of the Torture Convention is similar to Article 33 of the **Convention Relating to the Status of Refugees of 1951,** which prohibits the United States from returning any person to a country where he or she might be subject to persecution. But Article 3 of the Torture Convention and Article 33 of the Refugee Convention have important differences. First, several categories of individuals, including persons who have committed particularly serious crimes, are ineligible for the protections of U.S. laws that correspond to Article 33. Article 3 of the Torture Convention contains no such limitation. Second, Article 33 applies only to aliens whose life or freedom would be threatened on account of race, religion, nationality, membership in a particular social group, or political opinion. Article 3 covers individuals who fear torture that may not be motivated by one of the five grounds. Third, the definition of torture does not encompass certain types of harm that might qualify as a threat to life or freedom.

 **Tourist Visa**   See **visitor for pleasure.**

Transitional Immigrant Visa Processing Center   The **State Department** has set up the Transitional Immigrant Visa Processing Center (TIVPC) to centralize the initial processing steps in the immigrant visa process, from the receipt of the approved **visa petition** from the INS to the mailing of **Packet III,** which is the main application packet for prospective immigrants. The TIVPC was established to ensure that correct packets of applications are sent out in a complete and timely manner.

 **Treaty Investor**   See **investor visa.**

Treaty Traders   A **nonimmigrant** E-1 treaty trader visa is available to anyone who is entering solely to carry on substantial trade, including trade in services or trade in technology, principally between the United States and the foreign state of which he or she is a **national.** At least 51 percent of the trade must be between the United States and the alien's country. A purely domestic operation would not qualify.

Trade is the exchange, purchase, or sale of goods and/or services. Goods are tangible commodities or merchandise having intrinsic value. Services are economic activities, the outputs of which are other than tangible goods. Such service activities include, but are not limited to, banking, insurance, transportation, communications and data processing, advertising, accounting, design and engineering, management consulting, tourism, and technology transfer. In practice, most treaty traders will be engaged in an import-export business.

In order to qualify for a nonimmigrant treaty trader visa, the person must be a national of a country with which the United States has a treaty or agreement related to commerce. Those countries include Argentina, Austria, Belgium, China, Colombia, Costa Rica, Denmark, Estonia, Finland, Greece, Ireland, Israel, Korea, Latvia, Liberia, Luxembourg, the Netherlands, Nicaragua, Norway, Pakistan, Thailand, Togo, Turkey, United Kingdom of Great Britain and Northern Ireland, Vietnam, and Yugoslavia. Treaty trader visas are renewable as long as the person maintains the terms of **admission**. [8 U.S.C. §1101(a)(15)(E)]

TYDINGS-MCDUFFIE ACT OF 1934   After the U.S. victory over Spain in 1898, the Philippines became a colony of the United States. As a result, Filipinos became noncitizen **nationals** who could travel to the United States without regard to immigration laws. By the 1920s, calls for the **exclusion** of Filipino workers increased; violence and numerous anti-Filipino outbursts erupted between 1929 and 1934.

An unlikely coalition of exclusionists, anticolonialists, and Filipino nationalists banded together to promote the passage of the Tydings-McDuffie Act. Many of the exclusionists had initially wished to keep the Philippines, but they soon realized that to exclude Filipino laborers, they had to support Filipino nationalists and anticolonialists and grant the nation its freedom. Under the terms of the act, the Philippines would be granted independence in twelve years—1946.

Tydings-McDuffie was everything the exclusionists could hope for. When their nation became independent, Filipinos would lose their status as nationals of the United States, regardless of where they lived. Those in the United States would be deported unless they became immigrants. Between 1934 and 1946, however, any Filipino who desired to immigrate became subject to the immigration acts of 1917 (see **Asiatic barred zone**) and 1924 (see **national origins quota system**), and the Philippines was considered a separate country with an annual quota of only fifty visas.

U

UNAUTHORIZED ALIEN An unauthorized alien is a person who was not at the time of employment in the United States either (1) a **lawful permanent resident alien** or (2) authorized to be employed (or granted employment authorization) by the INS. An employer can be subject to **employer sanctions** and penalized for knowingly hiring an unauthorized alien. [8 U.S.C. §1324a(h)(3)]

UNDOCUMENTED ALIEN An undocumented alien or undocumented worker is a person who has entered the United States without inspection or surreptitiously, or a **nonimmigrant** (such as a visitor or foreign student) who has stayed beyond the time granted on his or her **nonimmigrant visa**. Such persons are sometimes derisively referred to as illegal immigrants.

UNGAR, DONALD (B. 1926) Donald Ungar is regarded by many as the preeminent immigration lawyer in the country. Now of counsel to Simmons, Ungar, Helbush, Steinberg and Bright, he was the senior partner at the firm until his semiretirement. He has been respected throughout his career as an expert in all aspects of immigration and citizenship law, from **asylum** and **deportation** to business and family visas. He has also been a law teacher and mentor to countless numbers of current immigration practitioners.

He is known for taking on difficult appellate work because such cases represent the most challenging aspect of immigration law, particularly when he can develop imaginative arguments on difficult immigration issues. A few of the many important cases he has handled are *Matter of Dunar* [14 I. & N. Dec. 310], in which the "well-founded fear" standard of the UN refugee convention lowered an asylum applicant's burden of proof long before the **Refugee Act of 1980**; *Bark v. INS* [511 F. 2d 1200], which held that a separate living arrangement between husband and wife does not mean their marriage is an immigration sham; and the Filipino war veteran litigation that spanned some twenty years and, after three trips to the Supreme

Court (*INS v. Hibi* [424 U.S. 5], *United States v. Mendoza* [464 U.S. 154], and *INS v. Pangilinan* [486 U.S. 875]), prompted Congress in 1990 to reinstate the veterans' right to be naturalized in exchange for their service with U.S. armed forces during World War II.

Ungar never thought he would be a lawyer. His first real job after attending the University of California at Berkeley was as a news writer and reporter for United Press International in Washington, D.C. Four years later, he returned to his hometown of San Francisco, went into public relations work, and attended law school at night. He decided that public relations did not suit him. He also remembered thinking, "I can do that," when he watched lawyers argue cases before the Supreme Court.

After graduating from law school, Ungar worked for a general practitioner for two years. He then became a naturalization examiner for the INS in Los Angeles. Six months later, he went to work for the late Milton Simmons back in San Francisco, eventually becoming his partner.

Ungar was the first lawyer to teach immigration law at a Northern California law school (Boalt Hall, 1972 to 1981), and he won the **American Immigration Lawyers Association**'s first Jack Wasserman Award for Excellence in Litigation and the Phillip Burton Immigration Lawyering Award from the **Immigrant Legal Resource Center.** Ungar received his J.D. from San Francisco Law School in 1959.

UNITED NATIONS HIGH COMMISSIONER FOR REFUGEES
In 1950, the General Assembly of the United Nations formally adopted the statute establishing the Office of the United Nations High Commissioner for Refugees (UNHCR), calling upon governments to cooperate with the office. The functions of the UNHCR encompass providing international protection and seeking permanent solutions to the problems of **refugees** by way of voluntary repatriation or **assimilation** in new national communities. Although the UNHCR has provided its opinion on cases involving individual **asylum** applicants in the United States, U.S. courts have not felt bound by the UNHCR's opinions. Nevertheless, the UNHCR's views and the guidance provided in the UNHCR *Handbook on Procedures and Criteria for Determining Refugee Status* has been influential in many cases. [*Immigration and Naturalization Service v. Cardoza-Fonseca,* 480 U.S. 421 (1987); *INS v. Stevic,* 467 U.S. 407 (1984); *Matter of Izatula,* 20 I. & N. Dec. 149 (BIA 1990)]. The current High Commissioner is Mary Robinson.

UNITED NATIONS PROTOCOL RELATING TO THE STATUS OF REFUGEES
In 1968, the United States became a

party to the United Nations Protocol Relating to the Status of Refugees, which obligates all parties to cooperate with the Office of the **United Nations High Commissioner for Refugees** with respect to the treatment of refugees. Importantly, under the protocol, the parties agree to the definition of **refugee** that is set forth in the **Convention Relating to the Status of Refugees of 1951.**

The legislative history of the **Refugee Act of 1980** reveals that that act was intended to bring United States law into conformity with the protocol. For example, the House of Representatives report accompanying the amendments declared that the "Committee Amendment conforms United States law to our obligations under Article 33 [of the Convention] in two of its provisions." And the conference report stated that the "conference substitute adopts the House provision with the understanding that it is based directly under the language of the Protocol and it is intended that the language be construed consistent with the Protocol." However, even prior to 1980, the United States was required to apply the provisions of the protocol by acceding to the terms in 1968.

Ideological and geographic restrictions in the U.S. laws prior to 1980 were inconsistent with the ideologically neutral protocol. For example, one provision, known as "seventh preference," favored refugees fleeing from "Communist-dominated" countries and those from the Middle East. So the United States attempted to jury-rig compliance by using the **attorney general's parole** authority. But that authority did not conform to the protocol's principles of neutrality either.

UNITED STATES CATHOLIC CONFERENCE, INC., MIGRATION AND REFUGEE SERVICES The United States Catholic Conference (USCC) is the public policy and social action agency of the Catholic bishops in the United States. Within USCC, Migration and Refugee Services (MRS) is the lead office responsible for developing conference policy on migration, immigration, and refugee issues, as well as providing program support and field coordination for a network of 110 diocesan refugee resettlement offices throughout the United States. USCC/MRS is a strong proponent of serving the pastoral and human needs and promoting the human dignity of migrants, immigrants, refugees, asylees, and people on the move.

USCC/MRS and its diocesan partners provide services to clients without regard to race, religion, or national origin. Migration and Refugee Services is a multi-unit management entity comprised of the Office of the Executive Director, the Office of Migration and Refugee Policy; the Office of Refugee Programs; and the Office for the Pastoral Care of Migrants and Refugees.

USCC/MRS is deeply concerned about the protection of refugees and internally displaced persons. To this end, close contact is maintained with the Office of the **United Nations High Commissioner for Refugees** and other international organizations. Field evaluations are carried out to evaluate the effectiveness of international communities' response to refugee emergencies.

Migration and Refugee Services carries out the commitment of the Roman Catholic bishops of the United States to serve immigrants, refugees, and other people on the move. This commitment is rooted in the Gospel mandate that every person is to be welcomed by the disciple as if he or she were Christ himself, and in the right of every human being to pursue without restraint the call to holiness. Migration and Refugee Services contributes to this commitment by:

- assisting the bishops in the development and advocacy of policy positions at the national and international levels that address the needs and conditions of immigrants, refugees, and other people on the move
- working with the federal government and with local churches in resettling refugees admitted to the United States into caring and supportive communities
- assisting local churches and specialized apostolates in responding to the pastoral needs of Catholics among these populations, thereby aiding in the development and nurturing of an ethnically integrated Church in the United States

UNITED STATES COMMITTEE ON REFUGEES The United States Committee on Refugees (USCR) was founded in 1958 to coordinate U.S. participation in the United Nations International Refugee Year (1959). In the over forty years since, the USCR has worked for refugee protection and assistance in all regions of the world:

- *Asia.* The USCR defended the rights of Vietnamese refugees who fled their country during the war and following the fall of Saigon in 1975. The USCR also brought the plight of Cambodians fleeing the genocidal Khmer Rouge to the attention of the American public and policy makers. In both cases, the committee was active until durable solutions were found for all survivors. The USCR has also worked to save the lives and restore the rights of Sri Lankans, Tibetans, Burmese, Thai, Afghans, Bangladeshi, and Chinese.
- *Africa.* Repressive governments, internal conflicts, and opposition to reforms have led to massive human rights abuse and displacement in

Africa. Since the early 1970s, the USCR has been a leading voice on behalf of uprooted people in Sudan and Uganda. The committee reported on the desperate plight of Ethiopian refugees, and it was one of the first to warn that the conflict in Somalia would lead to famine. The USCR has also provided groundbreaking reports on the brutal wars in Mozambique, Rwanda, Burundi, Congo/Zaire, Sierra Leone, and Liberia.

- *Middle East.* The USCR continues to closely monitor the situation of 3 million Palestinians living in Jordan, Iraq, Kuwait, Lebanon, Syria, the West Bank, and the Gaza Strip, including reporting on each of these groups every year in the *World Refugee Survey* and publishing expert analysis on the complex situation surrounding their plight. In recent years, the USCR has also conducted life-saving advocacy on behalf of Iraqi Kurds, an ethnic minority persecuted by that government.

- *Europe.* When war erupted in the former Yugoslavia, the USCR was among the very first in the field to travel to the region and to report on the ethnic cleansing and massive displacement of civilians. Its in-depth reporting and analysis put this very complex crisis in terms that policy makers, as well as the general public, could grasp. The USCR has also been outspoken on the effects of the European Union's efforts to limit numbers of asylum seekers in their countries by devising restrictionist asylum policies, a phenomenon known as "Fortress Europe."

- *The Americas.* The USCR was an effective advocate during the Haitian and Cuban refugee crises. Its recommendations on the establishment of temporary safe areas and on the humane treatment of those held in these areas saved lives and had a tremendous impact on the way those situations played out. The USCR has also documented human rights abuse and reported on displacement in El Salvador, Guatemala, Peru, and Colombia.

The USCR is often the first organization to document human rights abuses and is the most persistent watchdog for refugee protection and assistance. Examples of instances where the USCR has made a very positive difference include:

- *Serbia.* In 1996, the USCR advocated on behalf of nearly 800 Bosnian Muslims survivors of the 1995 fall (to Bosnian Serb forces) of Srebrenica and Zepa, Bosnian cities that had been guaranteed protection by the United Nations. Following the cities' capture, Bosnian Serb forces rounded up thousands of unarmed Muslim men and massacred them.

The Bosnian Serb government detained the group of 800 survivors in prisonlike barracks where they were not allowed to exercise, read, or work. Bosnian Serb officials indicated that they were willing to release the survivors, but no European government was willing to accept the men. Recognizing that the United States was the last and only hope for the jailed Bosnians, the USCR urged the U.S. government to rescue the men by offering them resettlement in the United States. Following the USCR's appeal, the U.S. government offered resettlement to the group.

- *Malaysia.* The USCR learned in 1990 that Malaysia was refusing Vietnamese boat people seeking shelter and safety. Worse, it was towing their rickety, dangerous boats back out to sea. In April 1990, the USCR reported that Malaysia had pushed back over 5,000 Vietnamese refugees since May 1989, and had towed more than 20 boats back out to sea within the past month alone. The USCR's report was cited in influential publications such as the *Economist* and the *Far Eastern Economic Review.* Congress responded to the news of Malaysia's treatment of the Vietnamese by barring Malaysia from receiving any International Military Education and Training Funds in the next fiscal year.

- *Somalia.* In 1987, the USCR brought the plight of Ethiopian refugees in Somalia to the world community's attention. The refugees were members of the minority Amhara ethnic group—a distinction that singled them out for ill treatment by the Somali government. Many were detained in Shelembod, a prison camp in a remote part of the country. The Somali government would not acknowledge the camp's existence. In the publication *Detained in Exile,* the USCR brought the problem to the world's attention. Following the USCR's report, a committee of the U.S. Senate called for the resettlement of the Shelembod refugees, and for international access to the refugees imprisoned there. In 1988, Somalia allowed the Red Cross access to the camp. Later, Canada resettled a substantial number of the refugees. The rest were able to return home to Ethiopia.

- *Iraq.* In 1996, Iraqi dictator Saddam Hussein's forces stormed into a region of northern Iraq that he had been warned to keep out of by the U.S. government. Hussein's past brutal treatment of the area's Kurdish inhabitants had forced the United States and its allies to declare the region "safe" after the 1991 Gulf War, and to make a commitment to protect its residents. Recognizing the danger of Hussein's invasion, the USCR warned that Iraqi Kurds employed by the U.S. government, as well as Iraqi aid workers employed by Western organizations, might need to be evacuated. The U.S. government evacuated its own employees. However, it refused to evacuate the 4,000 to 5,000 Kurds who had been working for American humanitarian organizations, even though Hussein's government had made it chillingly clear that it intended to target those individuals. In one incident, a Kurdish driver for Concern for Kids (an Atlanta-based charity) was dragged from a vehicle, stabbed, soaked in gasoline, and set on fire. Miraculously, he survived—but authorities deemed it a suicide attempt and threw him in jail. The USCR fought the U.S. decision to abandon the Kurdish humanitarian workers through opinion pieces in prominent newspapers, direct lobbying with high-level government officials, and a visit to the region by the USCR's Bill Frelick to get an accurate assessment of the problem. "We owe it to those who trusted us, who worked with us, who identified with us, and who have no place else to go, to get them out," Frelick wrote in the *New York Times*. Under pressure, the U.S. government changed its position in early December, and began evacuating the endangered aid workers. They were flown to Guam, in preparation for resettlement in the United States.

- In 1996, the **State Department** sought to have language removed from international agreements that protect refugees seeking to cross borders from being forced back into situations of tyranny, persecution, and danger. This change would have placed untold numbers of people at risk. The USCR brought the issue to the attention of Senator Ted Kennedy, the National Security Council, and the **United Nations High Commissioner for Refugees,** and worked with them to pressure the State Department. The State Department changed its stance, declaring its support for the principle of not forcing refugees back at international borders. The State Department official who announced the government's intention to stand behind the principle used wording that closely matched the language suggested by the USCR.
- In 1994, the INS proposed a $130 fee for applying for asylum. The USCR opposed the fee, out of concern that many asylum seekers arriving on America's shores have no money and often little more than the clothes on their backs. Fearing the tragic consequences of forcing people to return to persecution, torture, or death simply because they lacked $130, the USCR brought the proposal to Americans' attention in an article called "No Huddled Masses Need Apply," which ran in several newspapers.

Recognizing the uniquely vulnerable condition of the refugee, the USCR strives to make sure that when refugees flee, they have a place to flee to; that governments defend refugees' basic human rights; that persecutors and ethnic cleansers are not allowed to do their cruel work unnoticed; and that refugees are given a voice. Refugees need protection. Whether they are threatened by oppressive governments, warfare, ethnic cleansing, and closed borders, or by badly written laws, legal loopholes, and uncaring bureaucrats, the USCR is there to protect the rights of the world's most vulnerable people. The USCR defends the rights of all uprooted people regardless of their nationality, race, religion, ideology, or social group. Its work is based on the belief that once the consciences of men and women are aroused, great deeds can be accomplished. The USCR is guided by the following principles:

- Refugees have basic human rights. Most fundamentally, no persons with a **well-founded fear of persecution** should be forcibly returned (*refouled*) to his or her homeland.
- Asylum seekers have the right to a fair and impartial hearing to determine their refugee status.
- All uprooted victims of human conflict, regardless of whether they crossed a border, have the right to humane treatment, as well as adequate protection and assistance.

UNITED STATES EX REL. KNAUFF V. SHAUGHNESSY

This case [338 U.S. 537 (1950)] established the principle that the due process rights of aliens seeking to enter the United States can be severely limited by Congress. In this case, Knauff was excluded without a hearing, solely upon a finding by the INS that her admission would be prejudicial to the interests of the United States, even though she was the wife of a U.S. citizen who had served honorably in the armed forces of the United States during World War II.

Knauff was born in Germany in 1915. She left Germany and went to Czechoslovakia during the Nazi regime. There she was married and divorced, then went to England in 1939 as a refugee. Thereafter she served with the Royal Air Force honorably from January 1, 1943, until May 30, 1946. She then secured civilian employment with the U.S. War Department in Germany. Her work was rated "very good" and "excellent." On February 28, 1948, she married a naturalized citizen of the United States. He was honorably discharged from the U.S. Army, and became a civilian employee of the Army in Germany.

On August 14, 1948, Knauff sought to enter the United States to be naturalized. On that day she was temporarily excluded from the United States and detained on Ellis Island. On October 6, 1948, INS officials recommended that she be permanently excluded on the ground that her admission would be prejudicial to the interests of the United States for security reasons. She was thus excluded from entry without a hearing.

An alien who seeks admission to this country may not do so under just any claim of right. Admission of aliens to the United States is a privilege granted by the sovereign United States government. Such privilege is granted to an alien only upon such terms as the United States shall prescribe.

Exclusion of aliens is a fundamental act of sovereignty. The right to do so stems not alone from legislative power but is inherent in the executive power to control the foreign affairs of the nation. When Congress prescribes a procedure concerning the admissibility of aliens, it is not dealing alone with a legislative power. It is implementing an inherent executive (presidential) power.

Thus the decision to admit or to exclude an alien may be lawfully placed with the president, who may in turn delegate the carrying out of this function to a responsible executive officer of the sovereign, such as the attorney general and the INS. The action of the executive officer under such authority is final and conclusive. Whatever the rule may be concerning deportation of persons who have gained entry into the United States, it is not within the province of any court, unless expressly authorized by law, to review the determination of the political branch of the government to exclude a given alien. Normally Congress supplies the conditions of the privilege of entry into the United States. But because the power of exclusion of aliens is also inherent in the executive department of the sovereign, Congress may in broad terms authorize the executive to exercise the power, as was done here, for the best interests of the country during a time of national emergency. Whatever the procedure authorized by Congress is, it is due process as far as an alien denied entry is concerned.

In this case the attorney general and the INS, exercising the discretion entrusted by Congress and the president, concluded upon the basis of confidential information that the public interest required that Knauff be denied the privilege of entry into the United States. A hearing was denied because the disclosure of the information on which the opinion was based would itself endanger the public security. This was not improper.

🏛 *UNITED STATES V. WONG KIM ARK*   This case [169 U.S. 649 (1898)] is often cited for the proposition that anyone born in the United States is a U.S. citizen, even if the parents are undocumented. However, there continues to be some debate over that interpretation because the parents of Wong Kim Ark were actually legal residents of the United States when he was born.

Wong Kim Ark was born in San Francisco, California, in the late 1800s. His parents had become legal residents of the United States prior to his birth, but his parents were not eligible to become United States citizens because Chinese were not eligible for **naturalization** under the laws at the time. Therefore, the government argued that Wong Kim Ark could not be a citizen by birth in the United States since his parents could never become citizens.

To determine whether Wong Kim Ark was a citizen, the U.S. Supreme Court had to interpret the first sentence of the Constitution's Fourteenth Amendment: "All persons born or naturalized in the United States, and subject to the jurisdiction thereof, are citizens of the United States and of the State wherein they reside." The Supreme Court ruled 6–2 that Wong Kim Ark was a citizen because of the Fourteenth Amendment. The main purpose of the Fourteenth Amendment was to establish the citizenship of free African Americans who had been slaves. The court felt that the language of the amendment was not intended to impose any new restrictions on citizenship, or to prevent any persons from becoming citizens by the fact of birth within the United States. Thus, under the plain language of the amendment, Wong Kim Ark was a citizen because he was born in the United States and he was subject to the jurisdiction of the United States.

UNLAWFUL PRESENCE   The term *unlawful presence* is often used to describe the status of an alien who is in the United States without proper documentation. The person might also be referred to as an **undocumented alien.** The two primary means by which an alien assumes unlawful presence is by overstaying the permitted time attached to a **nonimmigrant visa** or by crossing a border into the United States surreptitiously.

Any alien who has been unlawfully present in the United States for a period of more than 180 days but less than a year, and who has voluntarily departed prior to any **removal** proceedings, is barred from **admission** (inadmissible) for three years. Any alien who has been unlawfully present in the United States for a year or more and who is seeking readmission will be barred for ten years. These are commonly referred to as the *three- and ten-year bars.*

Unlawful presence does not include any period of time that the person was under age eighteen, any time during which the alien had a bona fide **asylum** application pending, any time during which the alien had a nonfrivolous application pending for a **change of nonimmigrant status** or extension of status and did not work without authorization, or any time during which the alien was a beneficiary of **family unity** protection. This ground of inadmissibility also does not apply to an alien who was a victim of spousal or parental abuse when the unlawful presence is related to the abuse. [8 U.S.C. §1182(a)(9)]

Persons guilty of unlawful presence with certain U.S. citizen or **lawful permanent resident alien** family members can seek a discretionary waiver of the three- or ten-year bar. The INS or an **immigration judge** can grant a **waiver of inadmissibility** to an alien who is the spouse, son, or daughter of a U.S. citizen or lawful permanent resident, if refusing admission to this person would result in **extreme hardship** to the citizen or permanent resident spouse or parent.

URBAN INSTITUTE The Urban Institute has carried out many of the most important studies of fiscal impacts of immigrants performed in the last decade. Its studies of immigrants' fiscal impact on Los Angeles County and of recent immigrants' impact on the United States were instrumental in countering claims of anti-immigration advocates that immigrants were a costly burden on the native population. In September 1994, the Urban Institute released a report prepared for the Office of Management and Budget (OMB) that included estimates of fiscal impacts for **undocumented alien**s in seven states (California, New York, Texas, Florida, Illinois, New Jersey, and Arizona). Specifically, the institute estimated the state and local costs for primary and secondary education, state incarceration costs, and state Medicaid costs; the report also included estimates of federal and state income tax receipts, Social Security taxes, state sales taxes, and state and local property taxes.

The report to the OMB was well received in most of the states and led to revisions of California's widely publicized estimates of education costs. A General Accounting Office (GAO) review of the study's methods and competing estimates found the Urban Institute's methods to be sound. The Urban Institute's estimates of undocumented aliens incarcerated in state prisons were used to distribute funds to states under the Crime Act of 1994.

In recent years, the Urban Institute participated in a project with the Latino Institute carried out for the Illinois Immigrant Policy Project. The Latino Institute estimated the costs of welfare and education for immigrant populations and natives using methods developed by the Urban Institute. The Urban Institute estimated a range of taxes paid by various immigrant groups and natives. The major findings of the study were that overall, immigrants paid a higher proportion of taxes than their representation in the population in Illinois; that service use was proportionately less for immigrants; and that the federal government received a majority of immigrant taxes, but Illinois paid for a majority of services used by immigrants.

The institute's multiyear analyses of the implementation of five major provisions of the **Immigration Reform and Control Act of 1986 (employer**

sanctions, legalization, welfare verification, state impact aid, and new antidiscrimination safeguards) resulted in a large number of publications that have been widely cited by journalists, congressional leaders, and scholars.

V

VACCINATION REQUIREMENT Every person who seeks immigrant status must present documentation of vaccination against vaccine-preventable diseases such as mumps, measles, rubella, polio, tetanus and diphtheria toxoids, pertussis, influenza type B, and hepatitis B. A civil surgeon or approved physician examines each applicant's written history of vaccinations and certifies full compliance on an approved form. If the applicant has not received a complete series of each vaccine, the civil surgeon or physician can administer a single dose of each missing vaccine, or the applicant can have a private physician administer the dose and provide subsequent documentation to the official physician. [8 U.S.C. §1182(a)(1)(A)(ii)]

VAN DER HOUT, MARC (B. 1948) Marc Van Der Hout is one of the elite immigrant and refugee rights litigators in the United States. He is the founding partner of Van Der Hout & Brigagliano, an immigration law firm with offices in San Francisco and Palo Alto, California, and is certified as a specialist in immigration and nationality law by the State Bar of California.

Some of Van Der Hout's cases of national importance include *American Baptist Churches v. Thornburgh* [see **ABC asylum class**], a nationwide class action on behalf of Salvadoran and Guatemalan refugees that resulted in a settlement requiring readjudication of all denied asylum claims; *Escobar-Ruiz v. INS*, a Ninth Circuit Court en banc decision establishing a right to attorney's fees under the Equal Access to Justice Act in immigration proceedings; *American-Arab Anti-Discrimination Committee v. Reno*, a district court decision declaring unconstitutional ideological grounds of deportation under the **McCarran-Walter Act of 1952**; and a Ninth Circuit decision enjoining deportation based on selective prosecution, holding that aliens have the same First Amendment rights as U.S. citizens, and voiding on due process grounds the use of classified information to deny immigration benefits. He is currently involved in litigation challenging the new immigration laws, including restrictions on judicial review. One of his subspecialties is the immigration consequences of criminal activity, a subject on which he has lectured and written extensively.

Van Der Hout is a member of the Board of Governors of the **American Immigration Lawyers Association,** a past chair of and current member of the Board of Directors of the **National Immigration Project of the National Lawyers Guild** and the Criminal Trial Lawyers Association, and a member of the American Bar Association Coordination Committee on Immigration. He is a past national president of the National Lawyers Guild and has twice received the American Immigration Lawyers Association's Jack Wasserman Award. Van Der Hout has also been an adjunct professor of immigration law at Hastings College of the Law and Boalt Hall School of Law, University of California at Berkeley. He received his J.D. from Golden Gate University School of Law, San Francisco, California.

VANCE V. TERRAZAS In this case [444 U.S. 252 (1980)], the Supreme Court held that a person can lose U.S. citizenship through expatriation if, by the preponderance of evidence, the government establishes that the person intended to surrender citizenship.

Laurence Terrazas was born in the United States. Because one of his parents was a Mexican citizen at the time, Terrazas acquired both United States and Mexican citizenship at birth. While he was a student in Monterrey, Mexico, and at the age of twenty-two, he executed an application for a certificate of Mexican nationality, swearing "adherence, obedience, and submission to the laws and authorities of the Mexican Republic" and "expressly renounc[ing] United States citizenship, as well as any submission, obedience, and loyalty to any foreign government, especially that of the United States of America." The certificate, which was issued upon this application, recited that Terrazas had sworn adherence to the United Mexican States and that he "has expressly renounced all rights inherent to any other nationality, as well as all submission, obedience, and loyalty to any foreign government, especially to those which have recognized him as that national." Terrazas read and understood the certificate upon receipt.

A few months later, following a discussion with an officer of the U.S. consulate in Monterrey, proceedings were instituted to determine whether Terrazas had lost his U.S. citizenship by obtaining the certificate of Mexican nationality. He denied that he had, but the **State Department** issued a certificate of loss of nationality. The issue in this case was whether there was sufficient evidence that Terrazas had voluntarily relinquished U.S. citizenship as required in *Afroyim v. Rusk.* The Court held that in proving **expatriation,** an expatriating act and an intent to relinquish citizenship must be proved only by a preponderance of the evidence (e.g., more likely than not). When one of the statutory expatriating acts is proved, it is constitutional to presume it to have been a voluntary act until and unless proved otherwise by the actor. If he or she succeeds, there can be no expatriation. If he fails, the question remains whether on all the evidence the government has satisfied its burden of proof that the expatriating act was performed with the necessary intent to relinquish citizenship. The case was then sent back to a lower court. [8 U.S.C. §1481(a)]

Vargas, Arturo (b. 1962) Arturo Vargas is the executive director of the National Association of Latino Elected Officials (NALEO), a national membership organization, and the **National Association of Latino Elected Officials Educational Fund,** a national nonprofit civic participation and research organization. Vargas is one of the nation's leading advocates of full civic participation and acceptance of immigrants, and is regularly cited by major media outlets across the country. The NALEO Educational Fund is the leading organization seeking to empower Latinos to participate fully in the American political process, from citizenship to public service. The fund's primary programmatic activities include U.S. citizenship outreach and assistance, civic participation, campaign training, technical assistance to elected and appointed Latino officials, youth leadership development, research on Latino demographic and electoral trends, and policy analysis and advocacy on access to the democratic process.

Prior to joining NALEO, Vargas was the vice-president for community education and public policy of the **Mexican American Legal Defense and Educational Fund** (MALDEF). His responsibilities included supervision and direction of MALDEF's community education and leadership development programs. His prior positions at MALDEF included director of outreach and policy, where his responsibilities included the coordination of the organization's 1991 redistricting efforts, which led to a historic increase in the number of Latinos serving in the California legislature. Before that, he directed MALDEF's National 1990 Census Program, an award-winning national outreach and public policy effort to promote a full count of the Latino population. This program was recognized by the U.S. Census Bureau as the most effective outreach effort in the 1990 census.

Before joining MALDEF, he was the senior education policy analyst at the National Council of La Raza in Washington, D.C., where he focused on language issues, including bilingual education, the English-only movement, and literacy in the Latino community.

Vargas presently serves on the boards of the Edward W. Hazen Foundation, the Independent Sector, the National Civic League, the **National**

Immigration Forum, and Hispanics in Philanthropy. In January 1999, Vargas was elected to a second term as chair of the National Hispanic Leadership Agenda, an umbrella coalition of the leading national Latino organizations. He has received *Hispanic* magazine's 1995 Hispanic Achievement Award for Community Service, the National Federation of Hispanic-Owned Newspapers' 1998 Leadership Award, the National Association for Bilingual Education's 1999 President's Award, and has been included in *Hispanic Business* magazine's list of 100 influential Hispanics in 1996 and 1998.

Vargas holds a master's degree in education and a bachelor's degree in history and Spanish from Stanford University. He was born in El Paso, Texas.

 **VAWA** See **Violence Against Women Act.**

VERIFICATION PILOT PROGRAM This government program is available to employers seeking different means of verifying the work status of job applicants in order to make the **I-9 process** more efficient for purposes of avoiding **employer sanctions.**

For many years, controversy has swirled around the question of how employers should verify the work authorization status of job applicants. Opponents of the employer sanctions laws that make it illegal to hire unauthorized alien workers argue that employers will discriminate against authorized immigrant workers when there is some doubt or unfamiliarity with an immigrant's particular status. In fact, studies have shown that many employers admit that they have discriminated against immigrant workers because of the fear that an immigrant might not be authorized to work. This type of discrimination, however, can be a violation of discrimination laws.

In response to these concerns, supporters of employer sanctions laws have urged Congress to require that all authorized workers be issued national worker identification cards, or to set up some other type of verification system to assist employers in the hiring process. Over the objections of critics who argue that such procedures would constitute improper invasion of privacy rights or would be flawed, in 1996 Congress established three separate pilot programs to confirm an individual's employment eligibility in five states with the highest estimated population of **undocumented aliens**: California, Florida, Illinois, Texas, and New York. The three programs are: (1) the basic program, (2) the citizen attestation program, and (3) a machine-readable program. After the pilot period, Congress will consider whether to reauthorize the programs, possibly expanding or making the programs permanent.

The INS has created a toll-free telephone confirmation system that can respond to requests for identification and employment eligibility verification. The INS and the Social Security Administration have also established databases capable of verifying workers.

Any employer in a state with a pilot program may elect to participate, and can determine whether participation will apply to all its hiring, to hiring in the pilot program state, or to places within the state. Those participating in either the basic or citizen attestation programs also may elect to apply their participation in nonprogram states, with some restrictions. Participation may be required for employers found guilty of violations of certain sanctions provisions. The **attorney general** has the power to reject or terminate participation by employers.

For the basic program, employers are required to complete Form I-9 [see Appendix] with a more limited list of documents and obtain Social Security and alien number information for noncitizens. The employers then use a confirmation system to verify the information obtained within three working days of the hire. If the confirmation system is unable to confirm the information, the burden shifts to the employee to contest the nonconfirmation, but the nonconfirmation is tentative, and no employer can use it to terminate employment until final. If the nonconfirmation becomes final and the employer does not terminate the employee (or does not notify INS that the employee has been terminated), the employment becomes a knowing hire of an unauthorized alien.

For the citizen attestation program, if an employee attests to being a U.S. citizen, the employer may request documentation but is not required to do so or to seek confirmation. This pilot is limited to 1,000 employers.

The machine-readable program is limited to states where identification documents issued in the state include machine-readable Social Security account numbers. If the employee presents a document that includes such a feature, the employer must make an inquiry through the confirmation system by using the machine-readable information.

An employer who elects to participate is required to confirm an employee's identity and employment eligibility within three days by using a federal database. If an employer who participates in the pilot program obtains confirmation of an employee's identity and employment eligibility in compliance with the program, the employer may rely on a rebuttable presumption that the **Immigration Reform and Control Act of 1986** (IRCA) has not been violated. On the other hand, if the federal database shows that the individual is not authorized to work, then an employer who continues to employ the individual will be deemed in violation of IRCA.

⊞ VICTIM OF TORTURE

Under certain circumstances, the INS will issue a **stay of removal** of an alien who falls within the definitions of the **Torture Convention.** The Torture Convention is a multilateral United Nations treaty that was designed to prevent torture and to compensate and protect victims of torture. Torture is defined as

> [a]ny act by which severe pain or suffering, whether physical or mental, is intentionally inflicted on a person for such purpose as obtaining from him or a third person information or a confession, punishing him for an act he or a third person has committed or is suspected of having committed, or intimidating or coercing him or a third person, or for any reason based on discrimination of any kind, when such pain or suffering is inflicted by or at the instigation of or with the consent or acquiescence of a public official or other person acting in an official capacity. It does not include pain or suffering arising only from, inherent in or incidental to lawful sanctions.

Article 3 of the Torture Convention prohibits the return (nonrefoulement) of any person to a country when there are substantial grounds for believing that he or she would be in danger of being tortured. The INS has recognized the nonrefoulement obligation under the Torture Convention as an administrative matter. An informal procedure under which Torture Convention claims are addressed has been developed. To raise a claim, the applicant or his or her representative must contact the local INS district counsel.

⊞ VIOLENCE AGAINST WOMEN ACT

In 1994, Congress enacted the Violence Against Women Act (VAWA), which, among other things, allows abused spouses and children of **lawful permanent resident aliens** or U.S. citizens to apply for **cancellation of removal.** Like other forms of cancellation of removal, VAWA cancellation stops the removal of an alien and allows the person the opportunity to become a lawful permanent resident. VAWA cancellation requires the applicant to have continuous physical presence in the United States for the previous three years, to demonstrate that removal would result in **extreme hardship,** and to establish that he or she is a person of **good moral character.** Furthermore, the applicant must show that he or she has been battered or subjected to extreme cruelty in the United States by a spouse or parent who is a U.S. citizen or permanent resident, or he or she is the parent of a child who has been battered or subjected to extreme cruelty in the United States by a U.S. citizen or permanent resident parent. [8 U.S.C. §1229b(b); 8 C.F.R. §204.2]

VISA   A visa for a **nonimmigrant** is usually an endorsement made on a page in a person's passport by U.S. consular officials abroad indicating the type of visa (e.g., **visitor for pleasure, business visitor, intracompany transferee**) and a validity date. This can be represented by a multicolored rubber stamp in the passport. Some **nonimmigrant visas** might even be issued for an indefinite period. A visa for an **immigrant** may actually be included in a packet of materials issued by consular officials that is presented by the immigrant at the **port of entry** as proof that he or she is an immigrant.

VISA AVAILABILITY   When a person wants to immigrate to the United States, he or she must fit into an immigration category and not be subject to a ground of inadmissibility [see **inadmissibility grounds**]. Additionally, a **visa** must be available. Certain **immediate relatives** of United States citizens may immigrate to the United States without being subject to **numerical limitations** or quotas. Thus, visas are always available to immediate relatives of U.S. citizens as long as they are not inadmissible. However, other prospective immigrants who immigrate under the **preference system** are subject to two types of numerical limitations: a worldwide numerical cap and a country or territorial limit. The preference system provides separate systems for family immigration and for employment-related immigration.

Under the law, at least 226,000 family preference category visas are available annually on a worldwide basis. Although in theory the worldwide quota can be increased to 480,000 annually, the level likely will not be much more than 226,000. This is because the family preference category level is determined by subtracting the number of immediate relative entrants—generally well over 200,000 annually—from the maximum (480,000), with an absolute floor of 226,000. A separate **worldwide numerical limitation** of 140,000 is set aside for employment-based immigrants. Another 55,000 visas are set aside for **diversity visas** for immigrants on a worldwide basis.

The law also provides an annual limitation of visas per country of 7 percent of the worldwide quotas. Thus, assuming a 226,000 worldwide family visa numerical limitation and 140,000 for employment visas, 7 percent of the total (366,000) is 25,620 for each country. But 75 percent of the visas issued for spouses and children of lawful permanent residents (**second preference for relatives** 2-A) are not counted against each country's quota.

Prospective immigrants from countries with great visa demands such as the Philippines and Mexico face long backlogs. Until a visa becomes available, these individuals cannot immigrate to the United States. [8 U.S.C. §1152] See **visa bulletin.**

VISA BULLETIN   Each month the Visa Office of the **State Department** issues a bulletin that charts the availability of visas around the world for purposes of the **preference system.** A sample visa bulletin is contained in the appendix.

The chart contains a list of certain countries, as well as a general category for areas of the world that are not listed separately. The chart indicates visa availability from month to month with letters and dates. The letter *C* on the chart means that visas are currently available. The letter *U* indicates that visas are not available for that category. A date on the chart indicates that beneficiaries whose relative visa petition or **alien employment certification** applications were filed on or before that date may now apply for an immigrant visa. In other words, visas would be available to those beneficiaries whose **priority date**s have been reached.

Priority dates must be monitored month by month. As soon as a visa becomes available, the beneficiary should immediately apply for an immigrant visa abroad or for **adjustment of status** in the United States.

VISA PETITION   There are two types of forms that are commonly referred to as visa petitions. One is used for initiating the process to help a relative immigrate to the United States (Form I-130); the other is used for initiating the process for an employee to immigrate (Form I-140). The forms are filed with the INS. These two forms are included in the Appendix.

In the relative situation, the person who is technically completing the form is the U.S. citizen relative, who is known as the petitioner. The form is used for the **immediate relative** and for the family preference system categories. The prospective immigrant is known as the beneficiary of the petition. So, for example, if a U.S. citizen spouse wants to petition for the foreign-born spouse in the immediate relative category, the citizen spouse would file the Form I-130 visa petition on behalf of the foreign-born spouse. The form would be supported with evidence of the marriage (e.g., marriage certificate) and evidence that the petitioner is a U.S. citizen (e.g., U.S. birth certificate). Upon the petition's approval, the beneficiary would apply for **immigrant** or **lawful permanent resident alien** status through the immigrant visa process at a U.S. consulate abroad or through **adjustment of status** in the United States.

By the same token, an employer who seeks the services of a foreign-born employee on a permanent basis in the United States would file a Form I-140 petition for the foreign-born worker. The employer would be the petitioner, and the worker would be the beneficiary. When an **alien employment certification** is necessary, however, the Form I-140 cannot be submitted until the certification has been issued.

VISA WAIVER PILOT PROGRAM The **attorney general** has established a pilot program for **national**s of certain countries who need not possess a nonimmigrant visitor's visa (**business visitor** and **visitor for pleasure**) in order to be admitted as a visitor. The eight countries designated are Great Britain, Japan, Italy, Germany, France, the Netherlands, Sweden, and Switzerland. This means the visa waiver is available to visitors from those countries who are entering for no more than ninety days, who possess a round-trip ticket, who do not pose a security threat, and who have not previously violated conditions of a **nonimmigrant visa**. Furthermore, aliens seeking such a waiver must waive the right to review or appeal of an immigration officer's determination as to admissibility, including an appearance before an **immigration judge**, unless **asylum** is sought. This amounts to a waiver of the right to a **removal** hearing if the participant overstays the ninety-day period. [8 U.S.C. §1187; *McGuire v. INS*, 804 F. Supp. 1229 (N.D. Cal. 1992)]

VISITOR FOR PLEASURE Visitors for pleasure or tourists to the United States constitute approximately 80 percent of the **nonimmigrant**s who enter the United States annually. They are issued B-2 visas. Although visitors' visas are also available to visitors for business purposes, **business visitor**s are usually issued B-1 visas.

Visitors for pleasure are not permitted to engage in employment. However, they may enroll in a school as part-time students, so long as completion of the course is contemplated within the permitted period of stay indicated by the arrival-departure conditions on the **Form I-94**. With the exception of tourists from Canada and certain Mexicans who are entering on 72-hour shopping passes, visitors for pleasure must obtain a B-2 visa from an **American embassy** or consulate prior to arrival in the United States. The general requirement is that the nonimmigrant tourist must have a foreign residence that the person does not intend to abandon and that the visit is only temporary and for pleasure. A **visa waiver pilot program** is available for **national**s of certain countries.

Generally, a B-2 visitor for pleasure is granted permission to remain in the United States for six months. A six-month extension is also possible. Many visitors are issued B-2 visas that are valid for more than one entry into the United States. [8 U.S.C. §1101(a)(15)(B); 8 C.F.R. §214.2(b)]

VISITOR'S VISA   See **business visitor; visitor for pleasure.**

VOLUNTARY DEPARTURE   Instead of being removed (or deported) at government expense, most individuals who are placed in **removal proceedings** are granted the privilege of voluntary departure. A person who has departed voluntarily has a better chance of future readmission to the United States than one who was removed at government expense, assuming other admission requirements are met. In order to be granted the privilege of voluntary departure, the person must demonstrate a showing of **good moral character** for at least the preceding five years and must have sufficient travel funds. Aliens removable for security reasons or those who have committed an **aggravated felony** are barred from voluntary departure. If an alien is permitted to depart voluntarily and fails to comply within the specified time (usually thirty days), the alien can be fined up to $5,000 and is barred from further relief in the future. [8 U.S.C. §1229c]

W

WAIVER OF INADMISSIBILITY Even though a prospective **immigrant** or **nonimmigrant** may fall into particular immigrant or nonimmigrant category, he or she can still be denied **admission** if one or more of the **inadmissibility grounds** apply. However, some of the grounds of inadmissibility can be waived. In other words, even though someone is inadmissible, for example because of a **crime involving moral turpitude** conviction or visa fraud, it may be possible for the individual to apply for a waiver that, if granted, would in essence forgive the individual for the ground of inadmissibility and allow the person to immigrate or be granted a **visa.**

The determination of whether to grant a waiver of inadmissibility is usually in the hands of the INS **district director** or the American consul [see **consulate general**] who is deciding the application or visa request. The standards for waivers vary from one ground of inadmissibility to another. For example, a person with a prior history of mental disease may obtain a waiver if he or she is the spouse or unmarried son or daughter of a U.S. citizen or lawful permanent resident. A waiver for smuggling another person into the United States is only available to someone who assisted a spouse, parent, son, or daughter into the United States [see **smuggling of aliens**]. Someone who is subject to the three- and ten-year bar [see **unlawful presence**] can only be granted a waiver if **extreme hardship** is demonstrated. [8 U.S.C. §1182(d), (h)]

WELL-FOUNDED FEAR OF PERSECUTION In order to qualify for **asylum** or **refugee** status, an alien must be unwilling to return to his or her country of nationality due to a well-founded fear of persecution on account of race, religion, nationality, **membership in a particular social group,** or **political opinion.** The well-founded fear of persecution standard does not require a showing that it is more likely than not that persecution will occur. In some circumstances, even a 10 percent chance of being shot, tortured, or otherwise persecuted might be satisfactory [see *Immigration and Naturalization Service v. Cardoza-Fonseca*].

325

The person must simply show good reason why he or she individually fears persecution.

Persecution is broadly defined as the infliction of suffering or harm upon those who differ in a way that is regarded as offensive. Persecution can be inferred from a threat to life or freedom, or other serious violations of human rights, on account of race, religion, nationality, political opinion, or membership in a particular social group. Discrimination, however, amounts to persecution in only certain circumstances; persons who receive less favorable treatment are not necessarily victims of persecution. It is more likely that a claim of well-founded fear of persecution will be justified if the person has been the victim of a number of discriminatory measures, thereby involving a cumulative element. The suffering or harm inflicted must amount to more than mere harassment. However, persecution does not require physical harm or bodily violence, and can include the imposition of substantial economic deprivation.

A frequently used basis for seeking asylum is persecution on account of political opinion. This would include opinions not tolerated by the authorities that are critical of their policies or methods.

For purposes of asylum, a social group is normally made up of persons of similar background, habits, or social status. The **Board of Immigration Appeals** also requires that the members of the group share a common, immutable characteristic. Members of a taxicab driver cooperative and young single males from El Salvador have not been held to constitute social groups [see *Matter of Acosta*]. [8 U.S.C. §§1101(a)(42), 1158]

WESTERN HEMISPHERE IMMIGRANTS At one time, the immigration laws divided the world into Eastern and Western Hemispheres for purposes of visa distribution. For example, the **Immigration Amendments of 1965** set aside 170,000 for Eastern Hemisphere immigrants and 120,000 for Western Hemisphere immigrants. The Western Hemisphere was essentially all of North America, Central America, South America, and adjacent islands. The rest of the world was considered the Eastern Hemisphere. The law also imposed the **preference system** and a per-country quota on Eastern Hemisphere immigrants, but a first-come, first-served system on Western Hemisphere countries for the entire 120,000 pool [see *Silva v. Levi*]. The 1965 changes abolished the nonquota status of Western Hemisphere immigrants and classified them as **special immigrant**s. However, in order to immigrate, natives of the Western Hemisphere had to meet a rigorous **alien employment certification** requirement, with some exceptions.

Amendments to the laws in 1976 began to break down distinctions between the two hemispheres for visa purposes, and today **numerical limitations** and per-country limitations are calculated on a worldwide basis.

WHEELER, CHARLES H. (B. 1950)   Charles H. Wheeler

has been a senior attorney with **Catholic Legal Immigration Network, Inc.** (CLINIC) since 1996, and prior to that was the executive director of the **National Immigration Law Center** (NILC) from 1985 to 1996. He is a nationally recognized expert on public benefits, procedural, and farmworker issues in immigration law, writing and litigating extensively in the field.

Wheeler began his legal career as a staff attorney with the Colorado Migrant Council in 1977, then worked for Evergreen Legal Services in the state of Washington, before moving back to Colorado to serve as the director of the farmworker division of Colorado Legal Services from 1979 to 1985. Noteworthy in the lengthy list of publications he has written or co-authored are *Affidavit of Support and Sponsorship Requirements: A Practitioner's Guide* (CLINIC 1998); *Immigrants' Rights Manual* (NILC 1990, 1992, 1993, 1994, 1995); *Guide to Alien Eligibility for Federal Programs* (NILC 1992, 1993, 1994); and *Immigration-Related Employment Discrimination: A Practical Legal Manual* (NILC 1192, 1992, 1994). Wheeler's litigation has also been extensive. A sampling includes *Gillen v. Belshe* [E.D. Cal. 1994], a statewide class action challenging the legality of the provisions of **Proposition 187** that would restrict alien eligibility for health care and public social services; *Walters v. Reno* [W.D. Wa. 1994], a nationwide class action on behalf of persons placed in civil **document fraud** proceedings under 8 U.S.C. §1324c without being given adequate notice of the nature and consequences of such proceedings; *Naranjo-Aguilera v. INS* [30 F.2d 1106 (9th Cir. 1994)], a nationwide class action challenging the INS's implementation of the farmworker legalization (SAW) program; *Orantes v. Meese* [919 F.2d 549 (9th Cir. 1990)], a nationwide class action on behalf of Salvadorans that enjoined the INS from offering detained class members pre-hearing **voluntary departure** without first informing them of their right to apply for **asylum,** to request a deportation hearing, and to obtain free legal assistance; *Perez-Funez v. INS* [619 F. Supp. 656 (C.D. Cal. 1985)], a nationwide class action on behalf of all unaccompanied minors who are arrested or detained by the INS in violation of due process protections; *Alzalde et al. v. Ocanas* [580 F. Supp. 1394 (D.C. Colo. 1984)], in which sixty-four migrant farmworkers sued their farm labor contractor for numerous violations of the Fair Labor Standards Act and the Farm Labor Contractor Registration Act.

Wheeler has served on the boards or advisory committees of the **National Immigration Forum, National Immigration Project of the National Lawyers Guild,** and the Council of Advisors on Asylum and Refugee Protection of the **United Nations High Commissioner for Refugees** Washington Liaison Office. Wheeler graduated with honors from the University of Maryland School of Law in 1976.

WITHHOLDING OF DEPORTATION   Prior to 1996, withholding of **deportation** was a form of relief in deportation proceedings that was akin to **asylum** for aliens who feared persecution in their native country. After 1996, the terminology was changed to **restriction on removal.**

WONG WING HANG V. INS   Many decisions of the INS or an **immigration judge** are made as a matter of discretion. Unfavorable discretionary decisions can be reversed by a reviewing court only when there has been an "abuse of discretion." This case [360 F.2d 715 (2d Cir. 1966)] represents one example of a court's consideration of whether there has been abuse of discretion.

Wong Wing Hang was a 37-year-old native and citizen of China who entered the United States in 1951 on a false claim that he was the son of a United States citizen [see **paper son**]. Two years later, he fraudulently applied for a certificate of citizenship, giving false information as to his identity. Shortly thereafter he furnished the correct information when called before a grand jury, and subsequently revealed his identity to the INS and surrendered his certificate. In 1961 he was convicted on a plea of guilty to fraud and providing false testimony in court. He received a suspended sentence and was placed on probation for a year.

In 1963, the INS instituted deportation proceedings against Wong, who conceded deportability but sought suspension of deportation (a predecessor form of **cancellation of removal**). During the investigation, he falsely informed an investigator that his wife and children had never entered the United States and that they were living in Kowloon. In fact, Wong knew that his wife and children had fraudulently entered Canada in 1958 as the spouse and children of a Canadian citizen, and his wife eventually entered the United States as a Canadian citizen and was residing with Wong. Eventually, the whole scheme was unearthed by an INS investigator.

Wong's application for suspension was denied not for ineligibility but because he deliberately concealed the whereabouts of his family and permitted his wife to enter the United States with documents known to be fraudulent. Wong complained that he was being penalized for protecting his wife and children as any husband and father would. His position was that the **immigration court** had abused its discretion.

In ruling against Wong, the court of appeals set forth an analysis for abuse:

> "Abuse of discretion" has been given two rather different meanings. In one version it appears as a sort of "clearly erroneous" concept.... "When judicial action is taken in a discretionary matter, such action cannot be set aside by a reviewing court unless it has a definite and firm conviction that the court below committed a clear error of judgment in the conclusion it reached upon a weighing of the relevant factors."... Under a more limited notion discretion is held to be abused only when the action "is arbitrary, fanciful or unreasonable, which is another way of saying that discretion is abused only where no reasonable man would take the view" under discussion. A narrower meaning seems more appropriate when a court is reviewing the exercise of discretion by an administrative agency or an executive officer as distinguished from hearing an appeal from a decision of a judge— particularly so when the relevant statute expressly confides "discretion" to the agency or officer.... Without essaying comprehensive definition, we think the denial of suspension to an eligible alien would be an abuse of discretion if it were made without a rational explanation, inexplicably departed from established policies, or rested on an impermissible basis such as invidious discrimination against a particular race or group, or ... on other "considerations that Congress could not have intended to make relevant."

Here, Wong's falsehoods were prompted by the natural human motive to protect his wife and children and keep his family together. The court ruled that if the immigration authorities chose to say that a man who has gained entry by a false claim of U.S. citizenship, and has cooperated with others in similar efforts, can win their favor only by a spotless record in later dealings with them, and they apply this standard with an even hand, it could not find their decision so wanting in rationality as to be an abuse of the discretion that Congress vested in them.

WOODBY V. INS
This case [385 U.S. 276 (1966)] considered what burden of proof the government must satisfy in deportation or **removal proceedings.** The Supreme Court concluded that in such proceedings the government must establish the facts supporting deportability by clear, unequivocal, and convincing evidence.

The aliens involved in this litigation argued that the appropriate burden of proof should be that which the law imposes in criminal cases—the duty of proving the essential facts beyond a reasonable doubt. The government, on the other hand, urged that the appropriate burden of proof should be the one generally imposed in civil cases and administrative proceedings— the duty of prevailing by a mere preponderance of the evidence (more likely than not). The court basically adopted a standard in between.

> The hardship of deportation is great. Many lawful permanent residents have lived in this country long and established strong family, social, and economic ties. Thus, it is appropriate that no deportation order should be entered unless it is found by clear, unequivocal, and convincing evidence that the facts alleged as grounds for deportation are true.

WORK PERMIT   The term *work permit* is often used to describe a document that authorizes the holder to work in the United States. Such a document is important because after the enactment of the **Immigration Reform and Control Act of 1986** (IRCA), it became unlawful for an employer to knowingly hire an undocumented worker. A work permit for a U.S. citizen born in the United States is essentially a birth certificate presented with a Social Security card and drivers' license or a U.S. passport. A lawful permanent resident's work permit is his or her **alien registration receipt card** presented with another identification document. **Nonimmigrants**, such as tourists, foreign students, or temporary workers, must present their arrival-departure **Form I-94,** with a rubber-stamped "employment authorized" on the document and their passport.

An alien who wants a "work permit" may fall into a variety of situations. For example, a **foreign student** can work up to twenty hours per week on campus without INS permission. However, to work off campus, the student must remain in good standing, demonstrate economic necessity due to unforeseen circumstances, and obtain permission from immigration authorities. An electrical engineering foreign student who wants to work after graduation may seek *practical training* permission for up to a year, or possibly an **H-1B worker** visa as a software engineer or other specialty occupation requiring at least a bachelor's degree. [8 U.S.C. 1101(a)(15)(F) and (H); 8 C.F.R. 214.2]

WORLDWIDE NUMERICAL LIMITATIONS   Persons who seek to immigrate to the United States under the **preference system** are subject to two types of **numerical limitations**: a worldwide numerical cap and **country and territorial numerical limitations.** The law provides that at least 226,000 family preference category visas are available annually on a worldwide basis. Although in theory the worldwide quota can be increased to 480,000 annually, the level likely will not be much more than 226,000. This is because the family preference category level is determined by subtracting the number of **immediate relative** entrants—generally well over 200,000 annually—from the maximum (480,000), with an absolute floor of 226,000. Assuming that 226,000 is the operative figure, this means that in a given year, a maximum of 226,000 persons can immigrate to the United States under the family first, second, third, and fourth preferences. **Derivative beneficiary** immigrants are also counted in this numerical limitation. In contrast, because the immediate relative category is not subject to numerical limitation, in theory an unlimited number of immigrants could enter the United States each year in that category.

A separate worldwide numerical limitation of 140,000 is set aside for first, second, third, fourth, and fifth preference employment-based immigrants. Another 55,000 are set aside as **diversity visas** on a worldwide basis.

Each year, therefore, a careful allocation of immigrant visas under the preference system is made by the **State Department** Visa Control Division. Family preference visas are allocated in this manner: 23,400 to first preference, 114,200 to second preference, 23,400 to third preference, 65,000 to **fourth preference**. If the worldwide quota is actually more than 226,000 in a given year, the excess is channeled to second preference. The law also provides a flow-down effect for unused visas for the various preference categories. For example, unused visas from first and second preference categories can be used by third preference, and so forth. **Employment-based preference** visas are allocated as follows: 40,000 to first preference, 40,000 to second preference, 40,000 to third preference, 10,000 to fourth preference, and 10,000 to fifth preference. [8 U.S.C. §§1151, 1153] See **visa bulletin.**

Y

YICK WO V. HOPKINS This case [118 U.S. 356 (1886)] established early authority for the Supreme Court's close scrutiny of laws that looked neutral on their face, but were in fact racially discriminatory in their effect.

A San Francisco ordinance prohibited operating a laundry, except in a brick or stone building, without the consent of the county board of supervisors. The board granted permits to operate laundries in wooden buildings to all but one of the non-Chinese applicants, but to none of the approximately 200 Chinese applicants. Yick Wo, a Chinese immigrant who had operated a laundry for many years, was refused a permit and imprisoned for illegally operating his laundry. He successfully challenged his imprisonment in this case.

The Supreme Court found discrimination in the administration of the law:

> The facts shown establish an administration directed so exclusively against a particular class of person as to require the conclusion, that, whatever may have been the intent of the ordinances as adopted, they are applied by the public authorities charged with their administration with a mind so unequal and oppressive as to amount to a practical denial by the State of equal protection. Though the law itself be fair on its face and impartial in appearance, yet, if it is applied and administered by public authority with an evil eye and an unequal hand, so as practically to make unjust and illegal discriminations between persons in similar circumstances, the denial of equal justice is still within the prohibition of the Constitution. The present cases are with this class. While the consent of the supervisors is withheld from petitioners and from two hundred others who have also petitioned, all of whom happen to be Chinese subjects, eighty others, not Chinese subjects, are permitted to carry on the same business under similar conditions. The fact of discrimination is admitted. No reason for it is shown, and the conclusion cannot be resisted, that no reason for it exists except hostility to the race and nationality to which the petitioners belong, and which in the eye of the law is not justified.

YOUTHFUL OFFENDER EXCEPTION   Generally, a person who is convicted or formally admits the elements of a **crime involving moral turpitude** is excludable from **admission** to the United States [see **inadmissibility grounds**]. However, such a crime will not bar admission if the crime was committed while the person was under the age of eighteen, and the crime was committed or the person was released from prison more than five years prior to the application for admission. [8 U.S.C. §1182(a)(2)(A)(ii)]

Appendix

U.S. Department of Justice

Immigration and Naturalization Service

OMB #1115-0214

Affidavit of Support Under Section 213A of the Act

START HERE - Please Type or Print

Part 1. Information on Sponsor (You)

Last Name	First Name	Middle Name

Mailing Address *(Street Number and Name)*		Apt/Suite Number

City		State or Province

Country		ZIP/Postal Code	Telephone Number ( )

Place of Residence if different from above *(Street Number and Name)*	Apt/Suite Number

City	State or Province

Country	ZIP/Postal Code	Telephone Number ( )

Date of Birth *(Month, Day, Year)*	Place of Birth *(City, State, Country)*	Are you a U.S. Citizen? ☐ Yes ☐ No

Social Security Number	A-Number *(If any)*

FOR AGENCY USE ONLY

This Affidavit	Receipt
[ ] Meets	
[ ] Does not meet	
Requirements of Section 213A	

Part 2. Basis for Filing Affidavit of Support

I am filing this affidavit of support because *(check one)*:

a. ☐   I filed/am filing the alien relative petition.

b. ☐   I filed/am filing an alien worker petition on behalf of the intending immigrant, who is related to me as my _____ .
(relationship)

c. ☐   I have ownership interest of at least 5% of _____ .
(name of entity which filed visa petition)
which filed an alien worker petition on behalf of the intending immigrant, who is related to me as my _____ .
(relationship)

d. ☐   I am a joint sponsor willing to accept the legal obligations with any other sponsor(s).

Officer's Signature

_____

Location

_____

Date

Part 3. Information on the Immigrant(s) You Are Sponsoring

Last Name	First Name	Middle Name

Date of Birth *(Month,Day,Year)*	Sex: ☐ Male ☐ Female	Social Security Number *(If any)*

Country of Citizenship	A-Number *(If any)*

Current Address *(Street Number and Name)*	Apt/Suite Number	City

State/Province	Country	ZIP/Postal Code	Telephone Number ( )

List any spouse and/or children immigrating with the immigrant named above in this Part: *(Use additional sheet of paper if necessary.)*

Name	Relationship to Sponsored Immigrant			Date of Birth			A-Number *(If any)*	Social Security Number *(If any)*
	Spouse	Son	Daughter	Mo.	Day	Yr.		

Form I-864 (1/21/98)Y

Part 4.   Eligibility to Sponsor

To be a sponsor you must be a U.S. citizen or national or a lawful permanent resident. If you are not the petitioning relative, you must provide proof of status. To prove status, U.S. citizens or nationals must attach a copy of a document proving status, such as a U.S. passport, birth certificate, or certificate of naturalization, and lawful permanent residents must attach a copy of both sides of their Alien Registration Card (Form I-551).

The determination of your eligibility to sponsor an immigrant will be based on an evaluation of your demonstrated ability to maintain an annual income at or above 125 percent of the Federal poverty line (100 percent if you are a petitioner sponsoring your spouse or child and you are on active duty in the U.S. Armed Forces). The assessment of your ability to maintain an adequate income will include your current employment, household size, and household income as shown on the Federal income tax returns for the 3 most recent tax years. Assets that are readily converted to cash and that can be made available for the support of sponsored immigrants if necessary, including any such assets of the immigrant(s) you are sponsoring, may also be considered.

The greatest weight in determining eligibility will be placed on current employment and household income. If a petitioner is unable to demonstrate ability to meet the stated income and asset requirements, a joint sponsor who *can* meet the income and asset requirements is needed. Failure to provide adequate evidence of income and/or assets or an affidavit of support completed by a joint sponsor will result in denial of the immigrant's application for an immigrant visa or adjustment to permanent resident status.

A. Sponsor's Employment

I am: 1. ☐ Employed by _____*(Provide evidence of employment)*
Annual salary $ _____ *or* hourly wage $ _____ *(for* _____ *hours per week)*

2. ☐ Self employed _____*(Name of business)*
Nature of employment or business _____

3. ☐ Unemployed or retired since _____

B. Use of Benefits

Have you or anyone related to you by birth, marriage, or adoption living in your household or listed as a dependent on your most recent income tax return received any type of means-tested public benefit in the past 3 years?
☐ Yes   ☐ No (*If yes, provide details, including programs and dates, on a separate sheet of paper)*

C. Sponsor's Household Size   Number

1. Number of persons (related to you by birth, marriage, or adoption) living in your residence, including yourself. *(Do NOT include persons being sponsored in this affidavit.)*   _____
2. Number of immigrants being sponsored in this affidavit *(Include all persons in Part 3.)*   _____
3. Number of immigrants **NOT** living in your household whom you are still obligated to support under a previously signed affidavit of support using Form I-864.   _____
4. Number of persons who are otherwise dependent on you, as claimed in your tax return for the most recent tax year.   _____
5. Total household size. *(Add lines 1 through 4.)*   **Total**   _____

List persons below who are included in lines 1 or 3 for whom you previously have submitted INS Form I-864, *if your support obligation has not terminated.*
(If additional space is needed, use additional paper)

Name	A-Number	Date Affidavit of Support Signed	Relationship

Form I-864 (1/21/98)Y **Page 2**

Part 4.   Eligibility to Sponsor   *(Continued)*

D. Sponsor's Annual Household Income

Enter total unadjusted income from your Federal income tax return for the most recent tax year below.   If you last filed a joint income tax return but are using only your *own* income to qualify, list total earnings from your W-2 Forms, or, *if* necessary to reach the required income for your household size, include income from other sources listed on your tax return.   If your *individual* income does not meet the income requirement for your household size, you may also list total income for anyone related to you by birth, marriage, or adoption currently living with you in your residence if they have lived in your residence for the previous 6 months, or any person shown as a dependent on your Federal income tax return for the most recent tax year, even if not living in the household.   For their income to be considered, household members or dependents must be willing to make their income available for support of the sponsored immigrant(s) and to complete and sign Form I-864A, Contract Between Sponsor and Household Member.   A sponsored immigrant/household member only need   complete Form I-864A if his or her income will be used to determine your ability to support a spouse and/or children immigrating with him or her.

You must attach evidence of current employment and copies of income tax returns as filed with the IRS for the most recent 3 tax years for yourself and all persons whose income is listed below.   See "Required Evidence" in Instructions. Income from all 3 years will be considered in determining your ability to support the immigrant(s) you are sponsoring.

☐   I filed a single/separate tax return for the most recent tax year.
☐   I filed a joint return for the most recent tax year which includes only my own income.
☐   I filed a joint return for the most recent tax year which includes income for my spouse and myself.
    ☐   I am submitting documentation of my individual income (Forms W-2 and 1099).
    ☐   I am qualifying using my spouse's income; my spouse is submitting a Form I-864A.

Indicate most recent tax year _____
                                                (tax year)

Sponsor's individual income $_____

or

Sponsor and spouse's combined income $_____
(If joint tax return filed; spouse must submit Form I-864A.)

Income of other qualifying persons.
(List names; include spouse if applicable.
Each person must complete Form I-864A.)

_____ $_____
_____ $_____
_____ $_____

Total Household Income $_____

Explain on separate sheet of paper if you or any of the above listed individuals are submitting Federal income tax returns for fewer than 3 years, or if other explanation of income, employment, or evidence is necessary.

E. Determination of Eligibility Based on Income

1.   ☐   I am subject to the 125 percent of poverty line requirement for sponsors.
    ☐   I am subject to the 100 percent of poverty line requirement for sponsors on active duty in the U.S. Armed Forces sponsoring their spouse or child.
2.   Sponsor's total household size, from Part 4.C., line 5 _____.
3.   Minimum income requirement from the Poverty Guidelines chart for the year of _____ is $ _____ for this household size.   *(year)*

If you are currently employed and your household income for your household size is equal to or greater than the applicable poverty line requirement (from line E.3.), you do not need to list assets (Parts 4.F. and 5) or have a joint sponsor (Part 6) unless you are requested to do so by a Consular or Immigration Officer.   You may skip to Part 7, Use of the Affidavit of Support to Overcome Public Charge Ground of Admissibility.   **Otherwise, you should continue with Part 4.F.**

Part 4. Eligibility to Sponsor *(Continued)*

F. Sponsor's Assets and Liabilities

Your assets and those of your qualifying household members and dependents may be used to demonstrate ability to maintain an income at or above 125 percent (or 100 percent, if applicable) of the poverty line *if* they are available for the support of the sponsored immigrant(s) and can readily be converted into cash within 1 year. The household member, other than the immigrant(s) you are sponsoring, must complete and sign Form I-864A, Contract Between Sponsor and Household Member. List the cash value of each asset *after* any debts or liens are subtracted. Supporting evidence must be attached to establish location, ownership, date of acquisition, and value of each asset listed, including any liens and liabilities related to each asset listed. See "Evidence of Assets" in Instructions.

Type of Asset	Cash Value of Assets *(Subtract any debts)*
Savings deposits	$
Stocks, bonds, certificates of deposit	$
Life insurance cash value	$
Real estate	$
Other *(specify)*	$
Total Cash Value of Assets	$

Part 5. Immigrant's Assets and Offsetting Liabilities

The sponsored immigrant's assets may also be used in support of your ability to maintain income at or above 125 percent of the poverty line *if* the assets are or will be available in the United States for the support of the sponsored immigrant(s) and can readily be converted into cash within 1 year.

The sponsored immigrant should provide information on his or her assets in a format similar to part 4.F. above. Supporting evidence must be attached to establish location, ownership, and value of each asset listed, including any liens and liabilities for each asset listed. See "Evidence of Assets" in Instructions.

Part 6. Joint Sponsors

If household income and assets do not meet the appropriate poverty line for your household size, a joint sponsor is required. There may be more than one joint sponsor, but each joint sponsor must individually meet the 125 percent of poverty line requirement based on his or her household income and/or assets, including any assets of the sponsored immigrant. By submitting a separate Affidavit of Support under Section 213A of the Act (Form I-864), a joint sponsor accepts joint responsibility with the petitioner for the sponsored immigrant(s) until they become U.S. citizens, can be credited with 40 quarters of work, leave the United States permanently, or die.

Part 7. Use of the Affidavit of Support to Overcome Public Charge Ground of Inadmissibility

Section 212(a)(4)(C) of the Immigration and Nationality Act provides that an alien seeking permanent residence as an immediate relative (including an orphan), as a family-sponsored immigrant, or as an alien who will accompany or follow to join another alien is considered to be likely to become a public charge and is inadmissible to the United States unless a sponsor submits a legally enforceable affidavit of support on behalf of the alien. Section 212(a)(4)(D) imposes the same requirement on an employment-based immigrant, and those aliens who accompany or follow to join the employment-based immigrant, if the employment-based immigrant will be employed by a relative, or by a firm in which a relative owns a significant interest. Separate affidavits of support are required for family members at the time they immigrate if they are not included on this affidavit of support or do not apply for an immigrant visa or adjustment of status within 6 months of the date this affidavit of support is originally signed. The sponsor must provide the sponsored immigrant(s) whatever support is necessary to maintain them at an income that is at least 125 percent of the Federal poverty guidelines.

I submit this affidavit of support in consideration of the sponsored immigrant(s) not being found inadmissible to the United States under section 212(a)(4)(C) (or 212(a)(4)(D) for an employment-based immigrant) and to enable the sponsored immigrant(s) to overcome this ground of inadmissibility. I agree to provide the sponsored immigrant(s) whatever support is necessary to maintain the sponsored immigrant(s) at an income that is at least 125 percent of the Federal poverty guidelines. I understand that my obligation will continue until my death or the sponsored immigrant(s) have become U.S. citizens, can be credited with 40 quarters of work, depart the United States permanently, or die.

Part 7.   Use of the Affidavit of Support to Overcome Public Charge Grounds   *(Continued)*

Notice of Change of Address.

Sponsors are required to provide written notice of any change of address within 30 days of the change in address until the sponsored immigrant(s) have become U.S. citizens, can be credited with 40 quarters of work, depart the United States permanently, or die. To comply with this requirement, the sponsor must complete INS Form I-865. Failure to give this notice may subject the sponsor to the civil penalty established under section 213A(d)(2) which ranges from $250 to $2,000, unless the failure to report occurred with the knowledge that the sponsored immigrant(s) had received means-tested public benefits, in which case the penalty ranges from $2,000 to $5,000.

> *If my address changes for any reason before my obligations under this affidavit of support terminate, I will complete and file INS Form I-865, Sponsor's Notice of Change of Address, within 30 days of the change of address. I understand that failure to give this notice may subject me to civil penalties.*

Means-tested Public Benefit Prohibitions and Exceptions.

Under section 403(a) of Public Law 104-193 (Welfare Reform Act), aliens lawfully admitted for permanent residence in the United States, with certain exceptions, are ineligible for most Federally-funded means-tested public benefits during their first 5 years in the United States. This provision does not apply to public benefits specified in section 403(c) of the Welfare Reform Act or to State public benefits, including emergency Medicaid; short-term, non-cash emergency relief; services provided under the National School Lunch and Child Nutrition Acts; immunizations and testing and treatment for communicable diseases; student assistance under the Higher Education Act and the Public Health Service Act; certain forms of foster-care or adoption assistance under the Social Security Act; Head Start programs; means-tested programs under the Elementary and Secondary Education Act; and Job Training Partnership Act programs.

Consideration of Sponsor's Income in Determining Eligibility for Benefits.

If a permanent resident alien is no longer statutorily barred from a Federally-funded means-tested public benefit program and applies for such a benefit, the income and resources of the sponsor and the sponsor's spouse will be considered (or deemed) to be the income and resources of the sponsored immigrant in determining the immigrant's eligibility for Federal means-tested public benefits. Any State or local government may also choose to consider (or deem) the income and resources of the sponsor and the sponsor's spouse to be the income and resources of the immigrant for the purposes of determining eligibility for their means-tested public benefits. The attribution of the income and resources of the sponsor and the sponsor's spouse to the immigrant will continue until the immigrant becomes a U.S. citizen or has worked or can be credited with 40 qualifying quarters of work, provided that the immigrant or the worker crediting the quarters to the immigrant has not received any Federal means-tested public benefit during any creditable quarter for any period after December 31, 1996.

> *I understand that, under section 213A of the Immigration and Nationality Act (the Act), as amended, this affidavit of support constitutes a contract between me and the U.S. Government. This contract is designed to protect the United States Government, and State and local government agencies or private entities that provide means-tested public benefits, from having to pay benefits to or on behalf of the sponsored immigrant(s), for as long as I am obligated to support them under this affidavit of support. I understand that the sponsored immigrants, or any Federal, State, local, or private entity that pays any means-tested benefit to or on behalf of the sponsored immigrant(s), are entitled to sue me if I fail to meet my obligations under this affidavit of support, as defined by section 213A and INS regulations.*

Civil Action to Enforce.

If the immigrant on whose behalf this affidavit of support is executed receives any Federal, State, or local means-tested public benefit before this obligation terminates, the Federal, State, or local agency or private entity may request reimbursement from the sponsor who signed this affidavit. If the sponsor fails to honor the request for reimbursement, the agency may sue the sponsor in any U.S. District Court or any State court with jurisdiction of civil actions for breach of contract. INS will provide names, addresses, and Social Security account numbers of sponsors to benefit-providing agencies for this purpose. Sponsors may also be liable for paying the costs of collection, including legal fees.

Part 7.   **Use of the Affidavit of Support to Overcome Public Charge Grounds**   *(Continued)*

I acknowledge that section 213A(a)(1)(B) of the Act grants the sponsored immigrant(s) and any Federal, State, local, or private agency that pays any means-tested public benefit to or on behalf of the sponsored immigrant(s) standing to sue me for failing to meet my obligations under this affidavit of support. I agree to submit to the personal jurisdiction of any court of the United States or of any State, territory, or possession of the United States if the court has subject matter jurisdiction of a civil lawsuit to enforce this affidavit of support. I agree that no lawsuit to enforce this affidavit of support shall be barred by any statute of limitations that might otherwise apply, so long as the plaintiff initiates the civil lawsuit no later than ten (10) years after the date on which a sponsored immigrant last received any means-tested public benefits.

Collection of Judgment.

I acknowledge that a plaintiff may seek specific performance of my support obligation.   Furthermore, any money judgment against me based on this affidavit of support may be collected through the use of a judgment lien under 28 U.S.C. 3201, a writ of execution under 28 U.S.C. 3203, a judicial installment payment order under 28 U.S.C. 3204, garnishment under 28 U.S.C. 3205, or through the use of any corresponding remedy under State law. I may also be held liable for costs of collection, including attorney fees.

Concluding Provisions.

I, _____ *, certify under penalty of perjury under the laws of the United*
States that:

        (a) *I know the contents of this affidavit of support signed by me;*
        (b) *All the statements in this affidavit of support are true and correct;*
        (c) *I make this affidavit of support for the consideration stated in Part 7, freely, and*
            without any mental reservation or purpose of evasion;
        (d) *Income tax returns submitted in support of this affidavit are true copies of the returns*
            filed with the Internal Revenue Service; and
        (e) *Any other evidence submitted is true and correct.*

_____   _____
        (Sponsor's Signature)   *(Date)*

Subscribed and sworn to *(or affirmed)* before me this

_____ day of _____ , _____
                (Month)   *(Year)*

at _____ .

My commission expires on _____ .

_____
(Signature of Notary Public or Officer Administering Oath)

_____
                (Title)

Part 8.   **If someone other than the sponsor prepared this affidavit of support, that person must complete the following:**

I certify under penalty of perjury under the laws of the United States that I prepared this affidavit of support at the sponsor's request, and that this affidavit of support is based on all information of which I have knowledge.

Signature	Print Your Name	Date	Daytime Telephone Number
			( )

Firm Name and Address

U.S. Department of Justice
Immigration and Naturalization Service

OMB No. 1115-0136
Employment Eligibility Verification

Please read instructions carefully before completing this form. The instructions must be available during completion of this form. **ANTI-DISCRIMINATION NOTICE.** It is illegal to discriminate against work eligible individuals. Employers CANNOT specify which document(s) they will accept from an employee. The refusal to hire an individual because of a future expiration date may also constitute illegal discrimination.

Section 1. Employee Information and Verification. To be completed and signed by employee at the time employment begins

Print Name: Last	First	Middle Initial	Maiden Name
Address *(Street Name and Number)*		Apt. #	Date of Birth *(month/day/year)*
City	State	Zip Code	Social Security #

I am aware that federal law provides for imprisonment and/or fines for false statements or use of false documents in connection with the completion of this form.	I attest, under penalty of perjury, that I am (check one of the following): ☐ A citizen or national of the United States ☐ A Lawful Permanent Resident (Alien # A_____ ☐ An alien authorized to work until___/___/___ (Alien # or Admission #_____
Employee's Signature	Date *(month/day/year)*

Preparer and/or Translator Certification. *(To be completed and signed if Section 1 is prepared by a person other than the employee.) I attest, under penalty of perjury, that I have assisted in the completion of this form and that to the best of my knowledge the information is true and correct.*

Preparer's/Translator's Signature	Print Name
Address *(Street Name and Number, City, State, Zip Code)*	Date *(month/day/year)*

Section 2. Employer Review and Verification. To be completed and signed by employer. **Examine one document from List A OR** examine one document from List B **and** one from List C as listed on the reverse of this form and record the title, number and expiration date, if any, of the document(s)

List A	OR	List B	AND	List C
Document title: _____		_____		_____
Issuing authority: _____		_____		_____
Document #: _____		_____		_____
Expiration Date *(if any):* __/__/__		__/__/__		__/__/__
Document #: _____				
Expiration Date *(if any):* __/__/__				

CERTIFICATION - I attest, under penalty of perjury, that I have examined the document(s) presented by the above-named employee, that the above-listed document(s) appear to be genuine and to relate to the employee named, that the employee began employment on *(month/day/year)* ___/___/___**and that to the best of my knowledge the employee is eligible to work in the United States. (State employment agencies may omit the date the employee began employment).**

Signature of Employer or Authorized Representative	Print Name	Title
Business or Organization Name	Address *(Street Name and Number, City, State, Zip Code)*	Date *(month/day/year)*

Section 3. Updating and Reverification. To be completed and signed by employer

A. New Name *(if applicable)*	B. Date of rehire *(month/day/year) (if applicable)*

C. If employee's previous grant of work authorization has expired, provide the information below for the document that establishes current employment eligibility.

Document   Title:_____Document   #:_____Expiration   Date   (if   any):___/___/___

I attest, under penalty of perjury, that to the best of my knowledge, this employee is eligible to work in the United States, and if the employee presented document(s), the document(s) I have examined appear to be genuine and to relate to the individual.

Signature of Employer or Authorized Representative	Date *(month/day/year)*

Form I-9 (Rev. 11-21-91) N

U.S. Department of Justice
Immigration and Naturalization Service

OMB #1115-0009
Application for Naturalization

START HERE - Please Type or Print

Part 1. Information about you.

Family Name	Given Name	Middle Initial

U.S. Mailing Address - Care of

Street Number and Name	Apt. #

City	County

State	ZIP Code

Date of Birth (month/day/year)	Country of Birth

Social Security #	A #

Part 2. Basis for Eligibility (check one).

a. I have been a permanent resident for at least five (5) years .

b. I have been a permanent resident for at least three (3) years and have been married to a United States Citizen for those three years.

c. I am a permanent resident child of United States citizen parent(s) .

d. I am applying on the basis of qualifying military service in the Armed Forces of the U.S. and have attached completed Forms N-426 and G-325B

e. Other. (Please specify section of law)_____.

Part 3. Additional information about you.

Date you became a permanent resident (month/day/year)	Port admitted with an immmigrant visa or INS Office where granted adjustment of status.

Citizenship

Name on alien registration card (if different than in Part 1)

Other names used since you became a permanent resident (including maiden name)

Sex — Male / Female	Height	Marital Status: — Single / Married / Divorced / Widowed

Can you speak, read and write English ?   No Yes.

Absences from the U.S.:

Have you been absent from the U.S. since becoming a permanent resident?   No Yes.

If you answered "Yes", complete the following, Begin with your most recent absence. If you need more room to explain the reason for an absence or to list more trips, continue on separate paper.

Date left U.S.	Date returned	Did absence last 6 months or more?	Destination	Reason for trip
		Yes No		
		Yes No		
		Yes No		
		Yes No		
		Yes No		
		Yes No		

Continued on back.

FOR INS USE ONLY

Returned	Receipt

Resubmitted

Reloc Sent

Reloc Rec'd

| Applicant Interviewed | |

At interview
request naturalization ceremony at court

Remarks

Action

To Be Completed by
Attorney or Representative, if any
Fill in box if G-28 is attached to represent the applicant

VOLAG#

ATTY State License #

Form N-400 (Rev. 01/15/99)N

Part 4. Information about your residences and employment.

A. List your addresses during the last five (5) years or since you became a permanent resident, whichever is less. Begin with your current address. If you need more space, continue on separate paper:

Street Number and Name, City, State, Country, and Zip Code	Dates (month/day/year)	
	From	To

B. List your employers during the last five (5) years. List your present or most recent employer first. If none, write "None". If you need more space, continue on separate paper.

Employer's Name	Employer's Address	Dates Employed (month/day/year)		Occupation/position
	Street Name and Number - City, State and ZIP Code	From	To	

Part 5. Information about your marital history.

A. Total number of times you have been married ____ . If you are now married, complete the following regarding your husband or wife.

Family name	Given name	Middle initial

Address

Date of birth (month/day/year)	Country of birth	Citizenship
Social Security#	A# (if applicable)	Immigration status (If not a U.S. citizen)

Naturalization (If applicable) (month/day/year)   Place   (City, State)

If you have ever previously been married or if your current spouse has been previously married, please provide the following on separate paper: Name of prior spouse, date of marriage, date marriage ended, how marriage ended and immigration status of prior spouse.

Part 6. Information about your children.

B. Total Number of Children ____ . Complete the following information for each of your children. If the child lives with you, state "with me" in the address column; otherwise give city/state/country of child's current residence. If deceased, write "deceased" in the address column. If you need more space, continue on separate paper.

Full name of child	Date of birth	Country of birth	Citizenship	A - Number	Address

Continued on next page

Form N-400 (Rev. 01/15/99)N

◯   *Continued on back*   ◯

Part 7. Additional eligibility factors.

Please answer each of the following questions. If your answer is **"Yes"**, explain on a separate paper.

1. Are you now, or have you ever been a member of, or in any way connected or associated with the Communist Party, or ever knowingly aided or supported the Communist Party directly, or indirectly through another organization, group or person, or ever advocated, taught, believed in, or knowingly supported or furthered the interests of communism? Yes No
2. During the period March 23, 1933 to May 8, 1945, did you serve in, or were you in any way affiliated with, either directly or indirectly, any military unit, paramilitary unit, police unit, self-defense unit, vigilante unit, citizen unit of the Nazi party or SS, government agency or office, extermination camp, concentration camp, prisoner of war camp, prison, labor camp, detention camp or transit camp, under the control or affiliated with:
    a. The Nazi Government of Germany? Yes No
    b. Any government in any area occupied by, allied with, or established with the assistance or cooperation of, the Nazi Government of Germany? Yes No
3. Have you at any time, anywhere, ever ordered, incited, assisted, or otherwise participated in the persecution of any person because of race, religion, national origin, or political opinion? Yes No
4. Have you ever left the United States to avoid being drafted into the U.S. Armed Forces? Yes No
5. Have you ever failed to comply with Selective Service laws? Yes No
    If you have registered under the Selective Service laws, complete the following information:
        Selective Service Number:_____ Date Registered:_____
    If you registered before 1978, also provide the following:
        Local Board Number:_____ Classification:_____
6. Did you ever apply for exemption from military service because of alienage, conscientious objections or other reasons? Yes No
7. Have you ever deserted from the military, air or naval forces of the United States? Yes No
8. Since becoming a permanent resident , have you ever failed to file a federal income tax return ? Yes No
9. Since becoming a permanent resident , have you filed a federal income tax return as a nonresident or failed to file a federal return because you considered yourself to be a nonresident? Yes No
10 Are deportation proceedings pending against you, or have you ever been deported, or ordered deported, or have you ever applied for suspension of deportation? Yes No
11. Have you ever claimed in writing, or in any way, to be a United States citizen? Yes No
12. Have you ever:
    a. been a habitual drunkard? Yes No
    b. advocated or practiced polygamy? Yes No
    c. been a prostitute or procured anyone for prostitution? Yes No
    d. knowingly and for gain helped any alien to enter the U.S. illegally? Yes No
    e. been an illicit trafficker in narcotic drugs or marijuana? Yes No
    f. received income from illegal gambling? Yes No
    g. given false testimony for the purpose of obtaining any immigration benefit? Yes No
13. Have you ever been declared legally incompetent or have you ever been confined as a patient in a mental institution? Yes No
14. Were you born with, or have you acquired in same way, any title or order of nobility in any foreign State? Yes No
15. Have you ever:
    a. knowingly committed any crime for which you have not been arrested? Yes No
    b. been arrested, cited, charged, indicted, convicted, fined or imprisoned for breaking or violating any law or ordinance excluding traffic regulations? Yes No
(If you answer yes to 15 , in your explanation give the following information for each incident or occurrence the **city, state**, and **country**, where the offense took place, the **date** and **nature** of the offense, and the **outcome** or **disposition** of the case).

Part 8. Allegiance to the U.S.

If your answer to any of the following questions is **"NO"**, attach a full explanation:
    1. Do you believe in the Constitution and form of government of the U.S.? Yes No
    2. Are you willing to take the full Oath of Allegiance to the U.S.? (see instructions) Yes No
    3. If the law requires it, are you willing to bear arms on behalf of the U.S.? Yes No
    4. If the law requires it, are you willing to perform noncombatant services in the Armed Forces of the U.S.? Yes No
    5. If the law requires it, are you willing to perform work of national importance under civilian direction? Yes No

---

Continued on back   Form N-400 (Rev. 01/15/99)N

Part 9. Memberships and organizations.

A. List your present and past membership in or affiliation with every organization, association, fund, foundation, party, club, society, or similar group in the United States or in any other place. Include any military service in this part. If none, write "none". Include the name of organization, location, dates of membership and the nature of the organization. If additional space is needed, use separate paper.

Part 10. Complete only if you checked block " C " in Part 2.

How many of your parents are U.S. citizens?　　　One　　　Both　　(Give the following about one U.S. citizen parent:)

Family Name	Given Name	Middle Name
Address		

Basis for citizenship:	Relationship to you (check one):	natural parent	adoptive parent
Birth			
Naturalization Cert. No.		parent of child legitimated after birth	

If adopted or legitimated after birth, give date of adoption or, legitimation: *(month/day/year)_____.*

Does this parent have legal custody of you?　　　Yes　　　No

(Attach a copy of relating evidence to establish that you are the child of this U.S. citizen and evidence of this parent's citizenship.)

Part 11. Signature.　*(Read the information on penalties in the instructions before completing this section).*

I certify or, if outside the United States, I swear or affirm, under penalty of perjury under the laws of the United States of America that this application, and the evidence submitted with it, is all true and correct. I authorize the release of any information from my records which the Immigration and Naturalization Service needs to determine eligibility for the benefit I am seeking.

Signature　　　　　　　　　　　　　　　　　　　　　　　　　　　　　　Date

Please Note:　If you do not completely fill out this form, or fail to submit required documents listed in the instructions, you may not be found eligible for naturalization and this application may be denied.

Part 12. Signature of person preparing form if other than above. *(Sign below)*

I declare that I prepared this application at the request of the above person and it is based on all information of which I have knowledge.

Signature　　　　　　　　　Print Your Name　　　　　　　　　　　Date

Firm Name and Address

DO NOT COMPLETE THE FOLLOWING UNTIL INSTRUCTED TO DO SO AT THE INTERVIEW

I swear that I know the contents of this application, and supplemental pages 1 through____, that the corrections , numbered 1 through____, were made at my request, and that this amended application, is true to the best of my knowledge and belief.

_____
(Complete and true signature of applicant)

Subscribed and sworn to before me by the applicant.

_____
(Examiner's Signature)　　　Date

Form N-400 (Rev. 01/15/99)N

DEPARTMENT OF JUSTICE
Immigration & Naturalization Service

100 Typical Questions

1. What are the colors of our flag?
2. How many stars are there in our flag?
3. What color are the stars on our flag?
4. What do the stars on the flag mean?
5. How many stripes are on the flag?
6. What colors are the stripes?
7. What do the stripes on the flag mean?
8. How many states are there in the union?
9. What is the 4th of July?
10. What is the date of Independence Day?
11. Independence from whom?
12. What country did we fight during the Revolutionary War?
13. Who was the first President of the United States?
14. Who is the President of the United States today?
15. Who is the Vice-President of the United States today?
16. Who elects the President of the United States?
17. Who becomes President of the United States if the President should die?
18. For how long do we elect the President?
19. What is the Constitution?
20. Can the Constitution be changed?
21. What do we call a change to the Constitution?
22. How many changes or amendments are there to the Constitution?
23. How many branches are there in our government?
24. What are the three branches of our government?
25. What is the legislative branch of our government?
26. Who makes the laws in the United States?
27. What is Congress?
28. What are the duties of Congress?
29. Who elects Congress?
30. How many senators are there in Congress?
31. Can you name the two senators from your state?
32. For how long do we elect each senator?
33. How many representatives are there in Congress?
34. For how long do we elect the representatives?
35. What is the executive branch of our government?

36. What is the judiciary branch of our government?
37. What are the duties of the Supreme Court?
38. What is the supreme law of the United States?
39. What is the Bill of Rights?
40. What is the capital of your state?
41. Who is the current governor of your state?
42. Who becomes President of the United States if the President and the Vice-President should die?
43. Who is the Chief Justice of the Supreme Court?
44. Can you name the thirteen original states?
45. Who said "give me liberty or give me death"?
46. Which countries were our enemies during World War II?
47. What are the 49th and 50th states of the union?
48. How many terms can a President serve?
49. Who was Martin Luther King, Jr.?
50. Who is the head of your local government?
51. According to the Constitution, a person must meet certain requirements in order to be eligible to become President. Name one of these requirements.
52. Why are there 100 senators in the Senate?
53. Who selects the Supreme Court justices?
54. How many Supreme Court justices are there?
55. Why did the Pilgrims come to America?
56. What is the head executive of a state government called?
57. What is the head executive of a city government called?
58. What holiday was celebrated for the first time by the American colonists?
59. Who was the main writer of the Declaration of Independence.?
60. When was the Declaration of Independence adopted?
61. What is the basic belief of the Declaration of Independence?
62. What is the national anthem of the United States?
63. Who wrote the Star-Spangled Banner?
64. Where does freedom of speech come from?
65. What is the minimum voting age in the United States?
66. Who signs bills into law?
67. What is the highest court in the United States?
68. Who was the President during the Civil War?
69. What did the Emancipation Proclamation do?
70. What special group advises the President?
71. Which President is called the "father of our country"?
72. What Immigration and Naturalization Service form is used to apply to become a naturalized citizen?

73. Who helped the Pilgrims in America?
74. What is the name of the ship that brought the Pilgrims to America?
75. What were the 13 original states of the United States called?
76. Name 3 rights or freedoms guaranteed by the Bill of Rights.
77. Who has the power to declare war?
78. What kind of government does the United States have?
79. Which President freed the slaves?
80. In what year was the Constitution written?
81. What are the first 10 amendments to the Constitution called?
82. Name one purpose of the United Nations.
83. Where does Congress meet?
84. Whose rights are guaranteed by the Constitution and the Bill of Rights?
85. What is the introduction to the Constitution called?
86. Name one benefit of being a citizen of the United States.
87. What is the most important right granted to U.S. citizens?
88. What is the United States Capitol?
89. What is the White House?
90. Where is the White House located?
91. What is the name of the President's official home?
92. Name one right guaranteed by the First Amendment.
93. Who is the commander in chief of the U.S. military?
94. Which President was the first commander in chief of the U.S. military?
95. In what month do we vote for President?
96. In what month is the new President inaugurated?
97. How many times may a senator be re-elected?
98. How many times may a congressman be re-elected?
99. What are the two major political parties in the United States today?
100. How many states are there in the United States?

Answer Sheet

1. Red, white, and blue
2. Fifty (50)
3. White
4. One for each state in the union
5. Thirteen (13)
6. Red and white
7. They represent the original 13 states
8. Fifty (50)
9. Independence Day
10. July 4th
11. England
12. England
13. George Washington
14. [insert current President]
15. [insert current Vice-President]
16. The Electoral College
17. The Vice-President
18. Four years
19. The supreme law of the land
20. Yes
21. Amendments
22. Twenty-six (26)
23. Three (3)
24. Legislative, executive, and judiciary
25. Congress
26. Congress
27. The Senate and the House of Representatives
28. To make laws
29. The people
30. One hundred (100)
31. [insert local information]
32. Six (6) years
33.
34. Two (2) years
35. The President, cabinet, and departments under the cabinet members
36. The Supreme Court
37. To interpret laws

38. The Constitution
39. The first 10 amendments of the Constitution
40. [insert local information]
41. [insert local information]
42. Speaker of the House of Representatives
43. [insert current chief justice]
44. Connecticut, New Hampshire, New York, New Jersey, Massachusetts, Pennsylvania, Delaware, Virginia, North Carolina, South Carolina, Georgia, Rhode Island, and Maryland
45. Patrick Henry
46. Germany, Italy, and Japan
47. Alaska and Hawaii
48. Two (2)
49. A civil rights leader
50. [insert local information]
51. Must be a natural born citizen of the United States; must be at least 35 years old by the time he/she will serve; must have lived in the United States for at least 14 years
52. Two (2) from each state
53. Appointed by the President
54. Nine (9)
55. For religious freedom
56. Governor
57. Mayor
58. Thanksgiving
59. Thomas Jefferson
60. July 4, 1776
61. That all men are created equal
62. The Star-Spangled Banner
63. Francis Scott Key
64. The Bill of Rights
65. Eighteen (18)
66. The President
67. The Supreme Court
68. Abraham Lincoln
69. Freed many slaves
70. The cabinet
71. George Washington
72. Form N-400, "Application to File Petition for Naturalization"
73. The American Indians (Native Americans)
74. The Mayflower

75. Colonies
76. The right of freedom of speech, press, religion, peaceable assembly, and requesting change of government. The right to bear arms (the right to have weapons or own a gun, though subject to certain regulations). The government may not quarter, or house, soldiers in the people's homes during peacetime without the people's consent. The government may not search or take a person's property without a warrant. A person may not be tried twice for the same crime and does not have to testify against him/herself. A person charged with a crime still has some rights, such as the right to a trial and to have a lawyer. The right to trial by jury in most cases. Protects people against excessive or unreasonable fines or cruel and unusual punishment. The people have rights other than those mentioned in the constitution. Any power not given to the federal government by the constitution is a power of either the state or the people.
77. The Congress
78. Republican
79. Abraham Lincoln
80. 1787
81. The Bill of Rights
82. For countries to discuss and try to resolve world problems; to provide economic aid to many countries
83. In the capitol in Washington, D.C.
84. Everyone (citizens and noncitizens living in the U.S.)
85. The preamble
86. Obtain federal government jobs; travel with a U.S. passport; petition for close relatives to come to the U.S. to live
87. The right to vote
88. The place where Congress meets
89. The President's official home
90. Washington, D.C. (1600 Pennsylvania Avenue, N.W.)
91. The White House
92. Freedom of speech, press, and religion; peaceable assembly; requesting change of the government
93. The President
94. George Washington
95. November
96. January
97. There is no limit
98. There is no limit
99. Democratic and Republican
100. Fifty (50)

List of Schedule B
(20 C.F.R. 656.11) Occupations

Assemblers
Attendants, Parking Lot
Attendants (Service Workers such as Personal Service Attendants,
    Amusement and Recreation Service Attendants)
Automobile Service Station Attendants
Bartenders
Bookkeepers II
Caretakers
Cashiers
Charworkers and Cleaners
Chauffeurs and Taxicab Drivers
Cleaners, Hotel and Motel
Clerk Typists
Clerks, General
Clerks, Hotel
Clerks and Checkers, Grocery Stores
Cooks, Short Order
Counter and Fountain Workers
Dining Room Attendants
Electric Truck Operators
Elevator Operators
Floorworkers
Groundskeepers
Guards
Helpers, any industry
Hotel Cleaners
Household Domestic Service Workers
Housekeepers
Janitors
Key Punch Operators
Kitchen Workers
Laborers, Common
Laborers, Farm
Laborers, Mine
Loopers and Toppers
Material Handlers
Nurses' Aides and Orderlies
Packers, Markers, Bottlers and Related
Porters

Receptionists
Sailors and Deck Hands
Sales Clerks, General
Sewing Machine Operators and Handstitchers
Stock Room and Warehouse Workers
Streetcar and Bus Conductors
Telephone Operators
Truck Drivers and Tractor Drivers
Typists, Lesser Skilled
Ushers, Recreation and Amusement
Yard Workers

United States Department of State
Bureau of Consular Affairs

VISA BULLETIN

Number 7   Volume VIII   Washington, D.C.

IMMIGRANT NUMBERS FOR JULY 1999

A. STATUTORY NUMBERS

1. This bulletin summarizes the availability of immigrant numbers during July. Consular officers are required to report to the Department of State documentarily qualified applicants for numerically limited visas; the Immigration and Naturalization Service reports applicants for adjustment of status. Allocations were made, to the extent possible under the numerical limitations, for the demand received by June 10th in the chronological order of the reported priority dates. If the demand could not be satisfied within the statutory or regulatory limits, the category or foreign state in which demand was excessive was deemed oversubscribed. The cut-off date for an oversubscribed category is the priority date of the first applicant who could not be reached within the numerical limits. Only applicants who have a priority date earlier than the cut-off date may be allotted a number. Immediately that it becomes necessary during the monthly allocation process to retrogress a cut-off date, supplemental requests for numbers will be honored only if the priority date falls within the new cut-off date.

2. The fiscal year 1999 limit for family-sponsored preference immigrants determined in accordance with Section 201 of the Immigration and Nationality Act (INA) is 226,000. The fiscal year 1999 limit for employment-based preference immigrants calculated under INA 201 is 160,898. Section 202 prescribes that the per-country limit for preference immigrants is set at 7% of the total annual family-sponsored and employment-based preference limits, i.e., 27,083 for FY-1999. The dependent area limit is set at 2%, or 7,738.

3. Section 203 of the INA prescribes preference classes for allotment of immigrant visas as follows:

FAMILY-SPONSORED PREFERENCES

First: Unmarried Sons and Daughters of Citizens: 23,400 plus any numbers not required for fourth preference.

Second: Spouses and Children, and Unmarried Sons and Daughters of Permanent Residents: 114,200, plus the number (if any) by which the worldwide family preference level exceeds 226,000, and any unused first preference numbers:

A. Spouses and Children: 77% of the overall second preference limitation, of which 75% are exempt from the per-country limit;

B. Unmarried Sons and Daughters (21 years of age or older): 23% of the overall second preference limitation.

Third: Married Sons and Daughters of Citizens: 23,400, plus any numbers not required by first and second preferences.

Fourth: Brothers and Sisters of Adult Citizens: 65,000, plus any numbers not required by first three preferences.

-2- July 1999

EMPLOYMENT-BASED PREFERENCES

First: Priority Workers: 28.6% of the worldwide employment-based preference level, plus any numbers not required for fourth and fifth preferences.

Second: Members of the Professions Holding Advanced Degrees or Persons of Exceptional Ability: 28.6% of the worldwide employment-based preference level, plus any numbers not required by first preference.

Third: Skilled Workers, Professionals, and Other Workers: 28.6% of the worldwide level, plus any numbers not required by first and second preferences, not more than 10,000 of which to "Other Workers".

Fourth: Certain Special Immigrants: 7.1% of the worldwide level.

Fifth: Employment Creation: 7.1% of the worldwide level, not less than 3,000 of which reserved for investors in a targeted rural or high-unemployment area, and 3,000 set aside for investors in regional centers by Sec. 610 of P.L. 102-395.

4. INA Section 203(e) provides that family-sponsored and employment-based preference visas be issued to eligible immigrants in the order in which a petition in behalf of each has been filed. Section 203(d) provides that spouses and children of preference immigrants are entitled to the same status, and the same order of consideration, if accompanying or following to join the principal. The visa prorating provisions of Section 202(e) apply to allocations for a foreign state or dependent area when visa demand exceeds the per-country limit. These provisions apply at present to the following oversubscribed chargeability areas: CHINA-mainland born, INDIA, MEXICO, and PHILIPPINES.

5. On the chart below, the listing of a date for any class indicates that the class is oversubscribed (see paragraph 1); "C" means current, i.e., numbers are available for all qualified applicants; and "U" means unavailable, i.e., no numbers are available. (NOTE: Numbers are available only for applicants whose priority date is earlier than the cut-off date listed below.)

PREFERENCES	All Charge-ability Areas Except Those Listed	CHINA-mainland born	INDIA	MEXICO	PHILIPPINES
Family					
1st	01APR98	01APR98	01APR98	08AUG93	01OCT87
2A*	22FEB95	22FEB95	22FEB95	01FEB94	22FEB95
2B	01AUG92	01AUG92	01AUG92	01AUG91	01AUG92
3rd	01AUG95	01AUG95	01AUG95	01FEB91	01AUG87
4th	22JUL88	22JUL88	01OCT86	15MAY88	01MAR79

*NOTE: For July, 2A numbers EXEMPT from per-country limit are available to applicants from all countries with priority dates earlier than 01FEB94. 2A numbers SUBJECT to per-country limit are available to applicants chargeable to all countries EXCEPT MEXICO with priority dates beginning 01FEB94 and earlier than 22FEB95. (All 2A numbers provided for MEXICO are exempt from the per-country limit; there are no 2A numbers for MEXICO subject to per-country limit.)

-3-   July 1999

	All Charge- ability Areas Except Those Listed	CHINA- mainland born	INDIA	MEXICO	PHILIPPINES
Employment- Based					
1st	C	C	C	C	C
2nd	C	01SEP97	01OCT98	C	C
3rd	C	15JUL95	01SEP96	C	C
Other Workers	01JAN93	01JAN93	01JAN93	01JAN93	01JAN93
4th	C	C	C	C	C
Certain Religious Workers	C	C	C	C	C
5th	C	C	C	C	C
Targeted Employ- ment Areas/ Regional Centers	C	C	C	C	C

The Department of State has available a recorded message with visa availability information which can be heard at: (area code 202) 663-1541. This recording will be updated in the middle of each month with information on cut-off dates for the following month.

B. DIVERSITY IMMIGRANT (DV) CATEGORY

Section 203(c) of the Immigration and Nationality Act provides 55,000 immigrant visas each fiscal year to permit immigration opportunities for persons from countries other than the principal sources of current immigration to the United States. DV visas are divided among six geographic regions. Not more than 3,850 visas (7% of the 55,000 visa limit) may be provided to immigrants from any one country.

-4-   July 1999

For _July_, immigrant numbers in the DV category are available to qualified DV-99 applicants chargeable to all regions/eligible countries as follows. When an allocation cut-off number is shown, visas are available only for applicants with DV regional lottery rank numbers _BELOW_ the specified allocation cut-off number:

Region	All DV Charge-ability Areas Except Those Listed Separately		
AFRICA	AF 38,180		
ASIA	AS 11,970		
EUROPE	EU 22,340	EXCEPT: ALBANIA	EU 18,900
NORTH AMERICA (BAHAMAS)	NA 24		
OCEANIA	OC 1,012		
SOUTH AMERICA, CENTRAL AMERICA, and the CARIBBEAN	SA 2,850		

Entitlement to immigrant status in the DV category lasts only through the end of the fiscal (visa) year for which the applicant is selected in the lottery. The year of entitlement for all applicants registered for the DV-99 program ends as of September 30, 1999. DV visas may not be issued to DV-99 applicants after that date. Similarly, spouses and children accompanying or following to join DV-99 principals are only entitled to derivative DV status until September 30, 1999. DV visa availability through the very end of FY-1999 cannot be taken for granted. Numbers could be exhausted prior to September 30. **Once all numbers provided by law for the DV-99 program have been used, no further issuances will be possible.**

-5-   July 1999

C. ADVANCE NOTIFICATION OF THE DIVERSITY (DV) IMMIGRANT CATEGORY
   RANK CUT-OFFS WHICH WILL APPLY IN AUGUST and SEPTEMBER

For August, immigrant numbers in the DV category are available to qualified
DV-99 applicants chargeable to all regions/eligible countries as follows:

| | All DV Charge-ability Areas Except Those |
Region	Listed Separately
AFRICA	Current
ASIA	Current
EUROPE	EU 25,100
NORTH AMERICA	NA 24
(BAHAMAS)	
OCEANIA	Current
SOUTH AMERICA,	SA 3,071
CENTRAL AMERICA,	
and the CARIBBEAN	

For September, immigrant numbers in the DV category are available to qualified
DV-99 applicants chargeable to all regions/eligible countries as follows:

| | All DV Charge-ability Areas Except Those |
Region	Listed Separately
AFRICA	Current
ASIA	Current
EUROPE	Current
NORTH AMERICA	Current
(BAHAMAS)	
OCEANIA	Current
SOUTH AMERICA,	Current
CENTRAL AMERICA,	
and the CARIBBEAN	

D. ADVANCE NOTIFICATION OF THE DIVERSITY (DV) IMMIGRANT CATEGORY
    RANK CUT-OFFS WHICH WILL APPLY IN OCTOBER FOR THE DV-2000 PROGRAM

For October, immigrant numbers in the DV category are available to qualified
DV-2000 applicants chargeable to all regions/eligible countries as follows:

Region	All DV Charge-ability Areas Except Those Listed Separately	
AFRICA	AF	12,001
ASIA	AS	4,201
EUROPE	EU	14,016
NORTH AMERICA (BAHAMAS)	NA	10
OCEANIA	OC	738
SOUTH AMERICA, CENTRAL AMERICA, and the CARIBBEAN	SA	1,200

E. DETERMINATION OF NUMERICAL LIMITS ON IMMIGRANTS REQUIRED UNDER THE TERMS OF
    THE IMMIGRATION AND NATIONALITY ACT

The Department of State has determined the family and employment preference
numerical limits for FY-1999 in accordance with the terms of Section 201 of the
Immigration and Nationality Act. These numerical limitations for FY-1999 are as
follows:

    Worldwide Family-Sponsored preference limit: 226,000
    Worldwide Employment-Based preference limit: 160,898

Under INA 202(a), the per-country limit is fixed at 7% of the family and
employment preference annual limits. For FY-1999 the per-country limit is 27,083.
The dependent area annual limit is 2%, or 7,738.

-7-   July 1999

OBTAINING THE MONTHLY VISA BULLETIN: The Department of State's Bureau
of Consular Affairs offers the monthly "Visa Bulletin" on the INTERNET'S
WORLDWIDE WEB. The INTERNET Web address to access the Bulletin is:
                        http://travel.state.gov
From the home page, select the Visa section which contains the Visa Bulletin.

In addition to the INTERNET, the "Visa Bulletin" can be accessed and downloaded
from the Consular Affairs electronic bulletin board. Those with a computer,
modem, and communications software should dial (301) 946-4400. The login is
"travel"; the password is "info" (lower case required).

Individuals may also obtain the "Visa Bulletin" by FAX. From a FAX phone, dial
(202) 647-3000. Follow the prompts and enter in the code 1038 to have each
Bulletin FAXed.

(The Department of State also has available a recorded message with visa cut-off
dates which can be heard at: (area code 202) 663-1541. The recording is updated
in the middle of each month with information on cut-off dates for the following
month.)

To be placed on the Department of State's "Visa Bulletin" mailing list or
to change an address, please write to:
                             Visa Bulletin
                             Visa Office
                             Department of State
                             Washington, D.C. 20522-0106

Only addresses within the U.S. postal system may be placed on the mailing list.
Please include a recent mailing label when reporting changes or corrections of
address; the Postal Service does NOT automatically notify the Visa Office of
address changes. (Obtaining the Visa Bulletin by mail is a much slower option
than any of the alternatives mentioned above.)

The Visa Bulletin can also be contacted by E-mail at the following address:
                   VISABULLETIN@STATE.GOV

(The Visa Bulletin **is not** distributed by E-mail, however.)

Department of State Publication 9514
CA/VO:June 10, 1999

U.S. Department of Justice
Immigration and Naturalization Service (INS)

Petition for Alien Relative

OMB #1115-0054

DO NOT WRITE IN THIS BLOCK - FOR EXAMINING OFFICE ONLY		
Case ID#	Action Stamp	Fee Stamp
A#		
G-28 or Volag #		

Section of Law:		Petition was filed on: _____ (priority date)
☐ 201 (b) spouse ☐ 203 (a)(1)		☐ Personal Interview ☐ Previously Forwarded
☐ 201 (b) child ☐ 203 (a)(2)		☐ Pet. ☐ Ben. "A" File Reviewed ☐ Stateside Criteria
☐ 201 (b) parent ☐ 203 (a)(4)		☐ Field Investigations ☐ 1-485 Simultaneously
☐ 203 (a)(5)		☐ 204 (a)(2)(A) Resolved ☐ 204 (h) Resolved
AM CON: _____		

Remarks:

A. Relationship

1. The alien relative is my
☐ Husband/Wife ☐ Parent ☐ Brother/Sister ☐ Child

2. Are you related by adoption?
☐ Yes ☐ No

3. Did you gain permanent residence through adoption?
☐ Yes ☐ No

B. Information about you

1. Name (Family name in CAPS) (First) (Middle)

2. Address (Number and Street) (Apartment Number)

(Town or City) (State/Country) (ZIP/Postal Code)

3. Place of Birth (Town or City) (State/Country)

4. Date of Birth (Mo/Day/Yr)
5. Sex ☐ Male ☐ Female
6. Marital Status ☐ Married ☐ Single ☐ Widowed ☐ Divorced

7. Other Names Used (including maiden name)

8. Date and Place of Present Marriage (if married)

9. Social Security Number 10. Alien Registration Number (if any)

11. Names of Prior Husbands/Wives 12. Date(s) Marriages(s) Ended

13. If you are a U.S. citizen, complete the following:
My citizenship was acquired through (check one)
☐ Birth in the U.S.
☐ Naturalization (Give number of certificate, date and place it was issued)

☐ Parents
Have you obtained a certificate of citizenship in your own name?
☐ Yes ☐ No
If "Yes", give number of certificate, date and place it was issued

14a. If you are a lawful permanent resident alien, complete the following:
Date and place of admission for, or adjustment to, lawful permanent residence, and class of admission:

14b. Did you gain permanent resident status through marriage to a United States citizen or lawful permanent resident? ☐ Yes ☐ No

C. Information about your alien relative

1. Name (Family name in CAPS) (First) (Middle)

2. Address (Number and Street) (Apartment Number)

(Town or City) (State/Country) (ZIP/Postal Code)

3. Place of Birth (Town or City) (State/Country)

4. Date of Birth (Mo/Day/Yr)
5. Sex ☐ Male ☐ Female
6. Marital Status ☐ Married ☐ Single ☐ Widowed ☐ Divorced

7. Other Names Used (including maiden name)

8. Date and Place of Present Marriage (if married)

9. Social Security Number 10. Alien Registration Number (if any)

11. Names of Prior Husbands/Wives 12. Date(s) Marriages(s) Ended

13. Has your relative ever been in the U.S.?
☐ Yes ☐ No

14. If your relative is currently in the U.S., complete the following: He or she last arrived as a (visitor, student, stowaway, without inspection, etc.)

Arrival/Departure Record (1-94) Number   Date arrived (Month/Day/Year)

Date authorized stay expired, or will expire, as shown on Form I-94 or I-95

15. Name and address of present employer (if any)

Date this employment began (Month/Day/Year)

16. Has your relative ever been under immigration proceedings?
☐ Yes ☐ No Where _____ When _____
☐ Exclusion ☐ Deportation ☐ Recission ☐ Judicial Proceedings

INITIAL RECEIPT	RESUBMITTED	RELOCATED		COMPLETED		
		Rec'd	Sent	Approved	Denied	Returned

Form I-130 (Rev. 10/13/98)N

C. (continued) Information about your alien relative

16. List husband/wife and all children of your relative (if your relative is your husband/wife, list only his or her children).

(Name)   (Relationship)   (Date of Birth)   (Country of Birth)

17. Address in the United States where your relative intends to live

(Number and Street)   (Town or City)   (State)

18. Your relative's address abroad

(Number and Street)   (Town or City)   (Province)   (Country)   (Phone Number)

19. If your relative's native alphabet is other than Roman letters, write his or her name and address abroad in the native alphabet:

(Name)   (Number and Street)   Town or City)   (Province)   (Country)

20. If filing for your husband/wife, give last address at which you both lived together: From   To

(Name)   (Number and Street)   (Town or City)   (Province)   (Country)   (Month) (Year)   (Month) (Year)

21. Check the appropriate box below and give the information required for the box you checked:

☐ Your relative will apply for a visa abroad at the American Consulate in _____

(City)   (Country)

☐ Your relative is in the United States and will apply for adjustment of status to that of a lawful permanent resident in the office of the Immigration and Naturalization Service at _____ . If your relative is not eligible for adjustment of status, he or she will

(City)   (State)

apply for a visa abroad at the American Consulate in _____

(City)   (Country)

(Designation of a consulate outside the country of your relative's last residence does not guarantee acceptance for processing by that consulate. Acceptance is at the discretion of the designated consulate.)

D. Other Information

1. If separate petitions are also being submitted for other relatives, give names of each and relationship.

2. Have you ever filed a petition for this or any other alien before?   ☐ Yes   ☐ No
If "Yes," give name, place and date of filing, and result.

Warning: The INS investigates claimed relationships and verifies the validity of documents. The INS seeks criminal prosecutions when family relationships are falsified to obtain visas.

Penalties: You may, by law be imprisoned for not more than five years, or fined $250,000, or both, for entering into a marriage contract for the purpose of evading any provision of the immigration laws and you may be fined up to $10,000 or imprisoned up to five years or both, for knowingly and willfully falsifying or concealing a material fact or using any false document in submitting this petition.

Your Certification: I certify, under penalty of perjury under the laws of the United States of America, that the foregoing is true and correct. Furthermore, I authorize the release of any information from my records which the Immigration and Naturalization Service needs to determine eligibility for the benefit that I am seeking.

Signature _____ Date _____ Phone Number _____

Signature of Person Preparing Form if Other than Above

I declare that I prepared this document at the request of the person above and that it is based on all information of which I have any knowledge.

Print Name _____ (Address) _____ (Signature) _____ (Date) _____

G-28 ID Number _____

Volag Number _____

Form I-130 (Rev. 10/13/98)N

NOTICE TO PERSONS FILING FOR SPOUSES IF MARRIED LESS THAN TWO YEARS

Pursuant to section 216 of the Immigration and Nationality Act, your alien spouse may be granted conditional permanent resident status in the United States as of the date he or she is admitted or adjusted to conditional status by an officer of the Immigration and Naturalization Service. Both you and your conditional permanent resident spouse are required to file a petition, Form I-751, Joint Petition to Remove Conditional Basis of Alien's Permanent Resident Status, during the ninety day period immediately before the second anniversary of the date your alien spouse was granted conditional permanent residence.

Otherwise, the rights, privileges, responsibilities and duties which apply to all other permanent residents apply equally to a conditional permanent resident. A conditional permanent resident is not limited to the right to apply for naturalization, to file petitions in behalf of qualifying relatives, or to reside permanently in the United States as an immigrant in accordance with the immigration laws.

Failure to file Form I-751, Joint Petition to Remove the Conditional Basis of Alien's Permanent Resident Status, will result in termination of permanent residence status and initiation of deportation proceedings.

NOTE: You must complete Items 1 through 6 to assure that petition approval is recorded. Do not write in the section below item 6.

1. Name of relative (Family name in CAPS)   (First)   (Middle)

2. Other names used by relative (Including maiden name)

3. Country of relative's birth   4. Date of relative's birth (Month/Day/Year)

5. Your name (Last name in CAPS) (First)   (Middle)   6. Your phone number

Action Stamp	SECTION	DATE PETITION FILED
	☐ 201 (b)(spouse)	
	☐ 201 (b)(child)	
	☐ 201 (b)(parent)	
	☐ 203 (a)(1)	
	☐ 203 (a)(2)	☐ STATESIDE
	☐ 203 (a)(4)	CRITERIA GRANTED
	☐ 203 (a)(5)	SENT TO CONSUL AT;

CHECKLIST

Have you answered each question?

Have you signed the petition?

Have you enclosed:

☐ The filing fee for each petition?
☐ Proof of your citizenship or lawful permanent residence?
☐ All required supporting documents for each petition?

If you are filing for your husband or wife have you included:

☐ Your picture?
☐ His or her picture?
☐ Your G-325A?
☐ His or her G-325A?

Relative Petition Card
Form I-130 (Rev. 10/13/98)N

U.S. Department of Justice	OMB #1115-006
Immigration and Naturalization Service	Immigrant Petition for Alien Worker

START HERE - Please Type or Print

Part 1. Information about person or organization filing this petition.

If an individual is filing, use the top Name line. Organizations should use the second line.

Family Name	Given Name	Middle Initial

Company or Organization

Address - Attn:

Street Number and Name		Room #
City	State or Province	
Country	ZIP/Postal Code	

IRS Tax #	Social Security #

Part 2. Petition Type. This petition is being filed for: (check one)

a. ☐ An alien of extraordinary ability
b. ☐ An outstanding professor or researcher
c. ☐ A multinational executive or manager
d. ☐ A member of the professions holding an advanced degree or an alien of exceptional ability
e. ☐ A skilled worker (requiring at least two years of specialized training or experience) or professional
f. ☐ An employee of a U.S. business operating in Hong Kong
g. ☐ Any other worker (requiring less than two years training or experience)

Part 3. Information about the person this petition is for.

Family Name	Given Name	Middle Initial

Address - C/O

Street Number and Name		Apt. #
City	State or Province	
Country	ZIP/Postal Code	

Date of Birth (Month/Day/Year)	Country of Birth
Social Security # (if any)	A # (if any)

if	Date of Arrival ((Month/Day/Year)	I-94#
in the U.S.	Current Nonimmigrant Status	Expires on (Month/Day/Year)

Part 4. Processing Information.

Below give the U.S. Consulate you want notified if this petition is approved and if any requested adjustment of status cannot be granted.

U.S. Consulate: City   Country

Form I-140 (Rev. 12-2-91)   *Continued on back.*

FOR INS USE ONLY

Returned	Receipt

Resubmitted

Reloc Sent

Reloc Rec'd

☐ Petitioner Interviewed
☐ Beneficiary Interviewed

Classification
☐ 203(b)(1)(A) Alien of Extraordinary Ability
☐ 203(b)(1)(B) Outstanding Professor or Researcher
☐ 203(b)(1)(C) Multi-national executive or manager
☐ 203(b)(2) Member of professions w/adv degree or of exceptional ability
☐ 203(b)(3)(A)(i) Skilled worker
☐ 203(b)(3)(A)(ii) Professional
☐ 203(b)(3)(A)(iii) Other worker
☐ Sec. 124 IMMACT-Employee of U.S. business in Hong Kong

Priority Date	Consulate

Remarks

Action Block

To Be Completed by
Attorney or *Representative*, if any

■ Fill in box if G-28 is attached to represent the applicant

VOLAG#

ATTY State License #

Part 4.   Processing Information. *(continued)*

If you gave a U.S. address in Part 3, print the person's foreign address below. If his/her native alphabet does not use Roman letters, print his/her name and foreign address in the native alphabet.

Name   Address

Are you filing any other petitions or applications with this one?   ☐ No   ☐ yes attach an explanation
Is the person you are filing for in exclusion or deportation proceedings?   ☐ No   ☐ yes attach an explanation
Has an immigrant visa petition ever been filed by or in behalf of this person?   ☐ No   ☐ yes attach an explanation

Part 5.   Additional information about the employer.

Type of petitioner   ☐ Self   ☐ Individual U.S. Citizen   ☐ Company or organization
(check one)
                            ☐ Permanent Resident   ☐ Other explain_____

If a company, give the following:
    Type of business

Date established	Current # of employees	Gross Annual Income	Net Annual Income
If an individual, give the following: Occupation		Annual Income	

Part 6.   Basic information about the proposed employment.

Job Title	Nontechnical description of job

Address where the person will work
if different from address in Part 1.

Is this a full-time position?	☐ yes	☐ No (hours per week _____)	Wages per week

Is this a permanent position?   ☐ yes ☐ No   Is this a new position? ☐ yes   ☐ No

Part 7.   Information on spouse and all children of the person you are filing for.

Provide an attachment listing the family members of the person you are filing for. Be sure to include their full name,relationship,date and country of birth, and present address.

Part 8.   Signature. *Read the information on penalties in the instructions before completing this section.*

I certify under penalty of perjury under the laws of the United States of America that this petition,and the evidence submitted with it,is all true and correct. I authorize the release of any information from my records which the Immigration and Naturalization Service needs to determine eligiblity for the benefit I am seeking.
Signature   Date

Please Note: *If you do not completely fill out this form, or fail to submit required documents listed in the instructions, you cannot be found eligible for the requested document and this application may be denied.*

Part 9.   Signature of person preparing form if other than above. *(Sign below)*

I declare that I prepared this application at the request of the above person and it is based on all information of which I have knowledge.
Signature   Print Your Name   Date

Firm Name
and Address

Form I-140 (Rev. 12-2-91)

For Further Reading

Legal Treatises

These books are intended for lawyers and students of the law. The material in them tends to be technical. Nevertheless, much of general interest may be gleaned from them.

Aleinikoff, Thomas Alexander, et al. *Immigration and Citizenship: Process and Policy*. 4th ed. St. Paul, MN: West Group. 1998.
> A law school textbook with cases, laws, regulations, notes, and some historical information.

Boswell, Richard A. *Immigration and Nationality Law*. 2d ed. Durham, NC: Carolina Academic Press. 1992.
> A law school textbook with cases, laws, regulations, notes, and some historical information.

Gordon, Charles, et al. *Immigration Law and Procedure*. New York: Matthew Bender. 1999.
> A multivolume treatise on immigration law and procedure, with complete historical discussions and detailed explanations of current and past law.

Hing, Bill Ong. *Handling Immigration Cases*. 2d ed. Colorado Springs: Aspen Press. 1995.
> A detailed explanation of all aspects of immigration law and procedure with examples, sample forms, and commentary for practitioners.

Legomsky, Stephen H. *Immigration Law and Policy*. 2d ed. Westbury, NY: Foundation Press. 1998.
> A law school textbook with cases, laws, regulations, notes, and some historical information.

Lydon, Susan, et al. *A Guide for Immigration Advocates*. San Francisco: ILRC Publications. 1998.

A detailed explanation of immigration law with emphasis on family visas, deportation defense, asylum, and citizenship. Forms and examples are included.

Piatt, Bill, et al. *Immigration and Citizenship Law and Policy for the Twenty-First Century: A Modern Approach*. LEXIS Law Publishing. 2000.

An important overview of the law of immigration and citizenship, integrating technical rules with an understanding of a diverse society in which the laws are enforced.

General Reading

These books are intended for a general readership on immigration history and policy.

Bau, Ignatius. *This Ground is Holy—Church Sanctuary and Central American Refugees*. New York: Paulist. 1985.

A good description of the development of the sanctuary movement in the United States in the 1980s when church groups provided protection to refugees—many of whom were undocumented—from El Salvador and Guatemala.

Borjas, George J. *Friends or Strangers: The Impact of Immigrants on the U.S. Economy*. New York: Basic Books. 1990.

A description of how immigrants affect the U.S. economy.

Brimelow, Peter. *Alien Nation—Common Sense about America's Immigration Disaster*. New York: Random House. 1995.

An attack on current U.S. immigration policies, calling for an immigration policy that would favor English-speaking, white immigrants.

Chan, Sucheng. *Asian Americans: An Interpretive History*. Boston: Twayne. 1991.

A detailed, comparative history of Asian immigration to the United States.

Gitlin, Todd. *The Twilight of Common Dreams: Why America Is Wracked by Culture Wars*. Metropolitan Books/Henry Holt. 1995.

An expression of concern about separatism and identity politics in the United States.

Goodwill-Gill, Guy S. *The Refugee in International Law.* New York: Oxford University Press. 1983.

An excellent resource on an international perspective of refugee law and the rights of refugees under international instruments.

Handlin, Oscar. *The Uprooted.* 2d ed. Boston: Little, Brown. 1973.

A Pulitzer Prize–winning, classic account of the story of emigrants: their uprooting from a native soil and culture, and passage to the New World.

Higham, John. *Strangers in the Land: Patterns of American Nativism, 1860–1925.* New York: Atheneum. 1971.

Considered the classic book on the history of European immigration to the United States and the restrictionist movements against southern and eastern Europeans.

Hing, Bill Ong. *To Be an American: Cultural Pluralism and the Rhetoric of Assimilation.* New York: New York University Press. 1997.

A discussion of the social and economic impact of immigrants on society, using personal experiences of the author and a review of the most significant studies in the field, arguing that a new multicultural form of respectful pluralism with important core values is vital for the nation.

Hing, Bill Ong. *Making and Remaking Asian America through Immigration Policy, 1850–1990.* Stanford, CA: Stanford University Press. 1993.

A comparative history of exclusion laws that affect all Asian immigration to the United States, changes in the law, and the ultimate impact that immigration laws have had on the socioeconomic development of American communities of Chinese, Japanese, Korean, Vietnamese, Filipino, and Asian Indian descent.

Johnson, Kevin R. *How Did You Get to Be a Mexican? A White/Brown Man's Search for Identity.* Philadelphia: Temple University Press. 1999.

A personal search for racial identity by a second-generation immigrant whose mother was Mexican and father, a descendent of Swedish immigrant farmers.

Lind, Michael. *The Next American Nation.* New York: Free Press. 1995.

A critique of racial labeling and a call for dismantling multicultural America and restricting immigration.

Neuman, Gerald L. *Strangers to the Constitution: Immigrants, Borders, and Fundamental Law.* 1996.

A review of congressional power over immigration and the role of the judicial branch.

Schlesinger Jr., Arthur M. *The Disuniting of America: Reflections on a Multicultural Society*. New York: W.W. North & Co. 1992.

An examination of lessons from polyglot nations like the former Yugoslavia, Nigeria, and even Canada, arguing that efforts to preserve a plurality of cultures in the United States are threatening to tear the country apart.

Simon, Julian L. *The Economic Consequences of Immigration*. Cato Institute. 1989.

A description of most theories of how immigrants affect the U.S. economy and examples of how the theories work.

Takaki, Ronald. *Strangers from a Different Shore*. Boston: Little, Brown. 1989.

A comparative history of Asian immigration to the United States using the voices and anecdotal experiences of many of the immigrants themselves.

Walzer, Michael. *Spheres of Justice: A Defense of Pluralism and Equality*. New York: Basic Books. 1983.

A philosopical view of justice that includes arguments that immigrant workers permitted entry should be granted full benefits of citizenship.

Table of Cases

Index

Note: page numbers in **bold type** refer to main dictionary entries for that term.